ENTREPRENEURSHIP
in the SOCIAL
SECTOR

Dedicated to students, teachers, and practitioners of social entrepreneurship. May we all continue to learn together and advance our collective efforts to create a better world.

ENTREPRENEURSHIP in the SOCIAL SECTOR

JANE WEI-SKILLERN

JAMES E. AUSTIN

HERMAN LEONARD

HOWARD STEVENSON

Harvard Business School

SAGE Publications

Los Angeles • London • New Delhi • Singapore

For information:

Sage Publications, Inc.
2455 Teller Road
Thousand Oaks, California 91320
E-mail: order@sagepub.com

Sage Publications India Pvt Ltd.
B 1/I 1 Mohan Cooperative Industrial Area
Mathura Road, New Delhi 110 044
India

Sage Publications Ltd.
1 Oliver's Yard
55 City Road
London EC1Y 1SP
United Kingdom

Sage Publications Asia-Pacific Pte Ltd.
33 Pekin Street #02-01
Far East Square
Singapore 048763

Printed in the United States of America

Library of Congress Cataloging-in-Publication Data

Entrepreneurship in the social sector / Jane Wei-Skillern . . . [et al.].
   p. cm.
Includes bibliographical references and index.
ISBN 978-1-4129-5137-1 (cloth)
   1. Social entrepreneurship—Case studies. I. Wei-Skillern, Jane.

HD60.E56 2007
361.0068′4—dc22

2006101379

This book is printed on acid-free paper.

12   13   14   15   10   9   8   7   6   5   4   3

Acquisitions Editor:	John Szilagyi
Editorial Assistant:	Cassandra Margaret Seibel
Production Editor:	Denise Santoyo
Copy Editor:	Cheryl Rivard
Typesetter:	C&M Digitals (P) Ltd.
Indexer:	Kathy Paparchontis

Contents

Acknowledgments

We are grateful for the engagement and support from a number of individuals and institutions without which this book would not have been possible. We thank Greg Dees, who created the first Entrepreneurship in the Social Sector course at Harvard Business School, for his work as a pioneer in advancing the field of social entrepreneurship, and for being a faithful colleague and friend.

We also thank the many social entrepreneurs and their organizations whose work is profiled through examples in the text and the detailed case studies throughout the book. We are inspired by their vision, commitment, and the social impact of their endeavors. We appreciate their willingness to share their experiences by permitting us to develop the case studies included in the book. We also extend our gratitude to the other case study authors who have kindly allowed us to include their case studies in this book.

We are indebted to all the students who have taken our elective course, Entrepreneurship in the Social Sector, at Harvard Business School over the last decade, whose thirst for knowledge and passion about social entrepreneurship were the motivation for developing the course that led to this book.

Finally, we are grateful for support from the Harvard Business School's Social Enterprise Initiative and the School's Division of Research. We also extend our gratitude to Elizabeth Zeeuw, Jeff Cronin, and Jim Quinn for their professional editorial and research support.

Preface

Many of the ideas from this book were developed from the flagship Social Enterprise MBA elective course at Harvard Business School, Entrepreneurship in the Social Sector, which focuses on developing knowledge and skills for creating, leading, or supporting social purpose organizations through the application of entrepreneurial and managerial skills. Just as in our course, this book takes the reader through conceptual analysis and detailed Harvard Business School case studies of the critical components of social entrepreneurship, from starting, to growing, to enhancing the impact of social enterprises. The objective of this book is to enable the reader to develop an in-depth understanding of the distinctive characteristics of the social enterprise context and organizations and to develop concepts and tools that will enable them to pursue social entrepreneurship more strategically.

This book spans a range of social enterprise activity, with a primary focus on the social entrepreneurial process itself. The book introduces and develops the concept of social enterprise organizations, which are characterized first and foremost by their social mission, as well as by their innovative combinations of social and commercial approaches.[1] We define social entrepreneurship as innovative, social value–creating activity that can occur within or across the non-profit, business, or government sector. The distinct opportunities and challenges of creating and building sustainable social entrepreneurial initiatives require not only the application and adaptation of business skills to the social enterprise context but also the development of new conceptual frameworks and strategies tailored specifically to entrepreneurship in the social sector. To this end, this book not only draws on leading ideas and data from the field of social entrepreneurship today but also presents new frameworks based on several years of our own research and teaching. It is our ambition that this book will not only deepen interest and understanding of the practice of social entrepreneurship among students, instructors, and practitioners alike but will also enable social entrepreneurs to achieve mission impact as effectively, efficiently, and sustainably as possible.

NOTE

1. Dees, J. (1998). *The meaning of social entrepreneurship*. Comments and suggestions contributed from the Social Entrepreneurship Funders Working Group. Center for the Advancement of Social Entrepreneurship. Fuqua School of Business: Duke University.

A Note to Instructors

To receive the Teaching Notes to the cases you must first register. They are provided free of charge once the process is completed. Please follow the directions below. Thank you.

Instructions for university professors to register for Sample Area access:

Instructors who register at the HBS Publishing are usually verified within two business days. After being verified, instructors will have access to Harvard Business Review articles, Newsletter articles, Harvard Business School Cases and Teaching Notes. Sample copies of these materials are available to read at no charge and these will have the full text, however, they will have a DO NOT COPY watermark when printed out. Clean copies can be purchased with a Visa, Amex, or MasterCard. Also, the downloaded electronic files will be saved to "My Library," a storage area on the site that is exclusively yours and holds all your favorite links, product previews, conference materials and purchased or free downloads. You will also have the ability to manage your account, view your order history, reuse or track an order and print a receipt.

The direct URL to register as an educator is: http://harvardbusinessonline.hbsp .harvard.edu/b01/en/academic/edu_reg_info.jhtml

After a professor has registered and the teaching status has been verified by HBS Publishing, please remember to sign in so that the HBS system recognizes you as an educator. If you are searching for HBS cases on the site, please only enter the six digits for the case (for example, HBS case 9-801-361 would be entered as 801361 in the SEARCH box). IMPORTANT: When searching for case supplements or teaching notes, please enter the product number for the main case study and you will see any supplemental cases and teaching note(s) listed below if available. When you click on the listed supplement or teaching note, the following screen will give you the option to purchase a clean copy or to download a sample copy. General questions can be directed to HBS Publishing Customer Service at phone number 800-545-7685 (custserv@hbsp.harvard.edu) and technical questions can be directed to Tech Support at 800-810-8858 (tech-help@hbsp.harvard.edu).

CHAPTER 1

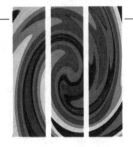

Social Entrepreneurship

Need and Opportunity

Societies worldwide are urgently seeking innovative approaches to addressing persistent social problems that afflict their communities but that have not yet been satisfactorily addressed by either governments or the marketplace. Historically, these challenges have been the domain of nonprofit organizations (also known as nongovernmental organizations or NGOs, or civil society organizations or CSOs), which operate in fields ranging from education, health services, social services, and environmental conservation to arts and culture. In response to the challenge of overcoming the increasingly complex social issues that societies face today, the social sector has grown vastly and continues to proliferate worldwide. In the United States alone, the sector is comprised of more than 1.5 million organizations[1] with combined revenues of over $700 billion, and it controls over $2 trillion in assets,[2] while internationally, hundreds of thousands of NGOs operate in both developed and developing countries with combined revenues on the order of tens of billions of dollars.[3] Despite the magnitude of the social sector, however, many of the challenges that these organizations seek to address persist to this day. While the social sector includes many activities that are critical to the well-being of society, many observers, both inside and outside the sector, have noted that traditional social sector approaches have made insufficient headway in addressing critical social problems. Many social problems have increased in intensity and complexity, crying out for more entrepreneurial approaches that create more social value with limited resources. Social entrepreneurship often exhibits some of the virtues commonly associated with commercial entrepreneurship, such as efficiency, dynamism, innovativeness, high performance, and economic sustainability. These approaches achieve better leverage on resources, enhance effectiveness through creative partnerships, raise expectations for performance and accountability, and ultimately achieve more sustainable social impact.

A CHANGING CONTEXT AND EMERGING OPPORTUNITIES

While the challenges in the social sector are many, the potential and opportunity for social entrepreneurship to be a powerful force for social value creation have never been greater. Financial pressures on most social sector organizations have increased in recent years and are unlikely to lessen. In much of the social sector, costs have been rising faster than inflation. For example, according to data from the U.S. Bureau of Labor Statistics, the Consumer Price Index rose 13.4% between 2000 and 2005, while during the same period, the price indices for education and medical care rose 35.7% and 24.0%, respectively.[4]

At the same time, in many social sector domains, government funding has decreased and private donations and grants have not made up the difference. President Bush's 2007–2012 budgets would cut direct federal funding of non-profits, excluding support of health services providers, by $14.3 billion. Research by the Aspen Institute estimates that about 20% of nonprofits' resources come from private giving, including individuals, foundations, and businesses; 30% comes from the state and federal government; while 40% to 50% is earned from service fees. According to Erica Greeley, deputy director of the National Council of Nonprofit Associations, which has more than 22,000 members in 45 states and Washington, D.C., "Federal budget cuts do have a major impact. There is no way that private giving can make up the difference."[5]

Even where public subsidies have not yet declined, they are under serious threat, as governments at all levels in most countries struggle to balance their budgets. This pressure on government and private funding, coupled with the proliferation of social sector organizations, has fueled intense competition for scarce funds (see Chapter 3). Consequently, many social enterprises are searching for new ways to control costs, increase revenues, and enhance effectiveness. More than ever, these organizations need to do more with less.

On the positive side, the economic boom of the 1990s in the United States generated significant new private wealth and fostered the emergence of many new philanthropists. At the same time, a new generation of leaders with managerial skills and entrepreneurial talent is growing and becoming increasingly engaged in the social sector. For example, the Masters of Business Administration (MBA) interest in the social sector has surged in recent years. Net Impact, an international organization whose membership is comprised of MBA students who want to use their business skills to make a positive influence on society, has seen their number of chapters almost double to 94 since 2000. Twenty-nine of the 30 schools on *Business Week*'s ranking of top business schools have a chapter on campus.[6] Growing numbers of MBA graduates have gone on to leadership positions in the social sector, whether as senior managers or volunteer board members. These social sector actors bring not only new capital, management expertise, and talent but also a drive to foster innovation to achieve increased social impact. Accompanying these trends have been a growing concern regarding the effectiveness and efficiency of traditional social sector approaches and an increasing demand for greater organizational accountability for social impact. Thus, an increased receptiveness toward new modes of operation has become a trend in the social sector.

As a result of the confluence of these trends, the nature of the social sector is changing. The boundaries between sectors, and indeed between organizations within sectors, are becoming increasingly blurred. Nonprofits are looking for more sustainable solutions to social problems and are sometimes experimenting with revenue-generating enterprises more commonly associated with the business world. As noted previously, fee for service income represents the major source of revenue for most nonprofits (see Chapter 4). They have a social purpose, but they are also economic enterprises. Social purpose business ventures are being established in sectors such as medical care, education, and human services—areas traditionally dominated by public and nonprofit organizations.

Innovative partnerships are being forged between nonprofits and businesses, often combining social and commercial goals (see Chapter 5). New organizational models are being created through creative alliances among nonprofits as well as between nonprofits and public agencies that enable the partners to better leverage their respective resources. As societies search for better ways to provide socially important goods and services, opportunities for experimenting with new approaches and organizational models for growing (see Chapter 6) to achieve social goals are continually emerging. An integral part of this activity is the development of effective performance management systems that enable more effective assessment and achievement of social impact (see Chapter 7).

SOCIAL ENTREPRENEURSHIP DEFINED

With the emergence of this range of innovative activity, the concept of social entrepreneurship has taken on multiple and varied meanings in popular discourse, as well as in the academic literature. The concept of social entrepreneurship has its roots in the broader field of entrepreneurship and draws on the definition of entrepreneurship as "the pursuit of opportunity beyond the tangible resources that you currently control."[7]

In this definition, a key focus is on how various individuals and groups identify and commit to an opportunity, how the entrepreneurial organization gains access and functional control over a network of resources that are not within its hierarchical control, and the way in which participants are rewarded.[8] The entrepreneurial organization focuses on opportunity, not resources. Entrepreneurs must commit quickly but cautiously so as to be able to readjust as new information arises. The process of commitment becomes multistaged, with minimal commitment of resources at each stage to allow for learning from experience and new knowledge before more resources are sought.

Definitions of social entrepreneurship have been based on this more general conceptualization of entrepreneurship and range from relatively narrow to more general.[9] Common across all these definitions is the fact that the underlying drive for social entrepreneurship is to create social value, rather than just personal and shareholder wealth.[10] Narrower conceptualizations of social entrepreneurship typically refer to the phenomenon of applying business expertise and market-based skills to the social sector, such as when nonprofit organizations operate revenue-generating enterprises.[11] More general conceptualizations of social entrepreneurship refer to innovative activity with a social objective in either the private or nonprofit sector, or across both, such as hybrid structural forms, which mix for-profit and nonprofit activities.[12] It is this latter, more general conceptualization of social entrepreneurship that we use throughout this book. *We define social entrepreneurship as an innovative, social value–creating activity that can occur within or across the nonprofit, business, or government sector.*

OBJECTIVES AND STRUCTURE OF THE BOOK

The opportunities available to a social entrepreneur are diverse and wide ranging, and they include everything from starting a social purpose commercial venture, to developing an innovative nonprofit model, to creating an entire network of alliances. The distinct opportunities and challenges of creating and building sustainable social enterprises require not only the creative combination and adaptation of social and commercial approaches but also the development of new conceptual frameworks and strategies tailored specifically to social entrepreneurship. Thus, successful social entrepreneurship requires an in-depth understanding of the distinctive management context of the social sector. Furthermore, although the field of social enterprise is relatively new and still emerging, and indeed many social enterprises are truly experiments in that they are often the first of their kind, social entrepreneurial success still requires a strategic and systematic approach.

Among the many characteristics that make social enterprise unique are the following:

- **The centrality of the social mission:** The creation of social value takes precedence over the creation of personal shareholder or stakeholder wealth.

- **Fragmented, heterogeneous capital markets:** Most social enterprises, to some degree, depend on the philanthropic capital markets for some portion of their funding. Funders have a wide range of motivations and expectations, often making funding unpredictable, highly restricted, and unsustainable. Yet social entrepreneurs must typically spend a majority of their time on an ongoing basis seeking funding from these sources since their operations rarely, if ever, become financially viable without some form of philanthropic support.

- **Human resources challenges:** Social enterprises, with their limited capacity for offering financial incentives, often pay below-market rates[13] and rely heavily on volunteer labor. Social entrepreneurs often must rely less on financial rewards and incentives and more on intrinsic motivators and creative strategies for attracting, motivating, and retaining staff.

- **Blending of social and commercial approaches:** Social and commercial approaches can sometimes be mutually beneficial, while other times they may conflict. Combining approaches for social value creation poses a unique set of management opportunities and challenges.

- **Alliance opportunities:** Because nonprofit organizations seek to create social value and do not necessarily require that all value created be captured within organizational boundaries, there is tremendous potential for new opportunities and models for collaboration and partnership within the sector. Unlike in the private sector, collusion is sometimes allowed and, in some cases, even encouraged by various stakeholders, from beneficiaries to funders.

- **Challenge of scale:** Although social needs far outstrip the resources dedicated to serving them, and demand for social programs and services is often virtually limitless, achieving large-scale growth and impact remains an elusive goal for most social enterprises.

- **Ambiguous market signals:** Despite its importance for effective management, performance measurement is a perennial challenge for social enterprises, as tools for measuring social impact are still in their infancy. Furthermore, because third-party payers often cover the cost of services due to an inability or unwillingness by customers to pay, market signals are often weak. Thus, high performance is not readily rewarded nor is poor performance readily punished.

- **Dispersed and distinct role of governance:** The board plays a central role in supporting the social enterprise leader and organization in generating social value, but there are important differences between social entrepreneurial governance and corporate governance. Some key differences include board leadership, composition, and membership.[14] Furthermore, many social enterprises have multiple governing bodies within a single organization. Even those organizations with a single legal governing board often have multiple local advisory boards that sometimes play a de facto governing role.

Through an examination and analysis of the critical components of social entrepreneurship, from starting, to growing, to enhancing the impact of social enterprises, this book will develop analytical frameworks that will enable readers to develop an in-depth understanding of the distinctive characteristics of the social enterprise context and organization and learn concepts and tools that will enable them to pursue social entrepreneurship more efficiently, effectively, and sustainably. By presenting a series of case studies on actual social enterprises, we will provide the reader with a firsthand look at the distinctive challenges and rewards of social entrepreneurship. Through analysis of the cases, our aim is for readers to develop the knowledge, skills, and attitudes necessary for responding creatively and effectively to the challenges of creating, building, and leading innovative social purpose organizations, and to provide an appreciation of how to approach the social entrepreneurial process more systematically and effectively.

We have organized this book around analytical frameworks and key action areas that social entrepreneurs are likely to face at various stages of their organization's development. We begin in Chapter 2 with an overarching framework for the social entrepreneurship process. The subsequent chapters address five specific action areas: resource mobilization, marketplace activation, alliances, growth strategy, and performance management. Each chapter will be introduced by an overview reading that explores critical dimensions of the topic and provides an analytical framework that can guide the examination of the corresponding critical action issues in the accompanying case studies.

Chapter 2, "The Social Entrepreneurial Process," sets forth a basic analytical framework that highlights the commonalities and distinctions between social and commercial entrepreneurship. This framework is applicable to the analysis of all the subsequent case studies. The cases in this chapter highlight some of the unique aspects of social entrepreneurship, including the centrality of social mission, the critical role of social and organizational networks, the idiosyncrasies of the capital markets, the imperative and challenge of growth, and the wide array of critical stakeholders that a social entrepreneur must build relationships with. These cases set the stage for further exploration of the distinctive aspects of social enterprise and their implications for social entrepreneurship in each of the successive chapters of the book.

Chapter 3, "Navigating the Philanthropic Labyrinth," examines key aspects of the philanthropic capital markets, as well as major trends and innovations that are emerging in the marketplace.

Chapter 4, "Earning Your Own Way," examines a number of creative market-based approaches and organizational structures used by for-profit and nonprofit organizations as a vehicle for generating the resources and services needed for social betterment.

Chapter 5, "Crafting Alliances," analyzes how a collaborative approach is becoming an increasingly integral part of social enterprise strategy and delves into some of the opportunities and risks associated with building innovative intrasector alliances among nonprofits, and intersector alliances between non-profits and business and between nonprofits and government.

Chapter 6, "Managing Growth," explores the distinctive challenges facing social entrepreneurs who successfully make it through the start-up stage and choose to expand their organizations to increase the organization's impact.

Chapter 7, "Measuring Performance," deals with perhaps the most compli-cated and distinctive managerial feature of social enterprises. Defining perfor-mance success and creating a measurement system to track a social enterprise's progress along these dimensions remain a perennial challenge.

NOTES

1. Independent Sector and the National Center for Nonprofit Boards. *What you should know about nonprofits.* Retrieved April 6, 2006, from http://www.indepen dentsector.org/PDFs/WhatUShouldKnow.pdf.

2. Oster, S. M. (2004). Foreword. In C. W. Massarsky & S. L. Beinhacker (Eds.), *Generating and sustaining nonprofit earned income* (p. xiii). New York: Jossey-Bass.

3. World Bank. *Nongovernmental organizations and civil society/overview.* Retrieved April 5, 2006, from duke.edulibraryhttp://docs.lib.duke.edu/igo/guides/ngo/define.htm.

4. U.S. Bureau of Labor Statistics. Retrieved July 6, 2006, from http://data.bls.gov.

5. Stapp, K. (2006, June 10). Federal budget tells the poor they're on their own [Electronic version]. *Inter Press Service.*

6. Di Meglio, F. (2005, January 6). B-school students with a cause. *BusinessWeek Online.* Retrieved July 6, 2006, from http://www.businessweek.com/bschools/content/jan2005/bs2005016_5334_bs001.htm.

7. Stevenson, H. (1983). *A perspective on entrepreneurship.* Harvard Business School Working Paper #9–384–131.

8. Stevenson, H. (1985, March-April). The heart of entrepreneurship. *Harvard Business Review,* pp. 185–208; and Stevenson, H., & Jarillo, J. (1991). A new entre-preneurial paradigm. In A. Etzioni & P. Lawrence (Eds.), *Socioeconomics: Toward a new synthesis.* New York: M.E. Sharpe, Inc.

9. Dees, J. (1998). The meaning of "social entrepreneurship." Comments and suggestions contributed from the *Social Entrepreneurship Funders Working Group.*

Center for the Advancement of Social Entrepreneurship. Fuqua School of Business: Duke University. http://www.fuqua.duke.edu/centers/case/documents/dees_sedef.pdf

10.   For example, Zadek, S., & Thake, S. (1997). Send in the social entrepreneurs [Electronic version]. *New Statesman, 26*(7339), 31.

11.   For example, Dees, J. (1998); Reis, T. (1999). *Unleashing the new resources and entrepreneurship for the common good: A scan, synthesis and scenario for action.* Battle Creek, MI: W. K. Kellogg Foundation; Thompson, J. (2002). The world of the social entrepreneur. *International Journal of Public Sector Management, 15*(5), 412–431; and Boschee, J., & McClurg, J. (2003). *Toward a better understanding of social entrepreneurship: Some important distinctions.* Retrieved April 5, 2006, from http://www.se-alliance.org/.

12.   Dees, J. (1998).

13.   Weisbrod, B. (1983). Nonprofit and proprietary sector behavior: Wage differentials among lawyers. *Journal of Labor Economics, 1*(3), 246–263; and Preston, A. (1989). The nonprofit worker in a for-profit world. *Journal of Labor Economics, 7*(4), 438–463.

14.   McFarlan, F. W. (1999, November–December). Working on nonprofit boards: Don't assume the shoe fits [Electronic version]. *Harvard Business Review.*

CHAPTER 2

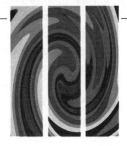

The Social Entrepreneurial Process

Despite the wide range of approaches through which social entrepreneurship is pursued, it is useful to analyze and understand the context and process of social entrepreneurship from a general management perspective. While ad hoc approaches may sometimes meet with success, we believe that a strategic approach to social entrepreneurship is more likely to achieve the objective of creating an entity that leverages resources most effectively to generate the greatest social impact. We start by introducing the key elements of a prevailing model used to assess the commercial entrepreneurship process. Second, we analyze the relationships between commercial and social entrepreneurship and then present the adapted framework as a tool to help social entrepreneurs achieve the greatest social impact.

COMMERCIAL ENTREPRENEURSHIP MODEL

Many different and useful approaches have been used to describe and analyze entrepreneurship. They have tended to fall within three main streams of research, which include a focus on the results of entrepreneurship, the causes of entrepreneurship, and entrepreneurial management.[1] In the former, economists have explored the impacts and results of entrepreneurship. For example, Schumpeter, in his seminal 1934 paper, examined entrepreneurship as a key process through which the economy as a whole is advanced. The second stream of research has focused on the entrepreneurs themselves. Research in this stream examines entrepreneurship from a psychological and sociological perspective. Finally, the third stream has focused on the entrepreneurial management process. This diverse literature included research on how to foster innovation within established corporations, start-ups and venture capital, organizational life cycles, and predictors of entrepreneurial success.

As is apparent from these three streams of research, earlier conceptualizations of entrepreneurship have often focused on either the economic function or the nature of the individual who is "the entrepreneur," whereas in recent years, significant research has focused on the search of the "how" of entrepreneurship. Among the many engaged in this area, Stevenson defined entrepreneurship in 1983 as "the pursuit of opportunity beyond the tangible resources that you currently control." With this definition, emphasis is placed on how opportunity can be recognized, the process of committing to an opportunity, gaining control over the resources, managing the network of resources that may or may not be within a single hierarchy, and the way in which participants are rewarded.[2] The entrepreneurial organization focuses on opportunity, not resources. Entrepreneurs must commit quickly but tentatively so as to be able to readjust as new information arises. The process of commitment becomes multistaged, limiting the commitment of resources at each stage to an amount sufficient to generate new information and success before more resources are sought. The entrepreneurial organization uses resources that lie within the hierarchical control of others and, therefore, must manage the network as well as the hierarchy.

Given our aim to develop a framework for how to approach the social entrepreneurial process more systematically and effectively, we draw on the literature focusing on the "how" of entrepreneurship. We use Stevenson's definition of entrepreneurship and build on Sahlman's analytical framework from the entrepreneurial management literature.[3] Sahlman's model succinctly captures the key elements that are critical considerations for commercial entrepreneurship, and therefore provide a strong basis for developing a framework for social entrepreneurship. This model stresses the creation of a dynamic fit among four interrelated components: the People, the Context, the Deal, and the Opportunity, or "PCDO." Because these elements are interdependent and situationally determined, the entrepreneur must manage the fit among them and adapt continuously to new circumstances over time. "People" is defined as those who actively participate in the venture or bring resources to the venture. They include both those within the organization and those outside who must be involved for the venture to succeed. People's skills, attitudes, knowledge, contacts, goals, and values provide the resource mix that contributes centrally to success. The presumption that economic self-interest drives most economic activity in organizations can lead to dangerous and expensive mistakes. Whether in nonprofit or for-profit organizations, the whole person with multiple motivations and capacities creates the energy and determines the nature of the outcome.

"Context" is defined as those elements outside of the control of the entrepreneur that will influence success or failure. Contextual factors include the macroeconomy, tax and regulatory structure, and sociopolitical environment. Economic environment, tax policies, employment levels, technological advances, and social movements such as labor, religious, and political are examples of specific contextual factors that can frame the opportunities and the risks that a new venture faces. With this definition, it is clear that one of the critical elements for success is defining those elements that must be consciously dealt with and those that can simply play out as they will. Attention to everything can mean attention to nothing. On the other hand, leaving out a single critical element of context can be the precursor of failure.

"Deal" is the substance of the bargain that defines who in a venture gives what, who gets what, and when those deliveries and receipts will take place. Each transaction delivers a bundle of values. They include economic benefits, social recognition, autonomy and decision rights, satisfaction of deep personal needs, social interactions, fulfillment of generative and legacy desires, and delivery on altruistic goals.

"Opportunity" is defined as "any activity requiring the investment of scarce resources in hopes of a future return." Change is motivated by the vision of the future that is better for the decision maker and by the credibility of the path presented to that desired future state. One of the historic difficulties in the study of entrepreneurship is that the definition of opportunity is not necessarily shared by the multiple constituencies who must work together to create change. Often, change affects power relationships, economic interests, personal networks, and even self-image. A critical factor in creating motivation for joint action arises out of the ability to create a common definition of opportunity that can be shared.

Even slight perturbation in one of these "PCDO" domains can have tremendous implications for the others. Changing people often requires significant modifications in the terms of the deal. Changing context can render the skill set of one group obsolete and make another group's skills more important. Different opportunities are perceived in differing contexts, and amending a deal may attract new players and/or drive away the old. Entrepreneurs must consciously manage a dynamic relationship among these elements. See Figure 2.1.

TOWARD A NEW FRAMEWORK

People and Capital

In many ways, the human and financial capital inputs that are essential components of the entrepreneurial venture are quite comparable between social and commercial entrepreneurship. Both commercial and social entrepreneurs must consider the managers, employees, funders, and other organizations that

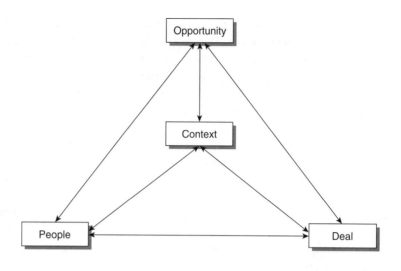

Figure 2.1   PCDO Framework

SOURCE: Stevenson, H., Roberts, M., Bhide, A., & Sahlman, W. (1999). Some thoughts on business plans. In *The entrepreneurial venture*. Boston: Harvard Business School Press. Used with permission.

are critical to their success and how to capture this human talent for their ventures. As noted by Sahlman, and Hart, Stevenson, and Dial,[4] two key determinants of whether a commercial entrepreneur will succeed in this effort are (1) entrepreneurs must know the industry in which they are seeking to mobilize resources and launch a new enterprise, and (2) they must be known by others for their abilities. Specifically, they must know the key suppliers, customers, competitors, and the talent that they need to bring into their organization. They must also be recognized by others for their reputations and capabilities in order to gain the trust of others who will be willing to work with and invest in them. While social entrepreneurs seek to attract capital for the social good rather than for financial returns, they rely just as much, if not more so, on a robust network of contacts that will provide them with access to funding, board members, management, and staff, among other resources. To attract these resources, social entrepreneurs, like their commercial counterparts, must have a strong reputation that engenders trust among contributors and a commitment to invest in the social enterprise and its mission.

Despite many similarities, the nature of the human and financial capital for social entrepreneurship differs in some key respects. Unlike a commercial entrepreneur who often has the financial capital or incentives to recruit and retain talent, social entrepreneurs are rarely able to pay market rates for key hires,[5] nor are they able to offer other equity incentives such as stock options. As noted by

Oster,[6] evidence for this pattern has been found in many nonprofit subsectors such as healthcare[7] and education,[8] as well as among various professionals in the sector, from lawyers to managers.[9] Furthermore, social enterprises often rely on volunteers to serve key functions, such as board members to help with fund-raising or to provide professional services, or to volunteer staff to deliver their services on the ground. An example of this reliance on volunteer staff is Ducks Unlimited (DU), the world's largest private waterfowl and wetlands conservation organization with a membership of nearly 800,000. In fiscal year 2005, DU volunteers held over 4,500 grassroots fund-raising events, which generated nearly 20% of the organization's $196 million in total revenue.[10] Clearly, this reliance on volunteers at the grassroots level for such core organizational functions presents a unique set of management challenges. Additionally, assuming that social entrepreneurs have the contacts and reputation to attract high-quality paid and volunteer staff, they must rely on creative strategies beyond offering financial rewards and incentives in order to recruit, retain, and motivate these contributors. Just as in the underfunded commercial start-up, social entrepreneurs must often find ways to accomplish more with few resources at their disposal.

Compared to the commercial capital markets, the philanthropic capital markets are highly fragmented. Social entrepreneurs rely heavily on a range of funding sources, including individual contributions, foundation grants, member dues, user fees, and government payments. Furthermore, these funders have a wide variety of motivations and expectations. In the commercial capital markets, the key motivation for all players involved is most often to build a profitable company and to earn an attractive return on investment. Thus, investors often provide a significant portion of relatively long-term funding, while at the same time, help raise additional funds for the venture. There are a multitude of competing financial institutions offering a wide range of financial instruments to meet the different needs of commercial entrepreneurs at distinct stages in their organizational evolution, once viability is demonstrated. The institutional breadth, flexibility, and specialization do not exist to the same extent in the philanthropic capital markets, thereby constraining the options of the social entrepreneur. Often, too, the social entrepreneur must rely on these sources in perpetuity since the operations rarely, if ever, will attain breakeven without some form of donor support.

Additionally, commercial entrepreneurs are generally given discretion to use the capital toward those activities that will add the most value to the venture. In the philanthropic capital markets, however, constraints on usage are common, in part because donor motivations are varied and often based on personal preference and values rather than on objective measures. Furthermore, the availability of funding is often extremely limited as competition has intensified. Motivations to invest in a social enterprise can range from pure altruism, to a belief in the social entrepreneur's vision and capabilities, to a desire for community recognition, among many others. Social enterprise investors generally invest a relatively small portion of the enterprise's capital needs for a relatively short period of time.[11] The social entrepreneur is thus required to spend a significant portion of his or her time, on an ongoing basis, cobbling together numerous grants, many of which come with spending restrictions and varied expectations of accountability, just to meet day-to-day operating costs. The duration of grants, often made on an annual basis, tends to be considerably shorter for social enterprises, thereby creating an ongoing need for social entrepreneurs to give fund-raising activities priority ahead of most other management demands.

In short, while the human and financial capital required for success is similar across commercial and social entrepreneurship, social entrepreneurs are often faced with more constraints. From limited access to the best talent, to fewer financial institutions, instruments, and resources, to restrictions that funds be used toward specific programs and activities, the social entrepreneur's ability to make decisions on how best to utilize resources to achieve the organization's ambitious goals is limited. To overcome some of these barriers, social entrepreneurs sometimes opt for a for-profit organizational form for a number of reasons, such as the ability to access the commercial capital market and pay more competitive wages to attract talent. However, even the corporate form does not remove all the constraints, as social entrepreneurs are then faced with the challenge of maintaining a focus on the social mission while generating a competitive return for investors.

Given these constraints, it is critical for the social entrepreneur to develop a large network of strong supporters and an ability to communicate the impact of their work in order to leverage resources outside organizational boundaries that will enable them to achieve their goals. The work of Steve Mariotti, founder of NFTE, the world's largest organization promoting entrepreneurial leadership among youth, illustrates the resourcefulness required of a social entrepreneur. NFTE was initially founded by Mariotti as a small operation run out of his apartment, with a small board composed of family and friends. Through building a powerful network of key staff and supporters, it has since grown dramatically, and the challenges it faced in this growth process are set forth in the first case study in this chapter.

Additionally, a social entrepreneur must be skilled at managing a diverse number of relationships with fewer management levers, as financial incentives are less readily available, and management authority over supporters, volunteer staff, and trustees is rather limited. These relationships may include funders, managers, and staff from diverse backgrounds, as well as volunteers, board members, and other partners. The diversity of relationships is also manifested in the different types of institutions, as social entrepreneurs may often need to work collaboratively with other nonprofit organizations, businesses, and government in order to attain the capital that is critical for the organization, such as partnerships that enable nonprofit organizations to pool resources to develop capabilities they could not afford to do on their own. Other examples include investing in systems, such as information technology for managing members, volunteers, and funders; or collaborating with other nonprofits to deliver programs or services; or cross-sector partnerships that bring valuable capital to the social enterprise while creating mutual benefit for the government or corporate partner. The September 11th Fund, one of the largest foundations established in the wake of the September 11 tragedies, provides an example of this resourcefulness. The foundation leveraged both intrasector and cross-sector collaboration to procure the capital necessary for its success. The fund-raising and grantmaking expertise of the founding partners, the New York Community Trust and the United Way of New York City, provided complementary skills, while support from businesses such as McKinsey Consulting and IBM provided additional managerial and technical expertise for creating the organizational infrastructure necessary for collecting the influx of donations. The evolution of this social enterprise is presented in more detail as the second case study in this chapter.

Another example might be contributing to and participating in sectorwide knowledge sharing or professional networks that broaden the knowledge base and talent pool available to the organization, and the sector as a whole. Social sector entrepreneurs often see others serving the same needs as competitors for funding, but these competitors can also be allies in the service of their objectives. For example, in the case of Women's World Banking (WWB), the organization invested heavily in building sectorwide networks among leading microfinance organizations to build joint knowledge and strengthen the sector's ability to affect banking regulations that affected microfinance. While the network members might have viewed each other as competitors, they have since found that participation in the networks furthered not only their own organization's objectives but also those of the microfinance sector as a whole.

To expand the organizational capacity with limited capital, the social entrepreneur must focus on building a rich network of contacts and capital, developing the skills to manage the various relationships in this network effectively, and seeking out creative arrangements to expand organizational capacity with limited capital. New Schools Venture Fund, a leading venture philanthropy fund in the education sector, established the New Schools Network, which exemplifies this approach. The network consists of a bipartisan community of education, nonprofit policy, and business leaders who work in collaboration toward the goal of education reform. In addition to New Schools' direct work of funding and providing support to promising education ventures, its network leverages resources outside the organization's boundaries to affect change in the public education system.[12] New Schools Venture Fund is presented in more detail as one of the case studies in Chapter 3.

While networks are important in commercial entrepreneurship, political and relationship management skills are of utmost importance to social entrepreneurs because such a large portion of the capital they rely on for success is outside of their direct control, from board members, to donors, to partners, to volunteers. Although nonprofits often earn a significant amount of their revenues through various earned income strategies (discussed further in Chapter 4), because the social sector organization relies so heavily on resources outside organizational boundaries, the social entrepreneur must not only continuously manage and cultivate the organization's network but should also ensure that key staff have and develop the skills to contribute to this critical task.

Context

The external context, defined as factors that affect the outcome of the opportunity but are outside the control of management, has considerable overlap for commercial and social entrepreneurship. In the social sector, factors such as interest rates, macroeconomic activity, government regulations, industry activity, labor markets, and the sociopolitical environment can be equally as important as in the commercial sector. Every organization faces competition for resources and for the goodwill of its employees and clientele.

The philanthropic market is highly affected by economic activity, as much philanthropic capital is derived in some form from commercial enterprise. Indeed, many nonprofit endowment funds are invested in the stock market, and individual contributions are tied directly to people's levels of discretionary income. Government regulations, in general, are relevant to both. Leaders must know the specific types of laws and regulations that affect their ability to function. Laws regulating the tax-exempt status or operations of nonprofits, tax policies that influence the amount of giving to the sector, and specific social policies affect social issues such as education, the environment, health, and housing. Finally, just as commercial enterprises compete for such resources as funding from investors, market share for customers, and the most talented employees, social enterprises compete for philanthropic dollars, government grants and contracts, volunteers, community mindshare, political attention, clients or customers, and talent within their "industry" contexts.

Although the critical contextual factors are in many ways analogous between commercial and social entrepreneurial opportunities, the impact of the context on a social entrepreneur differs from that on a commercial entrepreneur. The market selection mechanisms in the social sector are relatively less intense in that they tend to be less powerful and act over longer periods of time. For example, in many cases, a social entrepreneur can still meet with some degree of success while pursuing an opportunity, despite an inhospitable context. In fact, social entrepreneurs may choose to pursue opportunities to address social change not despite but because of an inhospitable context. As during harsh economic times, social needs tend to intensify, and many new social enterprises may be established to serve these needs, despite an adverse funding environment. In other cases, a social issue may be compelling to only a relatively small number of constituencies and have very low visibility, yet a social entrepreneur may seek to make an impact by raising awareness and attention to the issue.

A case in point is the National Organization of Rare Diseases, a federation of independent voluntary health organizations that is dedicated to helping people with rare diseases and assisting the organizations that serve them. The organization was founded in 1983 by members of patient support groups who worked together to get the Orphan Drug Act, which would provide incentives for the development of treatments of rare disorders, passed by the U.S. Congress and signed by President Reagan in 1983. In the 20 years since its legislation, the number of treatments developed for orphan diseases has increased more than 20 times compared to the previous decade.[13] In this case, the context was highly unfavorable, the issue had received relatively little attention, and it had a small number of supporters. Despite inhospitable contextual factors, the entrepreneurial efforts and innovative approach of the organization generated considerable social impact. In other cases, signals from the market are often difficult to decipher, and social entrepreneurs, driven by their social mission, may pay less attention to the contextual factors and forge ahead without a clear understanding of their implications. Even within nonprofit subsectors, although competition certainly exists among nonprofit organizations, social sector organizations are not often rewarded for good performance in the form of increased funding, nor are they readily penalized for ineffective performance. Aaron Lieberman, founder of Jumpstart, a fast-growing, early childhood education program, reflected on his experience, noting that "the connection between Jumpstart's success at demonstrating impact and its ability to fund raise is, at best, tenuous. Fund raising success comes primarily from building relationships based on trust and reputation—which can be completely disconnected from the actual performance of the organization."[14] Many have attributed this to the fact that impact and performance are notoriously difficult to measure in the social sector, and even if methods are devised to measure performance, the true organizational impacts often take a long time to manifest themselves.

While the social marketplace may not reward entrepreneurs for superior performance as readily as the commercial marketplace does for business entrepreneurs, neither does inferior performance get punished as readily. Some would argue that the discipline of the market applies less to social entrepreneurs. The for-profit entrepreneur often exits or is replaced if the financial measures of progress are not met. It appears that many social enterprises that are inefficient or ineffective at delivering their services can often continue for some time as long as their donor base recognizes the continuing need and does not necessarily demand hard measures of impact in exchange for further support. Many constituents, such as funders and board members, focus on the organization's social mission and fail to emphasize accountability and high performance for the organization.[15] The fact that their mission is to benefit others may insulate social enterprises from the same type of punitive discipline that occurs in the commercial marketplace. There tends to be a greater forgiveness factor or margin for error among capital providers, particularly because social enterprise performance is so difficult to measure. In short, market forces neither reward high performance nor punish poor performance as much or as readily as purely commercial organizations.

While the macroeconomic and social sector contexts undoubtedly have an impact on the outcomes of opportunities that social entrepreneurs pursue, as discussed previously, the impact of these contextual factors is often rather ambiguous. Social entrepreneurs may, therefore, have a tendency to pay less attention to the operating context since the consequences of doing so may manifest themselves slowly, if at all. Nonetheless, paying greater attention to the context and actively monitoring it for potential threats and opportunities can enable a social entrepreneur to develop an adaptive strategy that takes into account various contingencies. This proactive approach can ensure that the venture is better prepared to deal with sudden environmental shifts or changes.

The dramatic changes in the healthcare industry exemplify such contextual shifts. For example, the board of trustees of Mt. Auburn Hospital, a nonprofit community hospital in Cambridge, Massachusetts, recognized that the economic realities of their industry were leading to a major consolidation. Although they were in a solid financial position, their scanning of the environment led them to conclude that smaller facilities, like theirs, were an endangered species. Consequently, they took a very proactive approach to locating another, larger hospital with which they could merge.[16]

Perhaps more important than fending off threats, monitoring the context can enable a social entrepreneur to identify opportunities for the enterprise that might otherwise be overlooked. For example, political attention brought upon certain social issues, or emerging trends in the philanthropic capital markets, may provide social entrepreneurs who are astute enough to identify these shifts with valuable opportunities for new programs, fund-raising, and potential partnerships. To illustrate, the Sesame Workshop, a nonprofit educational organization best known for its flagship series *Sesame Street,* has a mission to make a meaningful difference in the lives of children worldwide by addressing their critical developmental needs. The organization, founded in 1968 with the aim of using television as a tool to help children learn, pioneered the concept of creating entertaining and enriching television for children. Today, the organization currently operates in a highly competitive context that is increasingly dominated by large, for-profit children's media companies. To continue to deliver on its mission in this context, it has sought to support its educational activities with revenue-generating activities that include global product licensing, book publishing, domestic and foreign distribution of local language television programs, coproductions, and overseas syndication of its portfolio of educational programs. In recent years, these self-generated revenues have become the largest contributor to the organization's capital and are central to furthering its educational initiatives worldwide.[17] The organization has grown to become an approximately $100 million revenue-generating entity.

While organizational survival in the social sector may not always seem to depend on responsiveness to the context, a social enterprise that monitors the context closely can develop strategies to minimize the impact of adverse environmental changes and capitalize on opportunities that might arise from favorable trends. Ultimately, this proactive management approach will best enable the organization to achieve the greatest social impact.

Opportunity

Opportunity is defined as the desired future state that is different from the present and the belief that the achievement of that state is possible. Opportunities in the commercial and social sectors require the investment of scarce resources with the hope of future returns. In social and commercial entrepreneurship, entrepreneurs are concerned with customers, suppliers, entry barriers, substitutes, rivalry, and economics of the venture, though perhaps to varying degrees due to differences in market dynamics between the sectors as previously discussed.[18] The key difference is that in the latter, the focus is on economic returns, while in the former, the focus is on social returns.

At a conceptual level, opportunities are quite similar across commercial and social entrepreneurship. However, in practice, this dimension of the framework is perhaps the most distinct. Commercial entrepreneurship tends to focus on breakthroughs and new needs, whereas social entrepreneurship often focuses on serving basic, long-standing needs more effectively through innovative approaches. For a commercial entrepreneur, an opportunity must have a large or growing total market size and the industry must be structurally attractive. For a social entrepreneur, a recognized social need, demand, or market failure usually guarantees a more than sufficient market size. The problem is not the existence of the need, but rather whether resources can be marshaled for the social entrepreneur's innovation to serve that need. The scope of opportunities for social entrepreneurs is relatively wide because they are able to pursue ventures that are both economically viable (i.e., financially self-sustaining) as well as those that require subsidies (i.e., donor supported). Unlike in the commercial sector in which unexploited, profitable, high-growth opportunities are relatively hard to capture, in the social sector, social needs, and hence opportunities for social entrepreneurs, often far outstrip the resources available to address them, particularly because the ultimate consumers are often unable or unwilling to pay for the costs of the goods or services. As a consequence, it is common that even before growth has been considered, much less a strategy for growth laid out, social entrepreneurs and their organizations are often pulled into rapid growth by pressure from funders or demand for their services and are pushed by their social missions to meet those needs, especially given the social entrepreneur's belief that his or her model is able to meet these needs in a superior way. Thus, a social enterprise may often launch into growth and expansion before much thought or planning.

A case in point is KaBOOM!, a nonprofit that has raised more than $10 million for community playgrounds since 1995. In 1998, during a period of particularly high growth in which revenues doubled, the organization encountered some difficulties managing all of its partner relationships. As one board member described, "KaBOOM! was building the plane while they were flying it, and they had to slow down to speed up again."[19] The KaBOOM! situation is presented in more detail as a case study in Chapter 5.

In comparing the nature of opportunities in the commercial and social sectors, it is apparent that in the latter relative to the former, there are abundant opportunities, which often lead to a situation in which organizational growth precedes planning. Opportunities for social entrepreneurship often seem boundless, in the sense that the demand for social programs and services usually far exceeds the capacity of the social enterprises to serve these needs. Initial successes often lead to increased demand for the social enterprise's programs, products, or services, or even requests to scale or replicate the organization in some form. For many of the employees and the outside funders, the growth imperative often becomes paramount (see Chapter 6). It fulfills their personal needs and builds on their values.

The growth may involve scaling the organization directly, working in partnership with other organizations to disseminate the social innovation, or some combination of approaches. A key challenge for social entrepreneurs is to resist the powerful demand-pull for growth and to be more deliberate about planning a long-term impact strategy. Social entrepreneurs should realize that they have great latitude in the ways that they can choose to pursue these opportunities. In some cases, growth may not be the best approach to achieving the organization's goals or having the greatest social impact. Growth for the sake of growth has the potential to squander organizational resources and can actually detract from the organization's overall impact. In other cases, organizational growth may in fact be the best path to optimizing social impact, but the organization may need to plan for a long-term growth strategy as it may not have the resources or the capacity to grow immediately.

The case of Guide Dogs for the Blind Association (GDBA), a social enterprise based in the United Kingdom and the world's leading breeder and trainer of seeing-eye dogs, illustrates the need for deliberate strategic planning for growth. The organization responded to the demand for expanded services in the early 1990s, adding hotel and holiday programs for the visually impaired to its services. While these new services were well received by some clients, they resulted in significant financial losses to the organization to the point where the long-term sustainability of the entire organization was threatened. In 1997, the financial state of the organization was so severe that the trustees hired a new CEO with a mandate to stem the losses while continuing to uphold the high-quality mobility service programs. Over a period of many years, GDBA established partnerships and transferred operations of the hotel and holiday programs through partnerships with other charities serving the visually impaired sector. At the same time, consistent with the organization's mission to provide guide dogs, mobility, and other rehabilitation services that meet the needs of blind and partially sighted people, the organization focused on enhancing the range of mobility services provided to clients such as reading, writing, and long cane training. A key challenge for the organization was how to manage its portfolio of services and growth options to achieve its mission. These challenges are presented in more detail in the case study set forth in Chapter 6.

As in the GDBA case, unbridled growth can often be ineffective at increasing organizational impact, be a drain on the organization's talent and resources, or worse, even undermine existing successes. In approaching any type of growth, whether expanding the range of services or expanding geographically through replication, a social entrepreneur must identify the relevant risks and approach all growth opportunities with disciplined, strategic thinking. Among the issues a social entrepreneur should keep in mind are the organization's mission and goals, how growth fits with those goals, the range of strategies that the organization can pursue to achieve these goals, and whether the human and financial resources available to the organization are consistent with these goals.

A FRAMEWORK FOR SOCIAL ENTREPRENEURSHIP

While the PCDO framework is in many ways applicable to the analysis of social entrepreneurship, we suggest that some adaptations might make it even more useful to both practitioners and researchers. To highlight the centrality of the social purpose in social entrepreneurship, we propose that this factor be the integrating driver of the framework. It is analogous to the "deal" variable in the PCDO in that it encompasses the terms of the undertaking, but those terms need to be related to and integrated by the core social value proposition (SVP). The distinctive nature and central role of the mission in social enterprises and the multifaceted nature of the social value generated give the SVP a logical centrality in the framework. We also believe that it would be analytically helpful to practitioners and researchers to separate out the economic and human resources as distinct variables. Our analysis revealed that the mobilization of financial and human resources for social entrepreneurship are each quite distinct from commercial entrepreneurship and from each other, and so merit focused attention.[20] The "opportunity" variable remains, although the nature of what is an opportunity is fundamentally different given the underlying generative effect of market failure. Contextual forces impinge on all the other variables and remain relevant to both forms of entrepreneurship, albeit often with fundamentally differing effects. What might be deemed an unfavorable contextual factor for market-based commercial entrepreneurship could be seen as an opportunity for a social entrepreneur who aims to address social needs arising from market failure. To enable a more disaggregated analysis of contextual forces that seem particularly relevant to social entrepreneurship, we added demographics, political, and sociocultural factors to the contextual factors presented in the original PCDO framework.

Figure 2.2 presents this revised Social Entrepreneurship Framework as a Venn diagram with the Opportunity circle at the top, because that is the initiating point for entrepreneurship. The two enabling variables—People and Capital Resources—are the bottom circles. The three circles intersect reflecting the overlapping and interdependent nature of the variables. At the center is the SVP as the integrating variable. Surrounding all three circles are the contextual forces shaping the other variables and requiring scrutiny by the social entrepreneur.

IMPLICATIONS FOR PRACTICE

Centrality of the Social Value Proposition

The foregoing analysis and framework underscore for practitioners the importance of a focus first and foremost on the SVP. This fact may seem patently obvious, as it is what drives most social entrepreneurs to pursue social entrepreneurship in the first place. However, in practice, it is often the case that the social entrepreneur becomes increasingly focused on organizational interests as a means to achieve social impact rather than on social impact itself. This phenomenon is not surprising given that the rationale is often that a larger, better-resourced

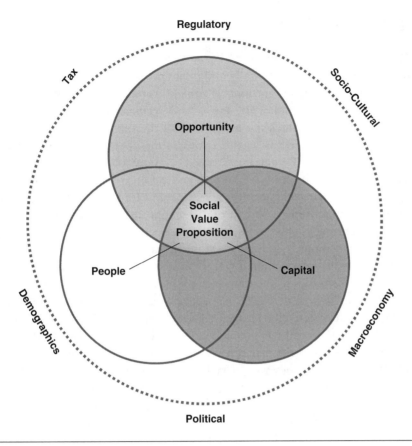

Figure 2.2   Social Entrepreneurship Framework

organization will be better able to deliver on its social mission. However, a number of factors limit the practicality of this approach. While people and resources to support the venture's growth are important and necessary, as our analysis has highlighted, mobilizing human and financial resources for social entrepreneurship is an extremely onerous task. The challenge of procuring resources for the organization can become so all-consuming for the social entrepreneur that it can become a primary focus of the organization's activities. The goal of furthering the organization may inadvertently become an end in and of itself, sometimes at the cost of social value creation. That is, social entrepreneurs may become so internally focused on procuring resources to support their organization's advancement that the paths to creating social value may become blurred. The resources are often a means to delivering on the SVP, but a broader perspective is needed.

Organizational Alignment

To deliver effectively on the SVP, the social entrepreneur must achieve a state of alignment both externally and internally among the key components of the framework: the Opportunity, People, Capital, and Context. For external alignment, one complicating fact is the dynamic nature of the context. Thus, the SVP that made sense at the time of the venture's founding may in fact evolve dramatically, as perturbations in the operating context are continuously occurring. Remaining attuned to how contextual changes can affect the opportunity and the human and financial resource environment causing the need for realignment is a critical skill for the social entrepreneur. Furthermore, practitioners should remain cognizant of a unique characteristic of the operating context, namely, that the societal demand for social value creation is enormous. This creates a plethora of opportunities for social entrepreneurs and a concomitant ever present temptation to address more and more of them. A social entrepreneur's task, then, is to determine at any given moment how to define the appropriate scope of the opportunity that can be pursued effectively. This requires ensuring that the scope is aligned internally with the available people and resources. Overextending the scope can cause a misalignment that could erode the core SVP. Seeking to address a very broad set of issues with very limited human and financial resources may actually result in low social impact because the organization's resources are spread too thin. While a social entrepreneur may devote considerable attention to achieving both external and internal organizational alignment, it is also important to keep in mind that social impact can often be more effectively generated from beyond organizational boundaries.

Organizational Boundaries

Although social value is very often created by bringing resources into the organization's boundaries and creating outputs directly, in other cases, the organization may actually have greater social impact by working in collaboration with complementary organizations, or even former or potential competitors. Indeed, greater social value can often be created by working collaboratively with other entities. The framework in Figure 2.2 helps to conceptualize this latter approach. By being closely attuned to the context in which the venture operates, a social entrepreneur can identify how best to mobilize resources both internally and externally. A social enterprise exists to create social value, regardless of whether that value is generated from within or outside the organization's boundaries. There may often be opportunities to leverage resources outside the organization's boundaries to create greater social value than could be generated by the organization alone. Although there are many obstacles to collaborating across organizational boundaries, such as concerns about organizational self-interest, or sharing proprietary knowledge, virtually all social issues require far more resources than any single organization is capable of mobilizing independently to solve. Building networks across organizational boundaries to create social value is a powerful strategy for social entrepreneurs because the objectives of creating social value do not require that value be captured within organizational boundaries. The social entrepreneurial venture can thus be conceptualized as a vehicle for creating social value, either directly or through facilitating the creation of social value with and by others.

CASE STUDIES

The social entrepreneurial process is commonly thought of as most important in the start-up phase of an organization. While thinking analytically about the various factors that will enable a venture's success at the outset is critical to ongoing success, social entrepreneurial skills are required at all stages to ensure ongoing mission impact. In the following two cases, we will examine two social enterprises as they were founded but also see the broader challenges that the social entrepreneurs must address as their organizations advance beyond their initial founding success. In just over two years, Steve Mariotti built the National Foundation for Teaching Entrepreneurship (NFTE) into an organization that had achieved national recognition for its work with economically disadvantaged and handicapped youth. Despite this accomplishment, questions were beginning to arise about the organization's overall strategy, funding, and management. The readings help us understand the institutional rationale for the creation of nonprofit organizations.

1. What were the key elements that enabled NFTE to be born?

2. What is your assessment of NFTE's launch and performance to date?

The September 11th Fund was created immediately after the September 11 tragedies through a partnership between the United Way of New York City and the New York Community Trust, New York City's two largest nonprofit funders, with assistance from McKinsey consultants. The case examines the role of institutional and individual social entrepreneurship in the creation of this new foundation. The reading provides an overview of some of the key legal and managerial issues to think about when starting a nonprofit.

1. What was it that enabled Dua to play the role that he did?

2. What are the critical factors that enabled the success of the partnership between the NYCT and the UWNYC? McKinsey and the UWNYC?

3. What factors would you identify as enablers or barriers to the three partners working together effectively?

NOTES

1. Stevenson, H., & Jarillo, J. (1991). A new entrepreneurial paradigm. In A. Etzioni & P. Lawrence (Eds.), *Socioeconomics: Toward a new synthesis* pp. 185–208). New York: M.E. Sharpe, Inc.

2. Stevenson, H. (1985, March–April). The heart of entrepreneurship. *Harvard Business Review,* pp. 85–94; and Stevenson & Jarillo (1991).

3. Stevenson, H., Roberts, M., Bhide, A., & Sahlman, W. (1999). Some thoughts on business plans. In H. Stevenson, M. Roberts, and A. Bhide (Eds.), *The entrepreneurial venture* (pp. 138–176). Boston: Harvard Business School Press.

4. Hart, M. M., Stevenson, H., & Dial, J. (1996). Entrepreneurship: A definition revisited. In W. Bygrave (Ed.), *Frontiers of Entrepreneurship 1995: Proceedings of the Fifteenth Annual Entrepreneurship Research Conference* (pp. 75–89). Wellesley, MA: Babson College.

5. Oster, S. M. (1995). *Strategic management for nonprofit organizations: Theory and cases.* New York: Oxford University Press.

6. Oster (1995).

7. e.g., Cole, B. (1982, December). Compensation. *Modern Healthcare,* pp. 67–90.

8. e.g., Freeman, R. (1979). The job market for college faculty. In D. Lewis & W. Becker (Eds.), *Academic rewards in higher education.* Cambridge, MA: Ballinger.

9. e.g., Weisbrod, B. (1983, July). Nonprofit and proprietary sector behavior: Wage differentials among lawyers. *Journal of Labor Economics, 1*(3), 246–263; and Preston, A. (1989, October). The nonprofit worker in a for-profit world. *Journal of Labor Economics, 7*(4), 438–463.

10. Ducks Unlimited Fact Sheet. Retrieved July 6, 2006, from www.ducks.org.

11. Letts, C., Ryan, W., & Grossman, A. (1999). *High performance nonprofit organizations: Managing upstream for greater impact.* New York: Wiley.

12. NewSchools Web site. Retrieved August 7, 2002, from www.newschools.org.

13. NORD Web site. Retrieved August 7, 2002, from www.nord.org.

14. Grossman, A., & McCaffrey, A. (2001). *Jumpstart.* Harvard Business School Case #9–301–037.

15. e.g., Letts, Ryan, & Grossman (1999).

16. McFarlan, F. W., & Elias, J. (1996). *Mt. Auburn hospital.* Harvard Business School Case #9–397–083.

17. Sesame Workshop Annual Report (2002).

18.   Porter, M. E. (1980). *Competitive strategy: Techniques for analyzing industries and competitors.* New York: Free Press; Porter, M. E. (1985). *Competitive advantage: Creating and sustaining superior performance.* New York: Free Press; Oster, S. M. (1994). *Modern competitive analysis.* New York: Oxford University Press; and Oster (1995).

19.   Austin, J. E., & Porraz, J. M. (2002). *KaBOOM!* Harvard Business School Case #9–303–025.

20.   The separation of economic resources might even be helpful for the PCDO framework's use for commercial entrepreneurship.

Case Study 2.1.

Steve Mariotti and NFTE

On a warm summer evening, Steve Mariotti paced around his one-bedroom apartment, which doubled as the headquarters of the National Foundation for Teaching Entrepreneurship to Handicapped and Disadvantaged Youth, Inc. (NFTE). He looked back over the past two and a half years with an understandable sense of pride. NFTE was not only up and running, it had gained national recognition for its work with inner-city youth. During 1989, it served over a thousand youths and raised nearly half a million dollars, and 1990 promised to be even better. Nonetheless, Steve felt in his gut that things had to change if NFTE was to continue on its growth trajectory. He worried about funding. "Can we simply count on the continued support of the foundations and individuals who helped get NFTE off the ground? Or do we need to look into alternative sources?" He worried about quality control. "Everyone raves about our program. How do we assure quality if we grow? How do we find dedicated people? How do we train them adequately?" He also worried about the increasing management burden he was feeling. "I love the teaching, but I could do without the administrative headaches. I don't want to expand if it means I do the administrative work and become a full-time executive." Steve needed to decide how to incorporate his personal goals and the goals of his staff with the larger organizational picture.

BACKGROUND

After an internal power struggle at Ford Motor Co. in 1979, Steve Mariotti lost his job as a financial analyst. Steve, a graduate of the Business School at the University of Michigan, moved to New York and founded the Mason Import-Export Company.

"When I came out of Ford, I was very bruised, real bitter. I had been in this hierarchy and I was on the bottom of it: I was a grade 7 and Henry Ford was a grade 27. I felt constant anxiety. I would go into work and they could pretty much do whatever they wanted with me. . . . But the minute I went into business for myself, I felt equal to Henry Ford psychologically. . . . I felt like, well, I'm president of this company, and he's president of a company. I just don't have as much capital as he does, and I don't really care. The effect that it had on my own psyche was enormous, marked, and immediate."[1]

During an evening jog in 1981, Steve was mugged by a group of youths demanding that he give them $10. Finding their victim penniless, they beat Steve severely. Steve felt confused; he was unable to understand why the kids mugged him over such a trivial sum. "I began to think that maybe it was related to a hierarchy, that these kids were viewing themselves at the bottom of some hierarchy like I had been at Ford. . . . And I just hooked it to my own experience of how I came out of the bottom of the heap by starting a small company."[2]

Realizing that he had developed an uncontrollable fear of the street kids he encountered daily, Steve visited a therapist who advised him to confront these fears. He liquidated Mason, and in 1982 he became a typing and bookkeeping teacher in the New York City public schools. Not only would this force Steve to confront his fears, but it would give him a chance to provide his students with a taste of the kind of empowerment entrepreneurship could offer. "I asked for the worst schools in the worst neighborhoods. . . . I'd go there and ask for troubled kids, because I view those kids as having special opportunities in the field of entrepreneurship. I think the best entrepreneurs have had trouble in a structured environment."[3]

From 1982 to 1986, Steve taught at 11 schools. "I was looked upon as a kook. It was very painful. I was very popular and I got along with the principals and the teachers, but the school system is very authoritative. It destroys the entrepreneur. Having the kids making products to sell didn't go over very well. People kept telling me to teach math and reading skills first. That seemed backwards to me. The students needed a reason to learn reading and math. Entrepreneurship provided that reason."

In 1987, Steve was teaching at Jane Addams Vocational High School in the Fort Apache section of the Bronx. Pat Black, the principal of the school, allowed Steve to teach a special class in entrepreneurial skills. The class was a success. This course eventually turned into the South Bronx Entrepreneurial Project, a "crash course in capitalism." It was given after school and was designed for the most troubled students. Many had been given the option of taking Steve's course or being kicked out of school.

"The kids filled out sole-proprietorship forms and got their stationery and business cards done. They wrote their business plans, their marketing plans. They did mock sales calls. I took them down to where you register businesses and introduced them to all the people there. I did everything I could to demystify the experience. Then I had them write to several [government-sponsored] Minority Enterprise Small-Business Investment Companies. . . . Right away I knew I had something. You'd have these guys sitting in the back and they'd be saying, 'Oh screw you, up yours, blah, blah, blah,' and two weeks later they'd be acting like MBAs." By the end of the year, 10 businesses had been started by Steve's students. He financed the student ventures partially through $1,000 in small grants from the Trickle-Up program. The Trickle-Up program provides small grants to young entrepreneurs, but most of the grants are awarded overseas, rather than in the United States. The rest of the money came out of Steve's own pocket. He quickly found himself $18,000 in debt, with a bad credit rating.

Steve had intended the hiatus from running his own business to be relatively brief. However, he loved working with the kids in his program and decided he wanted to make entrepreneurial education his full-time occupation. "Entrepreneurship is the catalyst that releases these students' creative energies, their sense of momentum and initiative, and perhaps, most important of all, it encourages them to take responsibility for their own lives. By helping disadvantaged youth improve their own future, we will be making a strategic investment in the future strength of our society—especially in the restoration of inner-city communities."[4]

At the end of 1987, Steve founded NFTE as an independent nonprofit organization. In 1988, NFTE received 501(c)(3) status as a tax-exempt educational organization. The mission of the foundation was "to promote entrepreneurial literacy among highly at-risk and economically and or physically disadvantaged minority youth living in America's inner cities and to help each one start his/her own business." See **Exhibit 2.1.1** for a brief description of NFTE's entrepreneurial education process.

MAKING IT WORK

Steve realized that he needed to raise money for his foundation. "I wrote to all the wealthiest people on *Forbes* magazine's list. I received only one reply from my 160 letters." The reply was from an individual in Newark, who introduced Steve to the Boys and Girls Clubs of Newark and the READY scholar foundation. Kids in the READY program who diligently attended a weekly, 4-hour after-school program from elementary school through high school would receive a free college education. "[This individual] called me two days later and wanted to see me. I had to borrow money from one of my special education students to make the trip. I got out my suit and took the train to see him the next day. He gave me good advice and encouragement. I was deeply grateful that someone understood what I was trying to do." Steve received similar support from Barbara Bell, CEO of the Boys and Girls Clubs of Newark, who had worked with the READY program for five years. She gave Steve his first contract—$60,000 to teach in the READY program. Each week, Steve spent 16 hours teaching elementary school kids and 6 hours teaching junior high school students. The Boys and Girls Clubs

We first have our students master basic reading, writing, and math skills (they learn to do their own bookkeeping and figure their own taxes); and basic human values (such as initiative, honesty, and persistence) are installed. We teach them to do the following:

- Identify and utilize basic economic concepts, such as cost-benefit analysis, supply-demand, and opportunity costs.
- Become alert to economic opportunities.
- Write a business letter, memos, and how to prepare a basic contract.
- Read the *Wall Street Journal* and do basic business research.
- Register the company with the proper municipal agencies and how to open a bank account.
- Print business cards, fliers, posters, and stationery.
- Find a product in the wholesale markets, set the price, and develop the techniques for marketing and direct sales of a product line.
- Sell by training with videotaped simulated sales presentations; this encourages self-analysis, builds self-confidence, and improves communication ability.
- Plan and write a business plan with a view to securing venture capital.
- Develop job-getting skills that include résumé preparation and interview techniques for those students who choose not to establish their own businesses right away.

The National Foundation for Teaching Entrepreneurship (NFTE) then arranges for on-site visits to, and internships in, successful businesses run by Black and Hispanic Americans and invites these established minority entrepreneurs to come to our classes to answer questions, share ideas, and, in general, be inspiring as role models.

Finally, NFTE has a graduation and awards ceremony. This serves as a formal recognition of the students' achievements and provides a source of positive feedback where there often had been none prior to the graduation.

After graduation, every graduate is encouraged to become a part of the NFTE Alumni Network and is invited to workshops via a quarterly newsletter published by the NFTE.

Exhibit 2.1.1   The Entrepreneurial Education Process

a. 1989 *Strategic Report*. National Foundation for Teaching Entrepreneurship.

Case Study

of Newark also hired Steve to run a separate program for high school students.

Having received his first contract, Steve needed another teacher. He asked Russell Kelly, a fellow faculty member at Jane Addams, to help him part-time with NFTE. Russell accepted and in essence became Steve's partner in the new venture. Russell had a bachelor's degree in business administration and was working toward his master's degree in journalism. Russell also had worked as a loan officer for the Small

Business Administration and had held various positions within the New York City Board of Education.

Steve set up an office in his apartment. He was assisted by his fiancée, Janet McKinstry. Janet held a bachelor's degree in marketing and an associate's degree in buying and merchandising. Having founded two companies herself, Janet also had a practical grounding in entrepreneurship. From the beginning, she helped Steve organize NFTE. Many of her ideas were incorporated into the NFTE curriculum. For example, Janet suggested that all the kids should be given a minimal amount of money and taken to wholesalers to buy merchandise for resale, a practice that became a standard part of NFTE's programs and a favorite with all of the students. Janet took a special interest in organizing NFTE's Physically Challenged Entrepreneur Program (PCEP).

Steve realized that he would need professional help with fund-raising and accounting. He hired Mike Caslin as part-time professional fund-raiser. Mike's company, the Caslin Group, advised small businesses and nonprofit organizations, specializing in turnaround situations and revenue growth. He worked from his home in Massachusetts, consulting with approximately ten clients each year. Mike agreed to assist Steve with strategic planning and public affairs. Steve also hired Ken Dillard to work part-time on the financial statements. Ken met Steve through Janet. He was a CPA who specialized in working with nonprofit organizations.

Later in the year, Steve hired yet another Jane Addams teacher, Chris Meenan, to run the Boys and Girls Clubs of Newark program for high school students. Chris had a bachelor's degree in political science from Loyola College and was working toward a master's degree in business education. He directed the Entrepreneur's Club at Jane Addams. Chris was unhappy teaching in the public school system and was seriously considering leaving the profession prior to Steve's offer. After working for Steve part-time for six months, Chris became a full-time teacher for NFTE.

During 1988, NFTE received a total of $189,000 in contributions from a variety of sources. Most of this was unrestricted seed

money, which NFTE could allocate within its stated mission as its management and board saw fit. The foundation helped start 32 businesses that grossed over $40,000. An additional 495 inner-city youth graduated from an NFTE program. Beyond the programs with the Boys and Girls Clubs and with the physically challenged, a number of efforts were initiated. These ranged from work with Riker's Island inmates to a two-week seminar at the Wharton School for promising high school students from West Philadelphia. The Wharton program was part of the University Community Outreach Program, funded by the Milken Foundation to stimulate business development in the inner cities. Steve received this contract with assistance from Lisa Hoffstein, the director of the program.

Steve's work began to gain recognition. In 1988, he was named the "Best Business Teacher of the Year" by the National Federation of Independent Businessmen, and he won first place in the New York State contest on teaching economics, sponsored by Mobil Oil Corporation. By 1989, NFTE had attracted an enormous amount of attention from the media. Steve was featured as ABC's "Unsung American" for the month of July, and NFTE's programs were covered in the "American Agenda" segment on ABC's *World News Tonight*. Steve and NFTE were also covered in *Inc.*, *USA Today*, the *New York Times*, and a variety of other publications. This media attention was unsolicited; it occurred as word spread about Steve and his foundation.

During 1989, existing programs grew rapidly, and a number of new programs were started. A franchise of the fast-food restaurant Jersey Mike's was opened on Rutgers University's Newark campus. The store would be operated by residents of the Ogden Residential Group Center for Boys (a division of Juvenile Services of the State of New Jersey) along with members of the Boys and Girls Clubs of Newark. NFTE's entrepreneurial education curriculum had been implemented in two New York City high schools during 1988. During 1989, NFTE organized a formal "master teacher" program to train teachers from participating high schools in the entrepreneurial curriculum. Master teachers would receive a monthly stipend for working with students, attending a 4-hour monthly training session at NFTE, and preparing four lesson plans each month. NFTE also established a junior teacher program. Students who were graduated from the general NFTE program were trained further to become assistants to the master teachers.

NFTE began an evaluation of its programs under the direction of three professors: two from Columbia Teachers College and one from the Pepperdine University School of Business and Management. The purpose of this evaluation was to track the long-term effects of NFTE's program on its students.

In 1989, Steve hired another full-time teacher, Scott Shickler. Steve met Scott at the annual conference of the Association of Collegiate Entrepreneurs. Scott was a senior at Fordham University and president of the Entrepreneur's Club at the university. Steve hired Scott to develop further the master teacher program, the junior teacher program, and to handle other requests for programs in Manhattan.

Now that Steve had a larger full-time teaching staff, he had a chance to work on developing an entrepreneurial education curriculum. He turned his attention to writing lesson plans with Tony Towle, a poet and writer, and with Rose Reissman, a specialist in curriculum development. Together, they developed 50 lesson plans for use in the classroom.

In this second year of existence, NFTE more than doubled its revenues to $494,000, largely on the strength of foundation grants. Nearly all the contributions for 1989 were restricted, earmarked for specific programs. Some $58,000 was given in small grants for students to start new businesses. In total, 1,173 youths participated in NFTE's various educational programs. Over 90 businesses were started, which grossed $150,000 in revenue.

FEELING THE STRAINS OF GROWTH

NFTE had expanded rapidly in the two years since its inception and planned to continue that high growth rate in 1990, setting a goal of over $1 million in contributions and 1,400 students (see **Exhibit 2.1.2** for a list of programs developed during 1988 and 1989, and the goals for 1990). With this growth Steve increasingly found himself on the phone and in the office playing the role of administrator. He was also teaching about 700 hours a year. He was personally feeling the strain.

One nagging source of concern was that NFTE lacked accurate and up-to-date financial information. While Ken Dillard had been doing the basic accounting, he worked only part-time and could not keep track of the daily inflows and outflows. Ken was assisted by Anne Hart, who worked three-quarters of a day each week. Anne was responsible for petty cash, and she did not have time to do more. Steve decided to hire

Direct Service Programs[1]

1. Boys and Girls Clubs of Newark. Elementary and high school students at the Boys and Girls Club are trained in entrepreneurial skills.

1988:	200 kids trained 17 businesses started
1989:	715 kids trained 20 businesses started Budget: $252,000
1990:	900 kids to be trained Budget goal: $383,000

2. Master Teacher and Junior Teacher Program (originally the South Bronx and Manhattan programs). Teachers receive entrepreneurial training from NFTE and teach this entrepreneurial curriculum in high schools in the South Bronx and Manhattan. It is anticipated that 6 master teachers and 12 junior teachers will be trained in 1990.

1988:	265 kids trained
1989:	300 kids trained Budget: $126,875
1990:	300 kids to be trained Budget goal: $170,000

3. Governor Kean's Entrepreneurial Education Program: NFTE runs an intensive two-week summer program held at Rider College and funded by Governor Kean for poor, inner-city youths. This is a pilot program to search for the most effective minority economic development program.

1988:	24 kids trained
1989:	35 kids trained Budget: $19,000
1990:	40 kids to be trained Budget goal: $25,000

4. Ogden Youth Home/Riker's Island. NFTE provided entrepreneurial education and training for Riker's Island inmates. In 1989, inmates from the Ogden Youth Home in 1989 were added to the program. A number of these youths work at Jersey Mike's, the fast-food franchise on Rutgers University's Newark campus.

1988:	55 inmates trained
1989:	60 inmates trained Budget: $35,000
1990:	75 inmates to be trained Budget goal: $38,000

5. University of Pennsylvania—Wharton School of Business: NFTE was selected as the most effective program in the nation to teach entrepreneurship to inner-city youth and runs an intensive two-week program in conjunction with the University of Pennsylvania Graduate School of

---

Exhibit 2.1.2   FTE Programs

Case Study

Business. These students are economically disadvantaged but are less poor than the students in New York and Newark. Most expect to go to college.

1988:   36 kids trained

1989:   40 kids trained
                 Budget: $25,000

1990:   40 kids to be trained
                 Budget goal: $25,000

6. Physically Challenged Entrepreneurs. Students with physical disabilities are trained in entrepreneurial skills.

1988:   2 kids trained

1989:   23 kids trained
                 Budget: $43,125

1990:   50 kids to be trained
                 Budget goal: $250,000

7. Madison Square Boys and Girls Clubs of New York. Elementary and high school students at the Boys and Girls Club are trained in entrepreneurial skills.

1990:   70 kids to be trained
                 Budget goal: $40,000

Support Programs

The following NFTE projects were undertaken to support the direct-service programs.

1. Telephone hotline for NFTE entrepreneurs. A hotline operating between 7 and 11 p.m., Sunday through Thursday. A consultant answers questions on small business and employment. Started in 1989, this hotline received an average of 19 calls each week. 1990 budget goal: $7,500.

2. Classroom curriculum program. In partnership with the Boys and Girls Clubs of Newark, NFTE is developing a complete curriculum to meet the special educational needs and skill deficits of economically and physically disadvantaged minority youth. 1990 budget goal: $100,000.

3. Public affairs for policy makers and educators. NFTE plans in 1990 to publish a book featuring a compiled series of articles by innovators in the field, a video with in-depth interviews of youths and the difficulties of starting their own businesses, and distribution of articles written by NFTE staff. 1990 budget goal: $74,000.

4. NFTE venture fund for Young Entrepreneurs. Funds would be used to support start-up and expansion of businesses. Young entrepreneurs presenting business plans would be eligible for grants of $100–$400. The maximum amount provided to any one person would be $10,000. Money for this fund is placed in a restricted NFTE bank account. 1990 budget goal: $78,400.

Exhibit 2.1.2

1. 1990 numbers are projected figures.

someone to manage the office. In late January, Steve hired Michelle Hori.

Michelle was graduating from the Fashion Institute of Technology (FIT) in New York, where she saw the job posted. Michelle wanted one day to run her own business. NFTE seemed an ideal place to acquire the necessary business skills. Michelle faced a formidable task in trying to organize the office, which was still in Steve's apartment. Steve acknowledged that he was primarily responsible for the mediocre performance of the office. He had been trying to minimize his administrative costs, because experience had taught him that foundations were reluctant to fund organizations with high overhead costs. However, Steve began to think that there was a trade-off between low administrative overhead and high-quality financial reporting.

"As executive director, I do not do an A+ job; it is more like a B–. We don't do any letter writing to speak of. Phone calls too often go unanswered. Much of the structure a good organization should have, we don't have. I would often take checks to go to one place or another. I would use them and sometimes they wouldn't get recorded in the checkbook. On several occasions, checks did not have a backup explaining why they were written. Our financial statements came out only every six weeks or so. Recently, I've turned over a new leaf. Ken will enter all checks in the books; he knows all the allocations. I don't touch the checkbook. I write down what checks I need written and why. Michelle writes them. Anne makes

sure that there is backup documentation for the checks and lets me know which ones don't have backup. Ken posts them in the ledger."

During the spring of 1990, Steve and Janet broke off their engagement. Janet decided to go to divinity school and announced that she would leave NFTE once she trained a successor. She chose Kevin Greaney, who had been helping with fund-raising for the PCEP program. A few weeks later, Janet agreed to continue to consult for NFTE on a part-time basis. She intended to start her own foundation, a job-placement and training agency for, owned, and operated by physically challenged adults.

The breakup with Janet threw Steve even more deeply into his work. He began to realize that his involvement in NFTE constrained his ability to maintain a personal life. This realization was magnified by the fact that NFTE still had its office in his apartment. A one-bedroom apartment with a loft, the apartment had no room for conferences or other private meetings, let alone personal space for Steve. Steve and Michelle began to discuss the feasibility of moving to new offices.

Steve's lack of private space was also important in terms of his work with his students. Steve had always believed that the effectiveness of NFTE was based 90% on camaraderie between the staff and the students. Steve was training youths who often had been physically or emotionally hurt, and he attempted to provide them with unconditional support. NFTE had a 24-hour, open-door policy. It had taken time, but Steve had built strong and unique relationships with the kids in his programs.

As often as three times a week, kids would show up at Steve's door after midnight. Steve would speak with them and try to help them out, but it began to overwhelm him. He did not believe that any of the kids would hurt him, but he began to be concerned that he was encouraging his students to be overly dependent on him.

The issue of dependence involved more than Steve's personal privacy. Steve had been criticized for giving the students grants instead of loans. He had tried both methods. "We feel the business start-up is very important. We give away 12% to 14% of our gross revenues to the kids. When I first started, before I had 501(c)(3) status, I gave the money as an investment. The kids had to sign a form saying they owed me money. It didn't work out at all because I became the collection agent. It ruined my relationship with kids. So now, everything we do for the kids, they own. I have been thinking that maybe with our best kids, the ones going to college [e.g., in the Wharton program], we could have them repay the money, make it more like the real world. But it adds a strain to the relationship. When you have to bring up money each time you see the kids, they stop coming over. You lose the camaraderie."

Steve was acutely aware of collection problems because NFTE was having difficulties collecting payments from the sponsoring institutions for its various programs. "A number of our big clients are late paying their bills. We are small, we cannot carry these multimillion-dollar places on our accounts receivable. I have to keep calling and saying, 'Look, I cannot do anything if I have no cash.' I know that our program has value for their clients. We attract donors to their programs and we help them make money."

"Our biggest problem is cash flow. We don't really have a credit rating, so we have to pay for things in cash. We have no reserves and the larger organizations don't pay us on time. It is very unpleasant and it puts a lot of my stress and time into accounts receivable. Plus, I begin to worry about the relationship when people don't pay. My relationships with these people are so tight, someone else calling them wouldn't be the same. By the same token, they know Michelle's salary depends on their money. So I call in the morning, and have Michelle call in the afternoon."

Steve resented the fact that so much of his time had to be spent on the phone and in the office. "At first, an organization needs a crazy guy willing to work seventy hours a week. But after a while, it definitely has some negatives for me and the company. It lowers productivity and morale; it is very difficult not to develop edges in my personality. I am here seven days a week. If I could get an MBA in here, and get a real office, it would help."

By June 1990, NFTE had raised $273,000 and was waiting to hear about a number of other large grants. Nevertheless, Steve was worried about the viability of relying on foundation money in the long term. "We cannot continue to rely on foundation money. They only want to fund a project for the first few years, not for the long term. I would think it wouldn't be too hard to raise the money from wealthy

1989

Mark Benenson, Esq., Partner, Benenson & Kates

Bella Frankel, M.A., Teacher, Jane Addams Vocational High School

Verne Harnish, President, Young Entrepreneurs Organization

Jack Mariotti, C.P.A. (Steve's brother)

Steve Mariotti, M.B.A., President/Founder, NFTE

Rev. John McKinstry, Otis, MA (Janet's father)

Eric Soto, Manager, Community and Government Relations, Con Edison, Inc.

June 1990

Al Abney, President, Abney Manufacturing

Mark Benenson, Esq., Partner, Benenson & Kates

Bella Frankel, M.A., Teacher, Jane Addams Vocational High School

Verne Harnish, President, Dolphins Development, Inc.

Steve Mariotti, M.B.A., President/Founder, NFTE

Leo McKenna, Director and Trustee, John Brown Cook Foundation

Eric Soto, Manager, Community and Government Relations, Con Edison, Inc.

Exhibit 2.1.3   NFTE Board of Directors

individuals if we could find the right folks." To facilitate fund-raising, Steve was advised to change the composition of his board of directors (see **Exhibit 2.1.3** for a list of original and new board members). "Up until five months ago my board was my friends and my brother. I started being attacked for that, so I brought in some outsiders. I was nervous at first, because I didn't know what they were going to say or do. In a nonprofit, since you don't own the business, you don't have control. If I lose one board vote, it's a serious issue."

The most difficult fund-raising issue revolved around whether or not to accept money from government sources. "I grew up in a libertarian family, where you do anything you want as long as it is not coercive. We believe in minimal government." On the other hand, Steve was committed to running a quality program, and NFTE would need money to maintain its quality. Steve commented on this dilemma. "What a hypocrite I have been. I don't feel that education should be publicly funded. Yet guess who was instrumental in helping many of our clients win government money? We need to come to terms with that hypocrisy and my uncertainty and think this through. Maybe it's not black or white. If we don't take these grants, someone else will get them. But I have seen how agencies that begin to rely on state funds lose their quality. I think it would be better if we gave vouchers to parents to spend on any school they want for their kids."

Steve examined the methods used by similar organizations to fund educational programs. The three primary ones were Edteck, Youth Entrepreneur Services (YES), and Junior Achievement. Edteck is a for-profit firm that operates out of Camden, New Jersey. It is funded primarily from city and government contracts and sells its own curriculum. Edteck has been in the field for over 20 years, but its programs have increasingly focused on adults and teacher training.

Like NFTE, YES and Junior Achievement are 501(c)(3) organizations and are funded through donations and contracts. YES is based in Berkeley, California, and is directed by Kathleen Black Sullivan. Steve and Kathleen have discussed working together. YES works primarily with young adults. Junior Achievement does not work with at-risk kids. It focuses on teaching the corporate model instead of concentrating on the sole proprietorship. Students work in teams of 30 or 40 and start small corporations. "Junior Achievement is somewhat of a thorn in our side," Steve commented. "When a foundation says 'no' to us, it is often because they have already given money to Junior Achievement. We then have to go into a long discussion of why we are different."

Steve was also considering how to best utilize his time and the time of his staff to meet the challenges of the coming year. Personally, Steve loved teaching and he was good at it. Eighty percent of his teaching was with elementary school kids in the READY scholar program; the rest was with

the prison entrepreneurs program and the Wharton program in the summer. Working closely with Lisa Hoffstein, Steve had agreed to duplicate the Wharton 2-week seminar at Columbia and Berkeley during the summer of 1990. Steve believed that these seminars were some of NFTE's best programs, and he was excited about leading more of them, but where would he get the time? He would not be able to lead more than a few seminars in one summer.

"So far, I have been able to lead these programs with Russell helping me. But next summer, I won't be able to run all of them. I need to find someone who can do it on their own. It's two weeks, eleven days for eight hours a day. It's very intense. How can I get my staff up to speed where I know they are going to do it just right? It's very difficult. You have to be able to anticipate problems, and you have to keep the kids interested. In the two years that we have done the Wharton program, we've had ninety-eight percent to ninety-nine percent attendance. This year, we had only three absences out of forty kids. It's very easy to slip just a little bit and have forty absences. There's an edge in education, where if you go over it, it's a free fall. Once you let the tension go, everything goes. You come in late, the kids don't show up. I always want to be on an edge where there is a tension and you are running an A to A-plus show."

Despite being somewhat protective of these seminars, Steve has been very pleased and impressed by the dedication and talent of his staff. "What I look for are people who are very entrepreneurial. I want them to believe that teaching is heroic, especially at the precollege level. In the public schools, everyone is so depressed. Teachers are low-level bureaucrats. There are no incentives to reward people. I try to treat my staff like tenured professors at Harvard. Their pay is much better than in the school system. Here, each person is in total control of their division. They raise their own money, and pay fifteen percent of these revenues into a general fund for administration.

"We don't really have a structure. Everyone talks to me. Still, the lack of structure has a tendency to work for us. We make decisions quickly. I began holding Friday staff meetings where we discuss lesson plans and present new ideas. It keeps us fresh. Everyone knows each other really well. We are very committed to the professionalization of teaching."

The NFTE staff expressed some of their opinions about the organization and its future.

Janet McKinstry: "I think it is easier to raise money as a nonprofit, but NFTE could be a for-profit. We could ask for more money for our programs. We have to run it like a business. First, we need new office space and room to train students in the office. Five years from now, we could sell the curriculum. We could train teachers that way and take the Wharton program national. Scott and Kevin have really expanded their programs. Maybe we could work in other cities, or even franchise. I think we should try to get more corporate involvement."

Russell Kelly: "I understand the concern about government money, but we need to

be flexible. I think we should take money wherever it comes from, to make sure we give quality programs to as many students as possible. Bureaucracy can be a problem. One issue we face is staff development. What sort of growth opportunities can NFTE provide beyond the classroom, beyond base programs? I have started my own consulting firm. One concern I have is drawing the line between my work for NFTE and work for my firm. Opportunities come along that do not suit NFTE. If they benefit the community and fit with my interests, I feel that I should pursue them outside of NFTE. Maybe we need a policy on this."

Chris Meenan: "I worry about how taking government money directly would affect my freedom in the classroom. I do not want to be constrained by government regulations. I had a bad experience with the board of education. But I am torn. The question is, How do we do the most good for the inner cities? Do we teach the kids ourselves, or do we teach the teachers? We need to decide what our philosophy is."

Scott Shickler: "NFTE needs to move away from relying heavily on donations. Over the next year, I would like to get eighty-five percent of my revenue in the New York City division from private contracts. These contracts, along with other youth-service organizations [i.e., Boys and Girls Clubs], would build long-term financial relationships while perpetrating our own mission to teach at-risk youth the fundamentals of economic and entrepreneurial concepts. NFTE adheres to the cost-effective philosophy that channeling money into education prevents, rather than corrects, the destruction of our inner city."

Kevin Greaney: "Corporations all complain about the inner city, but they won't give money. And no one wants to give money to overhead. Everyone here does their own fund-raising, which means we have some problems with communication and internal competition. We should concentrate on expanding geographically, first up and down the Eastern Seaboard and then in the South and California."

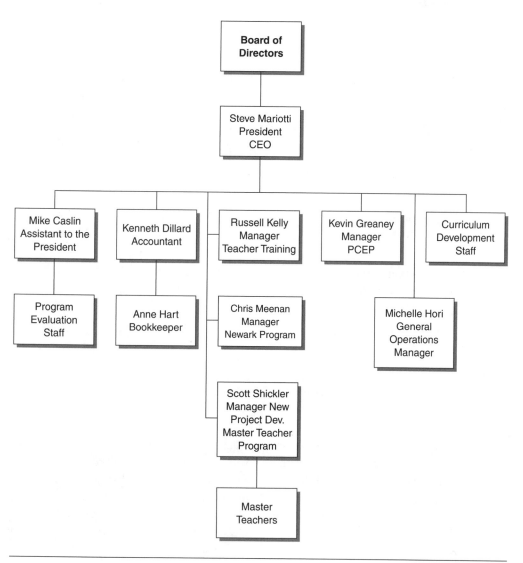

Exhibit 2.1.4   NFTE Organization Chart

	Dec. 31, 1988	Dec. 31, 1989
Assets		
Current Assets		
Cash	33,471	13,535
Prepaid Expenses	0	500
Other	0	3,735
Total Current Assets	33,471	17,770
Fixed Assets		
Furniture and Fixtures	0	8,453
Equipment	0	4,527
Total Fixed Assets	0	12,980
Depreciation	0	(1,246)
Net Fixed Assets	0	11,734
Total Assets	33,471	29,504
Liabilities and Fund Balances		
Current Liabilities		
Accounts payable and payroll taxes	1,036	11,061
Total Current Liabilities	1,036	11,061
Fund Balances		
Fund Balance - Unrestricted	23,435	1,808
Fund Balance - Restricted	9,000	16,635
Total Fund Balances	32,435	18,443
Total Liabilities and Fund Balances	33,471	29,504

Exhibit 2.1.5   NETE Balance Sheet

NOTE: The numbers in this exhibit have been adjusted for the purposes of the case.

Michelle Hori: "We generate so much paperwork, too much for me to handle by myself. I wish we could hire a full-time finance manager, so I could concentrate on coordinating programs and the logistics of the office."

Ken Dillard: "We have severe budget constraints. I would like us to have money where we can 'take it and run,' where we wouldn't have to be involved with the giver. We have a lean staff. Everyone is involved in so many aspects of the business. We generate a ton of paper, checks, et cetera; it is difficult to put them together. We need to get everyone together from a corporate standpoint. Everyone shares the same vision, but it shouldn't be competitive. We

	1988	1989	YTD Ending June 30, 1990
Support (Contributions)			
Corporations	61,600	8,620	2,000
Foundations	72,030	453,032	268,000
Federal Grants	24,641	19,000	0
Individuals	30,560	11,590	3,500
Total Support	188,831	492,242	273,500
Revenue			
Interest Income	120	1,602	200
Other Income	0	1,106	6,300
Total Revenue	120	2,708	6,500
Total Support and Revenue	**188,951**	**494,950**	**280,000**
Expenses			
Program	101,531	429,581	219,100
General & Administrative	29,620	23,248	54,900
Fund Raising	25,366	56,112	18,000
Total Expenses	156,517	508,941	292,000
Excess of Revenue Over Expenses	32,434	(13,991)	(12,000)
Fund Balances, Beginning of Year	0	32,434	18,443
Fund Balances, End of Year	32,434	18,443	6,443

Exhibit 2.1.6   NFTE Statement of Support, Revenue, Expenses, and Changes in Funds

NOTE: The numbers in this exhibit have been adjusted for the purposes of the case.

need to work together but give each other freedom to operate within that."

As Steve glanced around his apartment, he tried to sort out his own vision of the future. He had just been informed that one of his "kids" from Newark had been accused of murdering a woman. Sometimes Steve was overwhelmed by the violence that occurred daily in these kids' lives, but it further committed him to continuing his work with inner-city youths. He knew how he ideally would like to work. "I would like to just teach and do curriculum development. I would like to have one hundred lesson plans. I do not want to do research or evaluate results. I do not want to talk on the phone all day. I do not want to fundraise more than five hours a week. I don't want to be constrained in helping kids start new businesses. I'd like to have $200,000 to $300,000 to fund the start-ups.

Case Study

"I love my work [teaching]. I could do it all day, nonstop year-round. When I'm teaching, I feel zero stress. I am about the happiest man in the world. During the summer, I'm in ecstasy. Every day during the summer, I cannot wait to go to work. I'd like to do that year-round. I'd teach a two-week seminar, take a week to reorganize and correct my mistakes, and do it again. I would like to be the greatest classroom business teacher in the history of America. I do not have any desire to be a great administrator."

The objectives stated in the 1990 strategic plan summarized Steve's goals for the foundation. "After demonstrated success from 1990 to 1992, in the South Bronx, Manhattan, Brooklyn, and Newark, NFTE hopes to become a model for emulation by other inner-city areas throughout the country and by doing so empower a whole generation of minority youth to create their own wealth."

NOTES

1. *Inc.*, April 1989.
2. Ibid.
3. *New York Times*, Sunday, March 13, 1988.
4. 1989 Strategic Plan, National Foundation for Teaching Entrepreneurship.

Case Study

Case Study 2.2.

The September 11th Fund: The Creation

9/11/01

- **8:45 a.m.:** American Flight 11, carrying 92 people, crashes into the World Trade Center north tower.

- **9:03 a.m.:** United Flight 175, carrying 65 people, crashes into the World Trade Center south tower.

- **9:50 a.m.:** The south tower of the World Trade Center collapses.

- **10:29 a.m.:** The north tower of the World Trade Center collapses.

- **10:45 a.m.:** Lorie Slutsky, president and director of the New York Community Trust (NYCT) and board member of the

United Way of New York City (UWNYC), called her colleague Ralph Dickerson, president of the UWNYC, to discuss how they and their organizations could join forces, leverage their respective competencies, and create a single charitable fund to which people could give. They foresaw that many Americans would want to help victims, families, and communities affected by the terrible tragedies by giving to charities that would provide support and services in the wake of the disasters. As the two largest grantmakers in New York City, the NYCT and the UWNYC sought to jointly mobilize their resources and expertise to help channel the public's giving productively. Through a handshake deal, the two decided

Case Study

that their organizations would be equal partners in jointly setting up the September 11th Fund to receive financial donations from concerned Americans across the country. Slutsky and Dickerson each pledged $10,000 from their respective organizations to seed the fund.

The UWNYC, a dues-paying member of the United Way of America, the support organization for local United Ways, was a fund-raiser and grantmaker to a network of health and human service nonprofits and agencies in New York City. As with all local United Way organizations, the UWNYC fund-raising campaign took place annually through a single community-wide campaign that raised funds primarily through individual giving by company employees and corporate support. From 1999 to 2000, the UWNYC had fund-raised and spent $124.6 million through grants to local nonprofits. The New York Community Trust, the largest community foundation in the United States and the single largest grantmaker in New York City, consisted of over 1,500 charitable funds set up by high net worth individuals, families, and businesses. These donors tended to be fewer in number but gave in significantly larger amounts. In the year 2000, the NYCT, endowed with nearly $2 billion in assets, spent roughly $140 million, roughly the amount of annual earnings from its endowment, through grantmaking to New York City–area nonprofit organizations. The NYCT specialized in grantmaking to local nonprofits through a large staff of specialized program officers, who were skilled at administering unrestricted, field-of-interest, designated, and donor-advised funds.

- **11:15 a.m.:** The two nonprofits happened to be located in the same high-rise office building on 2 Park Avenue in Midtown Manhattan. Upon ending the phone conversation with Dickerson, Slutsky and the NYCT's general counsel, Jane Wilton, rushed down from the NYCT offices on the twenty-fourth floor to the UWNYC offices on the second floor to meet with the executive team of the UWNYC. The UWNYC executive team had gathered in the conference room to plan how their organization would respond to the crisis as the horrific events of that morning continued to play out just a few miles away. Ralph Dickerson, president; Larry Mandell, COO; Bertina Ceccarelli, senior vice president of marketing and communications; Chandra Anderson, senior vice president of resource development; and Lilliam Barrios-Paoli, senior vice president of agency services, and other key UWNYC staff met with Slutsky and Wilton to outline the general mandate and decide on a name for the newly created fund. In the meantime, the NYCT and the UWNYC had received calls from their respective national organizations, the Council on Foundations and the United Way of America, with pledges of support for the joint fund. United Way of America's pledge included a $1 million donation it had received from Williams Gas Pipeline.

- **4:00 p.m.:** By early evening, the UWNYC had set up a website to collect donations for the September 11th Fund, www.uwnyc.org/sept 11. The UWNYC and the NYCT issued a press release announcing the creation of the September 11th Fund. For both the UWNYC and the NYCT, the early work of the September 11th Fund proceeded at a frantic pace, with virtually no time for negotiating details, planning, or developing a strategy to address the fund-raising, operational and organizational issues, and distribution strategy that would ultimately need to be developed. Working at a breakneck pace, the UWNYC staff focused on one basic objective: to enable people to give in support of the victims, their families, and their communities.

Both organizations immediately began collecting donations for the September 11th Fund through their respective donor bases. The NYCT began collecting donations from individuals, families, and businesses that had established funds at the Trust, as well as from private foundations. The NYCT rarely raised funds through individual solicitations. Instead, funds were raised primarily through gifts and bequests of wealthy individuals and families. Thus, while the NYCT saw an increase in giving in response to the events of September 11, the magnitude was not so great as to stress the NYCT's systems for collecting and processing donations. Nonetheless, beyond fund-raising, there were countless issues around planning the distribution strategy that needed to be addressed immediately. The program experts at the NYCT set to work with the UWNYC on developing a set of guidelines for distributing the proceeds from the Fund.

Meanwhile, the UWNYC was instantly inundated with thousands of calls from individuals, corporations, and other non-profits with offers of help through in-kind donations or pledges of cash. Countless corporations with which the UWNYC had

developed strong relationships over many years called to offer their help. Donations to the UWNYC ranged from $10 to $100,000 to millions of dollars. Bertina Ceccarelli, senior vice president of marketing and a Harvard MBA, stated that the public's response "wildly exceeded anyone's expectations." In some cases, companies called with proposals for cause-related marketing campaigns in which products would be promoted as contributing to the Fund, and some portion of proceeds from the sale of such products would be donated to the Fund. While the UWNYC historically rarely received such proposals, it recorded over 1,540 such offers in the wake of September 11. Although the UWNYC was somewhat apprehensive about engaging in these partnerships, they were also reluctant to turn away well-meaning corporate partners' donations. These deals would need to be analyzed, evaluated, and negotiated on a case-by-case basis. Other companies called in simply to pledge cash, or other support, in the form of their products, services, or employee volunteers. Additionally, thousands of pledges from the public poured into the UWNYC via the Internet. At the same time, the UWNYC had to coordinate with other local United Way chapters to handle donations that were being called in from all over the country.

The UWNYC website was already set up to manage annual corporate giving campaigns, which take place year-round. The UWNYC had vast experience with fund-raising at this retail level, and its systems were well suited for this purpose. However, the magnitude and intensity of the response that began flowing in on September 11 strained the UWNYC systems. Virtually all donations to the Fund from the general public and companies came in via the UWNYC. According to Larry Mandell, the UWNYC essentially went into overdrive, "collecting approximately ten times the usual number of donations in 1/10 of the time."

- **5:00 p.m.:** Early that evening, Andre Dua, an associate principal at the McKinsey consulting company's office in New York, returned home after trying in vain to donate blood all afternoon. He had stood in line for hours, only to be turned away twice, because there were simply too many donors for New York City blood banks to handle at one time. He turned on the television and sat riveted, watching the coverage of events on CNN. Feeling utterly helpless, he wondered to himself, "How much longer can I just sit here watching?" Dua picked up the phone and called Ralph Dickerson, President of the UWNYC, whom he had come to know through work on a pro bono consulting project the previous year, to offer his help. Through a brief conversation, Dua was informed that the September 11th Fund had been created.

McKINSEY AND THE UWNYC: BACKGROUND

Typically, each McKinsey office committed approximately 5% to 10% of consultant time to pro bono consulting to nonprofit organizations in their communities on an annual basis. Consultants from the New York office of McKinsey had worked on a few pro bono projects for the UWNYC over the last decade. Dua's working relationship with UWNYC began in July of 2000 as engagement manager for a pro bono McKinsey project on a marketing strategy for the UWNYC. He had been at McKinsey just a couple of years, after having earned a law degree at Yale University. Dua had always had an interest in public policy issues and the nonprofit sector. While growing up in Australia, he had volunteered regularly in nonprofits and had founded a think tank, the Australian Youth Institute, while studying for his undergraduate degree at the University of Sydney. The Institute encouraged young people to become actively involved in social issues and provided an outlet for them to contribute their voice. Given these interests, Dua was enthusiastic about the prospect of working with a nonprofit organization through his work at McKinsey. The project had been the first pro bono McKinsey project with the UWNYC in approximately five years. The marketing strategic review had been initiated internally and was supported by the board of UWNYC. Board member Andrew Parsons, a senior partner at McKinsey, had offered the McKinsey team's services for the task.

Upon beginning work on that project, which focused on how the UWNYC could maximize giving from its largest donors, Dua and the rest of the McKinsey team hit the ground running with a focus on the task of developing a comprehensive marketing strategy. The McKinsey team, accustomed to working at a rapid pace under tight deadlines and, driven by the short-term goals of their project, worked assiduously to produce their recommendations for change. Realizing that the McKinsey team's competencies could only be leveraged through integrating the UWNYC's intimate knowledge of the fundamentals of fund-raising in the nonprofit sector with the McKinsey team's marketing analysis, Mandell sought to coordinate the McKinsey team's work with the UWNYC's internal marketing team. Dua reoriented the work style of the McKinsey team to work more closely with the UWNYC executive team to develop their recommendations jointly. In the remaining weeks of the project, the effectiveness of the working relationship between the McKinsey team and UWNYC staff steadily increased. By October of 2000, the project was completed and the jointly developed recommendations were ultimately well received by the UWNYC board.

Soon after the project, Dua was asked by the partners at his firm to run the annual United Way corporate campaign for McKinsey's New York office. This would be a real test of some of the recommendations that the McKinsey team had put forth earlier in their marketing strategy project for the UWNYC. Dua took on the challenge and increased giving in the McKinsey office by 42% from the previous year, making it one of the top two United Way corporate campaigns, in terms of percentage increase from the previous year, in New York City in 2000. In December, Dua and the other top New York City corporate fund-raiser were invited to present their approach to other corporate campaign managers. Shortly thereafter, Dua was asked to join UWNYC's marketing advisory subcommittee and continued an informal working relationship with some of his contacts at the UWNYC. Dua would sometimes initiate conversations with Dickerson and Mandell to follow up on his earlier work, and to seek their advice about how he could make a greater contribution in the nonprofit sector, and they, in turn, began to seek his counsel about ongoing issues at the UWNYC.

McKINSEY AND THE SEPTEMBER 11TH FUND

9/12/01

- **1:00 p.m.:** Dickerson called Dua at the McKinsey office in Midtown Manhattan to follow up on their conversation from the previous evening. Dua inquired about how the UWNYC was faring with the influx of public responses to the September 11th Fund. Dua guessed that the UWNYC could use some help given the magnitude of the task ahead. Upon ending the call, Dua headed directly to the UWNYC offices. There, he met with some key members of the UWNYC executive team, Ralph Dickerson, Larry Mandell, and Bertina Ceccarelli.

When Dua met with the UWNYC executives, they discussed a number of the critical issues that would need to be addressed: Had they registered an easy to remember Web site address for the September 11th Fund? How many hits could the UWNYC's existing Web site handle? Had they found out which newspapers would provide pro bono advertising for the September 11th Fund? Was there anyone working on the copy for ads announcing the creation of the September 11th Fund? Had the September 11th Fund's name and number been listed on the streaming crawlers on all of the television networks?

While the UWNYC had already dealt with some of these issues, their existing infrastructure was not designed to handle fund-raising of the magnitude after September 11.

With the public response growing seemingly without end, their existing infrastructure would eventually reach full capacity. The UWNYC staff did not have the time or the resources to manage all of these issues on their own. However, they had long-standing relationships with many of America's leading companies, many of which had already offered their resources or services.

Dua left the UWNYC offices, promising that he would get help from McKinsey. Dickerson and Mandell were enthusiastic to have Dua bring McKinsey on to help with the Fund. Dua thought that a dedicated McKinsey team could provide the resources to fill critical gaps at a time when the UWNYC's own resources were stretched to the limit.

• **4:00 p.m.:** Dua went to see Dana Norris, head of staffing at McKinsey, to see if it was possible to staff a team to help with the September 11th Fund. Upon hearing how McKinsey could make a difference, Norris agreed to staff the team. They would need to recruit an engagement manager and at least three additional team members.

• **6:00 p.m.:** Dua started calling prospective engagement managers for the project. To his surprise, some asked various questions about the project, wanted to think about it and weigh their other project options before getting back to him. Dua decided at that point that a key staffing criterion for this project would be that potential team members have immediate enthusiasm and commitment for the work. After a few more calls, he contacted Doug Tabish, a consultant with a military background who had been at McKinsey for about two years. Tabish received the call just

as he was leaving the office for the day. Upon hearing Dua's brief description of the project as a "way to help out," Tabish immediately responded, "Where do I sign up?"

• **7:00 p.m.:** Dua and Tabish met at once to begin creating a work plan based on Dua's meeting that afternoon with UWNYC staff on what needed to be addressed in the first few weeks of developing and managing the September 11th Fund. According to their plans, the overriding objective of this phase of their work would be to "maximize giving to the September 11th Fund by quickly executing an appropriate marketing plan and ensuring that the appropriate infrastructure is in place." For several hours, they worked on fleshing out the details of the tasks that needed to be accomplished to implement successfully the first few stages of the fund. The first stages of the project focused on marketing the fund to the general public, corporations, and foundations to mobilize resources for aiding victims. To manage this process successfully required a focus on the technology and back-office infrastructure that would be needed to handle the many donations. Over the next two days, Dua and Tabish recruited the remaining McKinsey team members, Joyce Liu, who had been at McKinsey for two years after completing her undergraduate degree, and Neal Zuckerman, a Harvard Business School alumnus who had been at McKinsey for a year after earning his MBA.

Zuckerman, who had also served in the military, recalled why he felt compelled to join the project.

The mission of my alma mater, West Point, is to train "leaders of character for a lifetime of service to the nation." That sense of awareness was heightened while I was at HBS. Service without personal gain is how societies are built. After I left school, I often asked how I could continue to serve the community. I became a board member for the local public radio station in New York City, was involved in Democratic politics, but still looked for other opportunities. This project was, for me, a clarion call.

McKinsey committed a team of five consultants to a seven-week project for the UWNYC and the September 11th Fund that would focus on three key areas: fund-raising and marketing, IT and operational infrastructure, and the organization and governance structure for the September 11th Fund.

9/13/01: Project Launch

On the morning of September 13, the McKinsey team kicked off the project. By the time the McKinsey project commenced, the UWNYC had already received an overwhelming response from the public and realized that its existing infrastructure would soon be unable to cope. Prior to September 11, the CFO had just retired, and the CEO was scheduled for major surgery within the next few weeks. As a consequence, the COO, Larry Mandell, had to coax the CFO out of retirement to ensure that appropriate financial controls were put in place and temporarily take on the additional responsibilities of the CEO.

Typically, the UWNYC raised approximately $45 to $50 million annually through their corporate campaigns over the course of many months. Now, they were bringing in over $2 million in donations per day. Their staff and systems were struggling to keep up with the influx of responses, as well as to manage the regular day-to-day operations of the UWNYC.

To begin, the McKinsey team met with key UWNYC staff members to get a sense of what was being done and how they could help with the monumental task of creating the fund-raising and operational infrastructure for the fund. Keeping in mind his previous experience in working with the UWNYC and recognizing the need for joint decision making, Dua knew that working hand in hand with staff was critical to McKinsey's ability to make a contribution. Mandell sought to integrate the McKinsey team with his executive team in order to augment the work that was already being done to build the fund. As Dua and Tabish had documented in their work plan, there were two issues of critical importance at this stage: to create (1) an orchestrated fund-raising marketing effort to publicize the creation of the fund and (2) the back-office infrastructure to manage the influx of donations and offers of help. (See **Exhibit 2.2.1** for initial work plan.) The goal of the first two weeks of the project would be to maximize fund-raising for the September 11th Fund. Although typical McKinsey consulting projects were focused on a clearly thought-out, detailed work plan, with clear roles and responsibilities outlined for each team member on the project, this project was unlike any other. Joyce Liu recalled,

OVERALL OBJECTIVE

Maximize giving the United Way "September 11 Fund" by quickly executing an appropriate marketing plan and ensuring the appropriate infrastructure is in place

1. Marketing

a. General Public

- Develop a set of marketing steps that leverage United Way's brand to maximize giving to the Fund by the general public—focus on the fastest, most cost-efficient and scaleable methods available.

b. Corporate

- Mobilize existing corporate-giving relationships to maximize giving to the Fund by both corporations and their employees—focus on using the companies' internal campaign network and infrastructure.

c. Foundations

- *Leverage relationships with key foundations to secure support.*

2. Infrastructure

a. Technology

- Ensure that the Fund web site can reliably scale to handle significantly more traffic and transactions ($10\times - 100\times$), and that the web site has appropriate information and functionality to encourage maximum giving.

b. Operations

- Ensure that back office operations are in place to support massive on-line, phone, and mail-in giving to the Fund (in particular, credit card processing, check processing, call center, and accounting & receipt generation).

Exhibit 2.2.1   McKinsey's original WorkPlan

SOURCE: McKinsey Internal Document.

It was so fast paced. There were so many issues to deal with. While we were working with a general work plan, new issues and challenges kept coming up. We weren't exactly sure of what we were doing at times; we simply had to work as fast as possible to get everything done.

To help focus the McKinsey team on these efforts, Dua set a fund-raising goal of one dollar for every single American, approximately $285 million.

Marketing and Fund-Raising

UWNYC Senior Vice President of Marketing and Communications Bertina Ceccarelli explained to Liu the existing efforts in publicity and fund-raising. Ceccarelli, who had over ten years of private sector experience working in direct marketing in the media, entertainment, and Internet industries, applied her skills to the challenge of mounting the fund's marketing campaign. Drawing upon her personal network of contacts, as well as those she had cultivated in her role at the UWNYC, Ceccarelli had begun to lay the groundwork for a comprehensive marketing strategy for the fund. By the time the McKinsey team came on board, the UWNYC already had a public relations firm and an advertising agency as partners to help publicize the creation of the September 11th Fund. Additionally, a number of television networks had begun including information about the Fund in the crawlers that appeared at the bottom of their continuous news broadcasts. In the two days since the

disaster happened, over 5,000 individuals and companies had contacted the UWNYC with various offers of help. Refer to http://www.uwnyc.org/sep11/donorlist.html for a list of donors and their contributions.

Liu worked closely with the UWNYC marketing staff to identify the key marketing pieces that were core to the fund's efforts and to create a framework to be used to prioritize and track the progress of TV, radio, Internet, and print advertising. TV news crawlers were of critical importance given the broad reach they afforded. Every last detail of the efforts needed to be monitored to ensure the accuracy of information being broadcast. For example, sometimes the crawlers on the networks inadvertently listed the wrong information or the crawlers were not appearing at all on stations that had agreed to run them. In the days following the tragedies, a coordinated marketing strategy was coming together in anticipation of a massive scale-up that would be necessary to handle the response as word about the September 11th Fund continued to spread.

National Telethon

On September 14, Ceccarelli was approached by ABC about a planned three-hour joint national telethon, titled "Tribute to Heroes," among all the major television networks, ABC, NBC, CBS, and FOX. All proceeds from the fund-raiser would be contributed to a separate fund within the September 11th Fund, the September 11th Telethon Fund. The television networks required that the telethon proceeds be restricted specifically to assist victims and families affected by the tragedies.

While the television networks would take care of the content and marketing for the telethon, the UWNYC was asked to handle the back-end infrastructure that would be required to collect and process all the phone and online pledges from the telethon. The telethon was scheduled to take place in just one week, on September 21. The McKinsey team set about doing a call volume analysis to get a sense of how many pledges they could anticipate during the telethon. They were confident that the fund's website, which was being supported through in-kind donations from leading technology companies, would hold up fine. The main concern was the need to assemble a total of 25,000 phone bank seats to handle the anticipated phone calls. They already had a commitment from Capital One for 5,000 seats and assistance with routing all the calls. Other commitments of large blocks from companies that had sizable call centers were desperately needed, as they had just days to pull everything together. Large blocks were needed in order to simplify training and coordination among the call centers and to spread the calls across a considerable number of companies in case any of the call centers went down during the television broadcast. Calling on the UWNYC's extensive network of corporate supporters, they secured commitments from nine corporate partners to provide the needed seats for the telethon phone banks. While the marketing team had already anticipated a massive scale-up before the telethon, one team member described their efforts to pull together and coordinate 25,000 staff to monitor the phone banks within days as a "mad rush."

The telethon took place as scheduled with great success, raising $120 million for the September 11th Telethon Fund.

Liu relished the opportunity to work in a hands-on way in helping to put the telethon together. She noted that the work was a lot more tactical than typical McKinsey strategy work streams. Given the unusual demands of this project, the challenge was to do everything as quickly as possible. Since Doug Tabish, the engagement manager on the project, was busy managing so many other issues, Liu took on a more prominent role than in traditional consulting projects. Liu had to take on the responsibility to make decisions on her part of the McKinsey team's work, to work directly with senior executives and partners, and to work not only on recommendations to UWNYC but also to assist the UWNYC marketing team with implementation of the marketing strategy. Liu reflected on the experience: "The McKinsey team brought the ability to disaggregate a highly complex problem, as well as the ability to take a step back and look at the problem in its entirety before making decisions. It was extremely gratifying to use what I know well, and translate it into social impact."

Reflecting on the UWNYC's work, Ceccarelli noted,

The pace of our work was like that of a dot com racing to go public, except that we were all doing it to help others. What I have found so rewarding about my work here at UWNYC, both before and after September 11, is that the singular focus on making an impact on the community fosters such a spirit of cooperation. While I am not on the front lines serving people in need directly, it's immensely satisfying to know that the behind-the-scenes work I do can help make even a small difference in our community.

IT Infrastructure

With the launch of the McKinsey project, Neal Zuckerman immediately became deeply involved with the UWNYC's IT group. Zuckerman worked closely with Ira Bellach, the UWNYC's chief technology officer, to create the technology infrastructure, specifically Web, database, and phone banks, to support the fund. The existing UWNYC website was not very scalable as there had never been a need to scale for a fund-raising effort of this magnitude, nor did the UWNYC have any prior need for phone banks to process calls. Bellach knew that the UWNYC's existing infrastructure had not been designed to manage the influx of calls and website hits that were coming in after September 11. Given the UWNYC's financial resource limitations and the extreme time pressure that they were working under, Bellach sought to outsource some of the critical pieces of the IT infrastructure.

Zuckerman and Bellach worked in collaboration to select and manage the relationships with the many corporate vendors that sought to donate their products and services to the fund. In the days immediately following September 11, the UWNYC was receiving more than 10,000 donations from individuals per day via phone and Internet. IBM, a longtime supporter of the

UWNYC, was among the first companies to offer extensive and substantial support on the order of millions of dollars. A representative from IBM was at the UWNYC offices on September 12 to help with the development of the September 11th Fund's IT infrastructure. Among the first tasks was the need to sort through the countless offers made by businesses and corporations for in-kind donations of technology and service support, to select the best vendors to serve the fund's needs, to negotiate terms with each vendor, and to coordinate work among them. This process was facilitated by the fact that the UWNYC already had strong working relationships with many of the companies, as they had been long-term supporters of the UWNYC and its work.

In negotiating with vendors, Zuckerman and Bellach found that most vendors wanted to handle all aspects of the project. Zuckerman and Bellach sought to choose the best elements of each and to get the vendors to coordinate with each other to create the best IT infrastructure to meet the fund's needs. In addition, Zuckerman soon learned that the project management role also required an understanding of and sensitivity to existing donor relationships. IBM provided the technical infrastructure for the September 11th Fund, while Microsoft provided the software for processing the pledges.

Bellach and Zuckerman focused their efforts on working with the vendors to create the infrastructure to handle the anticipated influx from the telethon and television marketing campaigns. The September 11th Fund IT infrastructure consisted of distributed pledge capture sources and an internal UWNYC systems database for consolidating, processing, and reporting. IBM already had a large-scale website platform up and running, as it had hosted the website for the U.S. Open tennis tournament, which had just ended a few days before September 11. Within 48 hours of the fund's creation, an international IBM project team of over a dozen people had adapted the U.S. Open website platform to host the September 11th Fund website, www.september11fund.org. The site described the fund's purpose and goals and could accept online donations. IBM initiated contact between KPMG and the UWNYC. Ultimately, KPMG was chosen to help with processing checks. Additionally, an unprecedented arrangement was made such that all credit card fees for credit card donations were waived with all five major credit card companies, a savings to the fund that amounted to millions of dollars. The September 11th Fund's website was ported to IBM on September 14 at 8 p.m. By that time, the UWNYC had already collected 33,000 pledges and $4 million on its own infrastructure and was nearing capacity. Meanwhile, Microsoft was at work building the database to accept the pledges captured by UWNYC's website, IBM's site, and other electronic sources.

Working with corporations to sort out who would do what and to coordinate their efforts on this project was unlike any other McKinsey project Zuckerman had worked on. McKinsey's expertise was project management, not technology management, per se. Additionally, Zuckerman noted that "traditionally, consulting firms play an advisory role, telling clients, 'You should do this . . . you could do that . . .'" Zuckerman was suddenly thrust into a situation where he had to execute at a rapid pace and work directly with the UWNYC team to make critical decisions for the fund's IT strategy. In this project, Zuckerman recalls that

> People were asking for our help day and night; we had to be executors working right alongside the UWNYC team. The work was very different from our usual course of business. We didn't spend time making charts or presentations . . . Decisions had to be made at lightning speed . . . In this crisis situation, we all had to trust our instincts, settle for "good enough" and do the best we could.

Fund-Raising Database

Zuckerman also worked with Chandra Anderson, senior vice president of resource development at the UWNYC, to create the call center infrastructure for tracking and managing the fund-raising effort. To manage corporate fund-raising, databases were created of existing UWNYC donors that had not yet contributed to the September 11th Fund, regular donors that had offered donations but whose calls had not yet been processed, and new potential donors that had never previously given to the UWNYC, but might give to the September 11th Fund. At Anderson's request, the McKinsey team created a strategy map to prioritize new and existing UWNYC donors for the fund. Given her extensive experience with managing long-term fund-raising relationships, Anderson stressed the need for the creation of a comprehensive database system to document all donations from individuals, businesses, or other organizations.

Since September 11, over 300 calls had come in from various corporations offering help, but there was no process in place to handle this scale. The development department was restructured, with over 90% of the employees being redirected to work full-time on the September 11th Fund. Volunteers were recruited from McKinsey and many other companies to staff a phone bank full-time. While the UWNYC managed the outpouring from corporations and individuals, its traditional giving base, the New York Community Trust, managed fund-raising from the third main donor group, foundations, its traditional funding base.

Doug Tabish, the engagement manager, had been involved with both the marketing and fund-raising and IT infrastructure development. He described his experience:

The first four to six weeks were phenomenal. What we were doing was really important. We were working as part of the UWNYC operations team. We were jointly managing various pieces of the project, not consulting. I loved being in the thick of things, in the trenches, helping make decisions, not just offering recommendations. It was not just independent analysis.

We were problem solving with senior clients in real time. First we had to gain their confidence, participate in meetings, and assure the staff that they could handle this. We could help provide the big picture, prioritize, and evaluate. We helped to identify big needs, leverage relationships, and determine what potential challenges might arise.

It was amazing how these organizations did come together to form something out of nothing. We may not have been able to always come up with the optimal solutions, with so little time and planning, but with everyone working for the common good, we were able to come up with workable solutions to these challenges.

Project Management

By the end of the first week of the project, after some of the most pressing fund-raising and infrastructure issues of the fund had been addressed, the McKinsey team had come to play a key project management role, helping to coordinate among multiple parties. Because the team members had been fully dedicated to the work of the September 11th Fund and were so deeply involved in advising and executing on decisions, they had come to be seen as part of the UWNYC operations team. According to Ceccarelli, "McKinsey provided the glue between innumerable companies and organizations." The UWNYC staff and the NYCT had to manage the work of the September 11th Fund alongside their normal jobs. The work on the September 11th Fund happened to coincide with the UWNYC gear-up for their annual corporate fund-raising drive that was to begin in September. The staff had hoped that the September 11th Fund efforts would only augment, not cannibalize, their ongoing fund-raising efforts. McKinsey helped to take some of the burden off by providing a team of dedicated staff. Ceccarelli reflected that

McKinsey provided a fresh team of really bright, dedicated people who were eager to help on anything and everything, even down to administrative tasks and phone calls. There was just so much to be done, it was physically impossible for the UWNYC staff to do it all. The McKinsey team just did whatever it took. It was inspiring for the UWNYC staff to see these volunteers stay until 2 a.m. to make sure that everything was happening.

Given his additional duties, Mandell, the COO, relied on the McKinsey team to perform some of the project management roles related to the fund. As the most immediate issues were being addressed, Mandell and Dua decided that a mechanism was needed to keep the UWNYC executive team abreast of major developments across all areas of work related to the fund. Mandell and Dua agreed to hold daily operating committee meetings to brief the entire UWNYC executive staff and McKinsey team on events and actions that were being taken on a daily basis. The meetings were designed to get everyone up to speed on the critical decisions that had already been made early on and to involve them in decisions that were still being made. Additionally, the McKinsey team was relocated to work in an office located on the same floor as the UWNYC's operations team. Mandell chaired the daily two- or three-hour-long operations meetings. Mandell later reflected that although the work could have occurred more quickly without these meetings, they "provided important structure for the senior management team, bonding, and sense of ownership of the work of the September 11th Fund among staff."

Dua recounts the early stages of the project when the team was so busy fighting fires,

It required a daily reorienting of our work. The most rewarding aspect was the hands-on work that we were doing, in a way that was really contributing. We had to first gain the trust of the UWNYC staff in order to be entrusted with and directly involved in making important decisions. Within a week or two, the UWNYC staff, McKinsey, and other donor companies were working side by side in a real partnership—it was immensely gratifying. Through our involvement in this project and through working with Larry, I learned a great deal about how to successfully manage a nonprofit through a crisis.

Dua found the many challenges and rewards offered by the work with the UWNYC and the September 11th Fund to be unlike other projects he had worked on. Reflecting on the experience, he said, "I would love to run a nonprofit someday—and have the impact that the UWNYC has."

Fund Distribution

Within the first days of the creation of the fund, the program staff from the UWNYC and the NYCT hosted a series of meetings with disaster relief and other nonprofit agencies to assess emergency needs and to coordinate their efforts. Participants included a dozen government agencies, 50 philanthropic groups, and over 300 non-profit organizations involved in providing disaster relief, food, or mental health support. Larry Mandell noted that this due diligence was a necessity, as "it would be dangerous to sit here in our offices at 2 Park Avenue and make funding decisions." As the largest charitable grantmakers in New York City, Joyce Bove, vice president of grants and special projects at the NYCT, and Lilliam Barrios-Paoli, the chief executive of agency services at the UWNYC, worked together on this effort. This process was facilitated by the fact that Bove and Barrios-Paoli had frequently worked together prior to September 11 to coordinate their efforts at the agency level. With the help from nonprofit consultants, Seedco, they jointly created a rough set of guidelines that could be used to process grant proposals and get grants out as quickly as possible.

When the UWNYC and the NYCT created the fund on September 11, they sought to define victims and their communities broadly, in order to ensure that the fund served a broader purpose than solely victims' immediate needs. Both organizations knew that early on, it would be virtually impossible to anticipate all the needs that would arise in the short term and long term from the disaster. The UWNYC and McKinsey teams contacted others with experience in dealing with crises and tragedies, such as those that provided assistance to victims and families of victims in Lockerbie, Scotland; Columbine High School in Colorado; and Oklahoma City. In these cases, funds were still being used to provide support to victims, their families,

and their communities, even six to seven years after the tragedies.

The UWNYC and the NYCT agreed on a set of seven areas that the fund would serve: immediate needs, direct cash assistance, big issues around economic recovery, mental health, environmental issues, rebuilding and reconstruction, and confronting bias and intolerance especially among young people. From the outset, it was decided that the bulk of the emergency-phase spending of the fund would be used to provide immediate support in the form of grants to established emergency assistance agencies with expertise in providing direct services and meeting victim and community needs, and to help coordinate the efforts of other nonprofit health and human service agencies, rather than attempting to provide services directly. Thus, the September 11th Fund reached out to prominent local organizations, such as Safe Horizon, New York City's leading provider of victim assistance, advocacy, and violence prevention services, to provide emergency financial assistance to victims and victims' families; the Legal Aid Society, to meet immediate legal assistance needs of victims; and other agencies, by providing grants to support the emergency relief efforts of these organizations.

Within New York City, both the NYCT and the UWNYC had a high level of expertise and a deep understanding of the provider bases across a variety of program areas. Outside of New York City, however, the two organizations had less expertise in identifying the various providers that should be given grants to assist victims of the terrorist attack on the Pentagon and

Case Study

in Pennsylvania and victim's families out-side of the cities directly affected by the attacks. Furthermore, the UWNYC and the NYCT had not reached agreement on the format and conditions that should be placed on these non–New York City providers that would do grantmaking on behalf of the September 11th Fund. The UWNYC thought that other local United Way chapters, sister organizations to the UWNYC, were appropriate vehicles for grantmaking outside of New York City, while the NYCT wanted to explore other options. The debate around how much involvement and control other local United Way chapters should have in dis-tributing proceeds from the fund to other communities affected by the tragedies, such as Washington, D.C., New Jersey, and southern Pennsylvania, was a source of continuing tension as fund distribution progressed.

To gauge the public's perception of what the work of the fund should be, the UWNYC marketing team and the McKinsey team commissioned two surveys, of 1,000 people each, within the first few weeks of the fund's inception. In the first survey, an online survey conducted by Lightspeed, a market research company that donated its services, respondents were asked their opinions about to whom and for what purposes they thought the fund's money should go. In the second survey, respondents were asked about how broadly they would define the pool of victims and who should, therefore, be eligible for sup-port. The UWNYC was particularly cog-nizant of the implications of their work on the September 11th Fund, for unlike the

NYCT, the UWNYC was one local organi-zation within a larger network of regional and national United Way organizations. Actions taken by the September 11th Fund would have repercussions on the United Way brand nationwide.

In light of these concerns, the UWNYC and the NYCT acted cautiously in the finan-cial management of the fund's resources, as they did not want their organizations to be accused of benefiting financially in any way from the fund. One hundred percent of all contributions donated to the fund were to be applied to relief efforts to aid victims, their families, and their communities. No admin-istrative costs would be covered through fund proceeds. Instead, a number of founda-tions had donated funds specifically dedi-cated to these costs. According to Mandell, "the UWNYC, already proud of its low administrative costs of 13%, did not want to take even 1% of the money to pay for the administrative costs associated with manag-ing the fund." Additionally, money in the fund would be invested, unless the donors directed otherwise, and all interest earned from the investment would be redeposited directly into the fund.

Beyond taking measures to make sure that careful thought and analysis had been put into administering the fund, the NYCT and the UWNYC had to ensure that these facts were communicated to their various con-stituencies effectively, especially in light of the widespread criticism of the fund-raising, administration, and grantmaking practices of various September 11 charities. Charges of wrongdoing ranged from misappropriation of funds, to disregarding donor intent, to unwarranted time delays in getting funds to those in need. The Red Cross's Liberty Disaster Fund, which had planned to set aside $200 million of the total $543 million collected to prepare for and to respond to future attacks, faced immediate backlash for disregarding donor intent. Despite a reversal of this strategy and a new commitment to dedicate all $543 million to victims of September 11 and their survivors, the Red Cross's public image was badly damaged. In the midst of the increased media and public scrutiny of September 11 charities, the September 11th Fund was also targeted at times. Early on, press releases were issued every few days to track the fund's fund-raising efforts and later the fund's grantmaking activities. Within three days of the fund's inception, over $60 million had been raised. By September 19, the fund reached $89 million. By September 24, it was announced that the fund had made its first grants to Safe Horizon, and the Community Resource Exchange, one of New York City's primary providers of technical assistance to the non-profit sector. By early October, over $300 million had been raised.

While a number of large grants were made quickly and early in the fund's life, the successful fund-raising efforts would mean that a comprehensive distribution strategy needed to be developed for allocating the more than $400 million that were projected to flow into the fund. Among the many issues yet to be addressed were (a) who should get the money, (b) how to prioritize giving among the potential recipients, (c) what support measures the funds should be allocated to, (d) what factors should be considered in determining the amounts to allocate to various recipients

for various purposes, (e) how to coordinate with other charities, and (f) what oversight to have over grantee organizations.

Organizational and Governance Structure

As the most urgent fund-raising and infrastructure issues were taken on by the UWNYC and the McKinsey team, and the UWNYC and the NYCT jointly worked on developing the fund's immediate and long-term distribution strategy, the need to clarify the organizational structure and governance system of the fund quickly became apparent. The UWNYC and the NYCT requested that the McKinsey team also turn its efforts to an analysis of the potential options for the September 11th Fund's organizational and governance structure.

Since Slutsky and Dickerson had agreed at the outset to the concept of the fund through an informal agreement on the morning of September 11, the specific details of the management and governance of the fund had not been established at the outset. Neither organization had had time to consider what the implications and challenges of coordinating the work between the two organizations would be. Slutsky remarked, "It would have already been difficult for a single organization to handle all of the work associated with the September 11th Fund. Yet here we had two organizations, two cultures, two missions, two boards, and two leaders who needed to execute at the speed of light."

The McKinsey team spent a week doing research on various alternatives for the organizational structure and proposed three potential options, confirming the initial options put on the table by Lorie Slutsky and Ralph Dickerson. They could leave it as it was, with the two organizations working together to manage the fund, or create an entirely separate legal entity with a dedicated staff to manage the fund. A middle option was to create a semi-independent organization that was governed in part by the two parent organizations, along with wider representation from other community representatives. Its board would have an independent chairperson and the fund would have its own CEO and staff.

Through their collaboration on the fund thus far, all parties involved knew there would be numerous points of disagreement over the details of the partnership and issues around control and management of the fund. There had already been instances in which negotiations around key decisions had become highly charged and contentious among the CEOs and Board Chairs of each organization. All aspects of the decision had implications for not only the fund but also

for the two partner organizations. Despite these challenges, it was their responsibility to create a sound organizational and governance structure for the fund that would enable it to deliver on its mission—"to meet the immediate and longer-term needs of victims, families, and communities affected by the terrorist attacks of September 11."

LOOKING FORWARD

The UWNYC, the NYCT, and the McKinsey team, in 30 incredibly intense days, had created and operationalized the September 11th Fund with the support of a multitude of other corporate and individual donors. The fund was up and running and beginning to fulfill its mission. Yet the leaders knew that to realize its full potential, they needed to refine the fund's distribution policy and resolve the organizational and governance issues. There was little time to savor a sense of accomplishment. The urgency of the tragedy continued to reign.

CHAPTER 3

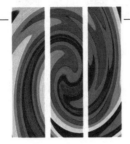

Navigating the
Philanthropic Labyrinth

In the Social Entrepreneurship Framework laid out in the previous chapter, mobilizing resources to pursue the opportunity stands out as the primordial challenge. This is an especially daunting task in the social sector because the philanthropic marketplace abounds with imperfections that greatly complicate the mobilization of resources. In this chapter, we will begin by presenting a profile of the sources of philanthropic funds. We shall then turn to some of the recent innovations in the philanthropic capital marketplace that have emerged, in part in response to weaknesses in the traditional philanthropic marketplace. The case studies at the end of the chapter portray some of these newer approaches.

THE SOURCES OF PHILANTHROPIC FUNDING

The best documentation of the philanthropic marketplace in the United States is compiled annually in *Giving USA* by Indiana University's Center on Philanthropy and published by the Giving USA Foundation, AAFRC Trust for Philanthropy. Accordingly, the statistics indicated below are drawn from that source unless otherwise indicated.

Some of the salient features of the marketplace are the following:

- *The pie is growing.* In inflation-adjusted terms, total giving has grown from $5.4 billion in 1954 to $248.5 billion in 2004. In only 10 of the past 40 years did total giving decline. There is not great volatility in total giving, with the biggest annual decline being −5.4%, the largest increase 14.5%, and the average +2.8%.

- *However, as goes the economy, so goes the giving.* The more money there is in their pockets and the more confidence they have in the economy, the more people and institutions give.[1] Individual giving as a percentage of personal income has fluctuated between 1.5% and 2.2%. Similarly, as a share of GDP, total individual and institutional giving since 1954 has ranged from 1.5% to 2.3%, moving up and down as the economy surges and recedes. For example, between 1973 and 1975, giving fell each year as the country slid into recession, and between 1996 and 2000, donations boomed as the stock market soared to record heights—and when the market crashed, giving fell into another three years of retrenchment. Thus, the entrepreneur's fund-raising task will vary in difficulty depending in part on the robustness of the economy.

- *Individual donors are the principal capital providers.* In 1964, they supplied 82.3% of total giving, slipping to 75.6% 40 years later: $187.9 billion in 2004. The vast majority of households in the United States give—between 70% and 80% of the population. The wealthy do not dominate this market: Fifty-nine percent of all giving comes from families earning less than $100,000 annually. But the rich do give mega gifts: The top 60 donors in 2004 gave $6.5 billion, and over 500 philanthropists made individual gifts in excess of $1 million. Bequests from individual estates account for another 8% of giving.

- *Foundations are the major institutional givers.* They accounted for 11.6% of 2004 giving, or $28.8 billion. In 1964, they provided only 6.1% of the giving pie, but over the past decade, they have more than doubled their giving and increased their share from 8.5% to 11.6%. Additionally, they have proliferated in number: from 21,877 in 1975 to 66,398 in 2003.[2] In the peak year 2000, on average, 17 new foundations were being formed every day. There are many more funding doors for entrepreneurs to knock on, and the foundations come in many different forms and sizes: In 2003, the nearly 59,000 independent foundations (of which 30,662 were family foundations) represented 88.8% of all foundations and accounted for 75.4% of foundation giving; corporate foundations were 3.8% of the total and provided 11.4%; community foundations were 1.1% and supplied 8.4%; operating foundations constituted 6.3% and represented 8.8% of foundation giving.[3] In addition to grants, many foundations offer program-related loans at submarket interest rates to nonprofits ($165 million in 2003). The amount foundations give is significantly tied to the value of their assets, causing variability with fluctuations in the stock markets in which those assets are invested. Between 1995 and 1999, foundations' assets grew in real terms an average of 15.3% per year, then slowed to 4.8% in 2000 and declined 6.5% and 8.3% the following two years, respectively. Foundation grants followed a similar pattern but with an approximate two-year lag and with the percentage changes being more moderate. Grantees' satisfaction with foundations is most dependent on the nature of the interaction: fairness, responsiveness, and comfort.[4]

- *Businesses are smaller but significant givers, and they give more than cash.* Corporate donations (from their foundations and from their other sources) accounted for 4.8% ($12 billion) of total 2004 giving, and around half of this comes in the form of in-kind goods or services rather than cash. Corporate giving in absolute inflation-adjusted terms has nearly tripled over the past four decades, but it fluctuates with profit levels and has a lag of about a year; annual giving amounts to about 1.1% of pretax profits.[5] Wal-Mart was the largest cash contributor ($170 million) in 2004, and Merck was the largest overall (cash and in-kind) contributor ($843 million) in 2003. However, businesses of all sizes contribute. Small social enterprises can match up with smaller, local businesses, not just giant corporations. Furthermore, businesses are also resource providers beyond their philanthropic giving. Many business interactions with nonprofits come out of the marketing and commercial sides and fall into the category of nonprofits' earned income activities, which are discussed in the next chapter.

THE USES OF PHILANTHROPIC FUNDING

Having looked at the supply side of the philanthropic marketplace, we flag some of the highlights on the demand side. Who gets how much in the social enterprise arena?

- *Religion gets most, but all sectors are getting more.* Religious organizations captured 35.5% of total 2004 giving. Just under half of all individual giving goes to religion; per capita annual giving to religion rose from $194 in 1964 to $300 in 2004. The remaining $100 billion of individual giving is still by far the major source for other sectors, all of which have experienced annual increases.

- *Giving is increasing faster than nonprofits are increasing.* There has been explosive growth in the number of nonprofits being created by social entrepreneurs as was indicated in our opening chapter. From about 500,000 in 1954, the sector has expanded to around 1,400,000 in 2004. However, the philanthropic capital market has grown even faster, such that the average amount received per nonprofit has risen from $75,000 to $180,000. There are many more competitors chasing the philanthropic capital, but there are also more dollars to be captured.

- *Some sectors dominate the market, but smaller sectors are growing faster.* If we remove donations to religious organizations from the capital supply, then the top three market share leaders are education (29.5%), health (19.1%), and human services (16.%), followed in the middle by arts, culture, and humanities (12.2%) and public–society benefit (11.3%).[6] The smallest slices of the charitable pie go to the environment (6.6%) and international affairs (4.6%). However, it is interesting to note that in terms of average annual growth rates, the ranking is almost the inverse: International is growing at 10.0%, environment 5.4%, public–society 5.2%, arts 4.7%, human services 1.5%, health 2.6%, and education 3.2%. Behind these multidecade averages there are also different dynamics. Human services appears to be the most starved sector with the lowest growth and also declines in 2002–2004. International has the greatest volatility, ranging from annual increases of 36.5% and declines of 8.8%. This may reflect the impact of natural or man-made disasters that trigger large-scale giving to meet the acute needs of emergencies. For example, following the December 26, 2004, tsunami disaster, of the more than $13.5 billion that was donated or pledged worldwide for emergency relief and reconstruction, 41% ($5.5 billion) came from private sources. The vast majority of these private donations came from the general public.[7]

- *Each sector faces different donor profiles, preferences, and practices.* For example, in 2003, corporate foundations placed their top priority (27.8%) on education, especially K–12. Public–society benefits followed (25.5%), but this significantly reflects giving to the United Way as part of the long-standing practice of employee workplace giving. International, environment, and health were not targeted areas. Independent and community foundations placed their highest priorities on education (24.1%) and health (21.2%), followed by public–society and human services, both at around 15%. Family foundations represent about half of the foundation universe in numbers and aggregate giving. While they also placed their highest priority on education, they were less likely to give to health, public–society, or human services. The 1,000 or so small foundations tend to give in their local community, and their grants average about $10,000. The social entrepreneur needs to identify and tailor the fund-raising approach to these varying preferences.

- *The big nonprofits get most, but the smaller ones are growing faster.* There are significant advantages that accrue to well-established, large nonprofits. Among these are long track records, high credibility, greater visibility, and larger fund-raising staffs. For example, the largest 30 environmental organizations capture 40% of the total giving to 10,000 environmental nonprofits. However, budding social entrepreneurs should not be totally intimidated by the big guys. Smaller nonprofits are speeding along the philanthropic highway. The average growth rate in 2004 over 2003 for small nonprofits (revenues under $1 million) was 8.31%, far outpacing the large nonprofits' (revenues above $20 million) 3.76%. Small organizations in human services and international, however, suffered declines of a little over 3%. Excluding these sectors would raise the small nonprofit growth rate to 13%. The smaller and start-up organizations have higher reliance on individual rather than institutional donors.

SOCIAL VENTURE PHILANTHROPY

During the late 1990s, a new entrant to the philanthropic marketplace emerged that has been referred to variously as social venture philanthropy, social venture capital, and high-engagement philanthropy. In part, this emerged as a response to what were deemed as some of the limitations of traditional sources of and approaches to philanthropy, both from foundations and individuals.[8] Funding from the traditional sources was generally on a short-term annual basis, obtained from many different donors with varying grant application and reporting requirements, restricted to programs or direct service rather than to strengthen organizational capacity, and very scarce for scaling up. Social enterprises cannot grow without increasing the funds invested in enabling the operation to function at higher and generally more complex levels. Getting bigger requires more cash for management functions and direct services. Growth can be fatal to an organization if it fails to also increase the cash flow. Creating the appropriate capital structure for each type of operation—with the right mix of assets and liabilities—is essential to sustainability.[9] Yet navigating this fragmented and demanding marketplace to get more funds, particularly unrestricted, is very time-consuming and costly. Executive directors of nonprofits have to spend inordinate amounts of time (up to 50% of their time is not unusual) in the capital-raising function compared to their corporate counterparts. The cost of funds mobilization for nonprofits is estimated at around 18% versus around 3% for businesses.[10]

As a way to overcome some of these problems, the idea emerged of utilizing the approach employed by venture capitalists in launching new businesses. In this venture philanthropy model, the donors engage more deeply with the recipient nonprofit organization. The relationship is seen as multiyear and ongoing. The capital disbursement is viewed more as an investment rather than a grant. There is a focus on strengthening the capability of the nonprofit to deliver on its mission more effectively. These social investors provide more than money. They deploy their other valuable assets such as skills, contacts, and credibility and allocate significant time and personal involvement to the nonprofit. Frequently, this engagement focuses on strategic planning and mobilizing resources that will enable the nonprofit to move to the next level of growth. These attributes can create a distinct relationship and dynamic between the social investor and the nonprofit compared with traditional donors. The deeper and longer commitment leads to more honest and transparent communications.

Rather than having to try to tailor program design to the specific interests of traditional donors, which can cause the nonprofit to lose focus and deviate from its strategy, or attempt to hide problem areas for fear of losing funding, the social investor and the nonprofit partner can concentrate their energies on jointly overcoming barriers that arise. This does not mean that the relationship is less demanding. In many ways, it is more demanding for both sides; the investor has to give more along many dimensions and the nonprofit has to respond to higher performance expectations. Nonetheless, it can be more efficient in that the amount of time previously channeled to fund-raising gets reallocated to enhancing the management of the organization.

While there are many attractive features of social venture philanthropy, it is still in its infancy. As of 2002, about 42 venture philanthropy organizations had emerged in the United States with a total capitalization of about $400 million.[11] On average, these organizations were disbursing investments of about $50,000 per year, with about seven investing over $1 million annually. All were providing nonmonetary assistance, the value of which often exceeded the cash grants. The financing was for four- to seven-year periods, frequently beginning with a one-year planning grant.

One of the pioneers in this movement was Social Venture Partners. This organization was started in Seattle by entrepreneur Paul Brainerd, who had invented the Pagemaker software program and was the founder of the Aldus Corporation that was later sold to Adobe. Brainerd was interested in engaging in philanthropy but was not satisfied by the traditional approach. He was captivated by the idea of deploying some of the techniques of private venture capital with which he was quite familiar. In good social entrepreneurship form, he mobilized like-minded friends and created an organization in which each member (partner) would ante up $5,000 annually for a three-year period, and this aggregated total would be the capital fund that the partnership would use to invest in screened nonprofits. By 2003, the Seattle undertaking had been replicated in 23 other cities in the United States and Canada, engaging 1,500 social venture partners. The concept aims not only to mobilize capital but also to educate young professionals about high-engagement philanthropy with the goal that they will subsequently invest higher resource levels. Various giving circles that are more focused on particular causes or groups have also emerged. Examples of such affinity groups are the Global Fund for Women, Funders' Collaborative for Strong Latino Communities, and the San Francisco Bay Area Quality Childcare Initiative.[12] Scanning for such targeted funders should be top priority for social entrepreneurs because matching mission to donor interest is key to triggering investment.

New Profit, Inc. (NPI) provides another nonprofit social venture philanthropy model. It raised around $10 million in an evergreen fund from a small number of individual donors. With this capital base it has identified nonprofits that had successfully demonstrated their basic concepts and wanted to undertake replication and significant growth. A multiyear investment was made in each organization, and intensive management advisory services were provided, including serving on their investees' boards of directors. New Profit created a strategic alliance with the Monitor Company Group, a leading management consulting firm, which allocated consultants to work alongside NPI's professional staff in strengthening the clients' strategies and performance measurement systems and in expanding operations.

One of NPI's portfolio nonprofit organizations was Citizen's Schools, an afterschool education program. President and Cofounder Eric Swartz had the following comment about the experience of working with New Profit and the Edna McConnell Clark Foundation, a traditional foundation that shifted its strategy and operations toward a venture philanthropy approach:

> Venture philanthropy has worked for us—big time. The clarity of our vision, tightness of our action plan, and power of our evaluation metrics are demonstrably greater than two years ago—and greater than they would have been without NPI and EMCF. In 18 months, we've more than doubled in size while improving quality and starting to replicate nationally. We're serving twice as many children and serving them better. Most importantly, we're building the capacity to continue to grow, improve, and creatively impact the field. Our venture partners trained us to use tools like the Balanced Scorecard (BSC) and introduced us to—and in several cases paid for—experts in the fields of evaluation, board development, technology, and business planning. They also provided me with an executive coach. In general, they motivated us to tighten up our strategic plan several turns more than we otherwise would have. They provided $3.75 million toward a $25 million, four-year growth plan—less than 20% of the total but vitally important to our momentum and ultimate success.[13]

Another pioneer in this field is Venture Philanthropy Partners (VPP), which was created in 2000 and mobilized $30 million from 30 technology and business leaders to create The Children's Learning Fund. This fund is targeted toward increasing the capacity of nonprofits in the Washington, D.C., area to serve the developmental and educational needs of children from low-income families. The fund provides cash investments and management assistance drawn from its network. VPP has also been a promoter of the very concept of high-engagement philanthropy, fostering ongoing research and learning about how to strengthen the philanthropic capital markets.[14]

Recently, many other successful businesspeople have made sizable allocations of their wealth to social investing, Bill Gates being the most prominent with the creation of the world's largest foundation and Warren Buffet's donation to the Gates Foundation as the largest charitable gift ever. The Bill and Melinda Gates Foundation stands out for its problem-solving focus. It selects a small number of critical and tenacious societal problems and then makes major, long-term investments aimed at achieving significant breakthroughs. Central to this approach is continual learning and adaptations based on ongoing findings, which is akin to what often happens in commercial venture capital. Such problems generally require multiple sets of distinctive competencies and resources and thereby call forth interorganizational collaborations. For example, the Gates Foundation partnered with the pharmaceutical company Merck and the government of Botswana to attack the AIDS epidemic ravaging that country. These lead investors attracted other partners from the United Nations, business, and philanthropic communities to create a coalition developing a multifaceted systemic solution that might also serve as a learning site for other countries' efforts.[15]

The venture philanthropy approach is also taking hold in other countries. For example, the Bridges Community Ventures and the U.K. Social Investment Taskforce are channeling venture capital into poor communities in England.

Many long-standing foundations continue to innovate in their approaches, with some having had impressive examples of venture philanthropy initiatives long before the term was invented. For example, the Ford Foundation played a key entrepreneurial role in creating and supporting the Local Initiatives Support Coalition (LISC), a national community development financial intermediary that became one of the pioneers in invigorating the national network of community development corporations and community development financial intermediaries (CDFI). The efforts of LISC and The Enterprise Foundation, among others, led to the creation of a low-income housing tax credit that propelled the low-income housing market and movement. Although these actors in the social capital market face many challenges stemming from the consolidation and penetration of the larger financial services industry, the approximately 365 certified CDFIs have $4.6 billion in assets deployed about half in housing and half in other community investments.[16]

Major foundations are also increasingly utilizing their capital base differently. Over 300 foundations made around $300 million in Program Related Investments (PRIs) to nonprofits. These loans are made at below-market interest rates and are considered as part of the foundations' 5% of assets disbursement rate required by the Internal Revenue Service. This provides a new form of longer-term capital for nonprofits. A small number of foundations have opted to spend down their endowments rather than maintain operations in perpetuity. Other major foundations have made fundamental shifts in their strategies to have a more focused and deeper engagement with their clients.[17]

Although Social Venture Philanthropy represents only a small fraction of the philanthropic capital market, it will continue to grow and evolve, and its practices will continue to influence the approaches of the larger traditional funding sources.

FINANCIAL CAPITAL MARKETS

The commercial capital markets have also begun to intersect with the social capital markets. Various funds and financial institutions have begun to offer investment opportunities to individuals and institutions that want their resources to both generate social good and provide them with an economic return. ShoreBank Corporation, a Chicago-based commercial bank, pioneered this approach in the 1970s with an explicitly dual economic and social goal. More recent entrants include Triodos Bank of Belgium and a variety of socially responsible investing mutual funds such as Calvert Group that screen companies based on their ethical, environmental, and social practices. Various new commercial venture capital firms, such as Generation Investment Management and Medley partners, are explicitly incorporating social and environmental criteria into their screening of companies because they deem those as enhancing the sustainability of the enterprises, thereby making them more attractive financial investments.

Partnering between philanthropic and commercial lenders to mobilize greater funds for social enterprises is also increasing. The Ford Foundation provided the community development nonprofit Self-Help with a grant of $50 million as a guarantee for mortgage loans. This enabled the group to parlay that into a $2 billion, five-year financing operation with Fannie Mae and 22 private lenders to enable home ownership for around 30,000 low-income families.[18]

Deutsche Bank mobilized $60 million from 25 other for-profit and nonprofit investors to create the Global Commercial Microfinance Consortium. This entity deposits cash as loan collateral in a bank that in turn issues a standby letter of credit to a local commercial bank. The letter-of-credit bank pays interest on the collateral deposit as well as a fee for the guarantee. The commercial bank also pays the letter-of-credit bank a fee for the guarantee, and then provides local currency loans to microfinance institutions double in amount of the letter of credit, thereby leveraging the original collateral guarantee.[19] *Compartamos* started out as an NGO doing microfinance lending in Mexico as part of the ACCION International network. It converted into a for-profit regulated financial intermediary and was able to raise 150 million pesos (about $15 million) through placements of notes with private investors. Subsequently, it raised another 500 million pesos with a public offering with a partial guarantee from the World Bank's International Finance Corporation.[20]

ePHILANTHROPY

Another addition to the philanthropic arena was ushered in by the Internet boom of the 1990s. There are two sides of ePhilanthropy. The first is the Web-based social enterprises (WEBSEs) that exist in their entirety as Internet entities, be they dot.coms or dot.orgs. These entities proliferated in many forms: online giving directories, charity shopping malls, online charity auctions, click-to-donate sites, workplace giving systems, online donor-advised funds (DAFs), alumni portals, nonprofit information hubs, and volunteer clearinghouses. As with their commercial sector counterparts, when the Internet bubble burst, the WEBSEs experienced a serious shakeout. Table 3.1 reveals that the population of these WEBSEs shrunk from 158 to 96, with only volunteer clearinghouses growing.

Table 3.1   Transactional WEBSE Shakeout

Transactional Enterprises	2001–2006 % Change
Charity Shopping Malls	–59
Click to Donate	–59
Online Auctions	–58
Alumni Portals	–50
Workplace Giving	–33
Online Giving Directions	–29
Nonprofit Information Hubs	–20
Online Donor-Advised Funds	–11
Volunteer Clearinghouses	+14

Numbers: 158 (2001) to 96 (2006).

In addition to the foregoing transactional WEBSEs, a group of support WEBSEs emerged to provide Web-based fund-raising and other services to operating nonprofit organizations. These too experienced a shakeout, as shown in Table 3.2.

These entities aim to integrate the Internet into the nonprofit sector and develop the capacity for online fund-raising within the nonprofit's operations.

Table 3.2   Support WEBSE Shakeout

Support Enterprises	2001–2006 % Change
Application Service Providers	–50
Internet Infrastructure Support	–44
Software Providers	–28
Miscellaneous	–43

Numbers: 110 (2001) to 64 (2006).

Table 3.3   Giving Growth Rates

	2000–2001	2001–2002	2002–2003	2003–2004
Online Giving	22%	46%	63%	58%
Total Giving	0.6%	1.1%	1.3%	5.0%
Online Share	0.46%	0.67%	1.05%	1.60%

NOTE: Source of Total Giving Data: Giving USA 2005.

This is the other side of ePhilanthropy. While the sector lagged in its adoption of Web-based systems relative to the business world, the penetration was nearly universal in the larger nonprofits. Among the top 400 nonprofits, online giving entities rose from 50% in 2001 to 90% in 2005. While online giving is not yet 2% of total giving, its growth rates are explosive compared to total giving, as shown in Table 3.3. Total online giving is estimated to have reached $3 billion by 2004 (see Figure 3.1).

The potential for expanding online giving is significant. As can be seen from Figure 3.2, about 73% of the adult U.S. population uses the Internet regularly, and about 67% of the population donates, but only 7.7% donates online. Consequently, the opportunity is to expand this base of 16.6 million current online donors by getting increasing numbers of the 158 million online users to donate and of the 145 million donors to do so online. There are significant incentives for nonprofits to move in this direction because there is evidence that online givers make larger donations than offline donors.[21] Furthermore, the cost

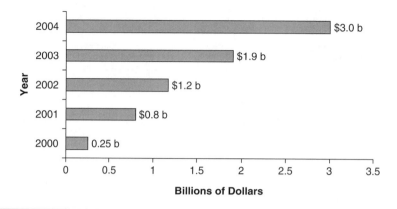

Figure 3.1   Annual Expansion in Online Giving

SOURCE: Used with permission of NPT Publishing Group.

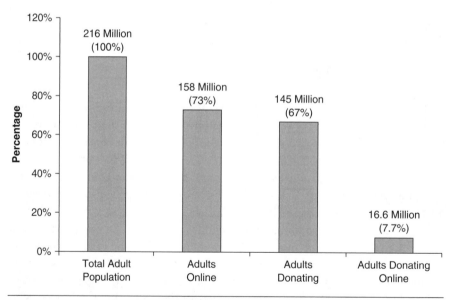

Figure 3.2   2004 ePhilanthropy Donations

SOURCE: Adapted from U.S. Census Bureau, *Current Population Reports.* From *Statistical Abstract of the United States* (2002); Giving USA Foundation (2006); www.pewinternet.org; Mary Malden, "Internet Penetration and Impact" (April 26, 2006); Kintera and Luth (June 2005), "Nonprofit Trend Report"; www.Kintera.com

of reaching a potential donor online is only about 20% of the cost of direct mail or telemarketing. Currently, ePhilanthropy giving growth tracks the growth in eCommerce. As the consuming public continues to incorporate online shopping into their consumption behavior, it is likely that it will also be accompanied by increased online giving. Furthermore, when time is of the essence, donors increasingly turn to the Web. The share of giving done online rose from 11% after 9/11, to 25% after the Asian tsunami, to 50% after Hurricane Katrina. Donors consistently give more in response to highly publicized and emotionally evoking disasters, and the more they do this successfully online, the more they are likely to do so for nonemergency giving. Online givers give to all sectors, with religion dominating as it also does with offline individual giving.

Online giving is mobilizing increasing funds, with the average raised per nonprofit as surveyed by the *Chronicle of Philanthropy* rising from about $175,000 in 2000 to almost $1 million in 2004. While online giving still represents a small share of most nonprofits' total receipts, many are pursuing this new channel aggressively. Mercy Corps generated 35% of its giving online, United Way of Atlanta 15%, Heifer International 13%, and the American Lung Association 12%. National Multiple Sclerosis increased its online donation from $10 million in 2003 to $16.5 million in 2004, and the American Heart Association–Dallas jumped from $6 million in 2003 to $10 million in 2004.

What is also important to note is that 60% of donors check out the organization's Web site before making a donation, whether it is on- or offline. This reveals what is perhaps the real importance of the Internet: It opens up a powerful new avenue for nonprofits to relate to their constituencies. We offer the following observations as guidance for social entrepreneurs utilizing the Internet.

1. CONNECTIVITY: The Internet transcends space and time and creates connection opportunities; this is its transformative effect.

2. CONVENIENCE: It has the potential to radically reduce transaction barriers and costs, but this potential is realized only if the nonprofit makes its site highly user-friendly.

3. CAUSE: This is the motivational engine that attracts the donor; Web site technology can present the cause in captivating Technicolor™ form and beauty.

4. CONTENT: You have to have substance behind the sizzle, and that requires a dynamic ongoing knowledge and story production process.

5. CREDIBILITY: Trust is the nonprofit's key intangible asset, but for online givers, this requires security, privacy, and transparency built into the site's system.

6. CONVERSION: This is the great power—converting the interested into the engaged, the e-mail newsletter reader into the donor, the donor into the advocate.

7. COMMUNITY: Durable conversion comes when the constituents feel they are a significant and engaged member of a group that has a common purpose and shared values, and this requires a site that enables two-way dialogue and multiple opportunities for interaction and contribution.

8. COMMITMENT: To obtain committed donors via the Internet, the non-profit must be committed to continually investing in its Internet presence.

9. CORE CAPABILITIES: This means that the Web should be viewed not as an administrative tool but as a strategically central capacity and mind-set.

MOBILIZING PEOPLE

As was emphasized in our Social Entrepreneurship Framework, the social entrepreneur must mobilize not only financial resources but also human capital. Beyond paid staff, volunteers play a vital part in the operations of social enterprises. In the United States in 2004, an estimated 109 million people (56% of all adults) provided 20 billion hours of volunteer labor valued at $225 billion.[22] In mobilizing people, social entrepreneurs should focus on four dimensions: role, recruiting, alignment, and managing of volunteers.

• *Role:* An important starting point is to establish clarity about where volunteers fit into the enterprise's value model. This requires an identification of the value added by volunteers. They are not a cost-free asset, so their benefits need to exceed the costs of acquiring and using them. While it is tempting to think of volunteers simply as a cheap labor source, they are usually much more. One way to sort out the benefits is to ask yourself: *Would I want them even if the organization had the funds to replace the volunteers with hired employees, and if so, why?* A healthy approach is to view volunteers as an integral part of the organization's human resources, rather than as a sideline activity.

• *Recruiting:* Just as a smart marketer thinks of distinct client segments for an organization's goods and services, so too should one segment potential sources of volunteers. For example, one can segment by age group, occupation, or institution. The Senior Corps of Retired Executives taps into the volunteer pool of more elder professionals interested in continuing to apply their management and technical skills in nonprofit organizations postretirement. Jumpstart recruits student volunteers to serve as mentors to disadvantaged preschoolers to prepare them to succeed when they enter school. For the United States as a whole, 59% of all teenagers volunteer.[23] Corporations have become a significant source of volunteers for many different nonprofit operations. Junior Achievement's model of providing in-school education about business depends critically on its corporate volunteers as teachers. In 2005, it mobilized 213,000 volunteers to work in 287,000 classes at 68,000 sites reaching over 7 million students. Many major corporations support community volunteering activities by their employees. Timberland, the leading boot company, provides its employees with up to 40 hours of paid time for community service of their choice. Of course, there are many other sources of volunteers. Over 400 communities in the United States and Canada have centers to facilitate the connection of interested volunteers and nonprofit organizations. As noted in the previous section, online volunteer clearinghouses were the only WEBSEs experiencing growth. Volunteermatch.org has made 2.5 million referrals. Networkforgood.org, founded by AOL, Cisco Systems, and Yahoo!, also includes opportunities for online volunteering. Regardless of the source, it is more powerful to approach recruiting as providing an opportunity rather than asking for a favor.

• *Alignment:* The contribution and engagement of volunteers will be greater when their assigned activities are aligned with their interests, skills, and time. People volunteer for a multitude of different reasons, so identifying their interests as part of the recruiting process is an important data point in the subsequent task of job design and assignment. Volunteers enrich the social enterprise's capability mix with the skills they bring, so matching specific organizational needs to those distinctive competencies will help maximize the value added of the volunteers, which in turn increases their motivation. It is also necessary to tailor the task to the time availability of the volunteer, both the absolute amount and the scheduling, so that they are compatible with the constraints imposed by the volunteers' other obligations.

• *Managing:* Volunteers should be managed as an integral part of the organization's personnel management system. It is more appropriate to view this as contracting individuals for designated jobs with specified responsibilities rather than bringing in volunteers. Nonetheless, because of their unpaid status, it is common for volunteers or paid staff to consider and treat each other as different. This can be counterproductive, so it is important to set forth very clear expectations up front and to execute performance accountability for the assigned responsibilities. Supervisory relationships, decision-making authority, and evaluation processes all need to be clearly delineated. While volunteers are not paid, they do require compensation in the form of psychological income. One should think through how this will be "paid" as carefully as one does for the organization's monetary compensation system. Fundamentally, one is valuing the volunteer's contribution through recognition and expression of appreciation. These can be both informal and formal, both private and public. But beyond issuing sincere thanks, it is probably most meaningful when one can attribute results to effort so that it is clear how that volunteer made a difference.

AT THE HEART OF IT ALL: THE VALUE PROPOSITION

The common central element critical to tapping any of the sources in the philanthropic capital market is the social entrepreneur's value proposition posited to the potential suppliers of funds, people, or other critical resources. Value creation is at the heart of the Social Entrepreneurship Framework that we presented in Chapter 2. It is the core motivator of the social entrepreneur and key to attracting most donors.

To construct the value proposition, the social entrepreneur needs to be able to set forth the organization's theory of change. Potential supporters want to know how their resources will be put to work to make a difference. One must delineate with clarity how the mobilization of various resources by the social enterprise can be deployed so as to bring about changes in the conditions that are causing the targeted problem such that it will be reduced or eliminated. This can be thought of as a logic model with resource inputs being transformed into activities that produce outputs that generate the desired outcomes. To be convincing, it has to be understandable, believable, and measurable. The measurability of outcomes is often surrounded with complexities, and these will be addressed more fully in Chapter 7. The goal is to demonstrate the "social return" that justifies supporters' investments and reveals mission attainment.

The foregoing stresses the analytical dimensions of the value proposition, but donors are also powerfully motivated by emotional dimensions. The social entrepreneur needs to capture hearts and minds. One way to accomplish this is to aim at creating empathy and sympathy for afflicted groups or issues. The hard data on the seriousness of a problem or the progress in alleviating it take on more meaning when connected with the human element through pictures and stories. It can be quite powerful if donors can interact directly with the groups being served. Most often this is not feasible, so one needs to have great skill in communicating and portraying the individuals being benefited. The Internet can be a powerful vehicle for doing this because of its multimedia formats and because it can transcend distance barriers and create communication linkages for donors with staff and clients in the field.

Resources are generally more forthcoming the more one can meet the supporters' motivations. This task is complicated because motivations are personal rather than standardized. While some will be interested in hard outcomes, others will be moved by human plight, yet others will be driven by their values, and some will be seeking social recognition, or some combination of all the above and others. Alignment can be elusive due to its heterogeneity. Just as businesses do consumer research, one should try to gather as much information as is feasible on supporters' orientation, but motivational understanding will be difficult to pin down with accuracy. This complication can be addressed in part by making one's case along many different dimensions, so that different donors can be reached across a motivational spectrum. This multifaceted approach also creates reinforcing arguments that make the whole case even more convincing.

One final cautionary note: The pressures facing chronically cash-starved non-profits create an ever present temptation to adjust or invent programs to fit donors' interests. This carries with it the risk of diverting resources away from the mission or losing focus and diluting efforts by spreading resources across an ever broadening set of activities. Although the added cash may help meet short-term exigencies, mission drift and focus dilution will almost always come back to erode effectiveness.

CASE STUDIES

One important player in the philanthropic capital markets is the community foundation. These entities mobilize donations from the community and then invest them in projects aimed at bettering the community. As such, they are an intermediate financial institution. One of the leaders has been the Peninsula Community Foundation (PCF) in the Silicon Valley area. After leading PCF through a period of tremendous growth, its president, Sterling Speirn, was faced with the prospect of a decline in the foundation's asset base for the first time in the foundation's history. In addition, the fact that commercial financial service companies had made significant inroads in the market for administering DAFs in recent years, an area that had been a key source for growth for community foundations for the past few decades, compelled Speirn to evaluate PCF's positioning in the market and to consider potential collaboration opportunities with these companies. Fidelity Investments had emerged as the major DAF competitor since it created its Fidelity Charitable Gift Fund in 1991, facilitating donations by its existing commercial clients. By 2005, it had 36,000 donors and had made $5.5 billion in grants to nonprofits.[24] In studying the PCF case, consider the following questions:

1. What are the key factors that enabled PCF to achieve its accomplishments to date?

2. How well do PCF's DAF services compare with other DAF options available to donors?

In the venture philanthropy arena, one of the early organizations to emerge was the New Schools Venture Fund. John Doerr, a partner in the venture capital firm Kleiner Perkins Caufield & Byers, decided in 1999 to apply his venture capital experience to philanthropy. His particular interest and frustration was with public education. He created the New Schools Venture Fund, led by CEO Kim Smith, as a venture philanthropy vehicle to enable higher performance in the organizations they would fund. The case highlights ways in which the private sector venture capital model can be applied to the work of foundations. The following questions can guide your examination of the case.

1. How does Kim Smith balance the realities of the nonprofit sector with the elements of venture capital and the expectations of the 18 New School Partners?

2. How may the criteria for funding developed by New Schools be objectively applied to a nonprofit organization?

3. To what extent do venture capital methods apply to social enterprise?

NOTES

1. Target Analysis Group Web site. Retrieved March 10, 2006, from www.target analysis.com.

2. The Foundation Center Web site. Retrieved March 10, 2006, from www .fdncenter.org.

3. Foundation Center, FC Stats. Retrieved March 10, 2006, from www.fdn.org.

4. Listening to grantees: What nonprofits value in their foundation funders. Retrieved March 10, 2006, from http://www.effectivephilanthropy.org/images/pdfs/lis teningtograntees.pdf.

5. Committee to Encourage Corporate Philanthropy, Annual Report 2005. Retrieved March 10, 2006, from www.corporatephilanthropy.org.

6. Public–society benefit encompasses civil rights, community improvement, scientific and social science research, and donations to the United Way and United Jewish Services.

7. Tsunami Evaluation Coalition, Synthesis report. Retrieved July 14, 2006, from http://www.tsunami-evaluation.org/.

8. Letts, C., Ryan, W., & Grossman, A. (1997, March–April). Virtuous capital: What foundations can learn from venture capitalists. *Harvard Business Review*, pp. 36–44.

9. For specific approaches to capital structure construction, see the publications of the Nonprofit Finance Fund: www.nonprofitfinancefund.org.

10. Bradley, B., Jansen, P., & Silverman, L. (2003, May). The nonprofit sector's $100 billion opportunity. *Harvard Business Review*, pp. 94–103.

11.   Venture Philanthropy Partners. *Venture philanthropy 2002*. Retrieved March 10, 2006. This document also provides detailed descriptions of these organizations. For details, please see venturephilanthropy.org.

12.   Fulton, K., & Blau, A. (2005). *The future of philanthropy*. Cambridge, MA: Monitor Institute.

13.   Venture Philanthropy Partners. *Venture philanthropy 2002: Advancing non-profit performance through high-engagement grantmaking*. Retrieved March 10, 2006, from www.venturephilanthropypartners.org.

14.   For an informative exposure to the perspectives of venture philanthropists and their partnering nonprofits, please see Community Wealth Ventures, Inc., *High-engagement philanthropy: A bridge to a more effective social sector*. Venture Philanthropy Partners, 2004, available from www.venturephilanthropypartners.org.

15.   Ruback, R. S., & Kreiger, D. (2000). *Merck & co.: Evaluating a drug licensing opportunity*. Harvard Business School Case # 9–201–023.

16.   Moy, K., & Okagali, A. (2001). *Changing capital markets and the implications for community development finance*. Retrieved April 2, 2006, from the Surdna Foundation and The Brookings Institute, http://www.brookings.edu/metro/capitalx change/article5.htm.

17.   Bailin, M. (2003, October). *Focusing in on an effective grantmaking strategy*. Speech delivered at the Center for Effective Philanthropy's Seminar on Foundation Effectiveness.

18.   Fulton, K., & Blau, A. (2005). *Looking out for the future*. Global Business Network and The Monitor Institute. Retrieved April 2, 2006, from http://www.future ofphilanthropy.org/files/finalreport.pdf.

19.   Emerson, J., & Spitzer, J. (2006). *Blended value investing: Capital opportunities for social and environmental impact*. Geneva, Switzerland: World Economic Forum.

20.   Ibid.

21.   Kintera, Inc., "Kintera/Luth Nonprofit Trend Report," June 2005, San Diego, CA.

22.   Network for Good Web site. Retrieved March 10, 2006, from www.network forgood.org.

23.   Ibid.

24.   Fidelity Charitable Gift Fund Web site. Retrieved March 10, 2006, from ww.charitablegift.org.

Case Study 3.1.

Peninsula Community Foundation

We are here to help realize and help shape the philanthropic dreams of individuals and organizations on the Peninsula and in Silicon Valley. Our customer is the community. We will serve the community and all who seek to improve and enhance it.

—Sterling Speirn, president of the Peninsula
Community Foundation, "Grassroots and Treetops," 2002

It was January 2003 and Sterling Speirn, president of the Peninsula Community Foundation (PCF), had just been debriefed on the contract details for Merrill Lynch's new donor-advised fund. His team had been talking with Merrill for the past few months about Merrill's plan to partner with community foundations around the country. Speirn was interested to see how the Merrill partnership was going to unfold, as the financial firm was pursuing an innovative approach to the growing market for donor-advised funds.[1] Rather than pursuing Fidelity's strategy of replicating some of the key functions that had traditionally been performed by local community foundations, Merrill was

SOURCE NOTE: Copyright © Harvard Business School Publishing, case number 9-304-015. Used with permission.

Professors James E. Austin and Jane Wei-Skillern and Alison Berkley Wagonfeld, Executive Director of the HBS Calfornia Research Center, prepared this case. The assistance of Senior Lecturer Bob Higgins is gratefully acknowledged. HBS cases are developed solely as the basis for class discussion. Cases are not intended to serve as endorsements, sources of primary data, or illustrations of effective or ineffective management.

seeking to partner with community foundations to leverage their collective knowledge about charitable giving, community needs, and local nonprofits. After months of discussions, Merrill was now looking for a solid commitment from PCF to be part of its network. Speirn was aware that this partnership would require a substantial investment from PCF in terms of time, money, and forgone opportunities. He was still unsure if this was the best path for PCF, but it was time to make a decision. Merrill was expecting a final answer by the end of the week.

This option to partner with Merrill came at an interesting time for Speirn and his team, as PCF's business was at a critical inflection point. During the economic boom of the late 1990s, PCF's assets had more than tripled, from $150 million in 1996 to nearly half a billion dollars by year-end 2001. This growth had been fueled by the widespread adoption of donor-advised funds, on the one hand, and the meteoric rise of the public equity markets, on the other. But now, in the wake of the capital market correction that began in March 2000, and with a field of powerful new competitors in the donor-advised fund business, future asset growth at PCF was far from certain. Indeed, PCF's assets contracted in 2002 for the first time in its nearly 40-year history. This trend concerned Speirn, in part because PCF derived its operating budget from fees charged on assets under management. Beyond the issue of fees, the recessionary climate increased the number of local nonprofits seeking grants from PCF, and the team wanted to support as many as it could.

PCF had worked closely and collaboratively with financial institutions for many years. In fact, firms such as Merrill and Goldman Sachs were a vital aspect of PCF's channel sales strategy, by which new donors were cultivated with targeted outreach to financial advisors, private bankers, estate-planning attorneys, and other professionals. However, the proposed partnership with Merrill appeared to be different, presenting unique issues that needed to be carefully examined. As Speirn and his team worked on their strategic plan, they thought about all the challenges and opportunities that lay ahead. Speirn predicted that PCF would look very different in 10 years, and that transformation might well depend in large part on the strategic decisions to be taken now.

COMMUNITY FOUNDATIONS

The first community foundation was started in 1914 in Cleveland, Ohio, in order to create economies of scale by pooling the funds of various individuals who wanted to allocate money for charitable purposes. Several banks invested the assets, while a community board oversaw the grants. Other regions set up similar foundations, and throughout the rest of the 20th century, the number of foundations and the assets under management continued to grow. By 2003, there were over 600 community foundations, responsible for over $30 billion in assets.[2] In 2002, they disbursed grants of $2.4 billion, representing 8% of the grants made by all types of foundations. Community foundations were public charities [501(c)(3) organizations], and as such, they were regulated by the Internal Revenue Service (IRS) on a national level and by attorneys general at the state level. Beyond legal regulations, community foundations had developed and published standards for voluntary adoption.

Nearly all community foundations focused on a designated geographical area within a specific state and played an important role in helping to fund and support nonprofit organizations that offered key community services in that designated area. Traditionally, most community foundation assets were obtained through gifts to a foundation's endowment, and each foundation had its own rules governing how endowment gifts were granted to nonprofits. Many endowment donors trusted community foundations to grant money in the manner that the foundation thought was most beneficial; however, other donors gave endowment gifts with restrictions (e.g., nonprofits focused on education). Endowment gifts were tax deductible at the time of the gift, and donors relied on the community foundation to do the due diligence and monitoring associated with grantmaking to specific community organizations.

By the mid-1970s, some community foundations started offering donor-advised funds (DAFs)—vehicles that allowed donors to have greater influence over how their charitable dollars would be allocated. A DAF allowed donors to establish their own accounts within a larger foundation and make specific requests as to how dollars in that account would be distributed. The advice provided by the donor had to be nonbinding (i.e., the community foundation had the right to deny a request), but most requests were accepted.

DAFs were seen as a great alternative or addition to contributing to a foundation's endowment, starting a private foundation, or sending out individual checks to each charity. One advantage was that a donor could receive an immediate tax deduction when donating money to a DAF and then request that the money be gifted to specific charities over the following years. A second

advantage was that the basis for the tax deduction was calculated at the asset's fair market value—a major benefit for gifts in the form of appreciated stock or real estate. For example, if a donor had $100,000 of stock that was purchased several years ago for $30,000, the donor could donate all $100,000 to a DAF and receive a tax write-off that year for the $100,000, up to 30% of his adjusted gross income (AGI).[3] Furthermore, the donor would not be required to pay capital gains taxes for the $70,000 profit from the sale of the stock. After making the onetime gift, the donor could then give $20,000 a year to various specified charities for each of the next five years.[4] In addition, the foundations that managed the donor-advised funds took care of issuing the individual checks and doing the paperwork. A third advantage—at least for donor-advised funds at community foundations—was that donors could use the foundation to learn about local community needs.

Donor-advised funds were also perceived as an alternative to private and independent foundations. A private foundation required a separate board of directors and extensive oversight responsibilities. Private foundations were also required to disburse at least 5% of their assets to nonprofits each year in order to retain their tax exemption, while DAFs had no minimum distribution requirements. Furthermore, donors were entitled to deduct their securities gifts to private foundations up to 20% of AGI and 30% of AGI for cash. For all of these reasons, a growing number of community foundations began offering donor-advised funds to complement their endowment funds. This trend contributed to the financial growth in community foundations—assets across all U.S. community foundations grew more than 1,000% from 1981 to 2001.

Most community foundations supported their operations by taking fees representing 0.5%–2.0% of assets under management. (Fees typically varied with the size and nature of a fund account.) Each foundation could choose how it wanted to invest its assets—some managed money on their own, and others outsourced this function to professional investment firms. Certain regions had only one community foundation (e.g., Boston), while other areas supported several. The San Francisco Bay Area was unique in that it had six community foundations. Although each covered a different set of counties, there was still some overlap. (See **Exhibit 3.1.1** for data covering the Bay Area community foundations.)

BACKGROUND AND HISTORY OF PCF

The Peninsula Community Foundation was founded in 1964 by Theodore and Frances Lilienthal. From 1974 to 1990, it was led by Executive Director Bill Somerville. Somerville was known for his creative approach to working with local nonprofits—he stressed the importance of establishing meaningful programs to help the community. Until 1989, the foundation had grown steadily from $400,000 in assets to $14 million. Many things changed in 1989 when an anonymous donor gave $25 million to PCF's endowment fund, propelling the foundation into one of the 25 largest community foundations in the country.

Shortly after receiving this gift, Somerville hired Speirn, whom he had known for several years, to help manage how the money would be granted to local nonprofits. Speirn had received his bachelor's degree from Stanford University and then went on to pursue a degree in law. He later decided to get a business degree as well, and in 1984, he started an MBA program at U.C. Berkeley. It was during a career night at school that he met Somerville. As Speirn recalled, "I remember hearing Bill speak and thinking 'that is what I want to do.' I introduced myself to him and asked if I could work as an intern at PCF during my second year at school. I believed that I had finally found the dream career." When Speirn left U.C. Berkeley, he took a job with Apple Computer as the manager of its national program for awarding grants to nonprofits. He enjoyed this position, but it ended abruptly in 1990 when Apple eliminated the division in an effort to cut costs. To Speirn's good fortune, the timing coincided with PCF's receipt of the $25 million gift. Somerville needed additional resources to help award grants, and he hired Speirn to be the program officer at PCF. However, shortly after Speirn started, Somerville decided to leave to start a new foundation. Within 15 months, Speirn was appointed to the position of president of PCF.

Speirn spent the next several years developing a plan for growing the foundation and made several changes to the seven-person team. (See **Exhibit 3.1.2** for management biographies.) In 1993, Speirn had the opportunity to attend the annual meeting for the top 25 community foundations in the country.[5] Speirn recalled: "I felt like the runt of the litter at the meeting, but it was a great learning experience. I sat there and absorbed everything I could. By the time I left, I had reached the conclusion that it would be hard to attract big endowment gifts if nobody knows you. I was convinced that donor-advised funds were going to play a major role in our growth."

Community Foundation—County or Counties Covered:

San Francisco Foundation—San Francisco, Alameda, Contra Costa, Marin, San Mateo

Peninsula Community Foundation—San Mateo and Santa Clara

Community Foundation Silicon Valley—Santa Clara and San Mateo

East Bay Community Foundation—Alameda and Contra Costa

Marin Community Foundation—Marin

Sonoma County Community Foundation—Sonoma

Bay Area Statistics (2000 Census):

County	Population	Median Household Income
Alameda	1,443,741	$55,946
Contra Costa	948,816	$63,675
Marin	247,289	$71,306
Napa	124,279	$51,738
San Francisco	776,733	$55,221
San Mateo	707,161	$70,819
Santa Clara	1,682,585	$74,335
Solano	394,542	$54,099

Exhibit 3.1.1   Map of Bay Area Community Foundations

SOURCE: www.bayareacensus.ca.gov/bayarea.htm, accessed May 29, 2003.

Case Study

Sterling Speirn, President   Speirn joined PCF in 1990 and has since launched the Center for Venture Philanthropy; cofounded the Peninsula Partnership for Children, Youth, and Families; and led PCF as it has grown from $44 million to more than $470 million in total assets. Prior to starting at PCF, Speirn worked at Apple Computer where he led the company's national computer grants program for nearly four years. He holds a degree in political science from Stanford and a law degree from the University of Michigan. He also attended the MBA program at U.C. Berkeley. Speirn is chairman of the statewide League of California Community Foundations, serves on the Board of Directors of the American Leadership Forum of Silicon Valley and the Northern California Grantmakers, and is on the Board of Advisors of Pacific Community Ventures and the Entrepreneurs' Foundation.

Vera Bennett, Vice President, Finance and Administration   Bennett is responsible for over-seeing all foundation investments and for managing internal operations, accounting, and information systems. Prior to her 13-year tenure at PCF, Bennett spent a decade as the finance officer for Kainos, a facility for developmentally disabled adults in Redwood City, California. She received her B.S. in business administration with an emphasis in accounting from the College of Notre Dame in Belmont, California.

Ellen Clear, Vice President, Community Programs   Clear is responsible for the foundation's community grantmaking to local nonprofit organizations. Prior to joining PCF in 1995, Clear worked with nonprofit agencies in San Francisco, Cambridge, Massachusetts, and Washington, D.C.; as a financial analyst for an investment bank in San Francisco; and as a newspaper reporter in Raleigh, North Carolina. Clear holds a master's in public policy from Harvard and a B.A. in political economy from U.C. Berkeley.

Ash McNeely, Vice President, Philanthropic Services   McNeely is responsible for the planning and implementation of the foundation's business development, donor services, and communication strategies. Prior to her work with the foundation, she served for eight years in development and marketing roles in Bay Area theater companies. She has also held external relations positions at San Francisco State and U.C. Berkeley. McNeely received an MBA in nonprofit management from Golden Gate University and graduated Phi Beta Kappa from Vassar College.

Terence Mulligan, Director of Outreach, Philanthropic Services   Mulligan joined the foundation staff in the summer of 2001. He is responsible for outreach to the professional advisor community. Prior to joining the foundation, he held a variety of customer-facing roles in both the public and private sectors, focusing on strategy and business development. Mulligan graduated summa cum laude with a B.A. in economics from U.C. Berkeley and holds an MBA from the Harvard Business School.

Exhibit 3.1.2   PCF Management Biographies

SOURCE: Adapted from the PCF Web site, May 2003.

Case Study

In 1993, nearly all of PCF's assets were part of the endowment. Some gifts were restricted to certain fields of interest, but for the most part, PCF had the authority to make grants as it deemed appropriate. Speirn explained, "Most community foundations grew up thinking that the primary goal was to get a big endowment and put together a process for giving it away." Speirn, on the other hand, believed that people should have the option "to give to PCF or through PCF." He continued, "We are here to put money to work today and in the future."

Speirn was pleased that his board supported these goals and encouraged him to grow the organization. In keeping with Somerville's strategy, Speirn wanted PCF to continue being creative and venturesome with the same spirit that had led PCF to describe its work as "venture philanthropy" in its 1985 annual report. (Venture philanthropy referred to applying certain practices of venture capital to the nonprofit community, such as investing the cash and expertise needed to build the capacity for high performance.) Speirn instituted a strong service ethic in the organization—he believed that PCF existed to serve the donors and nonprofits in the community. He hired people who "loved to talk with others about their philanthropic dreams." Speirn wanted PCF to be known for its cohesive organization and willingness to take risks. By 2002, the seven-person team had grown to 50 people focused on raising money, making grants, overseeing the finances, and managing special initiatives. The board continued playing an active role, serving on five different committees. (See Exhibit 3.1.3 for a list of board members.)

In the late 1990s, PCF had expanded on its commitment to venture philanthropy and set up a special "Center for Venture Philanthropy." The center worked with local donors to incubate new philanthropic programs and sponsored chartered bus tours (venture vans) to highlight social issues in the community. Speirn also teamed with various organizations in San Mateo County to develop a special series of programs targeting young children in the region. Speirn believed that PCF enjoyed a unique position as the hub between people wanting to give money and nonprofits looking to get money. He prided himself on PCF's ability to work effectively with both groups.

PCF Grants

From 2000 to 2002, PCF granted between $62 million and $65 million each year to nonprofits. This was about twice the amount it had granted each year in 1998 and 1999, respectively. Approximately 80% of the grants were from DAFs, with the remainder coming from the endowment and other funds such as special-interest funds.[6] In 2002, 55% of DAF grants were directed to nonprofits in the community served by PCF (Santa Clara and San Mateo Counties), while approximately 30% went out of state. (See Exhibit 3.1.4.) In order to recommend a grant, donors with advised funds at PCF had the option of using the Internet, fax, or mail to send in their recommendations. PCF used a third-party technology supplier to provide its Internet capabilities, and approximately 40%–60% of donors used the Web service (PCF Connect) to manage their fund accounts.

PCF had developed eight portfolios representing the areas in which it donated the majority of the annual grants from its

Patricia Bresee	**Linda R. Meier**
Retired Commissioner Superior Court of San Mateo Elected 1997	Community Volunteer Atherton Elected 1997
John H. Clinton, Jr.	**Karen V. H. Olson**
Retired Publisher Elected 1996	Independent Travel Consultant Bungey Travel, Palo Alto Appointed by President of Mills College, 1994
Bernadine Chuck Fong, Ph.D.	**Nancy J. Pedot**
President Foothill College, Los Altos Hills Elected 1999	Business Advisor/Consultant San Francisco Elected 1999
Susan Ford	**Jennifer Raiser**
President Sand Hill Foundation, Menlo Park Elected 1996	President Raiser Senior Services, San Mateo Elected 2001
Nylda Gemple, R.D./L.D.	**William L. Schwartz, M.D.**
Retired Public Health Administrator Hillsborough Elected 2001	Retired Internist, San Mateo Clinical Professor of Medicine, UCSF Samaritan House Medical Clinic Volunteer Elected 2000
Umang Gupta	**Donald H. Seiler, C.P.A.**
Chairman and CEO Keynote Systems, San Mateo Elected 2003	Founding Partner Seiler & Company, LLP, Redwood City Elected 1995
Charles "Chip" Huggins	**Warren E. "Ned" Spieker, Jr.**
President and CEO Joseph Schmidt Confections, San Francisco Elected 1999	Partner Spieker Partners, Menlo Park Elected 1999
Rick Jones	**Jane H. Williams**
Director E. Richard Jones Family Foundation San Mateo Elected 2002	President Sand Hill Advisors, Palo Alto Elected 2001
Olivia G. Martinez, Ed.D.	
Vice President, Institutional Development Canada College, Redwood City Trustee, Sequoia Union High School District Elected 1995	

Exhibit 3.1.3 PCF Board of Directors

SOURCE: PCF.

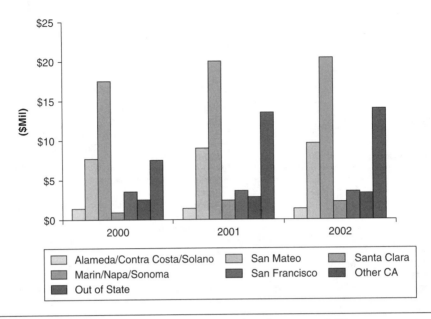

Exhibit 3.1.4   Geographical Distribution of Donor-Advised Grants at PCF

SOURCE: PCF.

endowment. These included First Five Years, In School & Out of School, Supporting Families, Health & Wellness, Strengthening Nonprofits, Community Building, Arts & Culture, and Environment. (See **Exhibit 3.1.5** for a detailed description of each category.) Nonprofits in each of these categories applied for grants, and the board helped choose the recipients of the larger endowment gifts. In 2002, PCF granted approximately $7 million to local nonprofits from its endowment fund.

PCF also assembled narratives describing causes that its staff found particularly worthwhile and shared these with donors interested in hearing about local philanthropic opportunities. PCF's Community Programs and Philanthropic Services departments together offered a program called Synergy Connection that enabled PCF to offer tangible and timely ideas to donors in a consistent manner. (See **Exhibit 3.1.6** for an example of a synergy listing.) As Ellen Clear, PCF's vice president of community programs, explained, "We believe that we can play an effective role of 'matchmaker' between donors who want to hear about opportunities and local nonprofits that are looking for donations for a specific need." In response to a charitable interest survey that PCF sent to its donors in 2002,

The First Five Years   This portfolio supports early childhood programs that promote positive child development by maximizing healthy physical and emotional development of infants and young children; nurturing a young child's love of reading and learning; and investing in quality child care, including professional development for child care workers and increasing the supply of child care for low-income families.

In and Out of School   The In School & Out of School Portfolio invests in programs that promote educational achievement and positive personal development in school-age children and youth, particularly those in low-income families. This portfolio supports a broad range of "in-school" strategies aimed at increasing schools' capacities to foster students' academic success. These include interventions that provide extra support and targeted instruction for students who need it, teacher professional development, and programs that encourage family participation in school. This portfolio also supports "out-of-school" strategies that provide homework assistance and academic support, enrichment activities, and programs that address working parents' need for safe, supervised activities outside of school.

Building Community   The Community Building Portfolio represents a spectrum of different funding strategies to support community building efforts: "street philanthropy" (being streetwise, able to react quickly and close to the pulse of community issues and organizations), civic engagement (building residents' involvement and connectedness to one another and their community institutions), and a comprehensive systems approach (impacting root causes of problems and influencing an entire service delivery system). Much of the work in this portfolio is supported by a series of private and public partnerships—some that catalyze relationships, others that bridge social networks, and all that strengthen communities.

Supporting Families   The Supporting Families Portfolio seeks to strengthen the human services safety net for low-income families and to help families of all kinds exercise their rights, fulfill their responsibilities, and realize their full economic and social potential. Our grantmaking supports nonprofit organizations that help low-income and disadvantaged children and adults meet basic needs for food, clothing, and emergency and permanent housing. The portfolio also targets organizations that address family violence, promote expanded opportunity for people with disabilities, and serve adults seeking to improve their economic prospects through literacy and employment development.

Strengthening Nonprofits   The Strengthening Nonprofits Portfolio supports the visions and infrastructures of nonprofit organizations in our community. The goal is to help exemplary programs continue to thrive within healthy organizations and to promote a stimulating nonprofit environment where exciting ideas can easily develop. This portfolio makes selected grants to foster leadership through staff and board development, strengthen organizations' fund-raising and development programs, support capital campaigns, build the capacity of organizations to improve or expand their services and operations, and build the capacity of the sector as a whole.

Health & Wellness   The Health & Wellness Portfolio promotes a healthy community and strengthens the health-care safety net for uninsured and underserved people. The foundation works in partnership with community-based organizations that target the health needs of diverse populations and geographic areas as well as public agencies that protect public health and ensure the availability of care for all. This portfolio supports strategies that prevent illness and promote health, enhance access to health services, initiate or strengthen services that promote recovery from illness and substance abuse, and involve community members in addressing local health needs.

Case Study

Exhibit 3.1.5   Overview of PCF Portfolios   *(Continued)*

(Continued)

Arts & Culture   The Arts & Culture Portfolio offers opportunities to artists and communities whose works we might not otherwise see and hear. We seek to increase artistic expression through support of individual artists, arts organizations, and arts programs for children and youth. Strategies supported by this portfolio include increasing the creation and performance of art forms reflecting the diversity of our community; supporting programs that offer children and youth experiences in the arts, both as participants and as audience members; and assisting organizations seeking to increase the venues for art exhibition and performances on the peninsula.

Environment   San Mateo and Santa Clara Counties have developed amid diverse ecosystems of biological richness including a marine coast, bay wetlands, fertile agricultural lands, and Pacific-temperate rain forests. The Environment Portfolio seeks to foster greater awareness of, access to, and stewardship of the natural treasures that grace the peninsula and Silicon Valley.

Exhibit 3.1.5

SOURCE: Adapted from PCF published materials.

32% of donors said they were interested in learning more about donor opportunities. PCF's recommendations generated $2.9 million of donations from DAFs in 2002—approximately 6% of all DAF grants at PCF that year. Speirn explained, "While this may seem low relative to all DAF donations, it increased our targeted local grantmaking by 40% to 45%. It had the same effect as adding $60 million to our endowment."

Clear managed a team of 11 staff, who were entirely focused on knowing all about the hundreds of nonprofits in the community. (See **Exhibit 3.1.7** for a PCF organizational chart.) Prior to recommending a nonprofit or approving a grant, Clear's team assessed the organization's management and program structure and reviewed its financials. Her team also compared nonprofits in various fields in order to determine which were being run the most effectively. Clear believed that "PCF was in the unique position of knowing more about all the local nonprofits and all the needs of this community than any other organization. This is one of the benefits for

donors who give money to us." It was this local knowledge that supported the synergy program and differentiated PCF from its commercial competitors. In a survey of PCF donors conducted in 2001, 72% of fund holders said they had recommended PCF to others. As Mike Spence, former dean of the Stanford Graduate School of Business, said, "PCF makes it easy to see what opportunities are worthwhile." Susan Packard Orr, a PCF donor and the chairman of the David and Lucile Packard Foundation, reinforced this sentiment: "I enjoy working with PCF because I know the depth of experience they bring to the table. There are few community foundations in the country that have pioneered as many initiatives and partnerships."

PCF Financials and Business Model

As of December 31, 2002, PCF had 583 fund accounts totaling $448 million of assets under management, making it the 16th largest community foundation in the country in terms of assets. Of the total

Synergy Connection:

Community Education Center

Type of Request: General operating support

Organization Mission/Background

The Community Education Center (CEC) offers a quality preschool experience in English and Spanish for low-income children in the Fair Oaks community adjacent to Redwood City. CEC was founded in 1964 by parents affiliated with the Carlmont Parents' Cooperative Nursery School in Belmont who recognized the need for a nursery school to serve the Spanish-speaking community. The goal of the half-day program is to provide each child with a sound foundation that will encourage future success in school and in life.

Project Description/Needs Statement

CEC can serve 96 children at two sites in morning and afternoon sessions that last three hours. Children ages 3 years and 9 months to 5 years are eligible to attend, and priority is given to those children who will enroll in kindergarten the following school year. The majority of the children come from monolingual Spanish-speaking families. Children participate in a variety of meaningful activities designed to help them develop abstract thinking, social skills, and an understanding of other cultures.

Although CEC has been in operation for nearly four decades, several things have occurred in recent years to cause its financial situation to change dramatically. CEC qualifies as a state-funded preschool, but the state reimbursement rate is far too low to adequately finance CEC's operations, particularly given the cost of operating on the peninsula. The United Way had provided core operating support of $30,000 until five years ago and then, when its funding priorities changed, began reducing its contribution until it ceased completely two years ago. CEC's executive director was seriously ill during the 2000–2001 fiscal year and was not able to keep enrollment at capacity. This current school year, CEC has operated without an executive director in an effort to reduce costs. Two members of the board of directors have worked intensely and effectively with the program coordinator to keep the school running smoothly, and all of the eight board members have been actively fund-raising.

Community Impact

CEC is well integrated into the Fair Oaks community, and parents trust the program and find the idea of sending their young children to school less intimidating. Parents are encouraged to become involved in their child's education and give their child a head start in school that will last a lifetime. Parents must volunteer in the classroom each month, and parent education courses are offered each month. CEC board members and administrators estimate that while more than 90% of the children entering the program do not speak English, more than 75% understand and speak English upon graduation. Younger children often repeat the program a second year.

Budget/Specific Request From PCF

The Community Education Center must raise $22,000 to finance its program through June 2002. Board members are actively seeking foundation support and individual donors to help the program regain financial stability. A contribution of $4,000 pays the cost of enrollment for one child for the school year.

Exhibit 3.1.6 Sample Synergy Listing

SOURCE: PCF.

Case Study

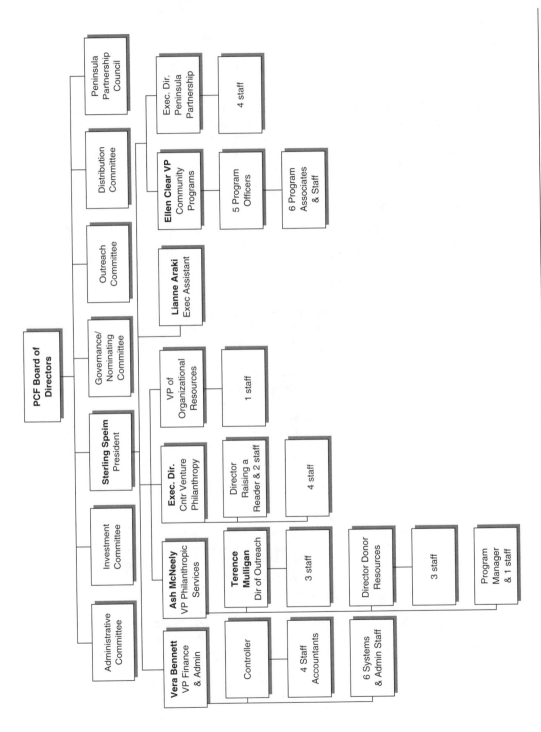

Exhibit 3.1.7 PCF Organizational Chart

SOURCE: Adapted from organizational chart provided by PCF.

assets, approximately $275 million (378 fund accounts) represented DAFs, $101 million represented the endowment, and the remainder was split among other smaller funds such as special-interest funds, scholarships, and charitable remainder trusts. (See **Exhibit 3.1.8** for assets by fund type from 1992 to 2002.) Gifts to PCF peaked in 2000 with $231 million coming in, $217 million of which was allocated to DAFs. (See **Exhibit 3.1.9.**) In 2000, about half of the incoming donations to PCF were from new donors establishing 130 new fund accounts and half from previous donors. PCF's minimum requirement to open a DAF was $5,000.

Between January 1, 2000, and December 31, 2001, PCF received 237 donor-advised fund gifts over $50,000. Of these, 48 (20%)

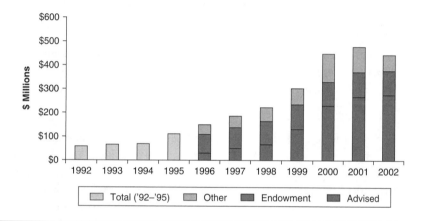

Exhibit 3.1.8   PCF Assets by Fund Type (1992–2002)

SOURCE: Adapted from information provided by PCF.

NOTES: Fund Type Definitions:

Other: Includes special-interest funds, charitable remainder trusts (CRTs).

Endowment: Represents money donated to PCF's primary endowment and available for general grant purposes.

Advised: Represents PCF's donor-advised funds.

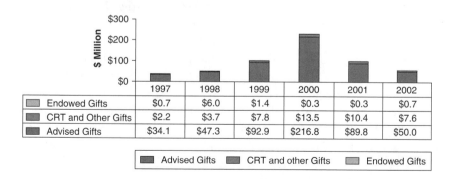

	1997	1998	1999	2000	2001	2002
Endowed Gifts	$0.7	$6.0	$1.4	$0.3	$0.3	$0.7
CRT and Other Gifts	$2.2	$3.7	$7.8	$13.5	$10.4	$7.6
Advised Gifts	$34.1	$47.3	$92.9	$216.8	$89.8	$50.0

Exhibit 3.1.9   Gifts to PCF by Type of Fund (1997–2002)

SOURCE: Data provided by PCF.

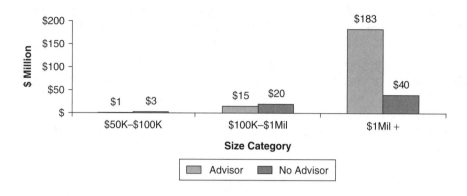

Exhibit 3.1.10   Source and Value of PCF Gifts by Advisor (January 2000–December 2001)

SOURCE: Data provided by PCF.

NOTE: Advisors include estate-planning attorneys, wealth-management advisors, accountants, financial planners, and trust officers.

represented 85% of the total dollar value. PCF found that 82% of its donors who set up fund accounts over $1 million were referred by advisors such as estate-planning attorneys, wealth-management advisors, accountants, financial planners, and trust officers. (See **Exhibit 3.1.10**.) These advisors were collectively seen as a critical channel to reach new donors. In 2001, PCF had hired Terence Mulligan (HBS '96) as the director of outreach to develop relationships with local professional advisors from firms such as Merrill Lynch, Goldman Sachs, and the region's many law and CPA firms. One of his goals was to highlight the services that PCF could provide to high-networth families. This was an important means of finding new donors, as PCF did little in the way of advertising. Speirn believed that Bay Area donors often chose a particular community foundation based on the quality of local services provided and the foundation's reputation. PCF did some direct mail and public relations targeted at

affluent families in the region, but word of mouth also played an important role in building PCF's presence in the community.

In connection with gifting assets to PCF, donors were able to recommend how they wanted the money invested. The foundation offered four portfolio choices: cash, fixed income, equities, and a balanced "socially responsible" portfolio.[7] Within each category, PCF selected a pool of three to five mutual funds from different investment firms. For example, the fixed-income pool consisted of the Vanguard Short-Term Corporate Fund Admiral Shares, the Merrill Lynch Corporate Intermediate Term Fund, and the PIMCO Total Return Institutional Fund. The funds in each of the pools were selected based on fund managers, performance records, and expense ratios. Speirn commented, "Until the mid-1990s, donor-advised funds were pooled with our endowment funds and collectively managed by investment managers hired by the foundation. But after the stock market downturn in

Case Study

1993 and 1994, we decided to separate our endowment funds from our donor-advised funds and to offer donors a wider choice in selecting and mixing investment strategies for their funds."

PCF assessed annual fees ranging from 0.5%–2.0% to cover the costs associated with providing its services. Fees were charged monthly based on the fund balance at the end of the month. The tiered fees were as follows:

Donor-Advised Funds	
On the first $3 million	1.0%
On the next $3 million–$10 million	0.75%
Funds in excess of $10 million	0.5%
Other	
Special-investment funds	1.0%
Agency funds	0.5%
Scholarship funds	2.0%
Field-of-interest funds	1.0%–2.0%
Unrestricted endowment funds	2.0%

According to Mulligan, fees for scholarship funds, field-of-interest funds, and unrestricted endowment funds tended to be higher because PCF needed to do more research and due diligence in order to make grants. In addition, the competition in the market for donor-advised funds forced PCF to keep its fees down.

Most contributions to PCF were in the form of cash or appreciated stock. However, PCF was willing to accept less "liquid" assets such as real estate, privately held securities, and partnership interests. For all gifts, PCF converted the assets to cash as soon as possible and donors were able to deduct the fair market value. PCF required that all assets be kept in the PCF investment pools (described above) unless a donor was interested in opening a fund account over $5 million. In that case, the donor was entitled to choose an alternative investment option or to keep the funds where they had been to date with the approval and oversight of PCF's investment committee. (In either scenario, the donor still paid fees to PCF based on the sliding fee schedule.) For example, if a $5 million-plus donor had been referred by Goldman Sachs and already had money invested with Goldman, that donor could keep its money with Goldman's asset management team and pay $37,500 (0.75%) each year to PCF for its work in distributing the money to charities.

In 2002, PCF earned a total of $5.2 million in fees. Of these fees, about half came from donor-advised funds. The foundation managed its expenses to its revenues and tried to finish each year with a small amount of "excess revenue." (See **Exhibit 3.1.11** for PCF's 2002 and 2003 operating budgets.) As Vera Bennett, vice president of finance and administration, explained, "We are not in a position to raise our fees, so we have to be cost-conscious."

In 2003, PCF was hoping to start charging fees to nondonors who wanted to tap into PCF's extensive knowledge about philanthropy in the Bay Area. As Clear described, "We have found that some of the smaller family foundations that do not have funds with PCF are interested in paying us for our expertise regarding local nonprofits. We're not sure how big an opportunity this is, but we are starting to make this service available." This was one of the areas that PCF was starting to explore in connection with its strategic plan.

Peninsula Community Foundation Summary of 2003 Operating Budget				
Revenues	2003	2002	$ Change	% Change
Cash Carryover (Estimated 2002 Surplus)	$ 186,617	$ 95,500	$ 91,117	95.4%
Administrative Fees from Funds	$ 5,164,940	$ 5,159,992	$ 4,948	0.1%
Fees & Events-External	$ 69,800	$ 127,000	$ (57,200)	−45.0%
Interest	$ 76,000	$ 420,000	$ (344,000)	−81.9%
Contributions/Grants	$ 121,827	$ 151,050	$ (29,223)	−19.3%
Total Revenues	$ 5,619,184	$ 5,953,542	$ (334,358)	−5.6%
Expenses				
Personnel	$ 3,800,261	$ 3,783,527	$ 16,734	0.4%
Travel & Professional Development	$ 72,713	$ 121,921	$ (49,208)	−40.4%
Association Memberships	$ 4,250	$ 39,000	$ (34,750)	−89.1%
Leases & Insurance	$ 576,776	$ 640,528	$ (63,752)	−10.0%
Office Expenses	$ 390,776	$ 316,460	$ 74,272	23.5%
Meetings & Cultivation	$ 30,117	$ 32,667	$ (2,550)	−7.8%
Audit & Accounting	$ 43,100	$ 37,750	$ 5,350	14.2%
Computer & Tech. Consultant	$ 148,363	$ 168,787	$ (20,425)	−12.1%
Outside Consultant	$ 147,038	$ 260,530	$ (113,492)	−43.6%
Legal Fees	$ 25,000	$ 13,500	$ 11,500	85.2%
Advertising	$ 33,800	$ 94,250	$ (60,450)	−64.1%
Special Events	$ 35,805	$ 133,950	$ (98,145)	−73.3%
Capitalized Equipment/Leasehold	$ 137,030	$ 163,440	$ (26,410)	−16.2%
Investment Consultant Fees	$ 103,500	$ 103,500	$ —	0.0%
Total Operating Budget	$ 5,548,485	$ 5,909,810	$ (361,326)	−6.1%
Budget Surplus/(Deficit)	$ 70,700			
Special Projects Budgets:				
NonProfit Center	$ 104,489	$ 120,942	$ (16,453)	−13.6%
Peninsula Partnership	$ 564,462	$ 652,675	$ (88,213)	−13.5%
EPA Neighborhood Improvement Program	$ —	$ 214,845	$ (214,845)	−100.0%
Children's Rpt. Card	$ 151,381	$ 193,595	$ (42,214)	−21.8%
Venture Funds (RAR & AFA)	$ 1,440,835	$ 173,961	$ 1,266,874	728.3%
Raising a Reader Business Fund	$ 822,496	$ 729,603	$ 92,893	12.7%
Packard Environmental	$ 1,079,798	$ 155,032	$ 924,766	595.5%
Total Special Projects	$ 4,163,459	$ 2,240,653	$ 1,922,806	86%
Interfund Transactions: (Amount contributed to operating budget from Special Projects)				
Personnel Cost Reimbursed to General Oper.	$ 49,565			
Overhead Paid to General Operating	$ 233,873			
Interfund Grants (RAR)	$ 374,851			
Total Interfund Transactions	$ 1,088,289			
Total Budget	$ 8,623,654			

Exhibit 3.1.11 PCF Operating Budget

SOURCE: Data provided by PCF.

U.S. MARKET FOR DONOR-ADVISED FUNDS

Since their inception in the 1970s, DAFs have become increasingly popular throughout the United States. In addition to community foundations, Jewish foundations were largely credited with increasing the availability of DAFs in the 1970s and 1980s. In 1992, Fidelity Investments was the first commercial/for-profit financial institution to offer its customers the advantages of contributing to a DAF. Other financial institutions followed Fidelity's lead, and by the end of 2002, there were 13 commercial investment companies that offered a significant DAF program.[8] In addition to the commercial investment companies and the community foundations, a number of religious organizations and universities started offering DAFs as well in order to build relations with their affinity groups. According to a survey conducted by *The Chronicle of Philanthropy*, assets held by a sample of the largest DAFs in the United States totaled $10.2 billion in 2002, a small drop from the $10.5 billion of assets in 2001.[9] (See **Exhibit 3.1.12** for 2001 and 2002 data for commercial funds and **Exhibit 3.1.13** for data from 1999 to 2002 for a broader set of the largest donor-advised funds.)

Commercial Investment Companies

Investment firms were eligible to offer DAFs as long as they established a nonprofit subsidiary and applied for 501(c)(3) status. Most investment companies did not purport to have in-depth knowledge about nonprofits throughout the United States; rather, they presented themselves as an effective tool for clients who already had a clear idea of their philanthropic-giving strategy. Customers could receive the tax advantages associated with gifting money through a DAF without moving their assets to another organization.

Fidelity Investments

Fidelity branded its offering under the name Fidelity's Charitable Gift Fund. Initially, Fidelity marketed its services primarily to its own customers, but it gradually grew more aggressive in its outreach. Speirn recalled a time in 1997 when one of his staff members came into the office with a letter from KQED, the Bay Area's local public broadcasting station, promoting Fidelity's Charitable Gift Fund. This was upsetting, as PCF had supported KQED with numerous grants over the years. Speirn felt that "Fidelity was buying its way into our community." In 1999, Fidelity had 16,458 fund accounts representing $1.7 billion. By December 2002, Fidelity had 31,002 fund accounts representing $2.4 billion of assets under management for its donor-advised funds. As Mulligan explained, "Fidelity's growth was unprecedented in the charitable-giving industry. Fidelity was the first organization to educate consumers about the market. They let people know that donor-advised funds were not only for the superrich—they communicated that 'you can have one too.'"

For clients who wanted to research charities, Fidelity offered links on its Web site to several resources. Ash McNeely, PCF's vice president for philanthropic services, believed that "Fidelity had a few people on its staff to

Organization	Assets			Amount Distributed to Charities			Number of Funds		
	2001	2002	Percent Change	2001	2002	Percent Change	2001	2002	Percent Change
Commercial Funds									
American Gift Fund (Newark, DE)	$ 5,960,591	$ 6,926,536	16%	$1,407,853	$ 1,269,930	–10%	134	138	3%
Calvert Social Investment Foundation (Bethesda, MD)	3,617,120	5,966,000	65	36,365	592,268	1,529	39	84	115
Fidelity Investments Charitable Gift Fund (Boston)	2,648,760,694	2,389,029,773	–10	735,914,318	750,975,802	2	27,601	30,112	9
Heartland Charitable Trust (Dubuque, IA)	4,734,285	4,652,612	–2	1,152,292	1,092,697	–5	102	102	0
Raymond James Charitable Endowment Fund (St. Petersburg, FL)	13,000,000	13,800,000	6	800,000	1,130,000	41	110	175	59
National Philanthropic Trust (Jenkintown, PA)	345,587,000	416,970,599	21	25,878,000	73,091,080	182	204	416	104
Oppenheimer Funds Legacy Program (Denver)	5,566,527	9,268,091	67	1,312,204	1,833,914	40	160	250	56
T. Rowe Price Program for Charitable Giving (Baltimore)	6,783,000	8,100,000	19	771,000	1,800,000	134	200	300	50
Renaissance Charitable Foundation (Indianapolis)	581,240	6,335,233	990	0	213,850	– ?	1	24	2,300
Schwab Fund for Charitable Giving (San Francisco)	139,513,683	200,080,456	43	43,035,392	52,731,810	23	3,369	4,451	32
SEI Giving Fund (Oaks, PA)	n/a	3,000,000	– ?	n/a	550,000	– ?	n/a	15	– ?
Vanguard Charitable Endowment Program (Malvern, PA)	291,412,593	383,041,593	31	45,051,829	64,813,601	44	2,099	2,750	31

Exhibit 3.1.12 Sample of Top Commercial/Financial Organizations With Donor-Advised Funds (2001–2002)

SOURCE: "Donor Advised Funds: Assets, Awards and Accounts at a Sampling of Big Providers," *The Chronicle of Philanthropy*, May 15, 2003.

Organization	Assets					Amount Distributed to Charities					Number of Funds				
	1999	2000	2001	2002	% Change ('99–02)	1999	2000	2001	2002	% Change ('99–02)	1999	2000	2001	2002	% Change ('99–02)
Fidelity Investments Charitable Gift Fund (Boston)	$1,700,000,000	$2,400,000,000	$2,648,760,694	$2,389,029,773	41%	$374,000,000	$574,000,000	$735,914,318	$750,975,802	101%	16,458	22,983	27,601	30,112	83%
Schwab Fund for Charitable Giving (San Francisco)[b]	n/a	72,000,000	139,513,683	200,080,456	n/a	n/a	14,000,000	43,035,392	52,731,310	n/a	n/a	1,500	3,369	4,451	n/a
Vanguard Charitable Endowment Program (Malvern, PA)	72,175,612	171,446,300	291,412,593	383,041,593	431	6,734,488	19,458,793	45,051,829	64,813,601	862	550	1,268	2,099	2,750	400
Boston Foundation	174,266,076	230,393,325	219,961,935	183,547,620	5	17,573,902	27,631,291	26,545,510	24,593,026	40	406	438	464	516	27
California Community Foundation (Los Angeles)	116,248,000	154,400,000	170,044,000	167,597,000	44	80,399,000	30,311,000	32,300,000	47,607,000	−41	369	464	531	601	63
New York Community Trust	n/a	711,000,000	648,000,000	650,000,000	n/a	n/a	102,000,000	87,100,000	87,091,000	n/a	n/a	841	928	948	n/a
Marin Community Foundation (Novato, Calif.)	41,000,000	47,000,000	47,251,000	55,757,414	36	5,900,000	7,200,000	8,764,000	15,080,768	156	72	94	111	142	97
East Bay Community Foundation (Oakland, CA)	27,916,000	40,502,000	53,500,000	57,184,000	105	4,052,000	6,065,000	11,500,000	6,884,500	70	200	270	178	224	12
Community Foundation Silicon Valley (San Jose, CA)	136,000,000	171,000,000	241,000,000	208,000,000	53	18,000,000	27,000,000	35,000,000	41,000,000	128	121	178	148	252	108
Peninsula Community Foundation (San Mateo, CA)	121,010,842	217,850,082	256,194,363	264,523,912	119	26,942,453	37,090,891	40,166,862	52,641,711	95	248	343	362	377	52

Exhibit 3.1.13 Selected Organizations With Donor-Advised Funds (1999–2002)

(Continued)

Case Study

(Continued)

Organization	Assets					Amount Distributed to Charities					Number of Funds				
	1999	2000	2001	2002	% Change ('99-02)	1999	2000	2001	2002	% Change ('99-02)	1999	2000	2001	2002	% Change ('99-02)
San Francisco Foundation	219,523,463	233,288,888	250,000,000	n/a	n/a	41,380,304	53,500,839	50,000,000	n/a	n/a	264	292	349	n/a	n/a
Sonoma County Community Foundation (Santa Rosa, CA)	n/a	8,489,700	11,156,766	17,716,026	n/a	n/a	2,157,009	3,792,5499	3,025,323	n/a	n/a	82	54	62	n/a
United Jewish Communities[c]	1,979,715,000	2,203,000,000	2,432,000,000	n/a	n/a	388,000,000	n/a	n/a	n/a	n/a	n/a	7,500	n/a	n/a	n/a
Jewish Community Federation of San Francisco, Peninsula, Marin & Sonoma Counties	n/a	n/a	200,085,000	187,600,000	n/a	n/a	n/a	39,800,000	37,600,000	n/a	n/a	n/a	672	713	n/a
Harvard University (Cambridge, MA)[d]	20,385,000	32,400,000	39,000,000	39,000,000	91	600,000	5,100,000	4,200,000	6,100,000	917	10	12	14	14	40
National Christian Charitable Foundation (Atlanta)	223,000,000	350,000,000	362,000,000	350,000,000	57	69,000,000	80,000,000	95,000,000	103,288,000	50	1,132	1,217	1,600	2,000	77
Tides Foundation (San Francisco)	122,000,000	157,000,000	155,900,000	138,829,231	14	28,000,000	56,000,000	76,300,000	59,536,000	113	275	300	314	314	14

Exhibit 3.1.13

SOURCE: Adapted from "Annual Donor-Advised Fund Survey," *The Chronicle of Philanthropy*, May 31, 2001; May 30, 2002; and May 15, 2003.

a. Fiscal years vary from June to December based on organization.

b. Data represent individual and corporate-advised funds.

c. In 2002, United Jewish Communities stopped reporting as a group.

d. Data represents estimates.

answer questions about nonprofits, but these people were responsible for covering the entire United States. As a result, they couldn't possibly have in-depth knowledge about local charities throughout the country." Fidelity required a minimum $10,000 gift to open a fund account and charged its donors on a sliding scale between 0.25% (for accounts over $2.5 million) and 1% of total assets (up to $500,000) on an annual basis. Fidelity also charged money-management fees, so total fees ranged from 0.67% to 1.87% per year. Donors were required to choose among four investment pools (money market, interest income, equity income, and growth), and all investments were kept with Fidelity fund managers.

Fidelity granted $750 million to nonprofits in 2002, more than double the $374 million it granted in 1999. The majority of donors used a Web-based interface to recommend a grant. Fidelity took care of disbursing the money and doing the record keeping. Fidelity also provided a Web site for donors to review the investment performance of their funds. During the mid-1990s, Fidelity had invested in a significant technology solution to support its donor-advised offering. Fidelity's technology platform was so robust that the firm started managing the "back end" for several other financial institutions as well. Along these lines, Fidelity provided private-label services for institutions such as asset-management firms and universities that wanted to offer DAFs but lacked the resources or desire to develop the infrastructure. The private-label division operated under the brand National Charitable Services and was also a not-for-profit operation.

Merrill Lynch

Merrill started offering donor-advised funds in 1995, but it took a different approach than Fidelity. Merrill partnered with local community foundations across the country in order to provide more robust philanthropic services. Initially, Merrill teamed up with a group of 170 community foundations and planned to refer clients to foundations as long as the foundations allowed Merrill to continue managing the assets. According to Bennett, "The Merrill arrangement from the 1990s was complicated, and I don't think it really panned out as Merrill had hoped. Neither Merrill nor the community foundations had the infrastructure in place to achieve Merrill's vision." There was no standardization across the country, so fees varied significantly from one region to another. In addition, most of Merrill's financial advisors were not informed about the partnerships, and they had no incentive to refer clients.

In 2002, Merrill revamped this strategy and started looking for a smaller group of foundations with which to have a closer relationship. The new plan, called The Merrill Lynch Community Charitable Fund, would require each of the participating community foundations to build a technical interface to Merrill's account systems through a third-party vendor. Merrill planned to start with 10 to 15 foundations and increase its network of community foundations to 60 foundations in two years.[10] Mulligan explained, "By adopting this strategy, Merrill hoped to give its clients the best of what was out there—detailed information about nonprofit organizations, high levels of local service, and a choice of investment options wrapped up by Merrill." According to H. King McGlaughon, Jr., former director of Merrill's Center for Philanthropy and Nonprofits, "Merrill will be the first to offer a uniform donor-advised program through community foundations nationally."[11] As of January 2003, Merrill planned to set the minimum investment level at $25,000.

Merrill informed PCF that donors could expect to pay fees of approximately 2.1%, 1% of which would go to Merrill while the other 1.1% would be divided among the local foundation and two different intermediaries helping with the interface between PCF and Merrill. Mulligan believed that "PCF would receive between 50 and 60 basis points of annual fees for each account. It was unclear, however, as to how much additional work would be entailed in providing services to Merrill's clients." For example, Merrill was expecting PCF to use customized donor correspondence as well as a customized Web site. In addition, PCF would need to manually synchronize all fund activity with its own database. These types of adjustments would cause additional work for PCF, while fees would be lower than those PCF received from its other DAF accounts.

Merrill planned to introduce its Community Charitable Fund in the spring of 2003 through a series of workshops for its 14,000 financial advisors across the country. If PCF signed the contract, McNeely and Mulligan would be invited to attend the workshop in San Francisco and make a short presentation about PCF's capabilities. Unlike the original plan in 1997, the new structure did provide some incentives to Merrill's financial advisors to refer clients to this new fund. According to McNeely, "Merrill was planning to position its donor-advised fund as another value-add that Merrill's

investment advisors could present to their clients. Nobody had a clear sense as to how many clients would be interested." While Merrill was universally regarded as one of the leading brokerage firms in the United States, it was not perceived as a large fund manager such as Fidelity or Vanguard. It was unclear how this reputation would affect its ability to attract sizable new DAF accounts. Merrill estimated that the average fund size would be approximately $150,000, with a 20% annual distribution rate.

Other Commercial Investment Funds

In addition to Fidelity and Merrill, there were a number of other investment firms that started offering DAFs. Vanguard introduced its fund in 1999 and had $383 million in assets by the end of 2002. In 2002, it granted $64 million on behalf of its donors.[12] Vanguard differentiated itself by being a low-cost provider and charging lower fees than any other provider of DAFs. Charles Schwab began offering DAFs in 1999 and had $200 million in assets by the end of 2002.[13] Given that a high percentage of Schwab's customers were from the Bay Area, PCF believed that Schwab drew donors from the same region covered by PCF.

An increasing number of commercial investment firms were interested in working with private-label companies such as those provided by Fidelity and its National Charitable Services division. This division allowed Bear Stearns and Goldman Sachs to enter the market relatively quickly, although the fees to donors were 1%–2% higher than those charged by Fidelity to account for the involvement of both financial organizations. Another firm—National Philanthropic Trust—worked with a for-profit Internet company called GivingCapital to run donor-advised funds for American Express, JPMorgan Chase, Legg Mason Trust, and Morgan Stanley.[14]

Community Foundations

Community foundations continued to play an important role in the proliferation of DAFs. Out of the list of 84 organizations with substantial advised funds in 2002 published by *The Chronicle of Philanthropy,* 49 of them were community foundations. The largest of these in terms of DAF assets was New York Community Trust with $650 million of assets in 2002 from 948 fund accounts. The next largest was Communities Foundation of Texas (Dallas) with $284 million of assets from 428 fund accounts in 2002. PCF was the third largest among the community foundations in terms of assets in DAFs. The combined DAF assets of the five largest Bay Area foundations were approximately $850 million in 2002.[15] The average size of DAF fund accounts at community foundations was $318,000, as opposed to $89,000 at the commercial investment firms.[16] Speirn believed that some of this difference could be attributed to the transactional nature of the commercial fund clients—he had heard that many of Fidelity's donor-advised fund holders had set up accounts in order to make gifts primarily to universities and religious institutions in a tax-efficient manner. In contrast, families that set up accounts at community foundations tended to want more advice and counseling because they had more money to give away.

While many community foundations offered DAFs, most of the foundations were run differently than PCF. McNeely explained:

Most community foundations focused the majority of their energy on the endowment, and DAFs were a small piece of the asset mix. Other community foundations also had fewer investment choices for their donors. They gave donors the impression that once money was given to the community foundation endowment, the donor was no longer involved. In contrast, PCF wants all its donors to feel like important customers, and it wants to be in the business of connecting them to community opportunities that match their philanthropic wishes.

McNeely wondered if these differences would become even more apparent as firms such as Merrill developed networks with multiple community foundations across the country.

Other Groups

In addition to investment firms and community foundations, religious groups and universities were the third major segment of DAF providers. The largest set of funds within this category was part of United Jewish Communities. As of December 2001, this set of organizations had $2.4 billion of assets.[17] The National Christian Charitable Foundation had $350 million from 2,000 fund accounts in 2002. By the end of 2002, a number of U.S. universities had started offering donor-advised funds to their alumni and affiliates. In 2002, Harvard University had $39 million of assets from just 14 fund accounts.[18] Universities often required that a large percentage of DAF contributions held with the university ultimately be donated to that institution, but as Mulligan explained, "Sophisticated development offices seemed able to attract some donors, particularly if those donors were not aware of other DAF options." Mulligan speculated that DAFs were becoming increasingly available, particularly through private-label options: "There are few barriers to entry in this market. Soon every insurance firm and local Rotary club will be offering donor-advised funds for their affinity groups."

PCF STRATEGIC OPTIONS

In light of the tremendous growth in donor-advised funds over the previous decade, Speirn believed that it was important for PCF to review its positioning in the market. PCF had grown accustomed to competing for donors with Fidelity and the other Bay Area community foundations, but as more organizations started offering DAFs, donors would have even more choices. PCF was optimistic, given that 4 million U.S. households had a net worth over $1 million and only a fraction of these already had DAFs or private foundations in place. In addition, analysts speculated that there would be a $41 trillion–$136 trillion intergenerational transfer of wealth during the next 50 years. A portion of this wealth was expected to be allocated to nonprofits, which could lead to growth for community foundations.[19] Nevertheless, PCF still needed to determine how it wanted to approach the market.

Competition

One option was for PCF to compete in all segments of the market with other institutions offering DAFs in the Bay Area. In this scenario, PCF would target everyone from young families hoping to give away $10,000 per year to retired CEOs looking to donate $2 million or more each year. PCF would continue to work with local professional advisors while also looking at broader marketing opportunities. To date, PCF had adopted the strategy of accepting any new donor with a minimum account of $5,000. Speirn explained, "At PCF, we have always believed in opening our doors to anyone that wants to be charitable—we do not say 'we don't want to work with this customer' because their giving goals are too small. We also see donor-advised funds as a gateway to a deeper relationship."

PCF could change its strategy and select one or two segments of the market in which to compete aggressively. For example, PCF could focus primarily on the wealthiest portion of the Bay Area population—the people who might be considering private family foundations as an alternative to a donor-advised fund. This group was likely to establish funds over $1 million and would be able to appreciate the breadth of philanthropic opportunities presented by PCF. In addition, this group might give a few large gifts rather than many small gifts—thereby reducing the workload on the staff at PCF. If PCF took a more segmented approach, it might choose to increase its minimum account size and develop new types of premium services.

Collaboration Opportunities

Speirn and his team were also considering establishing more collaborative relationships such as the potential relationship with Merrill. Speirn was pleased that the Merrill arrangement was designed to draw upon PCF's unique knowledge of Bay Area charities, but he wondered if this partnership would make it difficult for him to develop arrangements with other large commercial investment firms that already had sizable DAF assets. To date, Fidelity had not shown any interest in working with community foundations, but perhaps PCF could approach Fidelity with a proposed pilot project. Fidelity would not need any of the record-keeping services developed by PCF, but Fidelity's Bay Area clients could benefit from access to PCF's knowledgeable staff and list of synergy projects. Clear believed that "most Fidelity customers did not know what their local community foundation could offer in terms of grantmaking expertise and other services. Nearly all community foundations, including PCF, did not have advertising budgets to showcase their capabilities, so many Fidelity customers were unaware of other options." Schwab, with its headquarters in San Francisco, was also seen as a potential partner due to the high percentage of its clients in the Bay Area.

Speirn was aware that additional partnerships with financial institutions might further decouple what PCF had traditionally presented as a package, but he believed that "the situation was forcing us to examine our own core competencies and identify our marketable assets." McNeely commented:

Some of the options we are reviewing take us away from a business model tied only to assets under management. While there are benefits to diversification, it is important that we don't forget about our endowment. In many ways, our endowment serves as our research and development center because we continuously review grant requests from local nonprofits who are seeking funding. Conducting due diligence for these requests helps us stay in touch with the nonprofits in our community year after year.

Members of the PCF management team also discussed various private-label arrangements for the DAF business. On one side of the spectrum, PCF could develop the infrastructure to offer private-label services to other companies along the lines of what Fidelity had done with its National Charitable Services division. Local banks or Rotary clubs could be interested in leveraging what PCF had built to date. This strategy would require hiring additional people with the IT skills needed to effectively integrate multiple organizations. At the other end of the spectrum, PCF was even considering reducing the activities it performed in-house and engaging one of the national private-label organizations to do some of the complicated back-office and record-keeping tasks. PCF had invested in the technology and manpower to ensure that donors got accurate statements, but it was expensive. Bennett elaborated, "We like to give our donors choice, but it is very difficult to manage all the accounts. We have money in 115 funds across 38 financial institutions. In order to reconcile all the financials, we have to allocate returns among every account. It takes a team of five people to ensure accuracy and monitor all the investments."

PCF was not alone in thinking that it might be best to partner with other organizations. According to an article published in a large Bay Area newspaper, Community Foundation Silicon Valley was thinking along the same lines. The article stated:

"'When Fidelity launched its charitable fund, we went to Congress and the IRS. We tried to put them out of business,' recalled Peter Hero, president of Community Foundation Silicon Valley. 'In retrospect, we should have gone to them and collaborated.'"[20]

Other Options

Although donor-advised funds had become the largest part of PCF's asset mix, PCF also looked at the option of reducing focus on this competitive category. The foundation was aware that it was harder to attract endowment gifts, but once obtained, these gifts ensured a steady stream of management fees. To date, PCF had not undertaken a capital campaign, but that was a possibility for the future. McNeely also believed that board members had the potential to play a bigger role in attracting major endowment gifts. The management team was also reviewing records of the 1,200 independent or private foundations in the Bay Area and determining if some of them might be interested in tapping into the knowledge base at PCF. According to Mulligan, these foundations had assets of $10 billion in 2001 and were always looking for ways to give away money in a thoughtful manner.

On occasion, Speirn also wondered if it made sense to have six community foundations in such a small area. In 1995, the group had developed a "Statement of Principles for the Community Foundations in the Bay Area" that stated, "The Bay Area and its community foundations will benefit from *collaboration* in programming and

competition in their donor services." (See Exhibit 3.1.14 for the complete statement of principles.) Speirn believed that "although the six foundations were quite different in terms of focus and culture, they generally operated with collegiality and mutual respect."

CONCLUSION

As Speirn thought through all of the options available, he wondered just how much Americans valued the strong localized knowledge of community foundations. He questioned, "In an age in which people are less rooted and move frequently, what value do people place on having a strong community connection?" Speirn believed that deep, consistent relationships with donors and local nonprofits really made a difference. The success of the Center for Venture Philanthropy's first two social-venture funds (Assets for All Alliance and Raising a Reader) seemed to be perfect illustrations: The concepts were incubated with key nonprofit partners, and start-up funding had come entirely from people with donor-advised funds. Local families and private foundations later invested, and ultimately each initiative attracted federal funding and national attention.

The notion of venture philanthropy was based on working closely with a selected set of organizations for multiple years, and it was helpful to have philanthropists rooted in a community. PCF wanted its DAF donors to feel this same commitment to local nonprofits. Speirn believed, "In addition to funding programs, great community

Preamble.

The nine counties bounding the San Francisco Bay are fortunate to be served by six respected community foundations. It is uncommon for an American metropolitan region to enjoy such abundant community foundation resources. This statement of principles reflects the dedication of the community foundations bounding the Bay to work in close association, and to affirm as paramount to all else they do the encouragement of Bay Area philanthropy and the augmentation of Bay Area nonprofit services.

1) Shared interests.
    Many of the community foundations have overlapping service areas and all have intersecting program interests. Their characteristics reflect the regional nature of each community foundation.

2) Collaboration and competition.
    The Bay Area and its community foundations will benefit from *collaboration* in programming and *competition* in their donor services.

3) Program.
    On the program side of their activities, the foundations should seek every opportunity to increase community benefits through collaboration.

4) Donor services.
    On the donor services side of their activities, the foundations should be guided by the following principle: advancement of the community foundation field is the prerequisite of and fundamental to the advancement of individual foundations.

5) Good practice.
    Accordingly, the health growth and community respect and regard for all Bay Area community foundations requires us to abide by four basic rules of good practice:
    • inform inquiring prospective donors about other community foundations serving the communities in which they reside or work;
    • assist inquiring prospective donors in examining a full range of their private and community foundation options before they choose an institution to serve them;
    • avoid judgments or comparisons of community foundations;
    • seek opportunities to engage in collaborative efforts designed to promote philanthropy through community foundations and when addressing donors, prospective donors, professional advisors to donors, and the general public.

Peter Hero,
Community Foundation of Santa Clara County _____

Michael Howe,
East Bay Community Foundation _____

Stephen Dobbs,
Marin Community Foundation _____

Sterling Speirn,
Peninsula Community Foundation _____

Robert Fisher,
The San Francisco Foundation _____

Kay Marquet,
Sonoma County Community Foundation _____

Exhibit 3.1.14 Statement of Principles for Community Foundations in the Bay Area
SOURCE: Provided by PCF, dated June 21, 1995.

foundations help build organizational capacity within a nonprofit and are proactive with respect to launching and supporting new initiatives." This was done through money granted and time spent helping an organization understand how it could operate more effectively. Speirn and his team derived a great deal of satisfaction from watching donors observe the tangible benefit of their gifts. He enjoyed seeing donors increase their giving as they witnessed their impact. As he thought about the future direction of PCF, he wanted to ensure that the foundation did not lose the opportunity to help others realize their philanthropic dreams. McNeely elaborated, "At PCF we think about growth as more than bringing in money. It's also about giving it away and changing people's lives."

Speirn was concerned, however, about PCF's ongoing ability to increase its impact on the community. Unlike the commercial firms such as Fidelity, PCF perceived itself as both a provider of philanthropic services and a supporter of local community needs. He watched the financial services firms gather more fund accounts and wondered if the donor-advised funds would become nothing more than a commodity. He believed that "money managers have an incentive to keep money under management, not encourage it to be given away. In contrast, PCF measures itself by how much and how well the money is given away and the resulting impact on people's lives and our community." Speirn wondered if partnering with Merrill Lynch would just serve to strengthen the position that commercial investment firms had in the market. While PCF was interested in having access to Merrill accounts, the foundation

did not want to be marginalized in the process. Speirn noted the irony of community foundations being started by a banker who wanted the community to help give money away, and now bankers were figuring out ways to pull money back into their accounts. Donor-advised funds had proved to be a "sticky" asset, and financial institutions were positioning themselves to capitalize on the projected growth in the industry. While it might be necessary to work with more financial institutions, PCF needed to figure out what it could carve out for itself. This was particularly true as the financial firms wanted to control both the relationships and the money.

Speirn had overseen a tremendous expansion period for PCF during his decade as president, and he wanted to make the next decade even better. There was a board meeting scheduled for the following week, and Speirn needed to provide his recommendation for the Merrill deal. He knew that his recommendation should also include the implications for PCF's larger future strategy.

NOTES

1. Donor-advised funds allow people to contribute assets (e.g., appreciated stock) at a tax-advantaged time and then request that charitable grants be made on the donor's behalf at a time of the donor's choosing. A more detailed explanation of donor-advised funds can be found on pp. 2–3 of this case.

2. Peter A. Dunn, "Should You Create a Donor Advised Fund Program," *The Journal of Gift Planning,* third quarter 2002, pp. 17–18.

3. The 30% deduction represented the maximum deduction for securities. For cash donations, a donor could deduct up to 50% of AGI. (Any amount not deductible in the year the initial gift was made could be carried forward and used as a deduction in the five subsequent years.)

4. Any interest and/or capital gains/losses accrued over the five years are kept within the fund account, so the total amount available for donations at the end of the period would be $100,000 plus or minus the investment returns.

5. The annual Larger Community Foundations Meeting (sometimes referred to as the Peacock Meeting) was self-organized by the participating foundations. It was an opportunity for the board chairs and CEOs of the largest community foundations to get together and discuss strategy and best practices.

6. Special-interest funds allow donors to designate nonprofit grant recipients in a certain field of interest.

7. PCF defined "socially responsible" as a group of securities that have been screened using a standard avoidance list (e.g., tobacco) as well as for issues related to animal rights and international human rights.

8. "Donor-Advised Funds: Assets, Awards and Accounts at a Sampling of Big Providers," *The Chronicle of Philanthropy*, May 15, 2003.

9. Ibid.

10. Matt Ackerman, "Merrill Eyes Donor-Advised Fund for Charitable Giving," *Mutual Fund Market News*, March 10, 2003.

11. Ibid.

12. "Annual Donor-Advised Fund Survey," *The Chronicle of Philanthropy*, May 15, 2003.

13. Ibid.

14. Debra E. Blum, "Tailor Made for Charity," *The Chronicle of Philanthropy*, May 30, 2002, pp. 7–9.

15. Calculated from "Annual Donor-Advised Fund Survey," *The Chronicle of Philanthropy*, May 15, 2003.

16. Ibid.

17. "Annual Donor-Advised Fund Survey," *The Chronicle of Philanthropy*, May 30, 2002. (The United Jewish Communities started reporting separately for FY2002.)

18. "Annual Donor-Advised Fund Survey," *The Chronicle of Philanthropy*, May 15, 2003.

19. Terence Mulligan and Chris Nicholson, "The Community Foundation Value Proposition: An Introduction to Community Foundations and the Services They Provide to Estate Planners and Their Clients," *California Trusts and Estates Quarterly*, p. 27.

20. John Boudreau, "Philanthropy a Big Business Opportunity," *The San Jose Mercury News*, May 4, 2003, p. 5F.

Case Study 3.2.

New Schools Venture Fund

In December 1999, John Doerr—a partner with the venture capital firm Kleiner Perkins Caufield & Byers (KPCB) and a cofounder of the New Schools Venture Fund (New Schools)—reviewed a preliminary draft of New Schools' objectives for the year 2000. Doerr reflected on what New Schools—a $20 million nonprofit venture philanthropy fund started in 1998—had been able to achieve to date and what issues it faced going forward:

In the past year and a half we've invested in a number of education entrepreneurs attacking the problems in our public education system with scalable programs. However, the goal with New Schools is to provide far more than money—we also take board positions, offer advice to our ventures,

and connect educational entrepreneurs nationwide with each other. As we grow, it is important for us to think strategically about our network of supporters and donors to ensure we really add value to the ventures and make a difference in kids' lives.

New Schools (www.newschools.org) was one of the first funds focused on social entrepreneurs and "venture philanthropy." It borrowed the approach used in venture capital to invest in change in a specific philanthropic area. Social venture funds invested in high-potential entrepreneurial ventures that fit with the mission of the fund and provided ventures with strategic and operational guidance over the long term. Any returns generated by the investments were reinvested in the fund's ventures. New Schools' mission was to improve public kindergarten-through-twelfth-grade (K–12) education in the United States by (a) investing in entrepreneurial ventures targeting a vulnerability in the public education system and (b) creating a network of education entrepreneurs and New Economy leaders to both help New Schools' portfolio companies and build the field of education entrepreneurship as a whole. By late 1999, New Schools had made investments in five education ventures and had hosted a series of networking events, including a national conference for education entrepreneurs attended by 250 people.

New Schools' resources included 18 "partners"; among them were Doerr and cofounder Brook Byers—a fellow venture partner at KPCB—who contributed financial and/or intellectual capital to the organization. The group was comprised primarily of well-known venture capitalists and new-economy entrepreneurs, in addition to foundation leaders and educators. All of New Schools' partners were personally interested in the field of education and were committed to supporting entrepreneurs trying to create positive change within the public education system. The level of partner involvement in New Schools varied— some partners were very involved and had even accepted board positions within New Schools' portfolio companies; others were less actively involved but served as advisors on specific issues on an as-needed basis.

Kim Smith, president of New Schools, had prepared the organization's preliminary year 2000 objectives for New Schools' board of directors, which was comprised of Doerr, Byers, Smith, Dave Whorton—a former KPCB associate partner who had recently become CEO of Good Technologies—and Ted Mitchell, the president of Occidental College and former dean of UCLA's school of education. While Smith was pleased with New Schools' progress to date on the investment side, she felt that the organization needed to think more strategically about its approach to building its network of donors and supporters in order to both increase the level of support it provided to its portfolio companies and build the field of education entrepreneurship as a whole. Over the past year, Smith had seen that New Schools' portfolio companies needed more operational and strategic guidance than New Schools had the capacity to offer. Smith felt that in order to help each of its portfolio companies achieve its full potential, New Schools needed to do a better job of transferring the knowledge and experience of its partnership group to its education entrepreneur group.

One option was to expand New Schools' partnership group so that the organization had access to a larger pool of financial and intellectual resources. However, Smith believed that it was important to first develop a clear strategy for expanding the group, since there were many ways for partners to add value—they could contribute capital, investment advice, educational expertise, hands-on assistance for education entrepreneurs, board-level involvement in portfolio companies, and/or a broad network of contacts. Smith and her team had to decide which of these value-added services were most important since that would influence whom New Schools sought as partners. Another option was to partner with other organizations that could contribute support or specific expertise to education entrepreneurs. Smith knew that Doerr and Byers would be expecting her to have a recommendation on the most effective way of extending New Schools' network at their meeting the following week.

BACKGROUND ON NEW SCHOOLS

John Doerr first got involved with the issue of improving public education through a 1993 investment he spearheaded on behalf of KPCB in Lightspan Partnership Inc. (www.lightspan.com). Lightspan was a for-profit venture founded in 1993 that developed content and services for both K–8 schools and school districts, including curriculum materials, interactive software, and home-school connections using the latest technology. As part of Doerr's due diligence on Lightspan, he visited a number of public schools with the company's cofounders. Doerr reflected on what he learned through this process:

> We visited dozens of public schools, in both upscale and poor areas. In both places I saw schools that worked and schools that didn't. In the cases where they weren't working, the problem was practically criminal. It soon became clear that the U.S. educational system was the most screwed-up part of the economy. In fact, one study showed that over 40% of fourth-grade students in the United States were reading below their grade level—an astonishing discovery.

While the Lightspan investment highlighted the problems with the public education system, the idea for the New Schools Venture Fund actually came about during a roundtable discussion on education hosted by U.S. Vice President Al Gore. Doerr recalls Gore asking the group—which included a number of Silicon Valley executives—"If you Silicon Valley types are so smart, why can't you do something to create new schools?" Doerr came back from the conference energized to use his venture capital experience and network in the new economy to do something—possibly start a venture fund dedicated to education entrepreneurs. As Doerr explained,

> I thought we ought to be able to take what venture capital has been able to do in the Internet or in biotechnology and apply it to education. I guess if you're a carpenter with a hammer, everything looks like a nail. So as a venture capitalist in awe of the power of entrepreneurs, their ideas, and their ability to create large-scale change, when you see a large unmet need like school improvement, you want to apply the same hammer to it.

A few months later, the idea began to take shape. At a conference at the Aspen Institute, Doerr and Steve Case, CEO of America Online, discussed the problems with public education, and Case posed the question of whether Doerr's venture capital approach—which had proven so successful in spawning entrepreneurship and innovation—could be applied to education reform. On the plane ride back, Doerr talked over the issue with Byers and the two decided to seriously pursue the idea of starting a fund, which would raise money from donors to invest in high-potential education-oriented entrepreneurial ventures. They quickly incorporated the idea into a nonprofit 501(c)(3) organization and tested interest in the concept by putting up a Web site under the domain name NewSchools.org.

At the same time, Doerr and Jim Barksdale, at the time the president and CEO of Netscape Communications Corporation (Netscape), cofounded the Technology Network (Tech Net)—the technology industry's bipartisan public policy network formed to build relationships between technology executives and political leaders. One of the first education-oriented initiatives with which TechNet became involved was to reform California's charter school legislation. With leadership from technology entrepreneur Reed Hastings, the group was successful in passing a bill through the California legislature in 1998 that raised the statewide cap on charter schools from 100 to 250 in 1999 and by an additional 100 per year thereafter. As Doerr explained:

> Influencing public policy can be a very high-leverage way to create change. We spent $4 million on the campaign to put our charter school initiative on the ballot before the legislature agreed to include it in a pending bill. If you think about that from a return standpoint, over a 10-year period we will have 1,000 new charter schools in the state of California, which will each receive on average $3 million in state funding per year. So that's a $3 billion per annum return on a $4 million initiative campaign—an outstanding return, worth the time, worth the money.

Excited about the impact that a committed network of professionals had achieved, Doerr and Byers began to assemble a core group of passionate supporters to serve as partners in New Schools. Doerr estimated

that his role at New Schools accounted for 10% of his "professional" time.

Motivations for Partner Involvement

Brook Byers

Byers's interest in education traced back to his father-in-law, John Stremple, a former school superintendent who had spent his career working to improve public education and was an early New Schools partner. As Byers noted:

> What dictates a lot of philanthropic interests is being inspired by people you want to emulate. It really takes a one-on-one inspiration to develop a passion and motivate you. For me that personal inspiration came from my father-in-law, John Stremple, who for 17 years has taught me about the issues surrounding public education.

Byers estimated that he spent one day per month on New Schools business, which included attending New Schools' quarterly investment partner meetings

Reed Hastings

Hastings's involvement in education stemmed from a long-standing personal interest in the field dating back to his decision to become a high school math teacher with the Peace Corps in Swaziland, which is in southern Africa, after graduating from college. Hastings ultimately left the teaching profession and founded Pure Software, a company that made products to automate software development. After selling Pure Software in 1997 for $750 million, Hastings announced that he would begin a "new career in school reform." He was so committed that he enrolled in Stanford University's master's program in education in order to understand firsthand how the educational system worked. Hastings recalled the discussion with Mike Kirst, a professor in Stanford's program, that led to his decision to enroll:

> I met with Mike and said, "I really want to create some change in education and now I have the resources to do something meaningful. What should I do?" Mike's response was, "Well, you can either identify all the problems and work independently on solving them; then, after realizing that nothing has changed, you simply give up and go away. Or another approach would be to enroll in Stanford's master's program and understand the culture and theory behind education, because if you want to change what's here, you need to first understand the roots of the current model."

Hastings spent six months in the program before leaving school to spearhead the California charter schools initiative. As Hastings explained, "I thought, 'Here's my opportunity to really make a difference.'" Hastings believed that working to affect public policy was one of the highest-leverage mechanisms to create change in the educational system. It was through his work on the charter school initiative that Hastings learned of Doerr's involvement with New Schools. The idea immediately struck a chord with Hastings since he believed that

his philanthropic involvement would be more effective and emotionally fulfilling if he were part of a group focused on issues that mattered to him. Hastings reflected:

> In my view, the fundamental problem with philanthropy is that people don't pool their expertise together. Everyone does their own fragmented thing, which means that everybody has to figure out how to be most effective on their own. Since there's very little accountability in philanthropy, it's hard to assess whether you're having an impact or not. As a result, there's a lot of hit-and-miss philanthropy out there and most people don't develop an institutional framework for learning how to do it better.
>
> Mid-tier philanthropists tend to get randomly "pinged"—reacting to various incoming requests for donations. Decisions are made based on what other people are doing or on what's politically correct. As a result, the process becomes far more reactive than strategic. That's why I liked the idea of getting involved with a small but organized group where I could really have an impact. I thought that we could learn together as a group and evolve our institutional knowledge. Plus, from an emotional standpoint, I thought it would be more enjoyable to share the philanthropic experience with a group of like-minded people.

Hastings estimated that he spent a day a month working on New Schools–related business, including attending investment partner meetings and serving as a board member for one of New Schools' portfolio companies.

Ted Mitchell

Ted Mitchell had built his career in the field of education, first as a professor at Stanford's Graduate School of Education, later as Dean of the School of Education at UCLA, and most recently as president of Occidental College. He was a recognized national expert in the area of education policy. Mitchell explained his interest in New Schools:

I was attracted to New Schools for several reasons. The most important was that it represented some fresh voices in the school reform debate—fresh voices and fresh perspectives. Secondly, these people were serious, and although they were taking a new approach to changing education, they were genuinely interested in learning from people in the field, in knowing what sorts of things had worked and hadn't worked. Finally, and perhaps most importantly, I felt that New Schools and the distinctive strategy it represented had a chance to harness entrepreneurial energy in a way that most school reform efforts—and in fact most large bureaucracies—haven't been able to do.

Jim Barksdale

Barksdale's involvement in education reform also stemmed from a deep-seated personal interest. One of six boys raised in a highly literate household, Barksdale found himself unable to read by the end of second grade. However, working with a local tutor, Barksdale was able to overcome his reading problem and later excelled in school. After becoming CEO of Netscape and overseeing its highly successful IPO, Barksdale—a father of three—found himself in a position to give back to the community. After several discussions with his wife, Sally McDonnell Barksdale, the two committed themselves to improving education in his home state of Mississippi. The first initiative came in 1996 when Barksdale and his wife—both University of Mississippi graduates—donated $5.4 million to the University of Mississippi to establish the McDonnell-Barksdale Honors College, which offered college scholarships to top high school academic achievers. Barksdale also helped fund 12 scholarships for minority students applying to the university's medical school. In late 1999, Barksdale was contemplating his largest philanthropic effort to date—a $100 million donation to a literacy improvement program jointly developed by the state of Mississippi and the University of Mississippi. The donation would represent the largest ever to the field of literacy and one of the five largest gifts ever by a private individual or foundation to a public university. Barksdale reflected on how and why he got involved in New Schools in 1998:

John [Doerr] and I had a series of passionate discussions about reforming the public education system and he told me what he was doing with the New Schools fund. Quite frankly I got excited because *he* was so excited about it. I viewed it as an opportunity for Sally and me to both learn and contribute. Our family foundation is dedicated to improving education in our home state of Mississippi, but there are lots of different ways of doing that. I saw New Schools as a way to broaden our minds about what has been successful in both the for-profit and nonprofit arenas. I also felt that by investing in the fund, we would be demonstrating our commitment to the problem, which I think is important since I believe we all learn by example.

DEVELOPING THE STRATEGY FOR THE NEW SCHOOLS VENTURE FUND

In late 1997, Doerr had a series of meetings with Dave Whorton—who shared Doerr's interest in improving education—to explore and further develop the idea. After working together to develop the basic principles for the fund, Whorton and Doerr realized they needed an entrepreneur who could further flesh out the idea. "The issue was important enough that it deserved more attention and resources than we could devote to it," said Whorton. He recruited Kim Smith, a second-year student at Stanford's Graduate School of Business, to develop a detailed strategic plan for New Schools. Smith—a founding member of Teach For America[1] and later, the founder of BAYAC AmeriCorps[2]—agreed to take on the project as an independent study with the support of Paul Romer, a Stanford Business School professor, in January 1998.

Smith spent the winter quarter working on a paper that defined various segments within the field of social entrepreneurship, including venture philanthropy. During the spring quarter, Smith worked with Whorton to outline a strawman strategy for how New Schools should operate—what its mission should be, in what areas it should invest, and what criteria it should use to evaluate potential investment opportunities. To develop the strategy, Smith helped organize a series of "whiteboard sessions" with the core team—Doerr, Byers, Whorton, and Mitchell—to brainstorm and discuss ideas. Smith reflected on the process:

When I first started doing this project for John, Brook, and Dave, I thought I was trying to execute their vision. However, it quickly became clear to me that that was not how *they* saw it. They wanted someone who could flesh out their vision, ask them the right strategic questions, and propose various recommendations—an approach that comes from their experience in incubating companies. This was one of the first lessons I had to learn in working with them—they didn't just want an executor, they wanted an entrepreneur who would come up with new ideas and challenge them on theirs.

These "strategy sessions" in the spring of 1998 led to a number of important decisions regarding how to structure and position the New Schools Fund. Ted Mitchell, who participated in these early meetings, reflected on the thinking behind the fund:

There were a couple of founding principles behind New Schools. First, we believed that the spirit and energy of entrepreneurship was missing from public education and yet could have tremendous potential for changing schools. Second, we felt that the new-economy approach of identifying areas for investing and then capitalizing on them in a rapid way through experimentation and redesign wasn't being done in education, but again could have enormous potential. We wanted to be sure that New Schools didn't become just another foundation, so it was extremely important to us that we stay linked to the intellectual discipline of the venture capital approach used in the new economy.

One of the first decisions the group made was to invest in both nonprofit and for-profit ventures. The issue was complex. On the one hand, for-profit ventures typically had vastly greater access to financial and human capital than nonprofits and therefore had a far better chance of scaling quickly. On the other hand, for-profit ventures frequently had a more difficult time gaining acceptance by educators, who were typically wary of any venture that tried to make money off of educating children. After debating the issue, New Schools decided that its overarching criterion was whether the venture was going to improve education. As a result, they were willing to invest in both nonprofit and for-profit ventures depending on which structure (nonprofit vs. for-profit) would enable them to best achieve their educational goals. Working with a combination of nonprofit and for-profit educational ventures would also allow New Schools to contribute important intellectual capital to the dialogue about whether children are better served by for profit, nonprofit, or public providers of education services.

Another decision that these sessions resolved was in which sectors of the educational field the fund would invest. Smith had initially recommended that the fund focus on *one* specific area in order to have significant impact and develop deep institutional knowledge in that area. Smith recommended

that the fund focus on charter schools—an area she felt had the potential to have a major impact on students and the public school system as a whole by creating a sense of competition. However, after discussing the issue further, the team decided to broaden its focus beyond charter schools, but still use many of the criteria that made charter schools attractive to develop a framework for where the fund should invest. The team developed a framework that defined their target investment "sweet spot" as *scalable* ventures that had the potential to have a *direct* impact on student achievement. Given these criteria, a number of potential investment areas emerged, including charter school chains, comprehensive research-based curricula, and recruitment and training of teachers and managers. The group believed that other potential investment areas would emerge over time.

The group also developed a dual mission for New Schools—investing in scalable entrepreneurial ventures that would improve public K–12 education *and* creating a nationwide network that would connect education entrepreneurs to each other, leaders in the new economy, resources, and intellectual capital. The network would facilitate the sharing of information, ideas, and best practices and, thus, build the field of education entrepreneurship as a whole. This combined mission would help ensure that the fund leveraged its full potential for effecting innovation and change within the field of public education.

Finally, the team decided that the New Schools organization needed a leader that brought experience and expertise in both business and education. It was clear to Doerr, Byers, Whorton, and Mitchell that the best

Case Study

person for the position was Smith herself, even though she had always thought she would join a high-tech firm after graduating from Stanford. Byers reflected on what Smith brought to the table: "She had this amazing combination of an education background, urban and inner-city experience, a good heart for social good, a great analytical mind, a great network of contacts, and a proven ability to work with us and learn our approach." Kim accepted the offer to be president of New Schools in June, but she did not officially begin work until August 1998.

LAUNCHING THE NEW SCHOOLS FUND

When Smith joined in August, she set up shop in KPCB's offices to facilitate communication with Doerr, Byers, and Whorton and to learn KPCB's venture approach since New Schools intended to borrow heavily from it. During the first few months, Smith worked on building the New Schools internal organization, developing a perspective on whom the fund should target for investment partners, networking with educators and "edupreneurs," and continuing to develop New Schools' strategy and investment criteria.

As the New Schools organization grew, it was tempting to publicize the effort. However, instead of making a major public announcement about the formation of the fund, the group decided to keep a lower profile and let the results of the fund speak for themselves in the future. Smith explained:

Our priority was to do a "proof of concept" before we began to get the

word out about our efforts. As Brook often reminded us, in the end we would be defined by what we did, not what we said. We also wanted to save the publicity spotlight, in order to focus it on the education entrepreneurs themselves.

Doerr and Byers also pushed hard to start assessing investment opportunities quickly, since they believed that the process of determining whether or not to invest would force New Schools to develop and refine its investment criteria. Smith recalled:

John and Brook are strong believers in the "learn by doing" model. I was ready to take time to conduct research in order to identify high-potential areas in which New Schools could invest, but after we developed the first version of our investment criteria, I remember John saying, "We can't figure this out in the abstract. We need to look at some real investment opportunities and meet with our investment partners. By getting specific, we will learn a lot about what our criteria should be."

New School Partners

The New School fund involved partners in three different ways. First, there were Investment Partners who attended New Schools' quarterly investment partner meetings (e.g., Byers, Dees, Doerr, Mitchell, Stremple). These people were invited for their expertise or were donors who wanted to be actively involved. Second, there were Limited Partners who chose to play a more passive role in the fund, supporting entrepreneurs primarily through their donations to the fund. Third, some additional members of the network served as special partners by serving on the board of New Schools' ventures.

Early on, Smith recommended that New Schools increase the size of its investment partner group, by adding people with a passion for educational issues from a variety of backgrounds, including the venture capital community, entrepreneurs, educational leaders, and foundation leaders. Doerr and Smith encouraged a number of people to join New Schools, including John and Elaine Chambers (Cisco Systems), Jim Clark (Silicon Graphics, Netscape, and Healtheon), Steve Merrill (Benchmark Capital), Greg Dees (Stanford Graduate School of Business), Ann Bowers (Noyce Foundation), Doug MacKenzie (KPCB), Halsey and Deb Minor (CNET), Paul Lippe (Shine2000), Gilman Louie (In-Q-Tel), John Stremple (former school superintendent), Scott Cook and Signe Ostbey (Intuit), and Matt Glickman (BabyCenter).

Glickman—the founder of BabyCenter, which was sold to eToys in 1999—represented the type of partner who Smith believed could provide significant contributions to New Schools' portfolio companies. In addition to his work with Bain & Company and Intuit, Glickman had been the chief financial officer for Teach for America before going on to receive a dual master's degree in education and business from Stanford University. He was passionate and knowledgeable about educational issues, and he had experience in building a new-economy company. Glickman reflected on his decision to join New Schools:

Philanthropy starts with identifying where you want to get involved, and for me, that was clearly in K–12 education.

However, education is a huge field and I'm a big believer in being focused and going deep in a couple of areas. So I chose to get involved with two organizations: New Schools and Stanford's "I Have a Dream" program—a community-based program that "adopts" a third- or fourth-grade class and provides them with long-term mentorship and money for college. New Schools gives me the opportunity to be involved on a systemic, conceptual level in creating scalable solutions for problems with our educational system, whereas the "I Have a Dream" program gives me the opportunity to get involved in my local community and have a direct impact on the lives of a small group of people, which is extremely satisfying and important, even if it's not as scalable.

Developing Investment Criteria

The overarching goal of New Schools was to generate a high social return on its investments, as measured by the degree of educational impact on the "end consumer"— children themselves. As Doerr explained:

We are interested in initiatives that help make an "information literate" kid—one who can read, manipulate symbols, write, speak, and think critically in a world where they will be bombarded with information. That's what it takes to be a full participant in the new economy.

A secondary goal for New Schools was to contribute to industry knowledge about the effectiveness of various entrepreneurial approaches in creating change in the educational system. For example, New Schools purposefully invested in both a nonprofit and for-profit charter school venture to develop empirical evidence about which approach was more effective in terms of ability to scale, access to capital, access to people, and impact educational outcomes for children.

With these overall investment goals, New Schools had developed a specific set of criteria to assess investments. These included:

1. Scalability: The venture must have the potential to affect thousands of students.

2. Sustainability: The venture must have a sound business model and a credible plan for raising additional capital in the future.

3. Passionate leadership: The venture must have leaders with expertise in education and business management who have the ability to execute the venture's vision.

4. Opportunity for New Schools to make a difference: There must be a specific reason why New Schools' involvement will make a significant difference in the venture's prospects.

5. Significant opportunity: The venture must have the potential to make significant improvements to public K–12 education.

6. Specifically, the venture must
   a. Target a real vulnerability in the system.
   b. Have measurable educational outcomes.
   c. Be designed to overcome systemic inertia.

Scalability was of utmost importance to New Schools. Smith explained:

> I've run local programs that are not scalable, and they can be quite effective and important in children's lives. But we need to change an enormous and ineffective system, and our donors' experience is with the venture capital model and an emphasis on taking ideas to scale. They understand that scale matters if you're really going to change a $350 billion system.

Doerr emphasized the importance of scale, too. Doerr observed:

> We know how to make any particular school work and ensure that any individual kid can read. But I've come to the view that the important problems in public education are problems of scale. How can we rapidly improve tens of thousands of schools for millions of kids?

New Schools also placed significant emphasis on the strength of the venture's management team, since that had a direct impact on its ability to scale. Mitchell explained:

> Early on, we made the decision to focus on the venture's management team and their ability to get things done, which is remarkably different from how most foundations deal with granting. Foundations are more likely to look at the leader to see if he or she

has the right qualifications to get the project at hand done, not whether he or she can make widespread change with it. At New Schools, we have been relentless in our focus on whether the management team as a whole has the strategic and execution capability to truly scale the idea.

Another criterion of particular importance to New Schools was the ability to measure results. During the due diligence process, partners at New Schools encouraged education entrepreneurs to show what results their initiative had achieved to date and pushed them to think hard about how results would be tracked and measured over time. While measurement approaches and methods were often difficult to agree on, New Schools forced education entrepreneurs to grapple with the problem upfront since the ability to measure results was so important to the long-term success and impact of the fund. Barksdale explained:

Most people who give away serious money are looking for demonstrable results. Yet most philanthropic efforts and charities don't do a good job of measuring and communicating results. To the donor, it feels like your money just went down some hole—you think you did some good, but you don't really know.

By emphasizing measurable results, New Schools has the opportunity to make a major difference. If New Schools can prove its approach works, then it will be able to raise future rounds of capital and "copy cat" funds will emerge, which will further contribute to innovative solutions.

As New Schools assessed investment opportunities in the fall and winter of 1999, it became clear that the investment criteria they had developed represented a high hurdle. One of the most common dilemmas New Schools faced was that innovative ideas didn't always come complete with a strong management team. Greg Dees reflected on the challenge New Schools faced working with nonprofit entrepreneurs:

A fundamental question for New Schools is whether nonprofits can attract the capital and human resources needed to scale. They may have trouble attracting the human resources they need, because they cannot offer stock options and typically have pay scales below for-profit entities. Often the managers of nonprofits come from within the field and do not have a great deal of business experience or management training. They may be gifted managers, but we have to ask whether the nonprofit has a leadership team in place with the knowledge and skills to take them to scale. Of course, team issues arise with for-profits as well; it is just a more common issue on the nonprofit side.

One of New Schools' challenges was that since the field of education entrepreneurship was so new, there was a limited pool of experienced managers. In these situations, New Schools had to determine if they could either strengthen the existing management team through coaching or mentoring or recruit additional management team members to fill in for weaknesses.

Investment Process

The New Schools investment process was comprised of six separate steps, including:

1. Opportunity identification

2. Due diligence

3. Identification of a New Schools sponsor

4. Entrepreneur presentation to New Schools' investment partners committee

5. Follow-up due diligence

6. Investment decision and identification of a New Schools board member

Smith and her team were responsible for the initial screening of investment opportunities submitted to New Schools. She received business plans from a variety of sources, including her own broad network of education entrepreneurs, New Schools' investment partners, and other venture capital firms. Smith reviewed each plan to assess its fit with New Schools' investment criteria. If a plan met the criteria and Smith was personally intrigued by the concept, she would "recruit" a New Schools investment partner to sponsor the investment through the process. In some of the early deals, this was not necessary since one of New Schools' investment partners had brought the investment opportunity to the organization in the first place. The next step was to conduct due diligence on the opportunity, which included meeting the management team, conducting site visits, talking with industry sources, and evaluating the venture against other initiatives in the same area. New Schools had its own unique due diligence "check list" that Smith had developed based on research she had conducted on how other venture capital firms and foundations conducted due diligence.

Once an investment opportunity had successfully made it through the due diligence process, the next step was to invite the entrepreneur to present the concept at one of New Schools' quarterly investment meetings. While all members of New Schools' board of directors were in attendance at each of these meetings, the group of investment partners on hand sometimes varied. At the meetings, entrepreneurs would present their plan and then field questions from the group. New Schools' partners used these meetings to discuss and evaluate the level of risk involved in the venture. Byers explained:

In both venture capital and venture philanthropy, you can't avoid risk, so you have to decide which risks you're willing to take. Then you direct management time and capital toward eliminating those risks, while at the same time making progress against the venture's overall goal. For example, in a start-up, the initial capital goes to eliminating the white-hot risk, which is usually, Can we develop the product and will it work? Once that risk has been eliminated, the venture can start using capital to scale its organization, but you don't do that simultaneously. Lining up priorities is a good discipline.

The next question is whether there is a market for the product. For New Schools, this means, Will it be accepted by the educational community and can it scale? Because at the end of the day, education gets down to a teacher teaching a student, so you have to gain acceptance at that level. There are a lot of good ideas out there that are just too complicated for schools to adopt.

Even if the product works and gains acceptance, another question is, Will it always need philanthropic support to sustain itself, or is there a way for it to stand on its own? If it will depend on philanthropic support, who are the likely funding sources? Often entrepreneurs don't want to focus on this question, but we have to discuss it.

If the investment partners in the meeting supported the business plan and the management team, they would approve the investment contingent on any specific follow-up due diligence issues. Smith and her team would conduct the follow-up due diligence, which often entailed additional meetings with the management team or school administrators to answer questions raised in the New Schools investment meeting. If Smith and her team were comfortable with the answers to the follow-up questions, she would forward the investment opportunity to New Schools' board for their approval. While a majority vote was legally required, it typically turned out to be a unanimous decision.

New Schools also identified one of its own partners or an appropriate professional from their network of new-economy leaders to serve as a board member in the portfolio company on behalf of New Schools. While New Schools was willing to have someone other than one of its own investment partners represent New Schools on the board, that person had to understand and support New Schools' mission and had to understand New Schools' reasons for investing in the venture and its goals for the venture going forward. They also needed to offer expertise relevant to the venture's needs. Byers commented on New Schools' focus on board-level involvement:

> This is a signet of the venture capital model. To get a deal done in venture capital, several partners have to sponsor it and at least one has to offer to go on the board. Committing to a board seat injects discipline to the process. It avoids the practice of sprinkling money across multiple projects and simply hoping something happens.

New Schools Investments to Date

By December 1999, New Schools had invested in five education-related entrepreneurial ventures out of approximately 100 business plans received. Three investments—University Public Schools, LearnNow, and GreatSchools.net (GreatSchools)—fell into the category of offering parents "choice" in selecting public schools, through building charter schools or by providing parents with detailed information on public schools in their communities. The other two ventures—Success For All Foundation and Carnegie Learning Inc.—fell into the category of comprehensive research-based curricula for schools. Three of the five ventures were nonprofit entities, two were for-profits. The structure of New Schools' investments ranged from bridge loans to grants and equity investments. (See **Exhibit 3.2.1** for a brief description of each portfolio company.)

An Example of the New Schools Investment Process: University Public Schools

University Public Schools (UPS), a nonprofit charter school management organization, which planned to build clusters of elementary, middle, and high schools in ten California school districts, was New Schools' fourth investment. New Schools was introduced to Don Shalvey, the founder of UPS, through Reed Hastings, who had worked with Shalvey on the California charter school ballot initiative. Shalvey, a 34-year veteran of the public education system, had spearheaded the first charter school in California. After seeing the positive impact charter schools had on his own district, Shalvey became actively involved in trying to raise the statewide cap on charter schools. Following his work on that initiative, Shalvey teamed up with Hastings to found a nonprofit organization in November 1998 to build charter schools. To fund the organization, Shalvey turned to New Schools, in addition to state and federal grants, foundations, and individual gifts.

Shalvey's discussions with New Schools began in March 1999. New Schools' interest in UPS stemmed from UPS's plan to open 100 charter schools in California, which would enable them to test the hypothesis that when charter schools attract 10% or more of a district's students, they begin to serve as a major catalyst for non–charter school reform in their own and surrounding districts. Between March and September, Shalvey worked closely with New Schools to revise UPS's business plan to answer questions related to New Schools' investment criteria, talking with Smith and the New Schools organization several times a week. Specifically, New Schools sought changes in UPS's plan for building its management team, evaluating results, financing its growth, and raising future rounds of capital.

In terms of UPS's management team, New Schools made its funding contingent on three actions: first, that Shalvey devote himself full-time to UPS—which entailed resigning from his role as district superintendent and extracting himself from his other outside obligations—second, that UPS include two New Schools partners on its board, and third, that UPS expand its management team to include professionals from outside the educational sector who could contribute strong business expertise, particularly in the areas of finance and operations. Smith agreed to help UPS source qualified individuals by leveraging her own contacts and the New Schools network. In fact, in June 1999, UPS hired a consultant with a leading strategy consulting firm to be a senior manager at UPS, whom Smith had helped to recruit. Shalvey commented on the process:

The New Schools people worried much less about the money and future funding than they did about building a strong management team that would include both educators and MBA types who could help build the organization.

- **GreatSchools** Founded by Bill Jackson, GreatSchools was a nonprofit organization that provided a comprehensive online guide to K–12 public schools in California. The guide rated schools on a consistent set of measures, including academic performance and quality of teaching, leadership, and learning environment. The mission of the venture was to leverage the Internet to help parents and the community choose, support, and improve K–12 public schools. GreatSchools planned to roll out its online guide to communities nationwide. Based on what they believed was a highly scalable business model and a strong management team, New Schools invested $100,000 in GreatSchools even though it did not exactly fit with New Schools' criteria of investing in ventures that would have a *direct* impact on students.

- **Success For All** Designed by Drs. Robert Slavin and Nancy Madden of Johns Hopkins University, Success For All was a nonprofit organization that was best known for developing a highly structured approach to teaching children how to read. Specifically, the program set aside 90 minutes of each school day for students to work on building their reading skills in ability-based groups. One of the distinctive aspects of Success For All was its "whole school" approach. In fact, 80% of the teachers had to vote to have the curriculum adopted by the school before Success For All was willing to implement the program. Started in 1986 as a single-district effort to prevent at-risk schoolchildren from falling behind during their first few years of school, Success For All was now the nation's largest comprehensive school reform organization with its program being implemented in 1,400 mostly high-poverty schools in the United States. The goal was to roll it out to 3,000 schools within three years. New Schools provided Success For All with a 5-year, $1 million low-interest loan.

- **LearnNow** Founded by Gene Wade and Jim Shelton, LearnNow was a for-profit education management organization that planned to create and manage a national network of charter schools focused on math, science, and technology, for sixth- to twelfth-grade students from urban communities. Conceived by five Harvard University Law School students, LearnNow was originally founded as a nonprofit. The founders realized that it would be very difficult to raise the capital needed to go to scale as a national nonprofit, so they created LearnNow as a for-profit. LearnNow's mission was to prepare students from poor and disadvantaged communities to become successful college students and knowledge workers. LearnNow planned to open its first four schools in the fall of 2000 and ramp up to approximately 50 schools serving 46,000 students by 2005. New Schools invested $1 million in LearnNow.

- **University Public Schools** Founded by Don Shalvey—a charter school advocate and public school superintendent—University Public Schools was a nonprofit charter school management organization that planned to build clusters of elementary, middle, and high schools in ten California school districts. University Public Schools' mission was to provide a high-quality educational alternative to students in California by focusing on attracting and retaining outstanding teachers, and in the process, serving as a catalyst for change in the surrounding public school districts. New Schools provided University Public Schools with a $500,000 grant and agreed to provide another $500,000 in convertible debt if the organization met specific performance targets.

- **Carnegie Learning** Started as a research project by Professor John Anderson at Carnegie Mellon University, Carnegie Learning was spun out as a separate for-profit venture in 1999 that developed a comprehensive approach to teaching algebra and geometry, which combined classroom instruction and a learning-by-doing approach with an artificial intelligence-based computerized tutor. The program included extensive teacher training, which emphasized the importance of interactive learning. Backed by 15 years of research, the Carnegie Learning approach had demonstrated impressive results across class and ethnic lines, and in 1999 it was selected as one of the top five K–12 math curricula by the U.S. Department of Education. New Schools invested $500,000 in Carnegie Learning's first round of funding.

Exhibit 3.2.1   New Schools' Portfolio Companies (in chronological order of investment)

Case Study

That focus is very different than what is typically the case with foundation or government funders.

In terms of evaluation techniques, New Schools mandated that UPS develop a plan to be approved by New Schools for how the organization would measure its progress and its impact on students. As part of this effort, New Schools required that UPS hire an external evaluator to design and monitor measurements for student achievement. While UPS had initially considered bringing in an external evaluation firm to assist them, it was deemed too costly. However, New Schools placed such a strong emphasis on being able to measure results that the group increased the amount of capital they were willing to invest in UPS in order to fund an external evaluation effort. Shalvey explained New Schools' interest in measurement and evaluation:

When Kim started asking questions about our plan for evaluating student outcomes during our first few meetings together, I started to think that New Schools might be taking a typical Silicon Valley/corporate perspective of wanting results immediately, which in education never works well. It took a lot of conversations for us to see that what New Schools really wanted was not immediate *results,* but rather immediate *data collection* on baseline variables that we would need in order to test our hypotheses over time. New Schools forced us to be much more thoughtful than we would have been if we had been applying for a federal grant.

On the marketing side, New Schools pushed UPS to think carefully about how it would "brand" itself. New Schools felt that it was important for UPS to define what had to be part of every UPS school, as a way to differentiate its schools from other education alternatives, but also as a way to inject some discipline into the process of defining the core elements that had to be in place in every school across the system. "The brand represents what every parent can expect when they go to a UPS school," said Smith. "Identifying the few core variables that are critical for educational and operational success is also crucial if an idea like this is to be scaleable. UPS could not create a customized school for every group of parents if they want to get to scale." Shalvey commented on the difference in New Schools' approach:

Branding isn't something that public educators typically think about. The New Schools approach is to be much more forward and proactive with an edge of competitiveness and challenge. They tend to be much more evangelical and they like to focus on points of differentiation rather than similarities. That's really unheard of in the public school arena, where we tend to discuss how alike we are, because we don't want to alienate our colleagues at other schools.

Finally, in terms of development, New Schools pushed UPS to develop a two-year capital campaign plan that laid out their proposed funding sources for raising additional capital. Part of New Schools' motivation for this was to ensure that UPS was not going to be overly dependent on philanthropy in the future. New Schools also helped UPS bring in a former banker on a short-term volunteer basis to build a series of computer models that mapped out UPS's funding needs under a number of different growth and financing scenarios, specifically considering various debt strategies for facilities development.

After six months of discussions, New Schools committed to provide UPS with a $500,000 grant and another $500,000 if UPS met specific performance targets. (See **Exhibit 3.2.2** for UPS's performance targets.) While New Schools' due diligence process had been far more in-depth and lengthy than Shalvey had expected, he felt it had been well worth it in the long run. Shalvey commented:

> To be honest, the UPS team all wondered at different times whether we were being micromanaged by New Schools, because our interaction was so different than we were accustomed to when we applied for foundation or federal grants. Sometimes it felt like we were speaking two different languages, but the rigor of the process made for a stronger plan. New Schools really helped us integrate our mission, message, strategy, and budget. Every school district ought to write a business plan—which is vastly different than a grant—although you wouldn't want to have more than one New Schools–type partner! I can also say that out of hundreds of school board meetings I have been to, there have only been a handful that have been as mentally stimulating as UPS's first few board of directors meetings after our

New Schools board members had joined.

Smith conceded that New Schools had high standards. However, as she explained: "Our decision to invest is a long-term commitment, and over time, New Schools will add value in many ways, including helping the venture scale and securing future funding, so we want to work things out at the front end to make sure we are all talking about building the same thing."

Fulfilling the Second Half of the New Schools' Mission

Since joining New Schools, Smith had also worked hard to spearhead initiatives that would help the organization fulfill the second half of its mission—to create a network that connected education entrepreneurs to each other, leaders in the "new economy," resources, and intellectual capital. Leveraging her network from Stanford Business School, and her days with Teach for America and BAYAC AmeriCorps, Smith's first step was to host a series of dinners at her own home for education entrepreneurs and other leaders in the education field. These dinners served as a medium for Smith to discuss the goals of New Schools and to learn about various entrepreneurial efforts in a variety of areas within the education arena.

Smith also spent a significant portion of her time meeting with education entrepreneurs, educators, and foundations to communicate New Schools' mission and to keep abreast of trends and developments in the educational sector. She also hosted a

Case Study

	1999		2000	
UPS MILESTONES 1999–2000 SCHOOL YEARS	*Q3*	*Q4*	*Q1*	*Q2*
People				
Hire CFO		♦		
Hire Director of Development		♦		
Don starts full-time as CEO			♦	
Fund-raising and financing				
Develop 2-year capital campaign plan to raise $25 million		♦		
Secure $2 million start-up financing for next 3 schools			♦	
School results				
Start 1999–2000 school year fully enrolled	♦			
Start 1999–2000 school year fully staffed	♦			
Hire external evaluator		♦		
Receive positive midyear reviews from parents			♦	
Exceed 95% student reenrollment rate of eligible students				♦
Show significant improvement in student achievement				♦
Retain 95% of staff performing at or above expectations				♦
Growth				
Secure charters for Stanislaus County and San Francisco			♦	
Identify and secure 1–2 sites in Oakland			♦	
Identify and secure 1–2 additional sites in Central Valley			♦	
Establish partnership with organization(s) for new Central Valley sites				♦
Hire 2nd principal for Oakland				♦
Hire principal(s) for Central Valley				♦

Exhibit 3.2.2   UPS's Performance Targets

SOURCE: New Schools Venture Fund.

Case Study

series of focus groups with educators and education entrepreneurs to discuss and generate feedback on New Schools' strategy—a mechanism Smith found to be highly valuable in helping her think through a number of issues.

In January 1999, Smith hired Lisa Daggs, a former Teach for America teacher who had gone on to earn her master's in business and education at Stanford University, to be New Schools' director of educational operations. One of Daggs's first projects was to manage a national conference for education entrepreneurs. The conference—the Summit for Leaders in Education Entrepreneurship, cosponsored by the Stanford Graduate Schools of Business and Education—was held on October 30, 1999, at Stanford University. Over 250 education and technology entrepreneurs, educators, policy makers, industry analysts, and donors attended the event, which was designed to bring these groups together and provide a forum for discussing how new-economy principles could be applied to educational ventures. Breakout sessions focused on issues relevant to education entrepreneurs, such as how to design a scalable venture and whether to incorporate as a nonprofit or for-profit venture. New Schools intended to host other national conferences focused on improving K–12 public education in the future.

EMERGING ISSUES

In December 1999, Doerr sat down at his desk to review the preliminary set of year 2000 objectives that Smith had prepared. Doerr concurred with Smith that the organization had made excellent progress toward its goal of investing in high-potential educational ventures over the past year and a half, and that now was the time for New Schools to shift its priorities to strategically building its network.

Smith felt that New Schools could and should do even more to add value to its portfolio companies. In fact, as Smith and her fellow New Schools partners had found, New Schools did not have the capacity to offer the level of hands-on support and expertise that its portfolio companies often needed. For example, New Schools' portfolio companies sometimes needed help with corporate strategy, managing growth, building their internal organization, and recruiting people. However, given the prominence of New Schools' existing partners, many were too busy in their jobs to commit more than half a day to one day a month to New Schools, which included attending the quarterly investment partner meetings. Smith knew that in order to provide the type of hands-on assistance needed by some of New Schools' portfolio companies, the organization needed to think more strategically about how it went about extending and managing its network.

Smith believed that one option was to expand New Schools' partner group. However, she felt that it was important to first develop a set of criteria for what New Schools needed from new partners at this stage of the fund's development. There were many ways for New Schools to add value to entrepreneurial ventures, including contributing financial capital, providing ongoing mentorship and guidance by taking a board seat in the venture, providing targeted advice in a specific functional area, offering educational expertise, and providing networking support. It was virtually impossible to find a partner who could contribute in *all* of these areas. In fact, New Schools had already experienced some of the trade-offs; often the partners who could offer significant capital or extensive new-economy management expertise had very little time to invest in providing hands-on support to New Schools' portfolio companies. Similarly, partners with deep educational experience often lacked experience in the business side of the new economy. However, one thing was clear to Smith—over the past year, she had seen that human *time* was the critical factor in determining how much value New Schools could add to the ventures in which it invested.

Smith believed that there was a group of young, motivated, passionate people that New Schools had yet to tap into. In fact, Smith's personal network included many of these young professionals (e.g., friends from her business school class, colleagues from her work in the nonprofit arena) who were in their late 20s or 30s and had developed a specific functional or industry expertise that could be valuable to New Schools. Some in this group were already successful entrepreneurs, while others were at an earlier stage in their career. Smith explained the idea further:

Some of our partners already are sitting on six to eight boards, so we realized we just can't ask them to sit on multiple boards for New Schools. So that led us to explore our options. What if we brought in some younger professionals who each brought a particular expertise to the table? In some cases, they might even be experienced, talented, and interested enough to serve as board members on behalf of New Schools. In other cases, they could add value as a

hands-on team, helping us with due diligence, or helping CEOs with specific problems they are facing. We're not sure what the answer is, but we sense that this is a good resource that we aren't tapping into. We think that if we invited them to get involved, they would be very enthusiastic and would want to make a difference. The question is, How do we structure their involvement so that we can maximize the experience for them and their value to education entrepreneurs?

The opportunity to learn from and interact with New Schools' prominent partner group was a compelling reason in and of itself for some young professionals to get involved with New Schools. However, Smith wanted to be sure that people were joining based on a true desire to improve education as well. One New Schools partner reflected on this dilemma:

One of the problems that I see with the nonprofit and government sectors is that they ignore people's selfish motivations, instead of building off of them. The more you can align people's personal and organizational interests with their civic interests, the greater commitment you'll get. That said, New Schools does run the risk of having an adverse selection problem—people joining based on a belief that this is a great way to network with the organization's prominent set of partners, rather than to contribute to the goals of the organization. The challenge for New Schools will be to keep the networking benefits a secondary focus.

Smith had asked Glickman, Whorton, and two other colleagues with technology and marketing backgrounds—who all fit the young professional age demographic—to help her identify 20 potential young professional candidates who could contribute one of four types of expertise she felt that New Schools needed: entrepreneurial leadership and operations, venture due diligence, branding, and technology expertise.

The young professional group could potentially offer energy, passion, new-economy knowledge, and, in some cases, financial capital to New Schools. However, the question again came down to whether they had the time to contribute to the organization, given their professional and personal obligations. That raised another possibility that Smith had considered of attracting recently retired executives with an interest in education. The advantage of this approach was that these individuals might have more time and experience to contribute; the question was whether they had relevant start-up or new-economy experience and whether they were interested in learning about the education half of the equation.

Smith believed that precedent had already been set for partners to play different roles within New Schools. This raised the question of whether New Schools should better clarify its own expectations about the role each partner would play. This could be accomplished either through New Schools' initial discussions with each partner or through the use of different partner "categories." Perhaps New Schools should develop an explicit agreement with each partner as part of the recruitment process, which outlined the type of value the partner was agreeing to contribute to the organization.

Alternatively, New Schools could develop one or more partner categories for different types of contributions (e.g., financial, advisory). An analogy for this idea came from Silicon Valley where start-ups were increasingly making use of two boards—a board of directors made up of individuals who were very active with the company, had voting rights, and provided overall mentorship and a board of advisors made up of people who were less involved on a day-to-day basis, did not have a board vote, but served as on-hand advisors on specific issues. If New Schools decided to develop explicit categories of partners, Smith would have to think through who would be included in investment partner meetings and how New Schools would keep a larger group of partners feeling connected to the group and the goals of the organization.

Managing a larger group of partners brought up the issue of New Schools' internal infrastructure. New Schools had only three full-time staff members—Smith, Daggs, and Beth Sutkus—a recent Stanford graduate. As president of the organization, Smith was responsible for all internal and external issues related to New Schools. Daggs, New Schools' director of educational operations, split her time between conducting due diligence efforts for potential investment opportunities and building the New Schools network. Sutkus, New Schools' project manager, focused on New Schools' external communication efforts, including conferences and the organization's Web site. Responsibility for managing New Schools' network with its partners and with the external education entrepreneur community was shared among the group. Smith worried that adding additional partners might stretch the New Schools organization too thin. This represented even more of a concern since the New Schools board had all committed to ensuring that New Schools offer each partner a "high-engagement" way to get involved. Smith wondered what kind of team she would need to support a larger group of partners who sought high engagement.

Another idea for providing greater support to its portfolio companies was to develop partnerships with other organizations focused on serving educational ventures and/or nonprofits. While Smith hadn't compiled an exhaustive list of the types of organizations that might make sense, she had some early ideas, including consulting firms, executive search firms, education schools, and business schools. While this option clearly offered the advantage of having expertise "on call," Smith wondered whether it was important to develop this type of intellectual capital in-house rather than relying on external partners. By hiring more staff and developing these capabilities in-house, New Schools had the flexibility to share the knowledge developed with its other portfolio companies and with the education entrepreneur community as a whole. She also questioned whether this outsourcing approach would undermine the high-engagement approach for donors.

Smith knew that it was up to her to think through how to extend New Schools' network, since the board would

expect her to come to the meeting the following week with a recommendation. Smith believed that the board would support a plan to expand New Schools' network since they had both seen firsthand the power of a strong network through their experience at KPCB and TechNet. While Smith had a series of ideas on the table, she knew there were probably many more she hadn't yet identified. She planned to spend the next few days brainstorming with her internal team, New Schools' partners, and friends to test her ideas and potentially develop additional ones. While Smith looked forward to the challenge of developing a recommendation, she knew that it would be a difficult problem to solve, and she felt fortunate to be able to tap into such experienced entrepreneurial leaders for support.

NOTES

1. Teach for America was a national teacher corps that recruited, trained, and placed recent college graduates in teaching positions in underfinanced rural and urban districts with teacher shortages. As of 1999, Teach for America had helped bring over 5,000 new teachers into the profession.

2. BAYAC AmeriCorps was a consortium of 20 youth-serving nonprofit organizations dedicated to developing young leaders in education.

CHAPTER 4

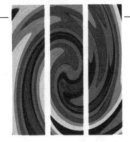

Earning Your Own Way

Mobilizing funds from the philanthropic market is clearly a major and challenging task of the social entrepreneur, as was evident from the previous chapter. Another, potentially complementary approach to funds generation is by earning it in the commercial marketplace through the sale of goods and services. In this chapter, we will first address the question: How important is earned income? We then analyze four important dimensions of this approach: portfolio management, mission relatedness, leveraging assets, and organizational form and capacity. We end with an introduction to the chapter's two case studies.

THE MAGNITUDE OF EARNED INCOME ACTIVITIES

Over half of all cash income of nonprofit organizations around the world is earned income. The Johns Hopkins Comparative Nonprofit Sector Project estimated that globally, 53% of revenues come from fees, 35% from government contributions, and 12% from private philanthropic giving. Furthermore, a significant portion of the government funding is via contracts or reimbursements for services rendered rather than grants, thereby magnifying the importance of earned revenue generation. Earned income is highest in developing and transitional countries at 62% compared to 45% in the developed nations. In some countries in the developing world, the importance of earned income is extremely high, for example, the Philippines at 92%, Mexico at 85%, and Kenya at 81%.[1] This in part reflects the relatively less developed private philanthropic market in developing countries. In the United States, fees account for 57%, government 31%, and philanthropy 13%. Table 4.1 shows regional

Table 4.1   Sources of Cash Revenue by Region (% of Total Cash Revenue)

	Fees	Government	Philanthropy
Latin America	75	15	10
Scandinavia	59	33	7
USA	57	31	13
Asia	56	22	12
Africa	55	25	19
E. Europe	49	31	19
Europe	38	56	6

SOURCE: Derived from *Global Civil Society: An Overview*, Figure 11, p. 32.

differences, which reveals Latin America as the highest earned income area and Europe as the lowest, where government contribution dominates.

While fees, including membership fees, are a prevailing mode in most types of nonprofit organizations, government funding is dominant in healthcare, and philanthropy is the primary source for religious institutions and international development organizations.[2] Within the United States, the revenues of the non-profit sector in the aggregate are estimated at about $700 billion, of which around $500 billion, or about 71%, comes from fees, including those paid to nonprofits by government agencies for goods and services provided.[3] Nonprofits are being created at a faster rate than for-profit businesses, and their revenue growth has expanded 78% faster than the GDP over the two decades of 1977–1997, with nearly half of that growth coming from fee income.[4] The growth of earned income is particularly relevant in the face of intensified competition for philanthropic giving and diminished government funding.

Social enterprises are serious businesses. Take, for example, Goodwill Industries. This group of 204 affiliated nonprofit member organizations operates in 24 countries, and in 2003, it generated $2.21 billion of revenue, 98% of it being earned income, with a 6.5% operating margin.[5] As a reference point, this was about the same as Starbucks' revenue in that year. It operated 1,950 retail stores that generated $1.3 billion of sales, which places Goodwill in the top 15 enterprises operating in the discount and value retailing segment. In addition, through its contracts, industrial services, and workforce development, it pursued its social mission by serving 616,000 disabled or disadvantaged individuals. The YMCA network is the largest nonprofit group with revenues of over $4 billion annually. In the United States, there are 2,500 Ys in 10,000 communities serving about 19 million people; globally, the organization operates in 120 countries and serves 45 million people.[6] It has evolved from being a charity formed in London in 1844 to a fee-for-service organization with major earned income services in health and fitness, child care, and camping, which some have criticized as unfairly encroaching on the terrain of for-profit businesses.[7] The biggest charitable-giving organization in Mexico is funded by the surpluses from its national network of pawnshops.

But earned income is not just for the Big Guys. Multitudes of nonprofits of all sizes engage in earned income activities, and interest is rising. In Chapter 2, we saw how Steve Mariotti launched NFTE by raising donations and using his own sweat equity, but he soon created products and services that could be sold to schools and other organizations.

Yet along with the benefits, there are many challenges, so let us provide some ways to think conceptually and operationally about different dimensions of earned income activity.

PORTFOLIO MANAGEMENT

It is useful to think of earned income activities as part of a social enterprise's total revenue-generating portfolio. We shall consider four dimensions of portfolio management: balance, roles, interrelationships, and alignment.

Balance. The viability and sustainability of a social enterprise is rooted in part in the entrepreneur's assembling a set of funding sources that will provide adequate resources to pursue effectively the organization's social mission. This requires an assessment of the mix of sources in terms of criteria such as their numbers, possible magnitude, stability, growth potential, and efficiency (dollar of surplus yielded relative to costs expended to generate it). One concept to consider is risk management through diversification. If one has multiple sources of earned and unearned income, you are diversifying the type of funds generated. If something goes wrong in the earned income operations such as a market downturn or a loss of market share due to new competition, the nonprofit may still have cash flow from its philanthropic fund-raising, and vice versa.

High dependency may also occur within either the philanthropic or earned income categories. If the social enterprise has only a few large donors, it is exposed to financial disruption if one of those sources dries up. Similarly, if the organization has only a single or very limited product line, it is at risk. For example, the Girl Scouts have been selling cookies since 1917, five years after the group's founding, and currently sell over 2 million boxes annually. It is the major revenue-generating activity for the organization and the local Girl Scout troops, which keep about 12%–17% of the revenue from their members' cookie sales. In 2004, an antiabortion group called for a boycott of the cookie sales because the Girl Scouts had supported a sex education program for girls sponsored by Planned Parenthood. Furthermore, the Girl Scouts named a Planned Parenthood executive as a "Woman of Distinction."[8] Nutritionists also were beginning to criticize the cookies as being fat-filled.

Pioneer Human Services provides a contrasting example. It was created in the 1960s with the mission of helping recovering alcoholics and released convicts to reintegrate into society. It started by collecting donations to provide living facilities and then generated government contracts to run its expanding alcohol treatment and prison release work programs, including subcontract work for the Boeing Company. Facing cuts in government funding, it chose to diversify its activities by developing over several years earned income operations in the form of manufacturing contract work for various industries, commercial catering, wholesale food distribution, and product assembly, fulfillment, packaging, and distribution services. Its early dependence on government funding dropped from 75% to under 33%, while earned income from the foregoing diversified businesses that employed the target populations became the dominant income source.[9] By the late 1990s, it was generating revenues above $40 million and a return on equity of 17% while serving a client population of over 5,000.

Roles. It is important to have clarity about the economic role and contribution that the earned income activity will play within the portfolio. Its role could be simply to generate a net surplus that can then be deployed into the mission-serving activities of the nonprofit. This surplus might play a distinctive role in the cash flow portfolio because as unrestricted funding, the organization could decide how to deploy it, which is generally not the case with philanthropic funding from foundations, governments, companies, and even individual donors. In assessing this role, however, it is important to have realistic expectations about cash flows.[10] One must recognize that earned income activities are initially, and on an ongoing basis, capital absorbing. You must first come up with the capital investment to generate the returns. And expanding enterprises require ever increasing working capital. Furthermore, one should scrutinize carefully the costs of earned income activities to ensure that all resources deployed, including top management and staff time, are included in determining surpluses. Some observers have reported undercounting, thereby giving an illusion of profitability.[11]

Earned income activities might not produce a surplus yet still play a desirable economic role. If the activities are part of the service operations that the organization would be providing to its clients, then the earned income aspects would be contributing to covering part of the fixed operating costs that would have been incurred in any case. If the earned income activities are serving non-target groups, then the justification can occur only if the marginal revenues from serving those groups exceed the marginal costs.[12] This added volume contributes to covering the common fixed costs. Assuming that the economics of the earned income activity are acceptable, there may be added benefits to the organization. In a survey of 72 social enterprises operating 105 ventures, 58% of the respondents reported that the most significant impact of the ventures was creating a more entrepreneurial culture in the organization.[13] This was rated even higher than achieving self-sufficiency, which was cited by 46% of respondents. Attracting and retaining staff was also deemed as an important effect.

Bill Strickland, president and CEO of Manchester Craftsmen's Guild and the Bidwell Training Center, remarked, "Entrepreneurship is not just a financial concept. Becoming more entrepreneurial is as much a shift in organizational culture as a broadening of economic opportunity. As we begin to think like entrepreneurs, we will become sharper and more focused. We will learn how to 'sell' our ideas to a much broader constituency. We will learn to evaluate staff and organizational capacity in a much broader way, and our commitment to entrepreneurship will have an impact on how we recruit and select board members." Thus, earned income activities can play a role of institutional enrichment from a noneconomic as well as an economic perspective.

If the discipline of the marketplace enables the organization to strengthen its total managerial capacities and thereby operate both its earned income and social service activities more efficiently, then significant economic gains could be forthcoming. One study indicated that there is wide variance in operating efficiency across nonprofits, even within the same subsector, and that if the organizations in the less efficient half could reduce administrative costs by 15% to improve to median efficiency rates, there would be a $7 billion savings for the nonprofit sector.[14]

Interaction. Within a portfolio, one wishes to avoid incompatibilities and to attain complementarity. For example, some critics of earned income activities in nonprofits have suggested that such activities can cause philanthropic supporters of the organization to stop giving because they assume that they are no longer needed or as important.[15] However, 36% of respondents in the above-mentioned survey of 72 nonprofits indicated that the earned income activities helped them attract donors. Many of the new philanthropic venture capitalists mentioned in Chapter 3 find investing in social enterprises' business ventures particularly appealing. Even the well-established foundations have invested. For example, the venerable Ford Foundation as part of its PRIs extended Pioneer Human Services a $2 million, 1% loan to enable them to acquire a for-profit going business.

Alignment. The final dimension of the financial portfolio management is to ensure alignment. The Social Enterprise Framework presented in Chapter 2 highlighted the idea that the entrepreneurial process requires the effective interaction of capital, people, and opportunity in pursuit of the SVP within a dynamic external environment. More specifically, it is important to understand how the earned income activities are aligned with the mission, the core assets, and the organization's structure and capacity. These are the dimensions we now turn to.

MISSION RELATEDNESS

How related the actual earned income activities are to the social mission of the organization is a fundamental issue. One way to envision this relates mission alignment and the importance of the earned income contribution to the financial flows of the organization. This is presented in Figure 4.1 below.

FINANCIAL CONTRIBUTION

If the earned income activity is contributing very little financially to the organization and is relatively unrelated to the mission (quadrant 1), then it is a

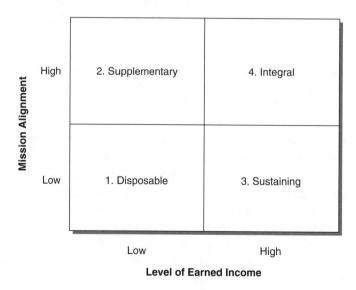

Figure 4.1

candidate for elimination, unless it is in a developmental stage that is expected to evolve into a more financially robust contributor. If it is a weak contributor but is quite related to the mission (quadrant 2), then it is playing a supplementary role in mission attainment. These activities should be scrutinized to see if the resources invested there could be managed in a different way that would enhance the economics while retaining the mission contribution. If not, then one needs to ascertain if this mission benefit could be obtained more efficiently by deploying the dedicated resources to non–earned income activities. If the earned income activities are a major contributor to the financial health of the organization, but are unrelated in any other significant way to the mission, then it is playing an organization-sustaining role (quadrant 3). As mentioned earlier, the largest nonprofit in Mexico is totally supported by the profits generated from its national chain of pawnshops, which have nothing to do with its philanthropic giving. In the United States, mission-unrelated commercial activities would be subject to income taxes by the IRS as unrelated business income. If the business is producing a healthy and sustainable return, then it should be managed independently as a cash generator. One risk of such undertakings is that they may begin to divert scarce management time or organizational energies away from the other mission-centric activities of the organization.

For many reasons, the category of choice is where mission relatedness and economic contribution are both high (quadrant 4). Goodwill Industries, Pioneer Human Services, Greyston Bakery, Rubicon Programs, and many others that have missions of assisting disadvantaged groups through job training, development, or placement generally have high mission alignment with their economic activities. Social enterprises promoting low-income housing are commonly earning their way through their real estate development activities with affordable housing. The Enterprise Foundation, for example, in 2004 helped create nearly 16,500 homes, and 80% of its $119 million in revenues came from mission-related earned income.[16]

But even where mission relatedness is high, there remains the risk of mission distortion in which the pursuit of the earned income causes the organization to dilute or adjust its mission in order to capture new revenues. This can happen even when the activity is more related to the original mission. The theatre company set up to foster innovative performing art begins to produce traditional popular shows to ensure attendance rather than experiment with riskier new productions. The social service agency begins to service higher-income clients and neglects uninsured patients. Pricing decisions can be problematic; one might raise the price of the nonprofit's service in order to generate more revenues so as to better serve the mission, but in the process, some of the clients most in need of those services might be excluded due to their financial inability to pay the higher price.[17]

There is a commonly present tension between market dictates and mission needs. The market imperatives must be dealt with by social enterprises, as revealed by George W. Kessinger, president of Goodwill Industries International, Inc.: "Just as in the private sector, nonprofit organizations must be able to meet customer needs and demands effectively and efficiently, to adapt and respond to shifting environments, and to hold to an ethical standard, so that the public, clients, employees, and other stakeholders can trust our results." Julius Walls, Jr., the CEO of the Greyston Bakery, a for-profit subsidiary of the nonprofit Greyston Foundation, commented,

> At Greyston, we don't employ people to make brownies, we make brownies to employ people. . . . But we cannot expect our business to succeed as a business if we are asking our managers to be social workers as well. . . . Good intentions alone are insufficient to support a premium-quality food product and a social mission. . . . For Greyston to become profitable, we had to professionalize our business by focusing on a few key lessons: Pay attention to the market, remain true to the vision, pay attention to the needs of the business, and don't force the business to be a social program.

In effect, social entrepreneurs must be mission driven and market sensitive . . . a challenging balancing act. In contrast to managing this tension to avoid adverse effects is the positive challenge of how to capture all the synergies between the commercial and social sides of the operations. Pioneer Human Services made its major shift to earned income activities to remove what it perceived to be a fundamental inconsistency between its mission and its dependency on grants. CEO Michael Burns stated, "Is it possible to teach others the importance of self-sufficiency and, at the same time, not be self-sufficient?" Pioneer's shift led to a transformation that enabled it to earn 99.6% of its $55 million revenues in 2003, thereby enabling the earned income activities to be a powerful reinforcement of the core social values. In turn, the social mission can also help the commercial side.

An integral part of Goodwill Industries' business model is the donation of used clothes and other goods. Attracted by Goodwill's social mission of recycling material to assist the disadvantaged, 50 million people donate their goods through 4,000 donation centers. Common Ground, a not-for-profit housing developer for the homeless, was able to obtain a Ben & Jerry's (B&J) franchise because of its social mission. The presence of the B&J outlet, in turn, enabled Common Ground to attract Starbucks to its new development, which was critical in revitalizing the retail environment in the neighborhood. Several of the retailers then agreed to employ a quarter of their staff from Common Ground's homeless clients. Pura Vida Coffee was organized as a for-profit social enterprise that would market gourmet coffee and channel its profits to assist poor communities in Central America.[18] Initially, the social entrepreneur, John Sage, focused on a very specific market segment: the church market and its widely practiced after-service coffee hour. The assumption was that Pura Vida could offer a double-value proposition: high-quality coffee that, through its purchase and subsequent donation of profits, would also benefit the needy. In effect, the social mission was put forth as a competitive differentiator among other high-quality coffees.

Clearly, there are important advantages to achieving alignment of income-earning activities and an organization's mission. But another, similarly important linkage is with the organization's key assets.

LEVERAGING KEY ASSETS

Social entrepreneurship is all about mobilizing the necessary resources to pursue opportunities. The pursuit of earned income opportunities by an existing nonprofit is often enhanced by leveraging the organization's key assets. The starting point is to identify those elements that are key to its current success such as its core capabilities, infrastructure, or reputation.

Share Our Strength is a leading antipoverty and antihunger nonprofit. Over the years, it had become creative in developing earned income partnerships with various companies and professional groups. It decided that this knowledge was a core capability that could be helpful to other nonprofit organizations. Accordingly, the company established the for-profit subsidiary Community Wealth Ventures to provide consulting services to nonprofits on how to discover and design earned income activities.[19]

One of its early clients was the Chicago Children's Choir, the largest children's choral education program in the country, dedicated to making a difference in children's lives through musical excellence. It serves over 3,000 youths of multiple racial and cultural backgrounds. An important part of its program is international tours, the expenses of which the choir had to try to cover via donations. With the assistance of Community Wealth Ventures, the choir generated earned income ideas based on leveraging its core capabilities: selling a musical curriculum, marketing a songbook, starting a choir school, and entering into corporate sponsorships to produce and sell CDs.[20] Similarly, the North Bennett Street School, a century-old fine crafts school in the North End of Boston, opened a retail store to sell graduates' works.[21]

Nation's Capital Child and Family Development operated 25 daycare facilities and produced a half million meals annually for those children.[22] The kitchen that was used to prepare those meals had an installed capacity to produce another 700,000 meals. It leveraged this underutilized support infrastructure to expand into institutional commercial catering serving other daycare and elderly care centers, the profits from which are channeled back into the support of the organization's core activities.

The Chilean Safety Association, which aims to enhance workplace safety and provide care for injured workers, was so effective in its injury prevention education that the number of workers requiring medical treatment dropped significantly. This desirable performance in attaining its mission had the secondary effect of reducing the demand for the medical services of the association's hospital, thereby creating excess capacity. The organization then leveraged this underutilized asset to provide for-fee services to outsiders, thus generating extra income for the nonprofit organization.[23]

Pioneer Human Services' birth involved the provision of housing for recovering alcoholics. As this expanded, it developed maintenance operations to service the residences. This set of learned skills provided the basis for developing a construction firm that provided remodeling and siding services to others.[24]

Nonprofits' reputations are their most valuable intangible asset. Embedded in their names—brands—is trust with their stakeholders and the public in general. It is an emotional connection, often quite deep, between the organization and the outside world. This type of connection is generally qualitatively different than that obtained by commercial firms and their customers and the public. Consequently, this has created an entrepreneurial earned income opportunity for nonprofits to interact with corporations. Such interactions have given rise to the cause-related marketing phenomenon in which corporations sponsor promotions or events of nonprofits. The companies receive the reputational benefits of positive associations with the nonprofit's brand and social cause in exchange for payments to the nonprofit. Table 4.2 indicates that fees earned by U.S. nonprofits through cause-related and arts sponsorships rose to $1.6 billion in 2005, a 33% increase since 2000. It is important to note that the bulk of this funding comes from corporate marketing budgets rather than their philanthropic giving (which amounted to $12 billion in 2004[25]) and thus represents new inflows from the commercial marketplace into the social sector.

While nonprofits understand that their reputations are extremely important, they generally do not know the true market value of their brands. In contrast,

Table 4.2   Corporate Sponsorship Fees to Nonprofits ($ Billions)

	2005*	2004	2003	2002	2001	2000
Causes	1.080	.988	.922	.835	.733	.700
Arts	.630	.610	.608	.603	.589	.548

*Projected

SOURCE: *IEG Sponsorship Report*, Chicago 2005.

corporations have relatively solid calculations of their brand value using fairly well-established marketing assessment methodologies. Recently, such methodology has begun to be applied to nonprofits. For example, Habitat for Humanity (HFH) hired Interbrand consultancy, which determined Habitat's brand value to be $1.8 billion, in the range of Starbucks' brand valuation.[26] With this more accurate assessment of their brand's value, Habitat was able to leverage this core asset more effectively, doubling the minimum threshold value for companies to qualify for partnering with them. They have been able to attract higher-quality partners and construct more leveraged, multiyear sponsorships. The next chapter will explore other dimensions of how to build strategic alliances.

ORGANIZATIONAL FORM AND CAPACITY

One of the well-known tenets in management is that structure follows strategy.[27] Accordingly, if an organization opts to undertake an earned income strategy, one of the core follow-up decisions is what type of organizational structure to create to implement that strategy. Social enterprises take many different legal forms ranging from nonprofit to for-profit, with various hybrids in between on the organizational spectrum.[28] This choice depends on which form is likely to offer the most advantages in a particular circumstance. For example, a for-profit corporation would have the possibility of raising capital from private investors who could receive a financial return on their investments as shareholders. While a nonprofit would lack that same possibility due to the legal constraint against distributing surpluses, it would have the advantage of being tax exempt as long as the earned income activities were deemed by the U.S. tax authorities to be relevant to the fulfillment of its social mission. If the activities are unrelated to the mission and therefore taxable, incorporating as a for-profit would likely make more sense.

Pura Vida Coffee, mentioned above, incorporated as a for-profit because the social entrepreneur, John Sage, who had previously been a successful executive at Microsoft, saw it as a more administratively simple way to start up and a legal form that would enable the organization to attract private capital. However, as part of his SVP to serve the poor, he had stated that all profits would go to charity. Consequently, he had self-imposed the profit distribution constraint, thereby eliminating the possibility of attracting private commercial capital into the venture, yet the company was also subject to taxation. He had created the worst of both worlds organizationally. Subsequently, John made some important adjustments. He created a nonprofit, to which the company would be a subsidiary; the nonprofit was able to raise charitable donations, thereby tapping into the philanthropic marketplace as a complement to the for-profit's engagement in the commercial market. He relaxed the total profit distribution constraint so that some profits could be reinvested in the company to meet its growing working capital needs. Furthermore, he sought commercial loans, which were forthcoming because the inventory was highly liquid and the accounts payable high quality. On the investment side, he created a novel financial instrument whereby investors would receive a return, which would go to the charity of their choice as a tax-deductible donation. This instrument and Pura Vida's social mission were able to attract socially oriented investors. In effect, Pura Vida created a hybrid organizational form and a mixed-funding portfolio.

Sometimes a social enterprise choosing a for-profit form can encounter resistance. Education Alternatives, Inc. (EAI), was formed to provide management services to public school systems. It won contracts to run school systems in Miami and Baltimore, but the mayor of Washington, D.C., withdrew an offer to hire the for-profit EAI to run the district's system because it "had proven to be too controversial and promised to create irreparable splits on the [school] board and within the city."[29]

Greyston Foundation set up the Greyston Bakery as a wholly owned for-profit subsidiary. While the bakery is seen as a vehicle for achieving its social mission of providing employment for the disadvantaged, it is managed with the typical discipline of a for-profit company. One risk for nonprofits is that they will not have the skills needed to be successful in the earned income business. Using existing talents that were sufficient to be successful as a nonprofit is seldom enough. As CEO Julius Walls, Jr., stated,

> It took about five years and significant growth in skills and manufacturing capacity for Greyston to break even . . . we are very strict about attendance, punctuality, attitude, and performance in the workplace. Because we are subject to the discipline of market competition, bakery employees develop skills that are genuinely valuable and marketable. This market pressure also holds our management team accountable and does not allow us to produce inefficiently or below market-quality standards.[30]

For nonprofits to have the organizational capabilities to run a nonprofit successfully, in addition to internal training, it is often necessary for them to recruit specialized talent from the outside. Mark Swann, executive director of Preble Street Resource Center, commented on this bottleneck when he was facing the creation of the Stone Soup Restaurant:

> Starting a nonprofit enterprise is a very messy and complex effort. It felt different from what we've always done as a social service agency. We needed different skills, different advice, and different kinds of people involved in the whole effort than we have on our parent board at Preble Street Resource Center, where our work is making sure that homeless people get access to the services they need. I know how to run a social service agency, but I don't know how to run a restaurant, even when it has a social mission.[31]

Success in starting businesses does not come easily or to all. About 4 out of every 10 small businesses fail.[32] Even the highly successful Pioneer Human Services encountered difficulties in its early attempts. They had to shut down a drug rehabilitation venture after three unprofitable years. Then-CEO Gary Mulhair remarked on the experience,

> We learned several lessons. First, we didn't understand the marketing knowledge needed to make a go of the venture. We didn't have the money for the television and other advertising and sales needed to compete. . . . We weren't operationally focused so our costs suffered. And don't kid yourself about the leverage of a not-for-profit status. The market doesn't care. Its decisions are economic. Know your market. Do your research.[33]

Understanding the target consumers and developing the capacity to meet their needs in a superior way are essential to success. Rochester Rehabilitation has been able to achieve a good fit between the capabilities of its mostly disabled employees and the requirements of Kodak for the reprocessing of its single-use cameras. Through its 15-year relationship with Kodak, it generates about $5 million annually, employs about 90 people, and recently recovered its 1 billionth camera.[34]

Because the earned income operations often require talents, systems, and behavior that are quite distinct from those on the social service side of the organization, organizational integration can be difficult. Jumpstart is a nonprofit that focuses on getting disadvantaged preschoolers ready for school through tutoring and enrichment programs. In an effort to generate earned income, Jumpstart created a for-profit subsidiary, SchoolSuccess.net (SSN), to sell its educational content via the Internet to other preschool education providers. It raised private capital, hired professional management and Internet specialists, and established a new board of directors. Then-CEO Aaron Leiberman commented on the resultant organizational dynamics: "Even though SSN is working just one floor up from Jumpstart, after an initial picnic involving the two organizations, we have been largely unable to bring the two staffs together, even though SSN was basically working on an electronic version of Jumpstart!"[35]

Sometimes the reactions can be even more extreme, such as that which occurred in an Oregon social enterprise working with psychiatrically disabled people. The organization added a production business to its social service operation. One of the leaders observed, "There was a demilitarized zone between the production people who ran the factory and the rehab people who provided social services. We had two very strong-willed managers and each of them had their own lieutenants and armies."[36]

Clearly, setting up business operations can create challenges to an organization's culture. Thus, a major organizational design issue is how separate to make the earned income activities. Here, one is balancing the need to ensure sufficient operating independence so that the entity can function efficiently in the marketplace against the desirability of capturing all possible synergies between the social and business sides of the organization. The ultimate goal is to find an organizational form that ensures strategic alignment.

CASE STUDIES

The following case studies will plunge the reader into the entrepreneurial challenges and opportunities of earned income activities and social purpose businesses. The first case, IPODERAC, started in a traditional way with the founding social entrepreneurs mobilizing philanthropic donations to support its orphanage. Its resource mobilization strategy evolved to encompass multiple sources including significant earned income activities. In studying the case, consider the following questions:

1. What is your evaluation of IPODERAC's past efforts to achieve financial sustainability?

2. What criteria should one use to evaluate the different revenue sources, both philanthropic and earned income?

3. What enabled the goat cheese operation to become so significant?

4. What recommendations would you make to IPODERAC regarding the future development of the goat cheese operation?

5. From a financial portfolio perspective, what is your assessment of IPODERAC's situation?

Newman's Own emerged as a social enterprise created by the actor Paul Newman. This provides an organizational contrast to the charity IPODERAC, as Newman's is operated as a for-profit commercial enterprise, the profits from which flow to charities. It has been very successful, having generated sufficient profits to have donated almost $100 million since its inception. Consider the following questions as you analyze this social enterprise:

1. Why has Newman's Own been so successful?

2. How does being a social purpose enterprise enhance or hinder the company's business performance?

3. How does being a for-profit entity enhance or hinder the creation of social value?

4. What would you recommend to the management of Newman's Own to strengthen its future success?

NOTES

1. Salamon, L. M., Sokolowski, S. W., & List, R. (2003). *Global civil society: An overview*. The Johns Hopkins Comparative Nonprofit Sector Project. Baltimore: Johns Hopkins University. While the sample in this country was limited to 32 countries and therefore is necessarily representative of all countries, it is the most thorough survey that exists to date.

2. Ibid.

3. Bradley, B. (2004). Foreword. In S. M. Oster, C. W. Massarsky, & S. L. Beinhacker (Eds.), *Generating and sustaining nonprofit earned income: A guide to successful enterprise strategies* (pp. xiii–xvi). San Francisco: Jossey-Bass.

4. Salamon, L. M. (Ed.). (2002). *The state of nonprofit America*. Washington, DC: Brookings Institution Press in collaboration with the Aspen Institute.

5. Goodwill Industries International, Inc., Annual Report. (2003). Rockville, MD: Goodwill Industries.

6. YMCA Web site. Retrieved April 10, 2006, from www.ymca.net.

7. Weisbrod, B. A. (2004, Winter). The pitfalls of profits. *Stanford Social Innovation Review, 2*(3), 40–47.

8. Severson, K. (2004, March 6). Controversy could crumble Girl Scout cookie sales. *San Francisco Chronicle*, p. A-1.

9. Heskett, J. L. (1999, April 7). *Pioneer human services (A)*. Denali Series, Manchester Craftsmen's Guild. Harvard Business School Case #MCG001.

10. Dees, J. G. (2001). Mobilizing resources. In J. G. Dees, J. Emerson, & P. Economy (Eds.), *Enterprising nonprofits: A toolkit for social entrepreneurs* (pp. 63–102). New York: John Wiley & Sons.

11. Foster, W., & Bradach, J. (2005, February). Should nonprofits seek profit? *Harvard Business Review*, pp. 92–100.

12. Young, D. R. (2004). Deploying resources effectively. In S. M. Oster, C. W. Massarsky, & S. L. Beinhacker (Eds.), *Generating and sustaining nonprofit earned income: A guide to successful enterprise strategies* (pp. 247–268). San Francisco: Jossey-Bass.

13. Community Wealth Ventures. (2003). *Powering social change: Lessons on community wealth generation for nonprofit sustainability*. Retrieved April 10, 2006, from http://www.communitywealth.org/Powering%20Social%20Change.pdf.

14. Bradley, B., Jansen, P., & Silverman, L. (2003, May). The nonprofit sector's $100 billion opportunity. *Harvard Business Review*, pp. 94–103.

15. Foster, W., & Bradach, J. (2005, February). Should nonprofits seek profit? *Harvard Business Review*, pp. 92–100.

16. The Enterprise Foundation Annual Report. (2004). Columbia, MD: The Enterprise Foundation.

17. Oster, S. (2004). Pricing goods and services. In S. M. Oster, C. W. Massarsky, & S. L. Beinhacker (Eds.), *Generating and sustaining nonprofit earned income: A guide to successful enterprise strategies* (pp. 61–76). San Francisco: Jossey-Bass.

18. Austin, J. E., & Grossman, A. (2002). *Pura vida coffee.* Harvard Business School Multimedia Case #9–303–051.

19. Austin, J. E., & Pearson, M. D. (1999). *Community wealth ventures, inc.* Harvard Business School Case #399–023.

20. Austin, J. E. (2000). *The collaboration challenge: How nonprofits and businesses succeed through strategic alliances* (pp. 46–48). San Francisco: Jossey-Bass.

21. Example provided by Alfred Wise, Community Wealth Ventures.

22. Community Wealth Ventures. (2003). *Powering social change: Lessons on community wealth generation for nonprofit sustainability.* Retrieved April 10, 2006, from http://www.communitywealth.org/Powering%20Social%20Change.pdf, p. 13.

23. Social Enterprise Knowledge Network. (2006). *Effective management of social enterprise.* Cambridge, MA: Harvard University Press.

24. Burns, M. J. (2003). Self-sufficiency: How important is it? In *Powering social change: Lessons on community wealth generation for nonprofit sustainability.* Retrieved April 10, 2006, from http://www.communitywealth.org/Powering%20Social%20Change.pdf, pp. 30–33.

25. Indiana University Center on Philanthropy. (2005). *Giving USA 2005.* AAFRC Trust for Philanthropy, p. 18.

26. Quelch, J. A., Austin, J. E., & Laidler-Kylander, N. (2004, April 1). Mining gold in not-for-profit brands. *Harvard Business Review,* p. 24. For further information on nonprofit brand valuation, see HBS Case #9–503–101 at www.harvardbusinessonline.org.

27. Chandler, A. D. (1962). *Strategy and structure: Chapters in the history of the industrial enterprise.* Cambridge, MA: MIT Press.

28. Dees, J. G. (2001). Social entrepreneurship. In J. G. Dees, J. Emerson, & P. Economy (Eds.), *Enterprising nonprofits: A toolkit for social entrepreneurs* (pp. 1–18). New York: John Wiley & Sons.

29. Elias, J., & Dees, J. G. (1995). *Education alternatives, inc.* Harvard Business School Case #9–395–106.

30. Walls, J., Jr. (2003). A successful social enterprise responds to the market. In *Powering social change: Lessons on community wealth generation for nonprofit sustainability.* Retrieved April 10, 2006, from http://www.communitywealth.org/Powering%20Social%20Change.pdf, pp. 26, 29.

31. Swann, M. (2004). A founder's perspective. In S. M. Oster, C. W. Massarsky, & S. L. Beinhacker (Eds.), *Generating and sustaining nonprofit earned income: A guide to successful enterprise strategies* (pp. 171–172). San Francisco: Jossey-Bass.

32. Foster, W., & Bradach, J. (2005).

33. Heskett, J. L. (1999, April 7).

34. Example provided by Alfred Wise, Community Wealth Ventures.

35. Austin, J., & McCaffrey, A. (2001). *SchoolSuccess.net.* Harvard Business School Case #9–302–008.

36. Boschee, J. (2006). *Migrating from innovation to entrepreneurship.* Minneapolis, MN: Encore! Publishing Company.

Case Study 4.1.

IPODERAC

For the first time in our thirty-two-year history, the possibility of achieving financial self-sufficiency is within our grasp. We must determine how to achieve and solidify this goal. This is a critical juncture for us.

In June 1998, Agustín Landa, the director of this Mexican civic association that housed and cared for abandoned street children, was optimistic but anxious about IPODERAC's future.

ORIGINS AND EVOLUTION

IPODERAC, Instituto Poblano de Readaptación, A.C. (Puebla Institute of Rehabilitation), was founded in 1966 by María Elena

Landa, María Elena Gomez, and a few other colleagues who had decided, according to Señora Landa, "to not waste their lives in daily routines and to make a contribution to the community." They began providing volunteer social counseling to male inmates at the prison in Puebla, a city of 2.5 million people located 80 miles east of Mexico City. They discovered that over two-thirds of the prisoners came from broken families, were abused as children, and were abandoned to a life in the streets. Many had been in youth correctional institutions in deplorable conditions that fostered further delinquency rather than rehabilitation.

The founding group decided to turn their efforts toward setting up a home for abandoned boys. They determined that it would be in a rural setting to avoid the temptations of the streets but near a small town so that services and public education would be available. With a bank loan, they purchased a nine-hectare site outside of Atlixco on a highway about 25 miles from Puebla. They named the site "Villa Nolasco" in honor of the founder of the Catholic Order of Mercy, whose members had encouraged and advised the founders. Servicing the loan was a constant struggle, as Sra. Landa explained,

In the beginning, we went out in the streets with collection cans to ask for money. It was embarrassing but none of us had a cent. Nonetheless, we fought for this goal. We pawned personal belongings and made other collections. It was a very difficult task, the results didn't appear as fast as we had hoped, and many who had been helping abandoned the effort. People give money and effort when they see something done. We only had a piece of land full of rocks.

Slowly the founders continued soliciting donations, and in 1969, the first house for eight boys in Villa Nolasco was inaugurated by the state governor. In 1971, a second house was added with funding from the Mary Street Jenkins Foundation. A third house was financed by the president of Mexico in 1972. Funding from the Puebla Municipal Board of Moral, Civic, and Material Betterment enabled the construction of the fourth house and a sports field in 1974. Funds raised by the IPODERAC board of trustees and friends provided the house furnishings. The fifth house was added in 1981 with another major private donation from a Catholic religious organization in Germany. By 1988, Villa Nolasco housed 60 boys whose average age was 8.3 years. In 1991, the Dutch embassy donated a health clinic. In 1992, IPODERAC was awarded the Luis Elizondo Humanitarian Prize in recognition of its social contribution. The boys remained at Villa Nolasco, on average, 10 years until their late teens, so a sixth house was added for older youth in 1994. In 1998, there were 72 boys ranging in age from 5 to 20 with the average being 14.6 years. A total of 550 boys had grown up under the care and guidance of IPODERAC. (See **Exhibit 4.1.6** for photos of the facilities at Villa Nolasco.)

Children's Care and Development

IPODERAC's initial mission was the personal and social rehabilitation of children from poor and disintegrated families. Street children are often sent out or abandoned by their parents to beg or even rob as part of their struggle to eke out an existence. The children are often abused and have little formal education. Their situation leads to frustration, low self-esteem, skepticism, mistrust, insecurity, independence, and aggressiveness. IPODERAC's aim was to provide a family environment with education and a moral orientation that would foster personal identity, self-esteem, and habits of cleanliness, order, discipline, and work. IPODERAC operated on the following premises: Street children need considerable help in gradually adapting themselves to society; they have the right to special attention and protection by the community; and they and their families are capable of communicating and deciding their own development and are not objects of charity.

These premises led to an open-door policy whereby boys would enter Villa Nolasco under their own volition and were also free to leave. Children were referred to IPODERAC by other social or governmental agencies who worked with street children and juvenile delinquents. Applicants would visit Villa Nolasco and learn about the community before deciding to enter. By living together in groups of 12, the boys had a "substitute family" environment. They attended public schools in the nearby town, thereby being integrated into a community as part of their educational and developmental process. In 1993-1994, over 90% of the boys passed their yearly exams and 10% finished in the top three places in their classes. Manual work was also seen as an integral part of the children's development. The principle was that the children should contribute to their own maintenance, and the goal was to inculcate them with an attitude that work was dignified and educational, that it builds character, and that you earn through effort.

The original model for the children's houses came from a conference on caring for abandoned and orphaned children in Chile sponsored by the Order of Mercy and attended by Sra. Landa. At Villa Nolasco, each two-story house had four bedrooms with three children in each, a dining and living area, a common bathroom, a kitchen, and a bedroom for the educator, who served as the primary caregiver. Each of the six houses corresponded to a specific age group, with the children moving into new houses as they reached the next age category.

The educators were the backbone of IPODERAC's caregiving system. They had to be over 25 years of age, single, and high school graduates. They lived with the children and had primary responsibility and authority. An educational director, Dr. Fernando Ballí, who also ran the health clinic, supervised the six educators. They received training on their duties, although the caregiving procedures and cumulative knowledge at Villa Nolasco were never documented in any manuals.

The educators stay, on average, about 3.5 years. Recruiting replacements is a difficult task because the work is very demanding. Most are found by word of mouth and indicate that they are motivated by the joy of caring for the children and by the pay, although it is very modest. The educators stated that it was difficult to balance being a friend to the children while also being the authority. The educators' and the children's days began at 5:00 a.m. and ended at 8:30 p.m. (see **Exhibit 4.1.1**). The educators received 2 days off every two weeks and 30 days of vacation annually. The house with the oldest youth did not have a resident educator in order to transfer greater responsibility and independence to them in preparation for their forthcoming graduation. In its early years, IPODERAC had a psychologist and a priest who provided counseling and support services, but these positions did not currently

5:00–5:15	Rise, make bed, get dressed [four youth rise at 4:30 to milk goats]
5:15–5:30	Wash, comb hair
5:30–6:00	Breakfast
6:00–6:45	Brush teeth, clean house
7:00–8:30	Transport to school (departure time varies by age)
8:30–9:00	Staff meeting
8:30–1:45	Attendance at school
1:45–3:00	Return from school, wash, change clothes, lunch
3:00–3:50	Clean up dining room, kitchen, bathroom
3:50–6:00	Study, workshops, or assigned work activities (e.g., goat care, gardening)
6:00–7:00	Games on the sports field or in the houses
7:00–7:30	Bath
7:30–8:00	Dinner
8:00–8:20	Clean up
8:20	To bed

Exhibit 4.1.1   Daily Schedule (Monday–Friday) of Children

exist. The combined living, working, and educational experience was aimed at creating a transformation process: developing values, attitudes, and behaviors that would enable the children to become independent, productive, and responsible members of society (see **Exhibit 4.1.2** for the developmental model).

Production Activities

From its inception, Villa Nolasco engaged in farming both to provide food and revenues as well as to engage the boys in structured work activities. The children were compensated for their work at the minimum-wage rate. From their savings accounts, the boys could draw out money for personal expenditures. At the beginning of the school year, the children are provided their school supplies by IPODERAC. Previously, the children could also get replacements for these supplies, but when it was discovered that they were selling them to their classmates at school, the children were required to replace any "lost" supplies from their savings accounts.

The various agricultural undertakings at Villa Nolasco met with mixed success. From the beginning, they planted vegetables to feed the children, with surpluses being sold in the nearby town. In 1974, they planted 1,100 avocado trees with technical and financial assistance from the government, including the installation of a drip irrigation system, a farming innovation that attracted considerable attention in the region. Avocado sales generated significant revenues, covering nearly half of Villa Nolasco's operating costs by the late 1980s. However, increasing supplies from other producing areas and theft of the fruit at night made the operation unprofitable. The farm started raising rabbits to eat and sell for skins and meat, primarily to the

TRANSFORMATION STAGES	➢	Values Affirmed in Each Stage
Alum follow-up		Connection with community
Graduation	➢	Adulthood
Preparation for independence	➢	Self-esteem, capability, liberty
Participative responsibility	➢	Service, coresponsibility
Facing up to past	➢	Pardon, hope, faith, love
Work	➢	Responsibility, self-esteem
Schooling	➢	Responsibility, friendship
Personal habits	➢	Responsibility
Acceptance that "I am here"	➢	Community
Entry and initial adaptation	➢	Friendship, community, self-esteem, happiness, respect
CHILDREN'S TIME IN VILLA NOLASCO	➢	

Exhibit 4.1.2   IPODERAC Transformation Process for Adolescent Development

cafeteria in the Volkswagen plant in Puebla. A disease threat led to a government embargo on rabbit sales, thereby ruining the business. Quails were raised for sale to nearby restaurants from eggs provided by a government incubator. However, when this government operation was privatized, the new owners stopped supplying outsiders with eggs, thus ending the quail operation. A similar experience occurred with ducks. The farm also raised a small number of cows and goats for milk for its own consumption. To feed them, they tried to use a system of hydroponics, but the resultant grass was not sufficiently nutritious. The lack of animal husbandry skills led to poor health and low productivity. They also produced small quantities of cheese for sale, but there appeared to be little demand. The disappointing efforts to generate earned income led to a rethinking of the traditional approach, which coincided with an unexpected change in the leadership of IPODERAC.

Leadership Change

In 1988, Sra. Landa, after serving 16 years as the director, suffered deterioration of her health, which led to her retirement. Finding a successor with the same deep level of commitment and energy as this founder was a major challenge for IPODERAC's board of trustees. Fortunately, Sra. Landa had recruited her nephew, Agustín Landa, an agronomist, to come to Villa Nolasco in 1987 to be in charge of the agricultural operations. When Sra. Landa was hospitalized and resigned, Agustín was named as the new director at the age of 26.

Agustín was exposed to IPODERAC as a child when his family would visit his aunt. When he was 19, he brought the first goats to

Villa Nolasco and was so deeply touched by the children and the mission that he recruited fellow university students to work as volunteers during the following four summers. He then decided in 1986 to leave his position as manager of his family's farm in Monterrey and come to Villa Nolasco full-time, with the idea of learning about vegetable and flower production for two years and then returning to Monterrey. When Sra. Landa resigned, Agustín decided, "This effort was very important and nobody other than the founder and I knew the internal system of education for the children and the basic principles that they wished to attain. So I decided to stay for two more years." In 1990, Agustín faced another crossroads. His father offered to give him the family ranch, worth over a million dollars, if he would return home to run it. This would be an opportunity to provide economic security to his young family, and he consulted his wife, who responded, "You said to me that God will provide for us if we concern ourselves with His realm, so what do you need the ranch for?" Agustín thanked his father and recommitted his energies to IPODERAC. His father sold the ranch.

Agustín lived with his family in a modest house next to the children's houses. His $600-a-month salary was many times less than what he could earn outside. To help out, an IPODERAC supporter committed himself to financing the education of the older of Landa's two children in private schools in Puebla. Agustín reflected, "There have been many other times that we have asked ourselves if we should leave or have thought that it was the moment for others to carry on, but we have always concluded that a better life we still could not find."

As director, Agustín was deeply involved in all aspects of the operation from administration to production and marketing to the boys' education to external relations and fund-raising. The staff was very small and dedicated, but it was difficult to attract highly talented people due to the low salaries and rural setting. **Exhibit 4.1.3** presents the formal organizational chart, but Agustín's reality was that "at times, I have to do some of everything." The organization's limited administrative resources also meant that only recently had they begun to develop formal and systematic management record keeping and procedures.

The 23 paid staff members were supplemented by volunteers and outside organizations, both local and international, who would primarily assist in activities with the students, such as tutoring, educational trips, and recreational activities. In 1997, 17 volunteers worked at Villa Nolasco between 15 days and a full year, providing an estimated 160 person-days of labor. Among the outside organizations sending volunteers was the British GAP and various local and overseas universities. A few corporations also provided volunteers; for example, 70 employees of General Electric Mexico spent a day painting the IPODERAC houses and interacting with the children on other occasions. Other companies provided summer internships for some of the youth, over half of whom were between the ages of 15 and 19. Various professionals provided special educational services to the children. IPODERAC had ongoing operational relations with 25 suppliers and financial or assistance relationships with 2 civic, 9 governmental, 10 philanthropic, 2 religious, and 69 business organizations (with the

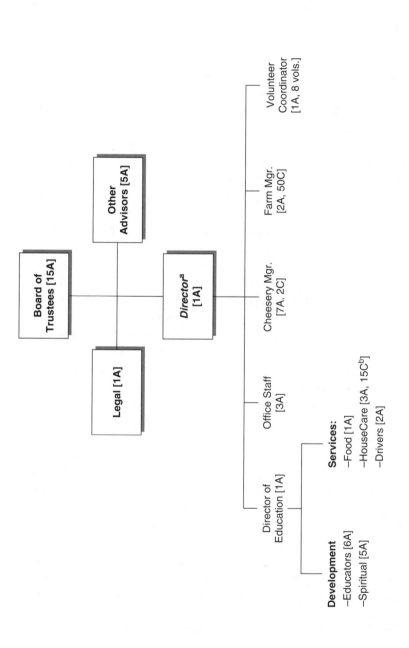

Exhibit 4.1.3 IPODERAC Organization Chart

NOTE: Bracketed figures indicate numbers of adults [A] and children[C] working in each activity.

a. In addition to supervising all the above direct reports, the director had primary responsibility for sales, fundraising, personnel administration, and public relations

b. Younger children engage in the cleanup of the common areas in the houses. In addition to the above, 2 adults and 20 older children work in the various construction projects when they arise; e.g., corral, building repairs.

157

majority of the latter being individual donors using funds from their businesses). Twelve of these various organizations were international.

Agustín was the primary person in charge of these external relationships. He was continually developing other contacts, generating new ideas, and starting projects aimed at generating funds or mobilizing resources in a constant search for solutions to PODERAC's problems and needs. However, the follow-through for many of these activities often was impeded due to the lack of time, organization, and staff capacity.

New Path Toward Self-Sufficiency

From its inception, IPODERAC depended primarily on donations in money or in-kind donations. The principal function of the 15-person board of trustees was fund-raising. Their main event was an annual raffle in November of a new car, but a variety of other activities also were used from time to time. In 1997, the raffle produced a net contribution to IPODERAC of 308,000 pesos. In 1994, Agustín, with the assistance of a General Electric executive and another Mexican colleague, created The Mexico City Group consisting of 17 professionals from various fields to assist IPODERAC in fund-raising, public relations, planning, mentorships, and internships.

The director also raised funds directly from foundations, corporations, government entities, and individuals, amounting to 614,000 pesos in 1997. Donations were tax deductible. IPODERAC had obtained donations from a few multinational corporations

and several large Mexican companies. Some firms provided in-kind donations; for example, Hewlett-Packard donated computers for the children; others gave foodstuffs, clothing, toys, and school supplies. Agustín indicated that the key to all donors was establishing a personal relationship, so much of his fund-raising time was spent in finding someone who could provide the personal contact within the donor organization. For corporate, foundation, or civic organizations, the personal relationship was more important than the nature of the project. In contrast, donations from foreign governments through their local embassy depended more on the nature and merits of the specific project, although having access to someone in the embassy was important. Donations from the Mexican government during the early years were very dependent on personal contacts and relationships. In recent years, however, federal government funding through the Social Conversion Fund was based on a proposal competition. Three times IPODERAC had won a 100,000-peso award. Agustín indicated that these competitions required only about three person-days to prepare the project proposal. However, they did not pursue this in 1998 because it was an election year and Agustín feared being used for political purposes.

IPODERAC also had created a Sponsor-A-Child program whereby for $150 per month, individuals or organizations could fund the living expenses of a specific child and have a personal relationship with him. As of mid-1998, 8 of the 72 children were sponsored, but up to 30 had been sponsored in the past. **Exhibit 4.1.4** provides financial statements for recent years.

Exchange Rate	6.17	7.57	7.88
INCOME	1995	1996	1997
Income generated by Board			
Scholarships	13	0.4	0.3
Events (annual raffle)	13	35	39
In-kind donations	2	—	—
	28	36	39
Income Generated by Management			
Scholarships	19	46	20
Donations for the Cheesery	30	1	—
Donations for fixed assets	1	23	15
FAPRODE	16	1	1
Other donations	58	22	23
Donations for goatherd	—	8	—
In-kind donations	7	25	18
Other income	0	0	—
	130	128	78
Self-Earned Income			
Alfalfa for goats (internal)	5	7	[a]
Milk for Cheesery (internal)	4	20	[a]
Milk for children (internal)	5	—	—
Sales of goats	1	7	9
Cheese sales	61	139	253
Other income, production	0	0	3
	77	173	265
Other income	—	—	1
Interest income	9	4	2
TOTAL INCOME	244	340	386
EXPENSES	1995	1996	1997
Production Expenses			
Alfalfa & Vegetables:	8	5	10
Children's wages	1	1	1
Depreciation and amortization	5	3	5
Others	2	2	4
Goats	17	38	28
Children's wages	2	3	4

Exhibit 4.1.4A   IPODERAC Financial Statements—Profit and Loss Statement
(in thousands of US$)   *(Continued)*

(Continued)

Exchange Rate	6.17	7.57	7.88
EXPENSES	*1995*	*1996*	*1997*
Salaries and benefits, others	1	2	2
Alfalfa Ipoderac	5	9	3
External feed	3	8	11
Depreciation and amortization	—	—	—
Others	6	16	8
Cheesery	39	77	99
Children's wages	3	2	2
Salaries and benefits, others	—	1	6
Milk	20	48	50
Depreciation and amortization	0	1	0
Others	16	24	41
Carpentry	—	5	—
Humus (Californian worms)	1	3	1
	65	128	138
Operation Expenses			
Administration	30	30	42
Salaries and benefits	16	14	17
Children	107	140	159
Salaries and benefits	13	20	22
Allowances	21	30	34
Annual event	—	5	—
Other expenses	—	14	—
	137	189	201
TOTAL EXPENSES	202	317	339
NET INCOME (LOSS)	42	23	47

Exhibit 4.1.4A

a. Net income from these internal sales unregistered in 1997.

The Cheese Opportunity

Soon after Agustín assumed the leadership, he and the board decided to make a more concerted and focused effort to generate earned income. They concentrated on cheese production and marketing for several reasons. Agustín's professional training was in agriculture and he was particularly interested in the goats. The market for goat cheese in Mexico expanded when the country's trade liberalization brought significant increases in imported goat cheese, which sparked demand. When Mexico's economy

Current Assets		Current Liabilities	
Cash and bank	41	Accounts payable	12
Accounts receivable	20	Taxes payable	1
Other	14	Subtotal	13
Subtotal	74		
Net Fixed Assets		Capital	
Land and equipment	22	Original patrimony	60
Office equipment	28	Retained surpluses	111
Buildings and furnishings	84	Current period surplus	47
Cheesery	13	Subtotal	218
Other	10		
Subtotal	157		
Total Assets	**231**	**Total Liabilities & Capital**	**231**

Exhibit 4.1.4B   Abridged Balance Sheet as of 12/31/97 (US$000)

went into crisis in 1994, imports fell, leaving a supply void in the recently expanded market for goat cheese. A retired Swiss executive from Nestlé volunteered his pro bono services to IPODERAC and provided the technical knowledge for making various types of high-quality goat and cow cheese.

In 1988, the small goatherd was increased, partially with donations from the Canadian government and a major Mexican company. Unfortunately, 16 of these new breeding-quality goats were stolen, slowing down the expansion, but by 1998, the herd had reached 148 producing milk or pregnant and 115 in development. One of the members of the Mexico City Group conceived of and launched in 1995 an "Adopt-A-Goat" program. For $125, individuals or groups could name a goat, receive a certificate of adoption with a photo, and receive a milk production report every six months for two years, at which time the adoption could be renewed. Thirty-two goats had been adopted. The

avocado plantation was replaced by alfalfa to provide feed for the goats. A new, small cheese-fabricating facility with a pasteurizer, hand-processing equipment, and refrigeration was developed with a $25,000 donation that came from the General Electric Foundation in Connecticut through the G.E. Mexico subsidiary. G.E. had selected IPODERAC as a recipient of its charitable donations only after surveying many other candidate nonprofit organizations. One of the G.E. executives also knew Agustín.

Marketing

Finding customers for the cheeses was a major challenge for Agustín. There was limited knowledge among food establishments about French-style goat cheese. He put his cheeses in an ice chest and headed off in the microbus to visit a few restaurants in Puebla, using contacts made through friends. Later he tried to penetrate the prime market of

Mexico City by approaching the classiest restaurants, again using personal contacts. To the manager of Maxim's, instead of trying to sell, he asked, "Tell me what's wrong with our cheeses." With this advice and the Swiss volunteer's expertise, IPODERAC made corrections in quality and packaging. Maxim's became a customer, and the manager also referred Agustín to a restaurant wine and food distributor of which he was part owner. The distributor facilitated their access to various other quality restaurants. In 1997, the Villa Nolasco cheeses were sold to the following clients in order of importance:

1. Unilac—A distributor of cold meats and cheeses, IPODERAC sells this cheese unbranded and Unilac sells it under its own name, mainly to supermarkets.

2. Ferrer & Associates—This wine distributor sells Villa Nolasco–brand cheeses to French restaurants, Price Club, and Carrefour Supermarkets.

3. Restaurants—IPODERAC sells directly to a few high-class restaurants in Mexico City, Puebla, and Cancún.

4. Supermarkets—Direct sales to HEBS, a Texas supermarket chain with two stores in Monterrey, and Soriana, a Mexican supermarket in Monterrey.

In addition to imports, Agustín cited three main competitors with brands, plus numerous small producers. Although he had little quantitative data on market size and growth, he pointed to imports as being over a million dollars in the first semester of 1994. Additionally, he indicated that he even had U.S. buyers interested. Agustín pointed to the quality of the Villa Nolasco cheeses as competitively important and to his policy of pricing slightly below competition, stating that "we believe in quality before charity. It's important that people come back and buy the cheese more than once."[1] The food and beverage buyer at the Four Seasons restaurant in Mexico City commented, "I can buy imported French cheeses for less money, but IPODERAC cheeses are such good products, I buy from them instead."[2] Agustín added, "Another competitive advantage is our character as a charitable organization. This makes the sale easier and the customer more receptive toward our conditions, such as only 15 days credit and no merchandise returns. My clients know that if they don't pay me on time, it is the children who will not eat." The Villa Nolasco label stated that "100% of the profits to the producer from the sale of this cheese is destined to the care, education, and development of abandoned children of our country."

The sales of cheese had grown to the point in mid-1998 that demand exceeded IPODERAC's production capacity. Agustín exclaimed, "Last week I sold 50,000 pesos of cheese but could not fill orders for another 12,000 pesos due to the lack of milk."[3] This situation focused attention on Villa Nolasco's goat milk production.

Production

Agustín had increased the size and quality of the herd from 30 to 263 through purchases, breeding, and artificial insemination, using semen imported from France. A goat begins milk production at 16 months and continues for 60 months. Each goat gives birth, on average, to 1.8 offspring, of which 45% are female. The males are consumed or sold. During its 305 days of lactation per year, the goat produces, on average, 2.5 liters per day or 750 liters annually, compared to national averages of 400 liters in Mexico and 900 in France. The expanding herd required increasingly careful attention in feeding, hygiene, and milking. The goats are fed alfalfa cut fresh daily from the farm's own fields; the climate allows ten harvests per year. Six acres can produce enough to feed 250 goats for a year. Additionally, purchased feed concentrate is fed to the goats (three kilos for every kilo of milk produced) while they are being milked in the milking stalls. The boys carried out these husbandry tasks under the supervision of one employee, an outside veterinarian, and Agustín. The growing demands of the operation led one of the educators to remark, "Here the goats are most important. They are capturing all of Agustín's attention."

To offset the shortage of milk from the farm, Agustín purchased goat milk from two nearby farmers whose operations were less technologically advanced than Villa Nolasco but still yielded an acceptable quality of raw milk. Other quality suppliers of goat milk had not been found. He also bought cow milk, which was readily available. The purchased goat milk cost about US$0.36/liter [3.10 pesos], which Agustín estimated to be slightly more than Villa Nolasco's cost of production and about $0.05 more than cow milk. In 1997, IPODERAC purchased 59,068 liters of goat milk and 43,062 liters of cow milk. Agustín believed that being able to offer the scarcer goat cheese is what enabled him to also sell the cow cheese.

Processing

The cheese production was done in a 170-square-meter building next to the farm's garage and near the bakery that produced the farm's bread. An expansion of the cheesery in March of 1998 gave it the capacity to process 3,000 liters per day. The operation processed daily an average of 350 liters of goat milk and 250 liters of cow milk to produce about 400 units of cheese. These included five types of goat cheese: Boursin (multiple flavors), Selles-sur-cher, Saint-Maure (aged and fresh), Valancay (with or without ash), and Feta; four types of cow cheese: Camembert, Fromage Blanc, Brie, and Reblochon; and two types of mixed goat and cow cheese: Tomme de Chevre and Flor de Atlixco. The cheese was made using French handmade techniques that did not use artificial colors or aromatics or chemical preservatives. Milk production was seasonal, peaking in July and August and lowest in November and December when demand was highest. To offset these cycles, the product could be stored in freezers until needed.

Quality control was handled through tasting by the Swiss expert and Agustín as needed but not on a regularly scheduled basis. The workforce in the processing facility was seven paid employees and only two boys, as the growing quality requirements and working hours no longer coincided with the children's abilities and schedule. One of the employees was an alumnus of IPODERAC who learned the cheese-making business at Villa Nolasco and returned to work there after graduating.

Challenges

Agustín was greatly encouraged by the progress made in the first four months of 1998 (see **Exhibit 4.1.5**, "1998 Partial

	Pesos		US$
INCOME			
Donations:			
Board fund-raising	57,995		
Director fund-raising	40,436	98,431	11,580
Production Revenues:			
Cheese sales[a]	770,582		
Goat sales	3,045	773,627	91,015
Total Income		872,058	102,590
COSTS			
Production:			
Alfalfa and vegetables	43,046		
Animals	68,218		
Cheesery	227,430	338,695	39,846
Children:			
Educators, housing, food, health, schooling		458,110	53,895
Administration:			
Salaries, taxes, office, depreciation		139,427	16,403
Total Costs		936,232[b]	110,144[b]
SURPLUS/(DEFICIT)		(64,174)	(7,550)

Exhibit 4.1.5   IPODERAC Financial Results, January–April 1998

a. Units of cheese sold—32,096 at an average price of 24.27 pesos.

   Liters of milk processed—Goat: 20,519; Cow: 50,829.

b. Total costs includes depreciation charges of 101,439 pesos.

Income Statement"), but he saw several operating and strategic challenges.

Milk Supply

To overcome the shortage of raw milk, Agustín formulated a proposal aimed at expanding the herd size at Villa Nolasco to 500. This herd would yield a daily production of 1,200 liters. This project also would promote the development of goat milking herds among small farmers in the area. The Villa Nolasco herd would be able to supply farmers annually 100 females ages 3 to 7 months and 43 males for breeding to create three herds of about 45 head.

The concept was for Villa Nolasco to act as a provider of animals and technical assistance to small farmers wishing to start or improve their goatherds and generate a new source of income. In the past, many farmers had visited the farm to learn informally about goat raising and milk production. Agustín explained that, in general, goats were "the poor man's cows." They often served as a "savings account," with a few being purchased young and raised and grazed in a rudimentary fashion by family members. The goats would be sold when there was a need for cash or butchered on special occasions. Generally they were not milked. In the proposed project, Villa Nolasco would donate the goats to a local development agency that would select and finance the small farmers, who would "pay" for the goats over five years with new goats bred from their herds. These goats, in turn, would serve to create milking herds for other farmers. Villa Nolasco would promise to buy the milk production of these new farmers at the prevailing market price, if they wished to sell to them.

To finance the project, Agustín planned to submit a request to the Mexican Foundation for Rural Development. The costs were estimated as follows:

1. Expansion of the corrals, food storage area, and watchman's room	$15,000
2. Alfalfa for 250 additional goats for one year	8,000
3. Feed grain for 7 months until birthing and lactation (0.3kg./day/goat = 21 tons @ $235/ton)	5,000
4. Goats—250 9-month-olds @ $165/goat	42,000
Total	$70,000

Marketing

Agustín was encouraged by the positive reception of his cheeses and by the strong demand. However, he was concerned by the potential competitive threat posed by the possible entrance of very large dairy products processors such as Nestlé and Alpura, who, Agustín believed, had made studies of the goat cheese market. In addition, he had just learned that Normex, a company in northern Mexico producing 10,000 liters of goat milk daily, had contracted a French specialist in goat cheese processing. He wondered what he should do to strengthen Villa Nolasco's market position. He also wondered whether or not he should pursue the export market in the United States.

Organization

IPODERAC's expanding commercial operations stretched Agustín's time even further. The growing demands also led him to express doubts about the adequacy of his managerial knowledge, in spite of his continuous process of self-education through reading and practice. He wondered what staff configuration and organizational structure would best equip IPODERAC for the future and what it would take to attract and retain talented and committed people.

He also wondered what, if anything, he should do with IPODERAC's board of trustees. The board ran the annual raffle and some other fund-raising events and met formally once a year. It basically went along with whatever the administration wanted to do. Most of the 15 trustees had served for over 10 years and several since the inception. Agustín indicated that most of the trustees felt that IPODERAC was quite successful and did not see any need for significant changes. However, one trustee who had been on the board for four years stated, "The board needs to be restructured; it needs younger people."

Case Study

One of Boys' Houses

Boys' Bedroom

Boys' Computer Room

Exhibit 4.1.6   Vistas of Villa Nolasco

Library; Volunteers With Boys

Vegetable Garden

Goatherd

Exhibit 4.1.6   *(Continued)*

(Continued)

Boys Tending Goat

Goat Milking Stalls

Cheese-processing Operations

Exhibit 4.1.6

Finished Cheese Products

Exhibit 4.1.6

Mission and Vision

The improving financial prospects of IPODERAC led Agustín and other staff members to engage in a collective reflection on IPODERAC's mission and vision. This led Agustín to propose the following possible mission definition:

> Our mission is to help the most unprotected children in our country and the organizations that assist them so that they have opportunities for a life of dignity and the capacity to improve their life conditions.

This would be achieved through the following programs:

1. Villa Nolasco

2. Financing and developing projects that care for abandoned street children

3. Financing projects that prevent children from turning to the streets

4. Direct help to organizations that work with rural people to enable them to remain in the countryside

Agustín thought that it was now important to indicate that IPODERAC had a mission larger than Villa Nolasco. However, the organization had to consider carefully the merits and feasibility of the strategic issue of whether to expand the number of boys cared for at Villa Nolasco or to set up similar centers elsewhere or to help others do that. Agustín knew that the decisions and actions taken now would fundamentally shape the direction and viability of IPODERAC as it entered the next century.[4]

NOTES

1. *Food Arts*, June 1997.
2. Ibid.
3. Exchange rate in May 1998 US$1.00 = 8.5 pesos.
4. Villa Nolasco is currently still in operation.

Case Study 4.2.

Newman's Own, Inc.

"Shameless exploitation in pursuit of the common good."

—Company motto

Paul Newman, distinguished actor and social entrepreneur, recalled in August 1998 the seeds that gave birth to his food company about twenty years earlier:

> We used to take the kids out and sing Christmas carols for the neighbors. One Christmas I decided to take old empty wine bottles and fill them with my salad dressing, put ribbons around them, and give them to the neighbors. Then about the middle of January there were all these people beating on my door, saying, "Where's my refill!" So I thought it would just be fun to throw it into a couple of local

SOURCE NOTE: Copyright © Harvard Business School Publishing, case number 9-301-038. Used with permission.

This case was prepared by Professor James E. Austin with assistance from Dr. Catherine Overholt to serve as the basis for classroom discussion rather than to illustrate effective or ineffective administration.

delicatessens and sell it. We had no aspirations for it. Nothing big time.

From this inconspicuous beginning, Newman's Own grew into a multiproduct company with 1998 sales projected at nearly $100 million. More distinctively, however, Newman donated all of the company's after-tax profits to charity. Over its life, this social enterprise had distributed about $90 million to nearly 1,000 nonprofit organizations. The entrepreneurial undertaking had achieved impressive and unexpected results commercially and socially but faced significant challenges for the future. Andy Crowley, president of Ken's Foods and the bottler of Newman's original salad dressing, put forth a basic challenge: "Paul has to figure out what to do to perpetuate this."

COMPANY ORIGINS

Newman recounted the first step: "When I got the idea to put this stuff out, I turned to 'Hotch' (A.E. Hotchner), who had written my first really critically successful television show, was a neighbor in Westport, Connecticut, and whom I'd known since 1955. Hotch did a lot of the early leg work."

Hotchner recalled, "If ever there was an accident that turned into a beneficial undertaking, this was it. For years, Newman had been making his own salad dressing. Even in restaurants he would sometimes embarrass us by asking the waiter to bring olive oil, vinegar, mustard, and what not to the table, and he would mix it up. When he said, 'Why don't we get a proper bottler and put a few bottles out,' I thought, 'well, I'll just humor him and the thing is going to evaporate.' But he sort of persisted." In seeking

advice from the president of a major marketing corporation, Hotchner learned that big companies that launch a new product do consumer panels in multiple markets. They stand to lose a million dollars in the first year of a new-product launch. Newman proposed that they just use friends for a taste test, invest $40,000, buy some bottles, and put them out. "We will have lost that, but at least we will have been in the business." After encountering considerable difficulty in obtaining a bottler, Newman recalled, "It went from just a lark to some kind of real challenge."

In the process, Hotchner got connected with David Kalman, a food broker. Kalman stated, "Because it was a small company consisting of an actor and a writer, they didn't have the business acumen for selling food. They knew they wanted to get involved but didn't know how to get there." Kalman approached a small bottler of salad dressing, Ken's Steak House in Boston (Ken's Foods), that sold its regionally marketed product to Stew Leonard's Supermarket in Norwalk, Connecticut, a Kalman client. Kalman recalled that the bottler's first response to the proposal was, "Are you crazy?" Andy Crowley, Ken's president, commented on his reaction then: "I wrote a memo to my father and business partner asking, 'Do we want to get involved with an actor, race car driver, and part-time cook?'" They decided to play it out and see what would happen.

Crowley indicated that over the next year, they prepared many different samples and often waited months to get a reaction from Newman, who was away making a movie. According to Crowley, there was "mounting frustration on all sides." Stew Leonard, owner of the Norwalk supermarket, finally arranged a meeting with Newman and Crowley on November 17, 1978, at his supermarket. They had a blind taste test of salad dressings using employees, and Newman's sample bottled by Ken's Foods ranked high. Leonard said, "Let's pack 2,000 bottles. You take 500 and I'll take the rest. You'll do it, right?" Crowley agreed.

With the bottler signed on, they turned to the label creation. When one of his associates asserted to Paul that "You will not be able to sell one bottle until you put your face on the label," Newman replied, "The chances of that are infinitesimal." The project hit a major roadblock. Newman explained how this deal-killer was averted: "When the face came on the bottle, I knew that the profits would have to go to charity. To make money off that would be so tacky. From this came the concept of circular exploitation. I allow my celebrity status to be exploited in order to sell stuff from which I then in turn channel the proceeds into good causes, hence the slogan of our company: 'shameless exploitation in pursuit of the common good.' It's a reciprocating engine." The label with Newman's likeness was drawn by the daughter of one of his buddies who was part of Newman's Formula One power car racing team.

Newman's Own was officially incorporated in 1982 as an S corporation with Newman as the sole stockholder.[1] They functioned for the first six months out of Newman's lawyers' office and then set up a small office in Westport. Newman recalled, "We were closing down our pool and so I took the pool furniture, umbrella and all, and put it in the office, where it still is today. A Ping-Pong table served as our conference table. It was all kind of a family operation." Hotchner managed the office and the staff of three. He pointed out, "The real challenge was that obviously Newman

wasn't a businessman nor was I, so very quickly, not only did we have to become businessmen, but we had to learn something about the food business, about the whole supermarket business, which is very complicated and ruthless. If you make a mistake, you can really get burned."

Newman's Own contracted Advantage Food Marketing, in which David Kalman was a partner, to serve as its master broker. Advantage managed all the sales and distribution functions, including recruiting independent brokers throughout the nation's main markets, negotiating and invoicing the supermarkets, managing the shipments from the company's manufacturers, and providing quality control of all products and processing facilities. Advantage received a 7% commission on sales net of trade discounts of which half was passed on to the independent brokers. Kalman stated the basic goal: "When you're a food broker, volume is the name of the game. We're looking to do more sales so that Newman can give out more money." To finance operations, the company borrowed from the bank with Newman's personal guarantee. Later the bank no longer required this. Newman's also negotiated a 20-day payment term from its contract manufacturers and a 10-day term from the supermarkets, although in practice, these clients took about 18 days to pay. The manufacturers held the inventories and billed Newman's Own when they shipped to the supermarkets.

PRODUCT DEVELOPMENT & GROWTH

From the original salad dressing, the company expanded its product line over the years to include other dressing varieties, spaghetti sauces and salsas, popcorn, lemonade, ice cream, and organic foods (see **Exhibit 4.2.1** for a timeline of product development and **Exhibit 4.2.3** for sales data). Hotchner described the product genesis process: "We don't really have a plan for a line of foods and when they will be introduced. We just get these ideas and then if something clicks, perhaps we'll go ahead." Newman continued to be heavily involved with tasting and approving every product: "We kind of do it on a case-by-case basis, but the products that seem to work best are the ones that people think that I could have somehow created in my kitchen." Kalman added another dimension: "Quality in food is the most important thing. We've always aimed to have the best in the category."

Salad Dressings

When Newman's first salad dressing was introduced, it was the only olive oil vinaigrette on the market with more than 51% olive oil. However, one *New York Times* food critic stated that it had a metallic taste. They quickly determined that this was due to the use of dehydrated garlic and onions, a standard industry practice. Newman switched to fresh ingredients, and, counter to industry people's assertions that it would spoil, this resulted in an even more novel and well-received dressing. Sales took off and the $40,000 original investment was recouped in a matter of months. Gross sales the first year were about $3.2 million, generating pretax profits of $373,000.

Andy Crowley commented on the process of developing the salad dressing line, "You can't market anything that Paul doesn't like, although you're not dealing with an ego and that makes him very easy to approach. He's been very intuitive and very prone to taking gambles. To tell him, 'You really can't do that,' his immediate response is, 'Why not?' For example, the industry wisdom is that labels should have a family appeal. His labels don't. The legends on the back labels are Paul. Each product and label is a character all to itself." Hotchner described the label creation process: "I usually write something and then Paul will poke around with the original. It is fun doing them and people get a chuckle out of them." (See **Exhibit 4.2.2** for label legend examples.)

After the initial adjustment to the ingredients, nothing further was done in salad dressings until the company agreed in 1990 to an exclusive placement of Newman's Own dressing in Burger King's salad section. Burger King also wanted to have Ranch, French, Light Italian, and Blue Cheese varieties in addition to the original, so Newman worked with a food consultant and his bottler, Ken's Foods, to develop these new formulations. These arrangements were made at very high levels and, according to Crowley, did not make the Burger King purchasing agents very happy because the Newman's dressings cost significantly more than generic alternatives. Newman's Own labels were displayed prominently in the salad bars. This relationship represented an important revenue source and continued for about 4 years. After it ended, Newman's Own added the Ranch dressing to its bottled line, because it had been so well received by Burger King customers. However, the bottled versions did not measure up to the quality of the Burger King offering. The unbottled form was more like a refrigerated

1982	*Oil & Vinegar Dressing*
1983	*Marinara Sauce* *Marinara Mush*
1984	*Jar Popcorn*
1986	*MicroWave Popcorn–Butter & Natural* *Sockarooni Sauce (August)* *Lemonade*
1990	*Diavolo Sauce (January)* *No Salt MicroWave Popcorn (June)*
1991	*Lite Butter/Lite Natural MicroWave Popcorn (April)* *Hot, Medium, Mild Salsa (April)*
1993	*Organic Pretzels*
1994	*Ranch Dressing (April)* *Bambolina Sauce (April)* *Caesar Dressing (June)*
1995	*Organic Candy Bar*
1996	*Say Cheese Sauce (October)* *Balsamic Vinaigrette Dressing (November)*
1997	*Garlic & Pepper Sauce (September)* *Pineapple Salsa (September)* *Peach Salsa (September)* *Roasted Garlic Salsa (September)* *FigNewman's*
1998	*Steak Sauce (April)* *Parisienne Dijon Lime Dressing (May)*

Exhibit 4.2.1   Newman's Own Product Introductions

Balsamic Vinaigrette

In 1602, in Modena, two brothers of the Vinegar clan, Balsa and Mick, due to a piddling insult, duelled to their deaths. Their grieving mother, Violetta Vinegar, who was pressing a new grape from their vineyard, named it in their memory—Balsa-Mick Vinegar. Thanks to Newman's Own, their names live on.©

Sockarooni Spaghetti Sauce

Sackarooni/Sock-it-to 'em Spaghetti Sauce all alone, by itself, just sitting there naked, will blow your socks off! Take yourself back to 1833 when Neapolitan adventures in St. Louis concocted this specific sauce, ingesting same, gathering strength, courage, endurance and wit to wrassle 1000 pound bears. 150 years later I fortify myself with Sockarooni to wrassle my own private bear—which is "jist gittin' through the day." ©

All Natural Salsa

Take some paper, take some glue,

Build a plane of balsa.

It won't fly as fast you

Can go on Newman's salsa. ©

Old Fashioned Lemonade

The marathon in Africa . . . I'm halfway out and barely chugging. Mountain coming! Liquid needed! What's around? Water's bitter! Beer's flat! Gator, Blah, Blah! . . . Fading fast. Then a vision—sweet Joanna!—tempting me with pale gold nectar . . . lemon is it? By golly! Lemonade? No, Lemon Aid! . . . Power added! Asphalt churning . . . Cruising home to victory! Hail Joanna! Filched the nectar (shameless hustler!)—In the market—Newman's Own!©

Picture Show Popcorn

I'll tell you how bad it is. Nobody gets trusted with popcorn—except me. That includes the FBI, the IRS, Tiffany's and concessionaires of any ilk. A good flick arrives on the local screen, you see ol' Newman scuttling across the lobby with a greasy brown paper bag of his homemade popcorn in one hand and—you guessed it—a machete in the other. Who's who lists a lot of one-armed people in my hometown. They got caught trying to muscle their way into my greasy brown paper bag. The way I feel—they got off easy. They should have been strung up.©

Newman's Own All Natural Ice Cream

In 1777, in the Alpine village of Uberotte, Baron "Buzz" Newman (The Original Newman from whence all subsequent Newmans sprung) was tending his herd of cows when a fierce, unforgiving ice storm flash-froze the entire herd and left them stark-stiff in their tracks. In the spring when the cows thawed, Buzz milked them like always. What came out Buzz sold as Iced Cream.

Every winter after that, Buzz froze all his cows stark-stiff in order to satisfy the growing demand for his Iced Cream. It was not until 1883 that Buzz's grandson, "Bubbles" Newman, the Rotter of Uberotten, invented the cuckoo clock and also hit upon the revolutionary idea of freezing the milk instead of the cows. He also created flavors by tossing in Alpine fruits like Elderberry, Youngerberry, and Berri-Berri.

The current Newman is not only proud to carry on the family tradition, but also honored to fulfill the exalted pledge of his ancestors:

"100% COW! NO BULL!!" ©

Exhibit 4.2.2   Newman's Own Label Legends

fresh delivery system with a three-month turnover in comparison to the bottled supermarket sales that spent up to 12 months on the shelf in nonrefrigerated conditions.

Newman's added Caesar in 1994 and Balsamic Vinaigrette in 1996, although the original Oil & Vinegar dressing remained the company's top seller. Salad dressings accounted for 38% of Newman's Own total revenues in 1998. Crowley discussed the salad dressing market: "The market has grown from $300 million to $1 billion since we began and expands about 2% annually. The novel varieties are where the growth is, although that is a coastal phenomenon. In the heartland, you still pave the street with Ranch. Ranch, Italian, Thousand Island are 85% of the market. Ken's produces 40 dressings under its own label, of which the biggest sellers are light Caesar and Light Raspberry Walnut. In a consumer focus group that we did for our products, we discovered that people consistently placed Newman's Own in the high-quality segment." In the 52-week period ending April 19, 1998, Newman's six salad dressings sales were $30.5 million, up 16.5% from the previous year, and amounting to a 2.6% market share (with an average unit price of $2.36). This compared to Kraft's market share of 29.5% (average price of $2.05), Wishbone's 17.2% ($1.94), Hidden Valley's 13.6% ($2.86), five other brands each at 5% or less, including private labels, and Ken's at 4.6% ($1.26).

Crowley indicated that "We're also a competitor of Newman's but we go to market differently. This does create tension at times with some people, but where are they going to go? They could go to some fringe players, but with us, Newman's has never ever been in trouble with one of its products. And when we negotiate with our glass

supplier for 8 million 8-ounce jars, his million jars are right there with ours. When we are shipping out a truckload to Stop & Shop and he has only three skids, his go out at the truckload rate. He derives the benefit. Over the 16 years, our unit price to Newman has increased only 9%. It's two-way. It's not a short-term situation. There's a mutual sense of loyalty, and Newman is a very loyal guy." Newman commented, "It's a long-standing relationship which is 99% friendly and 1% competitive. To some extent, they use their profits that they make from us to create another competitive line, which is troublesome, although we do try to stay out of each other's price range."

Since 1982, Ken's Foods grew from a $10-million company to $220 million. Newman's Own sales reached 18% of Ken's total business at one point and in 1998 constituted about 5%. Crowley commented on the relationship, "Monetarily they are significant but emotionally they're also very important to us. He forces you to get involved. You don't just pack for Newman and not give back. We're closer to him today at 5% than we were at 18%." Newman's also used a California bottler to handle its salad dressing production for the West Coast.

Sauces

About six months after the first salad dressing was launched, the second product category of spaghetti sauce was developed. Hotchner recalled the beginning: "Newman called me up one day and said that he'd just come home and found a bottle of spaghetti sauce that he tried out and he said, 'It's absolutely terrible; all full of sugar and preservatives, and it's got more chemicals in it than anything else. Why don't we come up with a spaghetti sauce that's full of fresh stuff?' Nobody had ever put out a sauce like that before. And we even had the audacity to call it 'Industrial Strength Spaghetti Sauce.' The naysayers said you have to put something like garden fresh on it, but they were proven wrong." But again, Newman's Own needed to find someone who would manufacture and bottle the product.

David Kalman approached Ed Salzano, executive vice president of Cantisano Foods, Inc., a private-label contract packer in Rochester, New York, and one of Advantage's clients. Salzano recalled, "David, being a very tenacious and brash guy, stuck a bottle of Newman's Own in front of me and says, 'Look what we've done for this. If you guys could make a great product, we could sell it.' So I came back at him and said, 'Give me Newman's recipe for his spaghetti sauce.' We played with it to see how we could commercially adapt it and were sending samples back and forth for Newman to taste. David would come back and say, 'Paul likes it, but try to change this.' We didn't know where we were going with it. One day David said to go buy *Time* magazine. Newman's picture was on the cover and there's an eight-page article about him and his company starting to give profits to charity. And there was one line in there that his next product will be his Industrial Strength Venetian Style Spaghetti Sauce. That's how in 1983 we found out that we were packing spaghetti sauce for them."

Salzano indicated that many personalities had approached the company to make a sauce, licensing their name to Cantisano for a royalty. "The difference with Paul Newman is that he took title to the goods and then he resold it. So the fact that he was willing to put his money at risk

made us feel that this man was really committed to this program. The relationship with Newman is one that is very unique, because we started to partner with him from the standpoint of looking at the good things that he was doing and said, 'Here's someone that has a tremendous name and a tremendous heart.' And if we can help his business grow, we always felt that it was in our business's best interest. We took a whole different approach to Newman's Own."

The initial Newman's Own sauces were the first of the chunkier, all-natural-types of sauces introduced to the marketplace. Cantisano played a supportive role in this development process, testing out recipe ideas from Newman and sharing theirs. Salzano commented, "We looked at Newman's as a place where we brought a new idea to first. We also tried to be proactive in analyzing for them the categories that we compete in because we have a greater level of sophistication in the food business." After producing several varieties of spaghetti sauce, Cantisano proposed developing in 1991 a very different type of salsa as a new-product category. "By that point, we had a good feel for what Paul's tastes were like: spicy, chunky, with a bite." In 1997, Newman's added three more salsa varieties. Newman's also sold in foreign markets a small pasta line produced in Italy.

Cantisano chose not to develop its own products in the premium end because "we felt why compete with a key customer." They also refused the request to pack a sauce for Frank Sinatra because they deemed that it would be a conflict of interest. Salzano stated, "Any connections that we had with the trade, we were willing to share with Newman's Own because of the good that he's doing. It really came down to the cause and the mission. We would even play on the strength of our relationship with the major grocery executives and say, 'Hey, the more money Newman gives you, the less he can help other people.' It's easier to beat up corporation XYZ because they're in it for the money. Newman's in it for the love."

Salzano indicated that the impact of Newman's on Cantisano Foods was significant: "It allowed us in our early stages of development to go forward and reinvest into our business because we looked at his brand as stability because of our commitment to Newman and his to us. Newman is an extremely loyal individual. It has been very good all the way around. Our company has grown much more than tenfold."

The total U.S. sauce market grew in size similar to that of dressings. Premium sauces constituted 25% of the total pasta sauce market. Newman's Own six sauces held a 7.3% share of the premium segment behind Classico (38.6%), Five Brothers (29%), and Barilla (16.2%). Newman's sauces were the lowest-priced brand in the premium segment, being 13% below Classico, 8% under Barilla, but 19% above the mainline segment. Sauce sales accounted for 31.7% of the company's 1998 revenues. The salsa products produced 11.5% of the company's sales. Salzano indicated that sales of private-label brands were increasing, particularly in the premium segment.

Popcorn

Newman stated, "I've always been a popcorn freak, so that was a natural."

But developing a product turned out to be difficult. Hotchner recounted, "That was the longest pursuit. Either the popcorn didn't pop right or taste right. It took us two years until we found a grower that produced a hybrid especially for us." The result was a higher pop ratio and a fuller bag that earned a Number 1 ranking in a consumer magazine. They developed kernels in jars in 1984 and then a microwave version in 1986 as that form became more dominant. Newman's offered four popcorn varieties, which accounted for 8.8% of company sales in 1998.

Lemonade

The idea for the lemonade came from Joanne Woodward, the renowned actress married to Paul Newman. In 1986, she provided a family recipe from her native state of Georgia. The concentrate for the lemonade was produced by a contract manufacturer in California and then shipped to dairies around the country. This first entrant into the beverage category accounted for 4.2% of sales.

Ice Cream

Unlike the other products, the manufacturer, Ben & Jerry's Ice Cream Company, proposed this product. Ben Cohen collaborated with Paul on various social sector undertakings. Newman noted, "We've had lots of products from manufacturers whom we've turned down because they didn't come up to quality or our taste." Ben & Jerry's paid Newman's Own a royalty and handled all the ice cream production and distribution. Tom Indoe, Newman's Own current chief operating officer, indicated that this type of licensing arrangement derived a smaller contribution than the other products marketed directly by Newman's Own.

Newman's Own Organics

One of Newman's five daughters was very interested in organic foods and had the idea. Newman recalled, "Nell came to me with a friend of hers, who had been in the swimming pool business, and proposed that they create the organic food subsidiary. So, they educated themselves and were on partial salary for some period of time to figure out what products they wanted to come out with." They produced pretzels as their main product. They became the dominant player in this small niche market. They also made an organic chocolate candy bar. Sales for the first seven months of 1998 amounted to $1.3 million.

An organic cookie to be called FigNewmans followed. Because of possible trademark infringements, Paul Newman wrote the president of Nabisco and asked for permission to use the name, indicated that it would not be competing against Nabisco's Fig Newtons, and that the proceeds would go to charity. The president wrote back indicating that they could not give permission because of the precedent it would set, but if Newman's would pay a royalty, say, $1, then it could be arranged. Newman agreed and thanked him for his

generosity. The cookie was launched in 1998 and sales for the first seven months were $751,000. Newman commented, "It's just delicious to watch the organic business grow."

Tom Indoe explained the relationship of the Organics operation to Newman's Own: "It's almost like a division. They're part of the S corporation and they have to survive on their own. We do their administrative stuff, help with quality assurance, and provide sales support, although they're more into health food stores than grocery stores. Through our relationship with KMart, we got them into that chain. If they need help, they've got it, and if we ask them to do something, they usually oblige."

PHILANTHROPIC ACTIVITIES

In 1997, Newman's Own generated gross sales of $62.6 million, producing a before-tax surplus of $8.5 million. These annual flows had enabled Newman to contribute over $90 million to charities since the inception of the company. (See **Exhibit 4.2.4** for balance sheet.)

Philosophy

Newman observed, "I wish I could lay claim to some terribly philanthropic instinct in my base nature, but it was just a combination of circumstances. If it had stayed small and had just been in 14 local stores, it would never have been charitable. It was just an abhorrence of combining tackiness, exploitation, and putting money in my pockets, which was excessive in

1982	3,204
1995	57,859
1996	60,498
1997	65,699

1998 *January–July*

(a) By Product:	Dressings	Sauces	Salsas	Popcorn	Steak Sauce	Lemonade	Pasta
	17,864	14,900	5,510	4,125	2,045	1,954	539
Gross Margin	48.4%	41.6%	44.2%	50.1%	66.7%	43.2%	20.2%

(b) Total	
Sales	46,937
Trade Allowances	9,908
Cost of Sales	25,276
Gross Profit	11,751
Directly Attributable Expenses	4,918
G&A	2,204
Misc. Income	435
Misc. Expenses	54
Pre-tax Surplus	4,999

Exhibit 4.2.3   Sales ($000)

every direction. I believe that people who acknowledge luck in their lives are more generous than those who only acknowledge their own rugged individualism. I am moved by the benevolence of luck in my life and the brutality of luck in others. One thing that really bothers me is what I call 'noisy philanthropy.' Philanthropy should be anonymous, but in order for this to be successful, you have to be noisy. Because when a guy walks up to the shelf and says, 'Should I take this one or that one?' you've got to let him know that the money goes to a good purpose. So there goes all your

ASSETS		LIABILITIES	
Current Assets			
Cash & Securities	2,442	Accounts Payable	2,429
Accounts Receivable	2,141	Commissions Payable	352
Inventory	1,964	Other Payables	610
Prepaid Coupons	394	Advance to N.O. Organics	26
Other	213	Total liabilities	3,417
Total current assets	9,781		
Fixed Assets		*CAPITAL*	
Furniture & Fixtures	398	Capital Stock	10
Less: Depreciation	314	Capital Surplus	1,000
Total fixed assets	84	Retained Earnings 1/1/98	815
		Operating Surplus 7/31/98	4,908
Other Assets	285	**Total capital**	6,734
Total assets	10,150	**Total capital & liabilities**	10,150

Exhibit 4.2.4   Statement of Assets and Liabilities as of 7/31/98 ($000)*

*Includes Newman's Own Organics: Assets—$820,000; Liabilities—$772,000; Capital—$820,000.

anonymity and the whole thing that you really cherish. Publicize the generosity in order to become more generous. That's been the most difficult part of it."

Beneficiaries

Hotchner was involved since the beginning with Newman in deciding to whom to give their social surplus. He explained an important juncture: "After some years, Paul said, 'We really ought to have our own charity. We don't have one that we're identified with. We've been getting a lot of requests from parents of children stricken with cancer. Why don't we set up a really unusual camp for these children where we can give them a wonderful time.' That was the beginning of the Hole in the Wall Gang[2] Camp in Connecticut." The camp was built in 1987 at an initial cost of $10 million, and now there are 5 associated camps in the United States, Ireland, and France, which have benefited 15,000 children. Each camp had its own board of governors and is largely financially independent of

Newman's Own, although Paul helped found each one and remained personally involved. Other leaders had been attracted to the cause; for example, General H. Norman Schwarzkopf was a cofounder of the Florida camp. (See **Exhibit 4.2.5** for the camp association's mission statement.)

Hotch, who is on the Connecticut camp's board of directors, remarked, "It's wonderful for these kids. That's been the major source of satisfaction for me and I'm pretty sure for Paul." Newman added, "It's certainly a big joy, but buying a bus for migrant farm workers in Florida can make the whole year work for them. And the ten grand that you give to some soup kitchen or the $25,000 that goes to a program for wayward kids makes huge differences, but we're very whimsical about how we choose these."

Grant Process

Newman's Own has one of its 15 employees dedicated full-time to handling the unsolicited grant requests. They receive hundreds weekly. Applicants can call the company's voice mail day or night to request an application. Hotchner heads the charity operations and discusses with Newman any requests that need immediate response. The majority of the requests are accumulated in a loose-leaf book broken down by category (arts, education, health, environment, children, elderly, animal protection, women's issues, and peace/human rights). Each page describes a charity, its request, and its overhead as a percentage of program costs. Usually in November, Newman and Hotchner sit down and go through the book, making their choices. They designate the remaining $3–$4 million not already allocated to preferred charities that receive annual repeat donations or to some organizations endorsed by their friends. Newman noted, "If their requests are worthwhile, why not let your friends use your money." There are no rigid allocation formulas, but they tend to spread

---

MISSION:

The mission of The Association is to foster The Hole in the Wall Gang Camp program for children who have cancer, leukemia and other serious diseases, and who, because of their illnesses, its treatments, or its complications, cannot participate in ordinary childhood activities. With all the amenities of traditional summer camps, each of these centers provide[s] support and education for children and families, and the volunteers, health professionals, and policy makers who serve these children.

PHILOSOPHY OF CARE:

The Hole in the Wall Gang philosophy holds that arts and adventure programming engages participants socially, emotionally, and physically, challenging them to grow beyond perceived limits, and enhancing their self-esteem—important for coping with a difficult present and future. The Hole in the Wall Gang centers provide 24-hour medical supervision and are recognized by doctors as important medical facilities for children who otherwise could not leave the vicinity of a local hospital or participate in ordinary childhood activities.

Exhibit 4.2.5   Hole in the Wall Gang Association

the donations across different sectors, geographically, and favor smaller non-profits that would have greater difficulty raising funds. Hotchner explained, "Overall our bent is towards the very young and the very old, who really don't get funded enough. We don't do much in the mainstream."

Involvement of Business Associates

Newman noted that "All of our partners have been very, very generous in terms of helping the camps and providing sponsorships." David Kalman recalled, "I was there when they announced the camp and I never knew that kids had cancer. I called my partner and said, 'We now have a charity.' My partners and I have given hundreds of thousands of dollars to the camp because we want to. Nobody told us to." Andy Crowley said, "We rent the Big Apple Circus for a day in Boston and invite 1,500 kids from the oncology wards. We do considerable fund-raising for the camp. Last year we raised over $150,000 squeezing our vendors. You wouldn't be a vendor if you weren't involved. It is a form of being loyal back. Everybody should do something. I could do it on my own or I could work at this." Ed Salzano spoke similarly, "We've made the Hole in the Wall Gang Camp our charity of choice, and I sit on the board of the camp. It has also exposed me personally and my associates to what a true philanthropist and what social consciousness is all about. It's different than organizations sponsoring things for the advertising value. Being involved in giving away $90 million to help other people and children with cancer is something that I could have never dreamed about."

The supermarkets also were involved. David Kalman pointed out that "Newman's Own's social purpose meant we have something to talk about other than price. What do you do when you walk into a chain store and you've got ten guys behind you in the waiting room all selling the same item? They bring the money bags with them and say, 'Okay, we're going to put in 10 SKUs'[3] and drop down $100,000. We can't do that." Newman's Own encouraged supermarkets to make suggestions of charities in their own communities. They called these "goodwill alliances." Newman had 85 such alliances in 1997 and contributed around $750,000 to these charities, which returned funds to the communities from which they originated.

MANAGEMENT TRANSITION

With the growth of the company came the need to strengthen the company's managerial resources. Newman explained, "About five years ago the company got to be around $60 million and was getting really complicated, yet it had a writer and an actor running it. We didn't have the marketing skills, the computer skills, any of the necessary skills. We really had to get a COO." The first operating executive the company hired was an individual with extensive consulting background but not in the food industry. Hotchner remarked on the transition, "It turned out to be difficult because this is no ordinary company and it doesn't go by ordinary rules. It requires a certain amount of imagination and certainly has to do with a relaxed attitude, and yet you have to watch the bottom line. One of our mottoes on the wall is '*If we have a plan, we're screwed,*' so we never had a plan. It was just sort of follow your nose and try not to make any major mistakes that would put you out of business." The new executive, who was engaged in late 1997, was Tom Indoe, whose whole career had been in consumer goods and food marketing. He commented on the challenge of taking charge, "You've got to establish credibility with Paul and everybody here. And I guess you have to have a small ego."

The New COO

Tom Indoe worked in sales and marketing for about three decades, first for Sterling Drug, then for RJR, which acquired DelMonte, Morton Frozen Foods, and Nabisco. Next he ran a $20-million food company. Newman commented on what he was looking for in a manager: "someone with a lot of marketing skills, who could run a business, was intimately connected with the grocery business, and really good with people. Tom fit the bill. I liked his personality—outgoing and straightforward. And Tom has made some sacrifices from a salary standpoint. It's not like you're working for a completely for-profit enterprise." Indoe commented on his motivation in joining Newman's Own as chief operating officer and senior vice president: "First, they had potential for tremendous growth. The second thing was the social benefit. I think everybody at one

point says, at the end of the day, what am I going to be known for? What did I really contribute? Is it that we put more Planter's Peanuts on the store shelf? So, here I get to run a consumer company that does a lot of good things." After joining Newman's on December 1, 1997, Indoe took actions in several areas.

Planning

When Indoe arrived, he was "shocked" to discover that the company had never had a budget, so he and the staff constructed one for 1998. He remarked, "We didn't know how well or poorly we were doing in specific areas so that we could focus against some of those. So we started to develop a game plan of what we were going to improve in our business." This plan encompassed several of the following initiatives.

Distribution

In order to manage the company's network of 69 independent brokers[4] more effectively, the four regional managers who worked under Advantage Food Marketing's operation were brought onto the Newman's Own payroll under the supervision of the COO. Newman's was a very important client for Advantage, and this shift of responsibility and authority caused some initial friction. However, David Kalman of Advantage remarked, "We've always wanted someone who understands the food business and knows what you're trying to say. We're on the same wave length and have the same aspirations to get the job done as Tom. But Paul is still boss."

Indoe's analysis of the distribution data revealed that all the supermarkets did not stock some products, for example, 16-ounce balsamic vinegar. "If we could get every store stocked up to 60%, it would mean an incremental $6 million in revenue." He organized his regional managers into a major effort to jack up distribution, paying the supermarkets "slotting allowances."[5] The result was a doubling of distribution in nearly every salad dressing. Before there were only two Newman's Own dressings in the grocery stores' top 100 sellers, and by August 1998, there were 5. For the sauce line, effort was concentrated on the best-selling products in the company's 15 core city and state markets.

Product Development

Newman's Own Ranch and Lite Italian dressings were not performing up to expectations and were deemed to be inferior to competition in quality. New and improved products were launched. A Parisienne Dijon Lime salad dressing was developed in collaboration with a French chef and was being market tested. The Steak Sauce was based on a recipe that Newman had discovered in California, and Indoe, whose previous work had exposed him to the attractive margins of steak sauce, pushed the product through to production by their California bottler. It was launched aggressively with $1 million in slotting allowances and other retailer discounts and coupons

(**Exhibit 4.2.6**). Sales for the steak sauce for the first seven months of 1998 were over $2 million.

Packaging

Two focus groups of 24 current consumers of Newman's Own products, all females, revealed that the quality of the pasta sauces was considered equal to competition but the packaging did not convey a premium sauce image. Working with Cantisano and the bottle vendor, Indoe improved the packaging without any incremental cost. Indoe also noted in his strategy plan that "the naming and labeling of pasta sauces have been very artistic by Newman and Hotch over the years with names like Sockarooni, Bombolina, and Say Cheese. We need to develop labeling that tells the consumer what is in the jar such as Tomatoes with Basil in the case of Bombolina." A labeling change was effected by August. Statements about Newman's charity efforts were placed on the labels and lid tops. A simple redesign of the labels was done to have consistency of Newman's face and some uniformity across all products. Indoe indicated that when he proposed the changes to Newman, Paul said, "I don't think this is a big deal. Use your own discretion."

Consumer Promotion

The consumer focus groups revealed several surprising findings to management: (1) Only about 35% knew that Paul Newman

Exhibit 4.2.6   Coupon Advertisement for Steak Sauce

donated all the profits to charity; (2) no one knew that over $90 million had been donated since the company's beginning; (3) less than 25% knew that the products were all natural; and (4) many were surprised by the broad range of products in the Newman line. In response, Indoe delivered hand tags to the brokers to place on the salad dressings that indicated the $90 million in donations and some of the charities that benefited. In response, 33 million Family Supplement Inserts with coupons, product picture, and the charity message appeared in Sunday newspapers in June (**Exhibit 4.2.7**).

Trade Promotion

In 1997, the company spent $6.9 million on 52-week discounts to the trade to create everyday low pricing to customers and another $6 million on advertising allowances. Indoe doubted the effectiveness of these discounts and allowances in terms of stimulating extra push by the trade and so he was reconsidering them.

FUTURE CHALLENGES

As Newman's Own moved into the twenty-first century, it faced several challenges and issues related to competition, advertising and promotion, products, and philanthropy.

Competition

Tom Indoe asserted, "The biggest challenge we have as a smaller company is how do we compete with Kraft? And there's

Barilla, Unilever, and Campbell's. These are billion-dollar companies." Hotchner added, "The competition is so demanding, we have to work hard just to keep running in place. The minute that we try to sit back on what we've got in the way of products or management or anything else, I think we're in trouble." Newman reflected, "My father ran a great sporting goods store in Cleveland, and although I worked there a lot as a kid, I never could find the allure of it. It wasn't until I got into the salad dressing business where the competition makes a killer out of you, could I understand what people mean by growing just for the sake of growing. There's no question there is a great romance to it. Our challenge is survival—just to stay alive in a competitive environment."

Ed Salzano pointed to the supermarket environment: "These chains today are so hungry that they really don't care whether they sell the product or not. When a new item comes out, manufacturers have to pay for the privilege of slotting that item on the shelf. Supermarkets look at what the profit is that supposedly this real estate generates and they secure that profit up front through slotting fees. If the product doesn't achieve the target sales figure within six months, it's discontinued. So they keep reselling these slots. There's product proliferation within categories, so there's always another manufacturer trying to come out with new things."

Advertising & Promotion

Newman contended that "One of the reasons this company really works is that

Exhibit 4.2.7   Sunday Newspaper Advertising Insert

we don't advertise. When the host of *Good Morning America* pulls our salad dressing out of his briefcase and talks about it, what do you need to advertise for? We penetrated the market very quickly because we didn't need to get name recognition." Hotchner added, "The expense of advertising for a company as small as ours is almost prohibitive today."

Salzano asserted, "You get to a point in a product development and a brand development that you either go up or down. You cannot stand still. And momentum is critical. The level that Newman's is at now, they must get the consumer to realize why they are on the shelf, why they're priced the way they are, and to make a consumer feel good about why they're buying that product. Not only does it taste good, but they're doing good. But Newman has been extremely shy about tooting his own horn about his charity work." Newman commented, "I'm not a very public person and all the public aspects of promotion are very difficult."

Crowley added, "All the other personality brands have profit motives. He has a distinctive difference: a good product at a fair price and all the profits go to charity. You had the Frank Sinatra spaghetti sauce, boom, gone. Paul is all on his own in this regard."

Products

The company needed to decide what actions were necessary regarding its product line. Was this the right mix? Should some be emphasized more than others? What new products, if any, should be developed and how?

One new product possibility was brought to Newman's attention by fellow actor Alan Alda, who discovered it while doing a documentary. It was a candy developed by a Yale doctor that helps treat the sores that develop inside the mouths of many people who have chemotherapy. Newman indicated, "We're toying with the idea of finding a candy manufacturer who would be willing to give up its profits and then possibly distributing through one of the pharmaceutical companies." Tom Indoe added, "In a normal company, you'd probably never be exposed to such a proposition. But at the end of the day, wouldn't it be neat to have this candy that takes pain away from these poor kids that have to go through chemotherapy." Tom continued, "This is really two companies, one that makes money and the other that gives it away. A big challenge is how do we measure ourselves."

New Philanthropic Initiative

Newman had been concerned for some time about the need to have corporations increase their philanthropic giving. He was joining with several other leaders, among whom were John Whitehead, the former chairman of Goldman Sachs; Paul Volcker, former federal reserve chairman; David Rockefeller and Walter Shipley, past and present chairmen of Chase; Ralph Larsen, chairman of Johnson & Johnson; Peter Malkin, a New York real estate developer; and Ben Cohen of Ben & Jerry's, to create a nonprofit center for promoting corporate philanthropy. Corporate contributions declined in inflation-adjusted dollars from a high of 2.3% of pretax profits in 1986 to 1.3% in 1996. The center's objective was to advocate for a 2% national goal. Corporate donations up to 10% of pretax income are tax deductible under existing laws. The center's founders viewed corporate philanthropy as "a strategic asset which contributes to improving stockholder value." They sought to represent the interests of shareholders of public companies who believe their companies should provide greater support to nonprofits. Achieving the 2% target would provide an additional $4 billion to the nonprofit sector.

Newman commented on the rationale, "The thing that makes the United States such an enviable place to invest in and to be in is that it's so stable. The more the gap starts to increase between the haves and have-nots, the rich and the poor, the employable and the unemployable, the less stability you're going to have, and the very great strength of the nation erodes. So if it's happening in your community today, you may be next week's victim. The whole sense of leadership is not to deal with things when they become crises, but to deal with them when they are problems. The second they become crises, they may not be manageable."

VISION

In looking to the future, Newman asserted that he would "like to see the company reach $250 million in sales and be able to support new philanthropic initiatives like the corporate philanthropy center. I don't want this thing to just dribble along and be a clearinghouse for a lot of people to collect salaries."

Continuity was on the minds of others. COO Tom Indoe stated, "Paul is 73, and unless he has a lease on life that nobody else has, he's not going to be here at some point." Ed Salzano echoed the concern, "If something happened to Paul, what happens to this business? The only threat there is to Newman's Own is not staying true to their mission. It's still a family-owned business, and how do you perpetuate a family-owned business?"

NOTES

1. S corporation profits are incorporated into the owner's total personal earnings and taxed accordingly.

2. The camp's name is derived from the Paul Newman–Robert Redford movie *Butch Cassidy and the Sundance Kid.*

3. SKU: Stock Keeping Unit refers to product category and subcategory, for example, Salad Dressing, 16-ounce & 8-ounce.

4. In addition to the grocery stores, Newman's had significant accounts with KMart (5.6% of 1998 sales), Amway-foreign markets (3.3%), the military (1.2%), and other sales to non-U.S. markets (1.9%).

5. Slotting allowances are like shelf space rental charges to get one's products into the stores.

CHAPTER 5

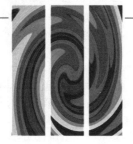

Crafting Alliances

Regardless of how successful a social enterprise is at mobilizing funds, most organizations will inevitably face resource and capacity constraints as a limiting factor to achieving their mission. The resources that any single organization brings to bear on a social problem are often dwarfed by the magnitude and complexity of most social problems. Thus, social entrepreneurs often pursue alliance approaches as a means to mobilizing resources, financial and nonfinancial, from the larger context and beyond their own organizational boundaries, to achieve increased mission impact. Social enterprise alliances among nonprofits, nonprofits and business, nonprofits and government, and even across all sectors in the form of tripartite alliances between nonprofit, government, and business have become increasingly common in recent years. Because alliances capitalize on the resources and capacities of more than one organization and capture synergies that would otherwise often go unrealized, they have the potential to generate mission impact far beyond what the individual contributors could achieve independently. This chapter first describes some alliance trends in the social sector and illustrates them with case examples. Next, we introduce a conceptual framework that can be helpful for developing an alliance strategy. Finally, we briefly introduce the chapter's two case studies, which offer readers an opportunity for in-depth analysis of a range of alliance approaches.

ALLIANCE TRENDS

Increased Competition

Increased competition due to a growing number of nonprofits coupled with recent overall declines in social sector funding have contributed to a dramatic increase in the number and form of social enterprise alliances. In the United States alone, the number of nonprofits doubled in number between 1982 and 1997,[1] and in the last decade, the number has increased an additional 64%.[2] Additionally, government funding, which makes up nearly one third of nonprofit revenues, has remained stagnant or declined over this same period,[3] while total giving has also declined. Beyond increased competition for funding, changes in public policy to foster competition such as vouchers for social services have also intensified competition among many social sector organizations.[4] Additionally, in many social sector industries in which private sector competition has been growing, such as in education and healthcare, nonprofit organizations may seek to partner with each other in order to compete with their well-financed corporate competitors.[5] For example, The Health Services Partnership, a management service organization, was founded through an alliance between two independent community health centers located just a few miles from each other in Dorchester, Massachusetts. In response to the increasingly competitive healthcare environment, the growth in managed care, and other Boston-area healthcare organizations joining forces and becoming more formidable competitors, Codman Square Health Center and Dorchester House Multi-Service Center established an alliance in 1998 to manage selected services, such as information technology, care coordination, and managed care contracting and member services for both centers, and to help each of them meet the various challenges that they faced. The alliance is focused on building an infrastructure to improve managed care participation and clinical performance, while at the same time supporting the public health and community missions of each health center.

Demand for Efficiency

Alliances are also being pursued as a way to achieve a range of efficiency gains, from achieving more with fewer resources to increasing the speed at which outcomes can be achieved. In recent years, there have been calls by many stakeholders for greater coordination in many social sector activities. Many donors have noted that there are too many organizations doing similar things, leading to a waste of resources and duplication of effort. Thus, many funders have come to view partnerships as a key way of achieving greater impact with their resources. Some funders have even stipulated specific partnerships among grantees as a requirement for receiving funding. A 2003 Urban Institute study on foundation attitudes and practices of 1,192 grantmaking foundations in the United States found that 69% reported that they actively encouraged collaboration amongst grantees, and 42% of these said that they sometimes required partnering as a condition for funding.[6] Alliance approaches are often pursued by social enterprises that seek to tap into these funding sources. Although efficiency gains from alliances can vary from basic reductions in administrative costs, to more significant gains such as increasing the resource flows and awareness of a social issue through coordination among network members, to mobilizing and deploying resources and expertise more optimally across network members through specialization, many nonprofits fail to realize the full potential of alliances because they pursue them in an opportunistic or ad hoc manner, often in an effort to secure funding. Such alliances often focus on a specific program or a peripheral organizational activity. The alliances themselves are not treated as an integral and strategic part of the organization's activities, and therefore the engagement and outcomes of such alliances can be limited. Indeed, alliance partners are often disappointed with the results of an alliance, feeling as if the collaboration did not adequately meet either of the partners' needs.[7] Outcomes of this type lie on one extreme of the outcome continuum.

In contrast, alliances that are viewed as core to the organization's strategy for achieving mission impact have much greater potential, including limiting redundancy, spreading costs across network members, drawing on expertise across the network, and attracting greater visibility and funding to the network members. These alliance outcomes can enable partners to generate greater mission impact than the individual entities acting alone. Alliances also have the potential to enable a social enterprise to achieve significant mission impact more quickly by mobilizing existing resources, infrastructure, and expertise than if organizations had to develop these assets independently from the ground up. Alliances are often viewed as a way to increase efficiency by spreading the costs for developing infrastructure such as performance measurement systems, and even leadership or employees, across more than one entity. For example, WWB is a microfinance NGO whose goal is to increase the economic participation of as many of the 500 million low-income women worldwide as possible by building performance standards and financial systems to serve their needs. WWB's strategy relies almost entirely on developing alliance networks of various organizations to expand services and coordinate microfinance services across the globe. Rather than seeking to offer microfinance services directly through a traditional hub-and-spoke model, WWB built a network of alliances among existing local microfinance organizations by providing and organizing support to network members to do their work more efficiently and effectively. Members of the WWB network have benefited from the availability of support that would have been cost prohibitive for NGOs working independently. While WWB affiliates focus on providing direct services, WWB staff concentrates on activities for which scale is beneficial and generates collective cost savings. This includes technical and financial services such as microfinance operations, market research and loan guarantees, and advocacy on microfinance policy and regulatory change. WWB staff also manages "learning networks," which diffuse best practices through meetings and exchange visits among members, reinforce network performance standards, and coordinate interactions among network members and policy makers. WWB achieves impact not only by supporting network members to get what they need to succeed but also by helping to shape financial systems and industry standards so that regulatory and legal structures continually evolve in favor of the microfinance industry. While individual NGOs could not easily justify these investments, network members invest collectively in order to learn from each other to improve their services and realize significant benefits because these scalable activities are performed on their behalf by WWB. For WWB itself, building alliances with and among other microfinance providers has made possible a greater increase in poor women's access to finance, knowledge, and markets, and enabled the organization to deliver on its goal of having a "major impact on expanding the economic assets, participation, and power of low-income women as entrepreneurs and economic agents" at a relatively low cost and in a timely manner.

Heightened Concerns About Effectiveness

In recent years, changes in both private and public funders' expectations have contributed to heightened concerns about accountability and effectiveness, which in turn have also contributed to an increased interest in alliance approaches. Alliances can offer a way to approach social problems in a more holistic and systematic way. Nonprofits can often identify complementary, or even competing, programs that could potentially increase the mission impact of their own programs or services. Working in alliance with such partners might enable nonprofits to offer more and better services to their beneficiaries, without causing mission drift or spreading resources too thinly across many activities for the organization. By generating synergies among collaborating programs and investing to build collective capacity to solve systemic problems, alliances have the potential to achieve not only greater efficiency and speed but also more sustainable mission impact. For example, Pratham, a nonprofit education organization in India, exemplifies how an alliance approach with other nonprofits, government, and business can be developed to achieve efficient, large-scale change and sustainable impact. The organization's goal to provide universal education to every child in India led it to work in close partnership with corporations, business, and other nonprofits to deliver early childhood education. By mobilizing various resources from its alliance partners, Pratham has been able to roll out educational programs across India with very little of its own capital and infrastructure. The organization is skilled at recruiting, training, and retaining local teachers directly from the communities in which they work.

Additionally, Pratham works with several prominent corporate partners, such as Industrial Credit and Investment Corporation of India and Hindustan Petroleum, that provide not only office space and equipment but also management talent for the organization's executive team. Alliances with municipal governments give Pratham classroom space and access to municipal schools to offer its remedial programs for children at risk of dropping out of school as well as those who have dropped out of or never enrolled in school. The organization also works with other nonprofits, such as a community-based health service organization, that work through Pratham's school network to deliver healthcare services and address some of the most common and pressing healthcare issues of Pratham students. Pratham has found that this health service alliance helps them achieve better educational outcomes with their students because, not surprisingly, students can concentrate better on their studies when their basic health issues have been addressed. Pratham's alliance approach to delivering its education programs draws on resources from all sectors through a series of alliances and enables Pratham to achieve scalable impact efficiently, effectively, and sustainably.[8]

ALLIANCE STRATEGY

Clearly, the fact that alliances can be a powerful mechanism to mobilize more resources, create synergies, and, ultimately, achieve greater social impact has led to increased interest and involvement in alliance opportunities of all types. However, despite their tremendous potential, the pursuit of alliance approaches is not something that should be undertaken without due consideration. Working via an alliance entails significant initial and ongoing investments of resources and time. Many challenges can arise as partners try to develop consensus, coordinate their activities, and adapt their cultures to achieving a shared vision. Indeed, working through an alliance can initially require more resources, effort, and patience than operating independently. Furthermore, because alliances often involve significant adaptations, development, and investments, the benefits realized from an alliance may play out over a long period of time. Alliance partners must be patient and committed to seeing the partnership through to the point where outcomes can be realized. To achieve greater mission impact through alliances, organizations must not only engage in individual alliances effectively but also actively manage their ongoing development and evolution, and, perhaps most importantly, create an overarching alliance strategy that guides individual alliance investments and decision making. Ultimately, the goal of the broader alliance strategy should be to construct individual alliances that together enable the most effective, efficient, and sustainable creation of social impact. The number and range of potential alliance opportunities available to a social enterprise are often far greater than can or should be pursued. Each alliance opportunity also entails opportunity costs and risks. Social entrepreneurs not only must analyze whether a particular alliance is worth engaging in at the moment but also must think strategically when deciding which alliance investments provide the greatest leverage and enable them to achieve the greatest impact relative to cost. Furthermore, organizations vary in the degree to which they engage in alliance approaches. On one end of the continuum are organizations for which alliances are peripheral activities that are not integrated into the organization's core operations. For example, alliances can be pursued at the program or project level to create efficiencies and synergies on a relatively narrow aspect of the organization's activities. Such alliances may require a relatively low investment of resources—the outcomes of these alliances will likely be commensurate with the investment. At the other end of the continuum are organizations for which alliances are integral to the way in which the organization generates value. In this case, a nonprofit seeks to develop a portfolio of alliances that when taken together enable a systemic, integrated approach to social value creation among network members. These types of alliances will require significantly greater investments but will also offer the potential of much more significant returns. Regardless of where along this continuum an organization may lie, a social enterprise must be clear on the role that alliances can play in achieving the organization's mission. While there is no single optimal position in which to be on the continuum, investment in an alliance strategy will help to guide individual alliance decisions and will enable the development of a portfolio of approaches that amounts to more than the sum of the individual parts.[9] Many organizations are so busy trying to manage their own day-to-day operations that when they pursue alliances, they tend to engage in a rather limited, transactional manner. Without a doubt, allocating the resources to building alliances is already a significant undertaking, and investing the time and effort to formulate a deliberate alliance strategy is even more resource intensive. However, if deliberate analysis and planning of a coherent alliance strategy can enable an organization to achieve the full potential of its alliances, it will more than justify the costs. Below are some of the key factors to think about in developing a comprehensive alliance strategy.

Focus on Mission and Vision

To engage successfully in any type of alliance, an organization must be clear about its own vision and mission and how the organization's overall strategy and programs serve to achieve these ends. By focusing on the vision and mission, and the role that their organization plays in moving society closer toward that vision, the organization can begin to identify other potential alliance partners that exist in the broader context, whether in the nonprofit, government, or business sector, and that can bring critical resources and capabilities to achieving the vision. The key objective to focus on in evaluating virtually all of the organization's alliance activities is mission impact, even before short-term organizational benefits. This requires an evaluation of whether the potential alliance will enable the nonprofit to achieve mission impact more efficiently, effectively, or more sustainably over the long term. The more adequately the alliance meets each of the three criteria, the more likely it will be worth the investment. Alliances may offer the potential to significantly enhance the organization's own activities in a number of ways. For example, in some cases, the organization's existing activities might be enhanced by working through alliances that enable efficiency or effectiveness gains through a combined effort, whereas in other cases, an alliance might fill a critical gap in the organization's own programs by contributing significantly to achieving the broader mission and vision. In still other cases, it may enable the organization to develop capacity in its partners to generate social value, thereby scaling social impact. Regardless of the specific alliances that are pursued, organizations should assess whether and how alliances might enable them to achieve greater mission impact. The work of HFH Egypt illustrates this unwavering focus on mission impact. HFH is known worldwide for its organizational model of mobilizing volunteers and donors to build or rehabilitate homes for homeowners with interest-free mortgages through thousands of affiliate organizations worldwide. The organization's mission is to eliminate poverty housing by building and rehabilitating houses in partnership with homeowner families. The organization traditionally invested in and built affiliate organizations as the primary means of delivering on its mission. In Egypt, the national director, Yousry Makar, remained focused on the *vision and mission* first and foremost, rather than the specific *means* by which to achieve mission impact. The country's overwhelming need for housing (approximately 20 million of the country's 70 million people live in substandard housing or are homeless) led Makar to pursue an innovative approach to delivering on the organization's mission. He established as the vision of HFH Egypt to directly empower communities to house 10% of those in need over 20 years, with an approach that could be spread independently to other local organizations, which in turn could begin to serve the remaining 90% *independent of HFH Egypt*. Although HFH brought considerable expertise for developing housing programs, and could commit a significant amount of financial and human resources toward this vision, Makar also noted that there were also tremendous resource constraints that limited HFH Egypt's ability to achieve its vision independently. Limitations ranged from the enormous administrative and organizational capacity that would be required, to the organization's limited knowledge of the local communities and lack of relationships that would facilitate homeowner selection, to the need to establish credibility and relationships in the community to mobilize volunteers, among other resources. In light of these tangible and intangible resource constraints in the Egyptian context, Makar believed that the feasibility of achieving this goal through the traditional HFH affiliate model was limited. Makar sought to achieve mission impact by building a series of alliances with existing national NGOs and local community development organizations, rather than seeking to build his own organizational infrastructure from the ground up and competing for scarce resources with other established community organizations. In Makar's view, investing in and mobilizing local community organizations to address the issue of poverty housing was the only way HFH Egypt could ever achieve significant and sustained mission impact.

Clarify Roles

In formulating an alliance strategy, it is critical for the organization to assess its own contributions as an alliance partner in order to be able to identify potential partners. Each organization must be clear on its own focus, competencies, and capabilities in order to identify what roles alliance partners can play in moving closer toward the vision. HFH Egypt illustrates how clarity about the organization's vision, key competencies, and the potential role to be played by alliance partners are critical to formulating a comprehensive alliance strategy. Makar developed a series of partnerships with established community development associations to mobilize the resources necessary to deliver on HFH's mission. HFH Egypt and its partners brought complementary skills and resources. The partnerships enabled HFH Egypt to build on their partners' established knowledge, credibility, and community development experience in the community. In turn, local partners recognized the tremendous housing need in their communities and wanted to leverage HFH's expertise and support to serve this need.

With each of its local partners, HFH Egypt sought to tailor the housing programs to each community to achieve efficiencies and enhanced impact by developing and leveraging existing local resources and expertise. HFH Egypt performed extensive due diligence of its partners' strengths and capacities, not only to ensure value alignment but also to be able to partner in a way that provided additional support only where it was needed. In some communities, issues of health or education already absorbed local leadership. Since it did not make sense for HFH Egypt to enter the community and attempt to compete for these resources in order to build its own infrastructure to address the housing need, HFH Egypt sought to work together with these leaders and their community organizations on their mutual interests, while at the same time adhering to the core principles of HFH's model. Makar estimated that HFH Egypt realized overhead savings of about $250,000 due to the cash and in-kind contributions from partners in the form of office space, staff, and training.

By developing a clear understanding of what their organization is capable of contributing to the cause and of what other critical assets potential alliance partners can provide, organizations can formulate a coherent alliance strategy that enables more productive movement toward the vision. The process of taking stock of the organization's role and key roles that can be played by others helps to identify potential alliance partners.

Define Values

While many might meet the criteria for an alliance partner from an operational and strategic perspective, not all of these entities would qualify on the basis of vision and values alignment. Clarity about the organization's values helps to define the key expectations, methodologies, and norms that will guide not only the organization's own activities but also its alliance activities. Values are the key guiding principle that defines what is negotiable and nonnegotiable in an alliance engagement. This is especially important because there is increased pressure to pursue alliances, and organizations may be drawn into forming them for the wrong reasons. Even if an alliance may appear to add value, if the potential risk of values incompatibility is high, then the chances of subsequent costly conflict increase and the partner's desirability decreases. Engagement in one alliance may often preclude the opportunity or ability to engage in others due to the opportunity costs of management and staff time. Although shared vision is fundamental, equally as important is a commitment among alliance partners to adhere to a shared set of values that will guide the activity of the alliance. While a shared vision is what motivates the partners to engage in an alliance, it is shared values that help to govern the relationship in formal and informal ways. Because it is virtually impossible to lay out every contingency and dictate every process for how work should be done in an alliance, shared values play a fundamental role in holding the alliance together and enabling it to function. To assess a potential partner's alignment on vision and values requires extensive due diligence on the part of each alliance partner. This includes investigating everything from alignment on vision, ability and willingness to commit resources and competencies to the alliance, and a proven track record for impact on key constituents and in the community. For example, in implementing its alliance strategy, HFH Egypt did extensive due diligence over a period of several months on potential partners. Most of their community partners were selected based on a successful track record in complementary community development areas such as microfinance, education, and health. In addition to their demonstrated performance, their work had been done in a way that was consistent with HFH Egypt core values, which included integrity as demonstrated by following through on commitments; diversity, as demonstrated by nondiscriminatory practices in providing services; and equity, as demonstrated by serving the needs of the community where they were greatest. To assess their potential partners' commitment to these values, HFH Egypt interviewed local leaders, local beneficiaries, and local NGOs to learn more about how their potential partner operated and what their impact was on the community. Before engaging in any alliances, an organization must commit the time and resources necessary to assess and evaluate whether there is sufficient common ground on which to build an alliance.

Invest for Impact

Alliance approaches require a willingness among nonprofit leaders, board members, and funders to broaden the ways in which they seek to deliver on the organization's mission and vision. Rather than viewing their own organization as the key mechanism for value creation, they must conceive of their organization's role within a larger constellation of other actors, as the engine for creating social value. Building such alliances not only requires significant initial and ongoing resource investments but also involves ceding control and sharing recognition for mission impact achieved with and through its network partners. Enhancing the organization's mission impact by working with and through other complementary and competitive entities is likely to be beneficial to a nonprofit over the long term; however, successful alliances require *more* than self-interest to endure and thrive. Although organizational benefits are a common outgrowth of alliances, a narrow focus on advancing individual or organizational agendas can undermine the trust necessary for an alliance to function productively. Instead, alliance partners must be committed to social impact as the key measure of an alliance's success. With this commitment, alliance members relate to each other as peers and equal contributors to achieving mission impact, each bringing critical resources and investing in a reservoir of goodwill that enables joint action. For example, HFH Egypt invested heavily in local entities to support not only the development of local capacity to deliver housing programs but also the development of a shared vision to address the root causes of poverty in their partners' communities. Even though HFH Egypt provided a large share of the initial financial capital, it acknowledges the equally valuable contributions of its partners in the form of staff, network relationships, and local expertise. HFH Egypt sought to work as peers with alliance partners, even forgoing some of the traditional organizational benefits an organization would typically gain, such as direct control over every aspect of the services, increased funding for HFH Egypt itself, and increased recognition and prestige associated with HFH Egypt. As a result, HFH Egypt built trust among its alliance partners that catalyzed the development and delivery of joint solutions that enabled them to effectively deliver on their shared vision, which was the ultimate goal. Makar viewed these relationships as going beyond transactional and opportunistic partnerships geared toward advancing HFH organizational interests. It was more important that the housing programs were delivered efficiently and effectively, in concert with other community development activities, than which organization controlled, managed, and received recognition for the outcomes. What he sought to do instead was to make significant investments in local capacity to drive the maximum creation of social value through HFH Egypt's network of alliance partners over the long term. With the goal of bringing the local community partners to the point of self-sufficiency, HFH Egypt could expand its mission impact by phasing out of successful partnerships in order to reallocate its resources into new communities. In effect, HFH Egypt played an enabling role through these collaborations, thereby leveraging its resources and creating a multiplier effect. In some communities, these partnerships were so successful that within certain villages, HFH's alliance partners began sharing their housing program expertise with their counterparts in other communities with little or no involvement from HFH Egypt, thereby achieving even greater mission impact for HFH Egypt. Indeed, some might question whether HFH Egypt gained sufficient organizational benefits or recognition for investing so much in building its alliance network. However, since HFH Egypt's leadership considered mission impact as the key measure of return on its investment, then the outcomes more than justified the cost. The alliances mobilized and coordinated a vast array of resources, expertise, and infrastructure to achieve mission impact far beyond what was possible by HFH Egypt acting alone.

CASE STUDIES

The case studies that follow expose the reader to a wide range of innovative alliances in action. The first case, Guide Dogs for the Blind Association (GDBA), profiles the newly appointed CEO and social entrepreneur Geraldine Peacock as she seeks to deliver on her organization's mission to improve the lives for the visually impaired by relentlessly striving for collaboration and alliance building within and across sector boundaries. This approach enables her to better serve her organization's mission by leveraging resources from outside GDBA. The GDBA case demonstrates the opportunity for generating enhanced social impact through the creation of new forms of social enterprise alliances, while at the same time illustrating the accompanying leadership and management challenges that must be overcome. As you read the case, think about the following questions.

1. What is your assessment of the hotel and holiday partnerships?

2. What are the critical elements of the Guide Dogs Mobility Service partnership? What is your assessment of this partnership?

3. What role should GDBA play in the visually impaired sector's umbrella organization?

4. What do you think of Geraldine Peacock's leadership? Why?

KaBOOM! is a nonprofit organization that builds and rehabilitates community playgrounds. The organization relies mostly on crafting corporate alliances to support and finance the construction of community playgrounds. The organization has undergone a period of rapid expansion through building a network of corporate partners. This case also serves to illustrate another dimension of the blending of social and commercial approaches and the mutual social and commercial value creation that can be realized through social enterprise collaborations. As you read the case, consider the following questions:

1. What is your evaluation of KaBOOM!'s use of corporate partnerships?

2. What are some of the benefits and risks that KaBOOM! and its partners get from working in partnership?

3. What should KaBOOM! do to deal with the increased competition?

4. In formulating its future strategy, how much weight should KaBOOM! give to the impact of this change on its corporate partners?

5. Based on the case, what are some key lessons on how and why partnering relationships evolve?

NOTES

1. The Independent Sector. (2001). *The nonprofit almanac.* New York: Jossey-Bass.

2. Talcott, S. Nonprofit mergers catch on in region. *The Boston Globe,* April 6, 2006. Retrieved April 6, 2006, from Factiva, http://www.factiva.com.

3. The Independent Sector. (2001). *The nonprofit almanac.* New York: Jossey-Bass.

4. Kohm, A., & La Piana, D. (2003). *Strategic restructuring for nonprofit organizations: Mergers, integrations, and alliances.* Westport, CT: Praeger.

5. Ibid.

6. Ostrower, F. (2004, September). *Attitudes and practices concerning effective philanthropy.* Retrieved April 6, 2006, from the Urban Institute Web site: http://www.urban.org/UploadedPDF/310986_attitudes_practices_ES.pdf.

7. Ostrower, F. (2005, Spring). *The reality underneath the buzz of partnerships: The potentials and pitfalls of partnering.* Retrieved April 6, 2006, from the Stanford Social Innovation Review Web Site: http://www.ssireview.org/pdf/2005SP_feature_ostrower.pdf.

8. Banerji, R., Chavan, M., Vaish, P., & Varadhachary, A. (2001). A point of light in Mumbai [Electronic version]. *McKinsey Quarterly,* Number 1.

9. Austin, J. E. (2003, Summer). Strategic alliances: Managing the collaboration portfolio. *Stanford Social Innovation Review, 1*(2).

Case Study 5.1.

Guide Dogs for the Blind Association

Case Study

Geraldine Peacock, chief executive officer of Guide Dogs for the Blind Association (GDBA), the recognized world leader in the breeding and training of guide dogs, reviewed her organization's mission statement: "Our mission is to provide guide dogs, mobility, and other rehabilitation services that meet the needs of blind and partially sighted people." GDBA had made substantial progress during her five years as CEO. The organization's reach had been considerably broadened, and costly losses from noncore activities had been contained or eliminated. Nevertheless, Peacock was concerned that systemic problems, including competition among organizations serving the visually impaired, program redundancy, and lack of optimum resource utilization in the sector, still prevented services from being delivered to many visually impaired people who needed such services. How these challenges could be addressed and what role GDBA and Peacock should play were not clear.

Peacock reflected on her past leadership experiences in the nonprofit sector and saw the potential to develop a broad, varied network of organizations that would cooperate in serving visually impaired people and leverage resources beyond traditional organizational boundaries. Peacock picked up the phone and called a kindred spirit, Stephen Remington, chief executive officer of Action for Blind People, who shared her concerns about the lack of cooperation in the sector, to discuss the idea of broad-based, pragmatic collaboration.

Peacock was aware that proposing that service providers work together was considered out-of-the-box thinking and was difficult in this insular sector of the nonprofit world and at GDBA itself. However, there had been a number of promising innovations in the sector over the past five years to support the possibility that this new approach might have merit. Despite this, convincing trustees, competitors, employees, and clients of the worth of a strategy to collaborate with organizations delivering many of the same services as GDBA would be a long, complicated process.

GDBA BACKGROUND

Guide Dogs for the Blind, a nonprofit organization in the United Kingdom (see **Exhibit 5.1.1** for cross-national comparisons of the nonprofit sector) with an annual budget of over £40 million[1] (see **Exhibit 5.1.2** for GDBA financials), had provided guide dogs to visually impaired people since its founding in 1931. Each year, GDBA bred and placed over 1,000 guide dog puppies and created over 800 new guide dog partnerships. As of 2002, GDBA had enabled over 21,000 people to experience greater mobility via guide dog assistance. A guide dog was given at no cost to any visually impaired person in the country who needed one. Each guide dog cost the organization £35,000 (breeding, feeding, veterinary care, etc.) over the animal's lifetime. The average dog could perform its duties for seven years. Upon retirement, a guide dog's owner, the owner's relative, or an individual on a waiting list would adopt the dog.

For many years, GDBA had been a highly successful organization by most measures. That changed during the early and mid-1990s with the introduction of increasingly noncore, complex, and varied service offerings, such as holiday and hotel programs for the visually impaired. By 1997, the organization was experiencing serious financial problems. In response to these difficulties, the trustees recruited Peacock, a seasoned nonprofit manager, to join the organization and change the way GDBA conducted its business. The board-mandated instructions were clear: "Focus the organization without shutting down services, stop the organization from bleeding at the jugular, maintain the quality and output of the core guide dog service, and work in partnership wherever possible."

Prior to joining GDBA, Peacock had been the first paid CEO of the U.K. National Autistic Society, where she had served from 1988–1997. Before that, she was deputy director of the London Boroughs Training Committee. At the time she was hired, she was serving as a trustee of the National Council of Voluntary Organizations, a member of the Council of the Industrial Society, and a member (and past chairman) of the executive committee of the Association of Chief Executives of Voluntary Organizations (ACEVO). She also served on the U.K. government's Treasury Task Force on Social Investment and the strategy unit's Review of Charitable Law and Regulation. In these capacities, and as part of her lobbying efforts for the interests of the fast-growing voluntary sector, Peacock met with politicians and members of key government departments.

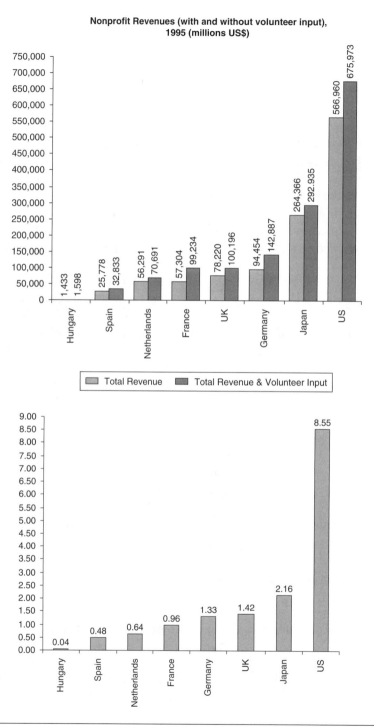

Exhibit 5.1.1   Cross-National Comparisons of the Nonprofit Sector, 1995

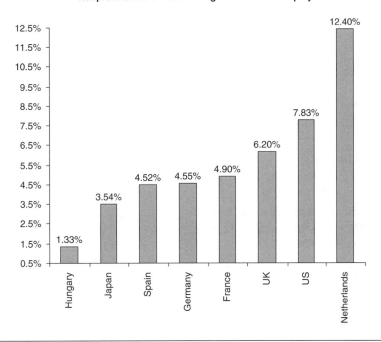

Nonprofit Share of Total Nonagricultural FTE Employment

Exhibit 5.1.1

SOURCE: Salamon, L., & Anheier, H. *The Emerging Sector Revisited: A Summary.* Baltimore, MD: Johns Hopkins University Institute for Policy Studies, 1998.

Within GDBA, Peacock faced daily challenges associated with working for an extremely cautious board (see **Exhibit 5.1.3** for GDBA Board of Trustees) in an organization that had undergone little organizational change for decades and where 70% of the employees had worked their entire working lives. Peacock knew she had to disturb "the temple of the dog" in order to truly serve guide dog owners, who increasingly were wanting more than "the perfect guide dog." "We needed to go from 'we do dogs, now who wants one?' to thinking more broadly about how to best serve the mobility needs of our clients," Peacock said. This reorientation was achieved through a wide and inclusive

consultation process with all of the organization's stakeholders. While Peacock reorganized the structure and invested in staff empowerment changes to realign GDBA internally, she sought to build alliances outside the organization that would help her enhance GDBA's impact.

At the time of Peacock's arrival, GDBA had annual revenues of £37 million and 4,610 clients, or guide dog owners. GDBA received 85% of its revenues from direct bequests and investment returns on its endowment. The remaining 15% of annual revenue came from branch fund-raising, corporate sponsorships, and other donations. GDBA received no funding from the

	2001 (£000)	2000 (£000)
Fixed assets		
Tangible assets	23,729	23,702
Investments	129,960	167,326
	153,689	190,398
Current assets		
Stocks	477	452
Debtors	7,094	7,875
Money market deposits	3,107	1,543
Cash at bank and in hand	1,497	726
	12,175	10,596
Creditors: Amounts falling due within one year		
Taxation and social security	256	517
Due to subsidiary companies	—	170
Other creditors	9,409	9,640
Accruals	52	56
	9,717	9,383
Net current assets	2,458	1,213
Total assets less current liabilities	156,147	191,611
Funds:		
General funds—Guide Dog Services	82,110	110,842
Designated funds		
Fixed assets	23,729	23,072
Guide Dogs Mobility Service development	28,319	31,323
New initiatives	18,865	19,736
Ophthalmic research	3,124	3,706
Hotels and holidays	—	2,932
	74,037	80,769
Total unrestricted funds		
Including a revaluation deficit of £8,044,000 in 2001		
and revaluation reserves of £9,883,000 in 2000	156,147	191,611
Restricted funds	—	—
Total funds	**156,147**	**191,611**

Exhibit 5.1.2   Balance Sheet, December 31, 2001

SOURCE: GDBA documents.

	General Funds (£000)	Designated Funds (£000)	Restricted Funds (£000)	TOTAL 2001 (£000)	As Restated Total 2000 (£000)
Incoming resources					
Voluntary	32,179	—	2,921	**35,100**	31,853
Activities in furtherance of the charity's objects:					
Continuing operations	442	243	—	**685**	752
Discontinued operations—Leisure services	—	353	—	**353**	536
Investment Income	4,434	—	—	**4,434**	5,334
Total incoming resources	37,055	596	2,921	**40,572**	38,475
Resources expended					
Cost of generating funds:					
Fund-raising and legacy marketing	5,866	158	—	**6,024**	5,272
Development of new fund-raising initiatives	1,823	—	—	**1,623**	1,342
Publicity	1,181	581	—	**1,762**	1,075
Investment management fees	386	—	—	**366**	290
	9,256	739	—	**9,995**	7,979
Net incoming resources available for charitable application	27,799	(143)	2,921	**30,577**	30,496
Charitable expenditure:					
Costs of activities in furtherance of the charity's objects					
Provision of guide dogs	29,600	1,368	1,313	**32,281**	32,108
Provision of visual-impairment support services	3,698	965	1,608	**6,259**	5,164
Training of visual-impairment support workers	1,817	146	—	**1,963**	2,069
New initiatives	—	749	—	**749**	135
Leisure services					
–Discontinued operations	—	3,894	—	**3,894**	1,883
Support costs included above: 2001 £5,521,000 (2000 £4,912,000)					
Grants payable in furtherance of the charity's objects	274	704	—	**976**	1,549
Management and administration of the charity	239	29	—	**288**	212

Exhibit 5.1.2   Cash Flow Statement for the Year Ended December 31, 2001
(incorporating an income and expenditure account)   *(Continued)*

(Continued)

	General Funds (£000)	Designated Funds (£000)	Restricted Funds (£000)	TOTAL 2001 (£000)	As Restated Total 2000 (£000)
Total charitable expenditure	35,616	7,855	2,921	**46,392**	43,120
Total resources expended	44,872	8,594	2,921	**56,387**	51,099
Net resources expended before transfers					
Continuing operations	(7,817)	(4,457)	—	**(12,274)**	(11,277)
Discontinued operations—Leisure services	—	(3,541)	—	**(3,541)**	(1,347)
Transfer between funds	(1,266)	1,266	—	—	—
Net resources expended	(9,083)	(6,732)	—	**(15,815)**	(12,624)
Net realized losses on investments	(7,874)	—	—	**(7,874)**	(4,459)
Net expenditure for the financial year	(16,957)	(6,732)	—	**(23,689)**	(17,063)
Net unrealized losses on investments	(11,775)	—	—	**(11,775)**	(4,909)
Net decrease in funds	(28,732)	(6,732)	—	**(35,464)**	(21,992)
Fund balances brought forward at January 1	110,842	80,769	—	**191,611**	213,603
Fund balances carried forward at December 31	82,110	74,037	—	**156,147**	191,611

Exhibit 5.1.2

SOURCE: GDBA documents.

NOTE: The net expenditure for the financial year under the historical cost accounting convention is £25,845,000 (2000, £19,108,000).

central or local governments to fund its guide dog service. GDBA had 1,240 employees and 27 offices throughout the United Kingdom, which were broken into seven regions, each with its own manager, who reported to two central client service managers. Peacock remembered:

The seven regions were like fiefdoms, and I had to try to remove barriers, both physically and mentally, and

create a truly national organization. This meant changing the culture from one of command and control to one of empowerment and creating new, cross-functional divisions and teams who worked together, supported each other, shared knowledge, and were accountable at the local level. We had to draw things into the center initially, invest in developing good staff and information systems, and then let go

	1992	1993	1994	1995	1996	1997	1998	1999	2000	2001	2002
Donations and fund-raising	7,789	5,685	5,385	4,236	6,174	5,823	6,673	6,396	6,833	7,633	7,649
Legacies	17,439	20,187	20,092	17,318	19,733	24,967	29,487	26,381	24,799	27,442	26,000
Investment income	6,297	6,414	6,111	6,522	7,063	6,035	6,391	6,468	5,334	4,434	4,375
Trading sub	419	248		624	505	503	639	335	221	25	
Rehab contracts									240	398	0
Funding for training rehab									512	287	
Leisure service income									536	353	0
Total income	31,944	32,534	31,588	28,700	33,475	37,328	43,190	39,580	38,475	40,572	38,024

Exhibit 5.1.2   Revenue Table

SOURCE: GDBA documents.

Geraldine Bounds   Date joined board: 1998
Bounds is Chair of the Board of Trustees of Liverpool Voluntary Society for the Blind. Geraldine has been a guide dog owner since 1956.

Tony Chignell   Date joined board: 1989
Chignell was Deputy Chairman for 2000 to 2002 Emeritus Consultant in Ophthalmology, teaching and advising in ophthalmology.

Sir Nick Fenn   Date joined board: 2002
Fenn spent 37 years in the diplomatic service as ambassador in Burma and Ireland and High Commissioner in India. He is blind for the early part of each day.

Bruce Gordon (Honorary Treasurer)   Date joined board: 1997
Bruce Gordon joined the board in 1997. Gordon is a chartered accountant and has been a partner for 10 years. He leads the Thames Valley practice of Deloitte & Touche in Reading and works with a number of large public companies and the U.K. operations of some of the worldwide firm's largest clients.

Nic Harper   Date joined board: 1989
Harper is a Fellow of the Royal Institution of Chartered Surveyors and the Central Association of Agricultural Valuers, and a member of the Lord Chancellor's panel of agricultural arbitrators. Since 1971 he has been with the London firm of Langley-Taylor and is currently Managing Partner of the practice.

Neal King (Deputy Chairman)   Date joined board: 1996
King has been a member of the British Veterinary Association Council since 1972 and of the Royal College of Veterinary Surgeons (RCVS) Council since 1988.

Richard Lane   Date joined board: 2001
Lane is currently working as Press and PR Manager for the *Lancet* medical journal. Richard became registered blind in 1992 and trained with his first guide dog in 1993.

Ken McFarlane   Date joined board: 2002
McFarlane, a chartered accountant, is a partner at Deloitte & Touche, in charge of the corporate tax practice for the firm.

Elaine Noad   Date joined board: 1998
Noad has worked in local government in Scotland since 1980 and is now Director of Social Work Housing and Health with South Ayrshire Council where she has worked since 1995. Elaine has been a guide dog owner since 1980.

Jean-Clare Schaw Miller   Date joined board: 1992
Schaw Miller was, until 1992, Scottish Chief Commissioner of the Girl Guides Association, an organization with which she has been involved since 1963. She is presently Chairman of the Guide Association (U.K.) Awards Committee.

Barry Weatherill (Chairman)   Date joined board: 1975
Weatherill has been Chairman since 2000. Weatherill was Senior Partner of Wedlake Bell Solicitors from 1984 to 1994 and until 2001 was head of his firm's Media and Intellectual Property team. He continues to practice as a corporate and IP lawyer.

Igal Yawetz   Date joined board: 1997
Yawetz is a chartered architect and planner by profession. He has been responsible for many major architectural projects including reconstruction of The Grand Hotel in Brighton, Metropole Hotels in London and Birmingham NEC, and conversion of the former KGB Headquarters in St. Petersburg to an International Business Center.

Exhibit 5.1.3   GDBA Board of Trustees

SOURCE: GDBA documents.

with trust. I decentralized the structure down to 32 linked district teams that delivered services locally to the service users in the most flexible, appropriate manner possible.

When Peacock arrived at GDBA, the organization only had several unnetworked computers in its head office. A network provider was contracted to place a computer with Internet access in all locations across the United Kingdom to foster better communication and collaboration among staff members in different offices and functions. The network included a logistics system, to better match people with dogs, and computerized veterinary records and genetic profiles, to better monitor dog health. For example, in the past, GDBA would not have known that an ideal dog for a person in England might be available in Scotland. With a new technology infrastructure in place, employees were able to make this type of match easily. In addition, the new technology enabled users to access video briefings, leadership development programs, and learning networks.

PATH TO PARTNERSHIP

Outsourcing Hotel Management

In 1990, GDBA's investments had performed so well that management was looking to broaden the range of services offered by the organization. Members of GDBA polled guide dog owners about what kinds of new services would be most valued. Guide dog owners said they wanted access to special hotels that would accommodate their needs. A staff member remembered: "Some guide dog owners did not like going to mainstream hotels because they didn't feel that they were properly cared for or attended to. They wanted to go to a hotel that was their hotel, where they were known, where they felt comfortable, unthreatened, et cetera. Guide Dogs had money to spare, so they started a new program."

GDBA bought two hotels in excellent locations. Cliffden (21 rooms) was a small converted retirement home located in Devon, an area by the sea in the southern part of the country. The other hotel, Windemere Manor (18 rooms), was north of London in the more mountainous heart of the Lake District. Under GDBA management, each of the hotels was run independently and therefore did not benefit from any overhead sharing or other economies of scale. Although one of the first things that Peacock did was merge the appropriate functions of the hotels, they were still too small to ever become profitable. This was true even if both hotels were booked to capacity every night. In 1997, the hotels were losing £1.4 million annually.

There were four nonprofit organizations running hotels for visually impaired people in the United Kingdom—Action for Blind People (AFBP), GDBA, Royal National Institute for the Blind (RNIB), and Henshaw's. GDBA proposed a three-way partnership among itself, AFBP, and RNIB. AFBP agreed, but RNIB would not commit to the deal in the time frame GDBA and AFBP proposed. Henshaw's had only one hotel, in North Wales, but it wished to retain its hotel as part of its range of local services.

AFBP, also with two properties, was having similar difficulties with GDBA. However, while Peacock wanted to gracefully bow out of the hotel business without alienating constituents, Remington, CEO of AFBP, wanted to scale the hotel business to the point of profitability, as leisure was part of its core business. Both executives believed that they would get further by collaborating rather than competing, so in 2000, they structured a mutually beneficial deal. Peacock noted:

> Managerially, we could see that the partnership made sense. It rationalized two businesses that were struggling and made one business that was profitable. Action for Blind People competed with us, but, in fact, the competition wasn't very intense because we still had more demand for beds than supply. The costing and the management structure were the real problems. Our hotels were running at a large deficit. So, we tried to think of how we could structure a partnership with another organization in the private or the voluntary sector that would keep the hotels open but make them cost-effective. People in the non-profit sector had done wholehearted mergers before, but people hadn't done strategic partnerships that left both companies alive and separate. We knew there was a good fit with AFBP because the provision of leisure facilities for visually impaired people was part of its core purpose.

AFBP managers would have to demonstrate to GDBA in a comprehensive business plan that running four hotels as a group was a sustainable business model. AFBP had experienced hotel management and was actively fund-raising to rebuild its Bognor Regis hotel. GDBA would invest in that project to accelerate its completion, as well as pay to expand its Cliffden hotel to provide more beds to enhance the hotel's financial viability. (When the hotel reopened, GDBA staff would be given first option on applying for new jobs.) GDBA would charge a "peppercorn"[2] rent to AFBP for the Cliffden and Windemere Manor properties to avoid giving up the title of its assets to the partnership. Also, by retaining ownership, GDBA would continue to influence the quality of services provided at the hotels. Ultimately, GDBA gave AFBP a 40-year lease for approximately £1 per year. GDBA would not receive any annual revenue, either from rent or potential profits; likewise, GDBA would not be responsible for any losses.

Outside authorities monitored quality standards at the hotels in areas such as customer care and dog care and issued quality ratings to the hotels. If the hotels received below a 70% rating, AFBP would have to agree to a plan of action with GDBA about how to improve. If improvements were not made within a specified time frame, GDBA could give AFBP a year's notice and then withdraw the lease and replace AFBP with another provider.

But Peacock was sure it would never come to that:

> Two of the hotels were completely overhauled, upgraded, and expanded,

so they now have much better facilities and are much more modern. We invested about £6 million in rebuilding and eliminating redundancy costs to make the project viable. The thinking of the trustees was that this was a one-off cost to the organization that would avoid a potential worst-case drain of nearly £2 million a year. When we handed the hotels over in 2000, the actual annual loss on the hotels had been reduced to £671,000.

When the deal was formalized, a small but vocal minority of guide dog owners began to register their discontent over the partnership. Some guide dog owners who were visitors at GDBA's hotels organized a sit-in in the bar of one of the hotels and called in the media to cover the event. Peacock herself received hate mail from angry guide dog owners. The controversy went on for some time, but GDBA and its partner forged ahead with the implementation of the partnership. Peacock explained: "There were a few difficult dog owners who didn't want to share their hotels with people who used canes. Most of all, they felt that they would be safe in hotels only if GDBA ran them. I knew this wouldn't be the case, but it required a leap of faith for the protesters."

Shortly after the new arrangement was put in place, gains in the hotels' quality of service as well as operational and financial performance were quickly realized. Most of the protesting guide dog owners were rapidly swayed by these outcomes. Some of the former objectors even wrote letters to GDBA, praising the move and questioning why these changes had not been implemented sooner.

An additional outgrowth of the hotel partnership program was the beginning of a dialogue with the Automobile Association (AA), the grading authority for mainstream hotels. After several discussions, GDBA, AFBP, and AA began to contemplate ways in which they might develop a standard for rating other hotels' accessibility for visually impaired guests. Peacock said:

Since The Disability Discrimination Act has been passed in this country, all sorts of businesses have to look at how they make their premises accessible to people with different kinds of disabilities. We are going to do some market testing to see whether hotels would pay to be inspected as user-friendly to visually impaired people and guide dog owners. If they would, in addition to getting rosettes for the quality of hotel service, they would also get marks for their user-friendliness for guide dog owners.

By 2001, the hotels had ceased losing money. By 2002, only two years after the deal was completed, the four-hotel chain was turning a small profit. It was planned that profits would be reinvested into the development of the business. Remington credited the hotel program with starting a wider dialogue among hotel providers toward people with a range of other disabilities. Based on the organization's strong track record, charities were now approaching AFBP about running their facilities.

Case Study

The Holidays Partnership

GDBA's Holiday Program, established in 1990, formalized what had previously been its informal volunteer holiday club, The Guide Dog Owners Adventure Group. This group participated in and sponsored a variety of adventures—from tandem bicycle riding to rambling, a structured but leisurely walking that is less strenuous than hiking. As the program evolved, GDBA provided even more adventurous trips by supplying sighted guides and developing comprehensive safety protocols. Guide dog owners paid membership fees and travel costs, while sighted people paid to travel on the adventure holidays as guides. Over the years, the range of travel options available grew, and GDBA became a substantial travel agency in its own right, packaging flights, organizing ground transportation, and arranging hotel bookings.

By 1997, the year Peacock joined the organization, GDBA was running 140 group holidays per year. The holiday offerings were very broad. People could opt for adventure trips including skiing, hiking near Everest, and rafting the Limpopo River. Guide dog owners and other visually impaired people loved the service, but GDBA was losing £761,000 per year providing it. Peacock sought to find a partner with expertise in the travel industry in order to stem the losses from GDBA's holiday operations. Peacock recalled the process of canvassing for appropriate partners: "We didn't really compete with anyone in adventure trips for the visually impaired because we had a unique service offering in that we were the only organization providing sighted guides. AFBP and RNIB did a little, but

nobody was doing what we were doing. It was quite an ambitious business, actually."

Peacock had discussions with several potential partners, but ultimately the best of a limited number of offers came from a nonprofit organization, The Winged Fellowship (TWF). While TWF was not a charity serving the visually impaired per se, its core business was providing holidays for people with a range of disabilities. One major challenge was that TWF had few reserves in the bank.

Peacock remembered:

TWF was a very small organization and going through quite a difficult time. They had just hired a new CEO, and he was looking at ways of securing their "market share." By taking on our holiday business, they could actually merge our respective infrastructures and be in a position to grow their business considerably.

It wasn't as easy or obvious as the hotel move. But TWF was clearly the most expert of the few companies we considered, so they were our choice. Also, I think, the trustees wanted this ongoing liability off our books. We found a pragmatic solution. Because we were partnering with another charity, which shared common values and had secured its positioning in the disability holiday market, the arrangement felt safe to visually impaired people, our core constituency.

TWF chief executive Pat Wallace agreed, and the two boards of trustees signed the deal in 2001. Wallace transferred the bulk of TWF's holiday office to the GDBA operation and hired GDBA's manager of hotels and holidays as the director of operations. Peacock and GDBA trustees felt there was a benefit to maintaining the Guide Dog Holidays brand, which was more established than the TWF brand, for a three- to five-year transition period. The outcome was that TWF's business was in effect integrated into that of GDBA's, and the new business was a considerably larger entity.

GDBA also provided financial support. "In essence, we gave them a front-loaded dowry for the first few years, because we wanted to support them while they developed their infrastructure and fund-raising capabilities," Peacock said. "We felt it was worth investing in making them secure because although the deal had no revenue-generating value, it stopped us from losing £761,000 the first year." By 2001, GDBA had created an annual subsidy schedule whereby it would pay out £2.9 million over five years. In 2001, GDBA gave TWF £565,000 and a £250,000 loan (to renew IT infrastructure). By 2002, when TWF offered 100 trips, the annual subsidy from GDBA had dropped to £484,000, and no loans were made.

GUIDE DOG MOBILITY SERVICE (GDMS) PROGRAM WITH LOCAL AUTHORITIES

Local Authorities in the United Kingdom

There were approximately 500 local authorities (local governments) in England and Wales, though Wales accounted for just 22 of the total. Because of its high population density, there were 33 local authorities in the city of London alone. Surrey, a large local authority that had a population of just over 1 million people, had a budget of £770 million a year. In contrast, the smaller Allerdale local authority had a population of 96,000 and a budget of £9.5 million per year. Local authorities raised money through local household property and business taxes. The taxes were set to meet the local budget in the area, and the national government approved the local government's budget. Local authorities were then responsible for providing a range of services, including education, fire, economic development, social services, and services for the visually impaired.

The central government provided financial support for all local authorities with cash payments intended to "top off" locally raised taxes. The emergency, primary, and secondary healthcare was provided and funded by the National Health Service and was not included in local authority budgets. Central government funding was also available for specific initiatives, such as environmental projects or road projects, that fit the political priorities of the government in power.

Changing the Course of Service Delivery

In most cases, a visually impaired person would receive a diagnosis to determine her condition, and if services were needed, she would go to the local hospital for treatment. She would then be advised to contact the social services department of the local authority in which she resided. The local authority would then assess the visually impaired person's condition, decide which services were needed, and build a care plan. The local authority would then most often issue contracts to nonprofit service providers for the required services or, much less frequently, provide the services itself. Services for the visually impaired fell into three categories: mobility services (guide dogs, long-cane training, orientation devices), communications skills (languages such as Braille and Moon), and independent living skills (learning to cook, clean, and shop).

Peacock said this process worked better in theory than in reality and explained why:

> Because local authorities have limited budgets, which are capped by the central government, they have to prioritize what's most important, which often means long waiting lists for the visually impaired. They typically don't have enough money to provide everything they're supposed to statutorily. So the local authorities tend to concentrate on crisis intervention like child protection. And visual impairment is often low down in the pecking order. A person might wait ages for an assessment of need. Once he finally gets his assessment, the local authority might not have, or be able to afford, the right services to meet that need.

GDBA had actually been one of the organizations receiving contracts to provide mobility services, and much less frequently communication and independent living skills, for a number of local authorities. In

addition, GDBA independently provided mobility services directly to visually impaired individuals who were entitled to receive them from local authorities but in fact had not been receiving them for some reason. The various GDBA locations had no coherent strategy for pricing the mobility services provided to the local authorities, and prices varied considerably from office to office. Historically, it was speculated within GDBA that the real reason for providing mobility services in the first place was to increase the number of guide dog placements. Consequently, the true costs of the service and the management required to effectively deliver the service did not garner significant organizational attention prior to Peacock's arrival. Other charitable organizations around the country, many of which competed with GDBA for service contracts, came to resent GDBA for its ad hoc approach to pricing, which was often below the actual cost of providing the services.

Peacock knew that the current system was not efficiently or effectively serving the needs of the United Kingdom's visually impaired population. In her view, the prime consideration for GDBA should be to ensure that mobility services were provided to as many people as possible, regardless of which organization ultimately provided the services. Peacock summed up her strategy for accomplishing this (see **Exhibit 5.1.4** for GDMS overview):

> By surveying visually impaired people in the United Kingdom, we learned that a lot of people were not getting either assessments or services from local authorities in their area. We

Focusing the Vision

In 1997, The Guide Dogs for the Blind Association carried out the charity's most extensive review to establish what services blind and partially sighted people need to become more independent.

Its findings were startling, revealing that 25% of visually impaired adults never leave home alone and 88% of visually impaired adults have never received mobility training.

Putting our extensive expertise and resources to use in totally new ways, we have established the Guide Dogs Mobility Service to help thousands more blind and partially sighted people in the United Kingdom get the most out of life in the 21st century.

The Guide Dogs Mobility Service—Your Essential Questions Answered

What Is the GDMS?

The GDMS is a new service with a single point of access to maximize the mobility of blind and partially sighted people, helping them to make the most of their remaining vision.

There are currently 200,000 blind and partially sighted people in the United Kingdom who could benefit from this service. While it would be impossible and inappropriate to provide them all with guide dogs, we can help them in many other ways.

An older person whose sight has deteriorated with age may want advice on low-tech aids like a long cane, while a young professional may be interested in the latest mobile phone technology that can help blind people. Our aim is to help them both. The service is designed to respond to people's needs making sure they have access to the best possible support and services.

How Will It Work?

The GDMS will establish an easily accessible, "single point of entry" for people in their local communities where they will be assessed to find out which services they would most benefit from.

It will be delivered locally, in partnership with local authorities, free to the individual user. As part of their commitment, local authorities will have to safeguard the money they currently allocate to visual impairment services for the duration of the partnership.

By working with other providers like the Royal National Institute for the Blind and local associations for the blind, we can coordinate these services under one umbrella, avoid duplication, and ensure that we focus our work where unmet need is greatest.

Where Will the Money Come From?

The new service is being set up with funds from designated reserves, although once up and running, it will be paid for entirely by voluntary income.

When Will It Happen?

Pilot projects are already established across the United Kingdom, and these are being reviewed annually. It will take between three and five years to assess demand for the service and to plan the training and development needs of mobility/rehabilitation workers.

How Will Guide Dogs Change to Deliver This Service?

To be effective, we have to bring our services closer to blind and partially sighted people in their own communities. We are restructuring our offices so we can provide mobility training from an extended number of small service bases across the United Kingdom.

Exhibit 5.1.4   GDMS Overview

SOURCE: GDBA Annual Report, 1999.

thought about how we might do a better job for the visually impaired in the face of competing interests at the local authority level.

Our proposition to the local authorities was, GDBA is a vision-impairment organization whose clients are telling us that they're not getting the services they need, or that they are getting good services from you but you're strapped for cash and can't do as much as you would like. Would you like to try a new partnership where together we could extend our collective reach?

We proposed that GDBA would deliver and fund the mobility component of a local authority's portfolio of services. In return, the local authority would contractually agree to reallocate the money it would save by not providing mobility services to the visually impaired to communications and independent living skills for the same population. The combined effect would be that the local authorities, by working with us, could improve and expand their overall services to the visually impaired without having to find more money in a cash-strapped environment.

The idea was that GDBA, working with a local authority, would establish a mobility budget that the authority would agree to assume for the upcoming year. Through a negotiated process, GDBA and the local authority would write a contract saying that GDBA would provide, or pay for, mobility services for X number of people at a cost of Y during the forthcoming year. In return, the local authority agreed to use the money saved by GDBA's assumption of the cost and delivery of mobility services to provide people on the waiting lists with other vision-impairment services. Under the terms of the contract, GDBA had the right to audit the local authorities to ensure that they lived up to their end of the bargain.

From Peacock's perspective, GDBA had been providing below-cost services to the local authorities all along, so the impact of this program to the organization was in essence not that different from an overall cost perspective. Additionally, by removing the mobility service component from their responsibilities, the local authorities could provide better-quality and broader communication and living services to the visually impaired through other visual-impairment nonprofit organizations that specialized in these particular services. This served Peacock's other agenda within GDMS, to build the capacity of voluntary sector organizations serving the visually impaired population of the country.

GDBA deal makers began approaching local authorities with the proposal but learned quickly that each local authority operated differently and that the negotiations for contracts would be more difficult than first assumed. Due to haphazard record keeping and variations in how local authorities conducted their affairs, the development of mobility budgets was time-consuming and far from uniform. For example, some local authorities used the number of past requests for service as the basis for developing a budget, while others used the number of people on a waiting list for service as a basis for establishing a budget.

Local authorities were not used to being approached in such a proactive fashion by a voluntary organization, and many were wary of an offer that seemed so unorthodox. Additionally, GDBA was still perceived by many in the sector as a provider of a simple service—guide dogs. Recognizing the organization as a significant provider of a broader range of mobility services and as a partner to the local authorities was a challenge.

Funding the GDMS Program

GDBA met with an unexpected economic obstacle, caused in large part by September 11 and the subsequent stock market crash. Peacock estimated that GDBA lost £27 million from its investment portfolio and £3 million more in lost fund-raising opportunities due to an outbreak of "foot and mouth" disease in the country. As a result, the £35-million budget the GDBA trustees had allocated for the rollout of the GDMS project in 1999 was under strain. This considerably slowed the national rollout of the GDMS partnership program. However, the pilot program, which involved 12 test sites, remained untouched, and even with a drastically reduced budget, working with the interest on the £35 million, GDMS was on track to sign an additional 43 partnerships by the end of 2002. Peacock noted: "With the initial £35-million budget, we were going to fundamentally change the delivery of services for visually impaired people in the United Kingdom. This was going to be Guide Dogs' gift to the nation. In three years, we could have rolled it out to every local authority in the country."

GDBA spent about £600,000 on the GDMS program in 2001, and it anticipated spending £1.3 million in 2002. GDMS was written into the GDBA core budget for 2003 at a guaranteed £2 million per year for the next three years.

Wider Implications for the GDMS Program

Peacock called the GDMS program the "most creative thing" she had done to date and wanted to explore further uses for her model. She wanted local authorities to think more creatively about the connections among the government, the voluntary sector, and the private sector. Peacock reflected on the implications of GDMS:

This could have a real impact in a short time frame. If we can develop a model of how service provision can be enhanced through new, cross-sector alliances that more effectively use private, public, and voluntary sector money, there's a win for everyone. It's really about working smarter and thinking laterally. There are always two maxims in the back of my mind— "less is more," and "together everyone achieves more [TEAM]."

This also shows how the culture and reputation of GDBA are changing—we've repositioned ourselves to be taken much more seriously by government and other agencies. This, in turn, allows us to fund-raise in new ways, because now different aspects of our work appeal to different segments of the public.

The U.K. Treasury, which was responsible for the national funding framework for welfare services in the United Kingdom, recently had committed £125 million over the next three years to build infrastructure and capacity for the delivery of public services by the country's voluntary sector. The Treasury had also introduced investment tax credits to encourage private investment. GDBA's management hoped that the GDMS program helped change people's minds about how the voluntary sector operated.

VISUAL-IMPAIRMENT SECTOR IN THE UNITED KINGDOM

GDBA was a "monopoly supplier" of guide dogs in the United Kingdom, but in the growing area of other mobility services, the organization coexisted alongside organizations such as the Royal National Institute for the Blind (RNIB), the largest national charity in the visual-impairment sector, and numerous large local associations for the blind. These organizations did not provide guide dogs but did offer a range of other rehabilitation services such as mobility services (long-cane orientation, electronic aids, etc.), independent living skills (cooking, cleaning, and shopping), and communications skills (languages such as Braille and Moon).

Each of these nonprofit organizations served many of the same client bases as GDBA and had unique funding models as well as distinct management and service-delivery approaches. Whatever their similarities and differences, all of the organizations were struggling to become sustainable. The question beginning to be asked by some in the sector was whether there were ways in which like-minded organizations might reduce redundancies, leverage their individual core competencies, and work collaboratively to enhance the services offered to the visual-impairment community as a whole. There was little precedent for nonprofits that competed in the same pool of funding and served the same constituencies to work together in a meaningful way.

Visual-Impairment Umbrella Organizations

In the mid-1990s, there were two umbrella organizations that represented the interests of the visually impaired population. One was the Visual Handicap Group (VHG), which was composed of the "of and for the blind" voluntary organizations. Members included GDBA, RNIB, AFBP, and numerous local associations for the blind. The goal of this umbrella organization was to foster collaboration among participants. Peacock described the organization itself as a "talking shop," where issues were discussed but nothing ever happened. The other umbrella organization was the United Kingdom Council for the Prevention of Visual Impairment (UKCPVI), which focused more on prevention of eye problems and diseases and was composed of the professional bodies from the eye care and eye health professions.

As one member observed: "The two umbrella groups, VHG and UKCPVI, didn't have a real dialogue between them. So you had the volunteer organizations [VHG] on one side, and the professionals [UKCPVI] on the other. There was talk of collaboration, but no one really seemed to have the appetite to do it."

Eventually, the Nuffield Trust was persuaded by Peacock, Remington, and other interested parties to hold a major seminar. As a result of the meeting, the separate umbrella groups decided that they could accomplish more together than they could apart. The groups combined in the late 1990s to form Vision 2020 UK.

Vision 2020 UK and the Future

Remington and Peacock were among the key drivers in the initiative to establish the emergent umbrella organization, Vision 2020 UK. They both became board members, and Remington served as the board's chairman.

Vision 2020 UK was registered as a national organization and was an affiliate of Vision 2020, an international organization. Participants included RNIB, AFBP, the Royal London Society for the Blind (RLSB), and the National Association of Local Societies for the Visually Impaired (NALSVI).

Neither Remington nor Peacock saw the organization as a direct-service provider, but rather as an entity that would have as its primary purpose the development of a unified advocacy agenda that would be embraced and promoted by all of its members. Additionally,

the umbrella organization would ideally facilitate the building of common infrastructures for nonprofit organizations that served the visually impaired. The objective was for the umbrella organization to achieve tangible benefits for its members by sharing common costs and attaining economies of scale. For example, one outcome could be that organizations in the sector could share "back-office" support services, such as payroll systems and purchasing systems. The thinking was that these new efficiencies would free up additional resources in the sector to flow directly to programs and services for the visually impaired population.

In 2001, working members of the umbrella organization agreed on a business plan for Vision 2020 UK. (See **Exhibit 5.1.5** for Vision 2020 UK working party members.) Highlights of the plan included the following:

Purpose

The purpose of the proposed National Agenda for action on visual impairment is to provide an agreed set of national aims that will enable organizations and individuals to determine their own future strategies in the knowledge that they are assisting with identified need. The agenda is intended to be relevant to visually impaired people and to all those working with them, as eye health professionals, educators, employers, in social services or in voluntary organizations.

A National Agenda will not only provide a framework in which organizations

- Ian Attrill, NALSVI
- Robin Birch, Age Concern (Chairman of the Low Vision Implementation Working Group)
- Ron Bramley, Gift of Thomas Pocklington
- Kathy Cash, NFB
- Gareth Davies, NLBD
- Professor Alistair Fielder, Royal College of Ophthalmologists
- Allen Forster, International Agency for the Prevention of Blindness
- Connell Gebbie, NFB
- Fazilet Hadi, RNIB
- Margaret Hallendorf, Royal College of Ophthalmologists
- Deane Houston, Blind Centre, Northern Ireland
- Robin Hill, Macular Disease Society
- Professor Gordon Johnson, International Centre for Eye Health
- Robert Leader, St. Dunstan's
- Allan Murray, Scottish National Federation for the Welfare of the Blind
- Geraldine Peacock, GDBA
- Paul Quin, UKCPVI
- John Canavan, Department of Health
- Stephen Remington, Action for Blind People
- Mary Robertson, Association of Directors of Social Services
- Tim Smith, Royal College of General Practitioners
- Vanessa Webb, Wales Council for the Blind
- Dr. Michael Wolffe, College of Optometrists
- Sue Wright, Opsis
- Mike Brace, Development Director
- Margaret Alexander, Secretary

Exhibit 5.1.5   Vision 2020 UK Working Party Members, 2002

SOURCE: Vision 2020 UK documents.

can determine their own strategies, but also be a powerful tool for influencing government and for articulating the key issues to the public. Such an Agenda could provide a framework for detailed objectives of a U.K. Forum (if one is created) and could be reviewed and revised by the Forum over time.

Background

A national agenda would provide all those concerned about visual-impairment issues with the following:

- A shared set of priorities to which they can refer in determining their own strategies
- New opportunities for partnership and collaborative projects
- A means of identifying gaps in, or duplication of, provision
- Its not being designed to remove the autonomy of any organization, to restrict its right to act alone or outside the priorities of the agenda, or to eliminate the benefits of positive competition between organizations

The items on a national agenda must meet the following criteria:

- Be achievable in the sense that there must be the serious prospect of progress
- Be nationally relevant
- Satisfy identified need
- Make sense externally and be expressed in jargon-free language
- Be empowering, not prescriptive, and allow individual organizations to pursue their own strategies within the greater context of the agenda
- Encourage cooperation between organizations to help with information exchange, good practice sharing, and project partnerships

Agreement on the national agenda would imply the need to map current provision, to assess its quality, and to agree on priorities for action. This would then enable statutory, voluntary, and private organizations to assess how best to deploy available resources. (See **Exhibit 5.1.6** for the balance of the Vision 2020 UK proposal for a national agenda for action on visual impairment.)

Although it was intended for Vision 2020 UK to remain lean, staffing was necessary. A development director, Mike Brace, was hired to move the agenda forward. Brace described his progress:

I have established a quarterly newsletter directed at both members and other interested parties to let them know what I and we are doing in their name. The net result of a year's work is that member organizations are now coming to me with ideas that they wish me to explore. They want to know if others share their ideas and are willing to form partnerships to move forward. I am also initiating projects or facilitating interest groups to get discussions under way or take proposals forward that members are unwilling to have any other single member take the lead on. When consulted by government bodies, I have endeavored to discuss the issues with members in advance to gain their view. Often the members' views are uniform enough that I can then represent them as the voice of Vision 2020 UK.

Raising Awareness

There is a universal need to improve the understanding among the general public and decision makers of the needs of visually impaired people and of their actual and potential contribution to society.

The distinct needs of, and opportunities for, visually impaired people are often overlooked. For example:

- The waiting times for cataract operations are longer than for any other treatment, and yet this is one of the top ten most cost-effective health interventions.
- Generic social workers are unable to give priority to visually impaired people.
- The employment situation is far worse for blind and partially sighted people than for any other group of disabled people, but policy is being developed generically.
- Many other excellent causes have gained a higher profile with the public, and visual impairment has become a lower priority for donors.

Rights and Responsibilities

The rights of visually impaired people must be promoted by common consent and, where necessary, supported by law. These include the right:

- To live free from discrimination
- To exercise choice and control over their lives
- To receive information in accessible formats
- To be able to safely navigate the external environment
- To have equal access to education and employment
- To enjoy the opportunities and services they need to lead fulfilled lives
- To be supported and encouraged to take part in democratic, economic, and community life and to be empowered to play a full part in determining service priorities and choices affecting them

People who do not have a visual impairment should be encouraged to learn to understand the varied needs, the achievements, and the potential of those who do.

Visually impaired people have the same rights and responsibilities as everyone else. There is a current tendency, however, to treat all people with disabilities as a generic group. This leads to the marginalization of visually impaired people with fewer opportunities and poorer services. This trend must be corrected.

Improved Prevention, Cure, and Amelioration of Visual Impairment

The ideal must be the eradication of all visual impairment, so we should continue to encourage and fund research, both medical and nonmedical. Until we attain that ideal, we must reduce the personal, social, and economic impact of visual impairment by:

- The vigorous application of current medical knowledge uniformly across the country
- Promoting the importance of early diagnosis by regular sight tests and public education
- Providing effective support and services to people who are visually impaired
- Providing effective low vision services that are consistent across the country
- Providing a range of services that ensure that visually impaired people, in all aspects of their lives and wherever they live, enjoy opportunities equal to those of other members of society

Exhibit 5.1.6   Vision 2020 UK Proposal for a National Agenda for Action on Visual Impairment

The eradication of all sight problems is unattainable for now, so we need to ensure the best possible and most timely diagnosis, treatment, amelioration, and support for all visually impaired people in all parts of the country. Examples include promoting the benefits of cataract extraction, identifying the most efficient and cost-effective means of improving the consistency and quality of eye care, and the reduction in waiting lists. We need also to address the needs of groups that are particularly at risk—elderly people, people with multiple disabilities, and children with other sensory impairment.

We must provide services that not only help to compensate physically for loss of sight but that also ensure that the disadvantages of visual impairment are relieved through the provision of specially designed and adapted services and facilities in all aspects of life.

Improving Quality of Services and Opportunities

We must seek continually to improve the quality of all the services and opportunities for visually impaired people and promote the use of standards where the results are measured primarily by client satisfaction.

This might be achieved by measuring and monitoring outcomes.

Standards based on the statistical measurement of inputs and outputs have some use but are no substitute for measures of the actual achievements of visually impaired people.

A large number of high-quality services and opportunities are available for visually impaired people around the country. But not only is the provision uneven in quantity and geographical spread (see Extending Reach, below), the quality varies widely even where services are nominally available. The aim of this agenda item is to help those providing services and opportunities to improve their own standards by sharing the experiences of others and, above all, by working with visually impaired people to measure their achievements against their aspirations and to offer them choices and opportunities to enable them to achieve more.

Extending Reach

This includes increasing the numbers of people served and increasing the geographical spread of services and opportunities and improving access to them.

Just as quality varies around the country, so does the availability of the services and opportunities that are essential to ensure the prevention, cure, and amelioration of visual impairment. Issues of particular concern include the following:

- The provision of health and social services and the contributions of local and national voluntary organizations are so variable and diverse, that it is hard to make judgments on where is the greatest need for action.
- People from ethnic minorities seem to be poorly served.
- People with dual sensory loss or with multiple disabilities need specialist attention that they often do not receive.

Exhibit 5.1.6

SOURCE: Vision 2020 UK documents.

- Action for Blind People
- Albinism Fellowship
- Association of Blind Asians
- Association of Directors of Social Services
- Blind Centre for Northern Ireland
- British Computer Association of the Blind
- British Orthoptic Society
- British RP Society
- Calibre
- Christian Blind Mission
- Circle of Guide Dog Owners
- College of Optometrists
- Fight for Sight
- Guide Dogs for the Blind Association
- HSBP Henshaw's
- Impact Foundation
- International Glaucoma Association
- International Centre for Eye Health
- Iris Fund
- LOOK
- Macular Disease Society
- National Association of Local Societies for Visually Impaired People (NALSVI)
- National Federation of the Blind
- National League of the Blind and Disabled
- National Library for the Blind
- Nystagmus Network
- Opsis
- Partially Sighted Society
- Retino Blastoma Society
- Royal National Institute for the Blind
- Royal College of General Practitioners
- Royal College of Ophthalmologists
- Scottish National Federation for the Welfare of the Blind
- Share the Vision
- Sightsavers
- Society of Blind Lawyers
- SPECS
- St. Dunstan's
- TNAUK
- Thomas Pocklington Trust
- Torch Trust
- VIEW
- Vision Aid Overseas
- Wales Council for the Blind

Exhibit 5.1.7   Vision 2020 UK Provisional Members, 2002

SOURCE: Vision 2020 UK documents.

Peacock and Remington were pleased that Vision 2020 UK was established, had articulated a common agenda, and was beginning to move forward. They were also encouraged that participating agencies were standing on equal footing, regardless of their respective sizes, and that the larger participants had assumed funding the organization's basic costs for the first three years of its operation. (See **Exhibit 5.1.7** for Vision 2020 UK provisional members.) Nevertheless, both were also well aware that this was only a first step and that over time, they would have to charge membership fees to remain sustainable. They also knew that in order to grow, the umbrella organization would likely have to consider various strategic alliances and merger options. The challenges for making Vision 2020 UK effective did not stop there. Could all of the member organizations really speak with a unified voice to all the varied stakeholders interested in the visual-impairment sector? What would it take to move from words in a document to executing the plan and achieving meaningful cost-saving efficiencies among members? How would they justify that this approach would be the best utilization of scarce human and monetary resources and was the most effective mechanism for serving the United Kingdom's visually impaired? From GDBA's board's perspective, was this the best use of Peacock's time?

Peacock strongly believed that if the nonprofit sector was going to succeed in serving the needs of the visually impaired population over the next five years, this newly constituted network would have to be made to work. Peacock pondered how to make that happen and what her and GDBA's role should be in that effort.

NOTES

1. £ = pound sterling; £1 = $1.65 as of November 27, 2002.

2. This is a term for a nominal amount of consideration, equaling roughly one British pound.

Case Study 5.2.

KaBOOM!

KaBOOM! attempts to do what we know is so important and that is to provide spaces and playgrounds in neighborhoods around the U.S., particularly very tough difficult neighborhoods where they haven't had a playground for many years because of violence and gangs, drugs and some of the other challenges they face.

—Hillary Rodham Clinton[1]

In April 2002, Darell Hammond, CEO and cofounder of KaBOOM!, looked back over the past seven years since he had decided to found a nonprofit organization with the mission of ensuring that every child, through the participation of their communities, had healthy play opportunities.

He had grown the organization from a $25,000 start-up in 1995 into a lean, highly innovative, national nonprofit with a $5-million annual budget and 17 full-time staff members who led efforts from offices in Washington, D.C., San Francisco, Chicago, Atlanta, and Burlington, Vermont. Using its signature "community-build" playground process, KaBOOM! had involved more than 65,000 volunteers in the hands-on construction of 338 playgrounds, primarily in urban and low-income communities (see **Exhibits 5.2.1 and 5.2.2**).

Year	1997	1998	1999	2000	2001	2002 (p)
Total income	1,812	3,785	2,540	2,900	6,356	n/a
Total expense	1,300	2,416	3,157	3,383	4,681	n/a
Net income	512	1,369	(617)	(483)	1,675	n/a
Net assets	519	1,987	1,370	873	2,548	n/a
Playgrounds	38	40	51	29	83	97
Active funding partners	3	8	7	4	21	26
Retention of funding partners	66%	63%	71%	100%	81%	n/a

Exhibit 5.2.1   Financial Performance and Program Results of KaBOOM!

SOURCE: Guide Star.com, and KaBOOM! internal documents.

(p) = preliminary.

n/a = not available.

KaBOOM! had generated more than $14.5 million in contributed revenue for community playgrounds, largely through business/social sector partnerships with The Home Depot, CNA Insurance, Ben & Jerry's Homemade, Target Corporation, Kimberly-Clark Corporation, Motorola, Computer Associates, Snapple, Sprint, and more than 40 other corporate partners.

Hammond was proud of the success KaBOOM! had achieved and felt that the organization had now reached the critical juncture where it was ready to turn an effective, tested program model into a systemic solution. But to do this implied a significant shift in strategic focus. Rather than just continuing to directly build playgrounds with its corporate partners, KaBOOM! would increase its emphasis on indirect builds by providing training and grant programs to help communities independently replicate the community-build playground model. Additionally, KaBOOM! would become a knowledge leader and advocate for children's right to play.

The KaBOOM! staff and board of directors were considering the opportunities and challenges of broadening their strategic direction. Competition had increased from several nonprofit organizations and for-profit companies that offered similar services for building community playgrounds. How would the new strategic direction affect the position of KaBOOM! in this landscape? How would the new strategy impact relationships with current funding partners? What type of new partners should KaBOOM! pursue to support the new strategy? Would support for the proposed program strategies hinge on new types of business/social sector partnerships? What would be the organizational implications if such a broadened strategy were pursued?

CHILDREN'S RIGHT TO PLAY

Benefits of Children's Play

Playing has a very important role in the development and learning of children, building imagination and promoting social skills among other things. As Karen DeBord

Current Partners	Past Partners
• AARP • Aid Association for Lutherans/Lutheran Brotherhood • American Academy of Dermatology • American Academy of Orthopaedic Surgeons • Armstrong Foundation • BASF • Ben & Jerry's Homemade, Inc. • Chicago Housing Authority • CNA Foundation • Computer Associates International, Inc. • Deloitte Consulting • Discover Financial Services • Motorola • NASCAR • National Society of Collegiate Scholars • Odwalla • Oregon Association of Orthopaedic Surgeons • Snapple • Sprint Foundation • Target Corporation • The Boston Consulting Group • The David and Lucile Packard Foundation • The Home Depot • The Washington Redskins • ZS Associates *Major Individual Donors* • Aly, Stacey, & Bruce Bloom • Mr. Webb Sowden • students of American University • Mr. Doug Finlay • Ms. Nancy Rosenzweig & Friends Foundation • Family & Friends of Daniel Soloma • Radian Guaranty/Radian MI	• Akin Gump Law Firm • Black Entertainment Television • British Airways/Patterson Communications • Cafritz Foundation • Chicago Park District • Chicago Tribune Foundation • CoStar Realty Information, Inc. • Epstein, Becker & Green • Erik Jonsson Community School • First Steps to School Readiness of South Carolina • First Union Corporation • Fred C. Rummel Foundation • Freddie Mac Foundation • Illinois Attorney General's Office (for the dissolved Dixmoor Park District) • John Nuveen & Co. • Jewel/Osco, an Albertson's Co. • Kankakee Valley Park District— • Orthopaedic Associations of Kankakee • Kimberly-Clark Corporation • Nike/Reuse-A-Shoe Program • Novus Services • Primordial/Zoob® • Prudential Foundation • Redwood City School District • Retired Peace Corps Volunteers • RREEF Funds and RREEF Funds –Dallas • San Francisco Promise • SOME (So Others Might Eat) • The Cheesecake Factory • The John Buck Company • Timberland • USAA A Charitable Trust • Village of Sun River Terrace • Walgreen's • WTTG-TV/Fox • Yahoo! Employees Foundation

Exhibit 5.2.2   List of KaBOOM! Partnerships

SOURCE: KaBOOM! internal documents.

and Nick Amann, two researchers from North Carolina State University, reasoned:

> Play is to a child what work is to an adult: It is what they do. It is through play that children learn about their world and the things in it. Play allows children the chance to explore their environment, to learn how it works and how they relate to it. A child can express feelings and emotions through various types of play activities (play, art, stories, etc.) far earlier than they can express them in words. For older children, play may be the outlet through which they convey emotions that they are either unwilling to share verbally or do not have the sufficient vocabulary to express. Through play, children can be anyone, at anyplace, at anytime.[2]

Furthermore, through physical play activity, children are able to stay in shape and reduce the incidence of obesity-related diseases like diabetes, sleep apnea, or gallbladder disease. A study by the National Center for Chronic Disease Prevention and Health Promotion said, "The proportion of discharges (of children) with obesity-associated diseases has increased dramatically in the past 20 years. This increase has led to a significant growth in economic costs:"[3] In the past 20 years, hospital costs for diseases related to childhood obesity increased 260% in real terms, from $35 million in 1979 to $127 million in 1999 (in constant 2001 dollars).

Current Status of Playgrounds

Children are playing less and in less than ideal places, such as alleys, streets, and decaying buildings. Darell stated, "If children are our future, why are we allowing them to play in garbage-strewn lots, abandoned cars, bushes riddled with crack vials and needles, and boarded-up buildings? It is unacceptable for children to grow up without a safe place to play."[4]

Not only is there a shortage of playgrounds, but four out of every five are considered unsafe (see **Exhibit 5.2.3**).[5] Playground accidents are a leading cause of injuries to children. According to the U.S. Consumer Product Safety Commission, every three minutes, a child in the United States sustains a serious injury from a playground accident.[6] That means that every year, more than 200,000 children suffered playground-equipment injuries that required emergency room treatment, with many requiring operative intervention.[7] The playground injury rate has more than doubled in the last 20 years.[8] Darell asserted, "Community residents need to know that they are not powerless against the statistics which say that neighborhood playgrounds are full of safety hazards."[9]

DARELL HAMMOND

A charismatic 30-year-old social entrepreneur, Hammond's accomplishments were achieved in the face of several challenges. He had no formal training in community development or nonprofit administration, but he had many innate talents. Additionally, he was challenged by dyslexia, but he had tenaciously applied himself to understand the business of his mission, taking a small start-up investment and turning it into a multi-million-dollar social enterprise. He did not complete college, but he had attracted stars for his staff, recruiting them from for-profit, government, and nonprofit sectors—many alumni from top universities.

- 80% of the playgrounds lacked adequate protective surfacing, which was the most critical safety factor on playgrounds because approximately 75% of all injuries were caused by falls.

- 48% of playgrounds had climbers and 36% had slides where the height of the play equipment is greater than six feet high, which was higher than necessary for play value, and only served to increase the risk of injury.

- 47% of all playgrounds had peeling, chipped, or cracking paint on equipment surfaces.

- 38% of playgrounds had small gaps, open S-hooks, and other protrusions, which posed clothing entanglement hazards, in particular, drawstrings on clothing.

- 38% of playgrounds had unacceptable dangerous equipment, such as chain or cable walks, animal swings, and individual climbing ropes or exercise rings.

- 34% of playgrounds had improperly sized openings in the play equipment that posed a head entrapment hazard that might lead to strangulation.

- 31% of slides and climbing equipment did not have an adequate fall zone under and around the play equipment. Other equipment and obstacles in the fall zone posed hazards where a child might fall.

- 27% of playgrounds with swings had some swings that were either too close together or too close to swing supports, which increased the risk that a child could be hit by a moving swing.

- 13% of playgrounds with swings had swing seats that were made of wood, metal, or other rigid material, which increased the severity of injury if impact occurred.

Exhibit 5.2.3   Public Playground Safety Statistics

SOURCE: Adapted from U.S. Public Interest Research Group, The Consumer Federation of America. "Playing It Safe: June 2000. A Fifth Nationwide Safety Survey of Public Playgrounds," viewed at <http://www.pirg.org/reports/consumer/playground2000/playgroundreport2000.PDF> (April 2, 2002).

Hammond believed that he shared many qualities with children—including curiosity, boundless energy, and a willingness to pick himself and those around him up and to keep going during challenging times. These traits were helpful to the organization in its first two years, which were rocky and marked with a high staff turnover and, he quickly admits, memorable missteps of his own. Over time, he believed that he had evolved into a mature operational and people manager, running an organization with high donor and staff retention rates, plus award-winning program innovations.

The seeds of his lifelong commitment to this cause come from his experience growing up with his seven brothers and sisters in a children's home in Mooseheart, Illinois, which was funded by the local and national Moose Lodge community of 1.7 million men and women. The experience shaped both his perspective on the power of volunteer service and his commitment to give children opportunities to play. He had become a passionate advocate who "eats, sleeps, and breathes" play. He developed an encyclopedic knowledge of everything that touched the cause—from community engagement in child's play, to playground equipment design, to ADA guidelines, to emerging community development theory, to pending legislation, to the intricacies of business challenges facing myriad prospective corporate partners.

Hammond credited a number of mentors for helping him shape his leadership philosophy, most notably Marian Wright Edelman, founder of the Children's Defense Fund; Suzanne Apple, vice president of community affairs for The Home Depot; Billy Shore, founder of Share Our Strength; Michael Brown, cofounder and president of City Year; and Dr. John Kretzmann, codirector of the Assets Based Community Development Institute at Northwestern University, each of whom had helped him understand the challenging work of building a citizenry in a community of people who have the skills, know-how, and resources to create a stronger neighborhood and democracy.

KaBOOM!

History

In 1995, armed only with this vision, $25,000, and a lot of motivation, Hammond and KaBOOM! cofounder Dawn Hutchison began to seek partners to support their endeavor. In 1996, Hammond met Suzanne Apple, vice president of community affairs at The Home Depot, when they spoke on a panel at a housing conference. A few months later, Hammond was able to get the support from The Home Depot and from community members, who raised $9,000 for the project. Together, members of The Home Depot and community volunteers joined their efforts to

create the first-ever KaBOOM! playground in Washington, D.C.

The KaBOOM! vision, from the outset, was "to help develop a country in which all children have within their communities access to equitable, fun, and healthy play opportunities, with the participation and support of their families and peers." The community component of this vision was key, as the organization believed that disconnection among neighbors eroded civic life and undermined a community's ability to respond to and prevent serious social problems. KaBOOM! aimed to provide an antidote for this disconnection: a catalytic cause that would inspire hands-on, collaborative civic engagement. Every KaBOOM! playground project, therefore, was driven by the families and children who would use the playground, and funding partners were coached to "do with, don't do unto" so that at the end of a playground partnership, the partners would have built a strong community through the process of building a playground.

During 1997, KaBOOM! started its LET US PLAY campaign to fulfill a commitment to General Colin Powell's "America's Promise: The Alliance for Youth" launched at the president's Summit for America's Future. Through the campaign, KaBOOM! committed itself "to build, renovate, or provide technical assistance to develop 1,000 community-build playgrounds by the end of the year 2000."[10] The goal was to enrich more communities with playgrounds, enable more children to play safely together, and encourage more neighbors to meet, work, and solve their problems together. By the end of the year, KaBOOM! had raised $1.8 million and created 38 playgrounds with Kimberly-Clark and CNA as new corporate partners.

In 1998, KaBOOM! found itself with more resources than it could administer. Revenue doubled to $3.8 million through eight corporate partnerships that supported 40 builds, registering a net income of $1.3 million for the year. However, because of the unprecedented growth and the lack of systems in place to manage that growth, some partners complained that it was hard to work with KaBOOM! When there was a problem, Hammond said he "would jump on a plane and solve the problem; but that was the problem." Apple said, "KaBOOM! was building the plane while they were flying it, and they had to slow down to speed up."

As a result of these problems, several partners decided to reduce or terminate their involvement with KaBOOM! In 1999, KaBOOM! revenues fell by one-third to $2.5 million through seven partnerships (see Exhibit 5.2.1). However, KaBOOM! decided to increase the number of playground builds to 51, which generated a deficit for the year of $617,000. The appearance of a deficit was also created by the fact that accounting standards required KaBOOM! to book revenue received in advance for multiyear programs in the year that the grants were received.

Faced with key partners indicating that their support to KaBOOM! would end unless things changed, Hammond started to surround himself with people with operational experience that could help KaBOOM! improve its operations. He invited Pete D'Amelio, senior vice president of operations of The Cheesecake Factory, to become a board member and hired a more seasoned management team. Since then, KaBOOM! has dedicated considerable energy to improving its product consistency and management of the partnerships. As a result of these efforts, KaBOOM! revenue, partnerships, and builds grew consistently. By year-end 2001, KaBOOM! reported total income of $6.3 million, 83 playgrounds built, and 21 partnerships.

Organization

To carry out its mission, KaBOOM! employed 17 full-time staff with an organization structure driven by work process (see **Exhibits 5.2.4, 5.2.5, and 5.2.6**). Project management staff ("Playground Dream Builders") were responsible for coordinating and executing KaBOOM! playground-build projects and leading community partnership development. "The Administrators of Play" provided administrative support to KaBOOM! operations. Marketing and development staff ("The Pep Squad") were responsible for marketing, development of revenue-generating partnerships, account services, and public relations. From the perspective of external partners, the KaBOOM! structure mirrored that of a small marketing agency, as staff were also organized into project-specific account teams with billable hours and account management systems.

Hammond explained that "human resources are absolutely, no doubt, one of our biggest challenges going forward . . . retaining, training, and recruiting new people are critical activities for us achieving our new plan." As a result, by 2001, KaBOOM! had implemented an approach aimed at having "the right people in the right place, at the right time, and with the right training." This involved paying competitive salaries and implementing an incentive system that rewarded employees when corporate goals were met or exceeded. The incentive system for 2001 was structured so that all employees would receive a bonus of up to $3,000 if certain metrics for success were accomplished by the entire team.

Operations

To ensure that every child has healthy play opportunities, KaBOOM! historically had focused on its core strategy of community builds financed through corporate partnerships. With sustainable partnerships with major corporations, the organization remained focused on this program with a steady growth rate. However, KaBOOM! was now on the brink of implementing its three-part program strategy (lead, educate, and advocate) in a bolder, more assertive fashion—maintaining the pace of its community-build playground projects, maintaining its educational programs such as the Playground Institute, and maintaining its position on the child's right to play, but "turning up the volume" on the latter two areas to extend its impact (see **Exhibit 5.2.7**).

Leading

Broad-based community participation, grassroots volunteerism, and a self-help spirit were the hallmarks of a KaBOOM! community-build playground process. KaBOOM! typically worked with volunteer leaders to plan and design a playground over a 27-week period, applying best practices from their work on an eight-step project plan to research, conceive, plan, design, coordinate, build, celebrate, and maintain a community playground. This documented process, the "KaBOOM! Roadmap," helped communities and funding partners leverage their existing assets, get creative in their approach to event organizing, access templated project materials, and ensure a safe, fun playground project. (See **Exhibits 5.2.8** and **5.2.9**.)

The playground Build Days were high-energy events that involved from 50 to 500 volunteers who built the playground from the ground up in a single day. They were barn-raising events, with an urban twist. The day began with an empty site and ended with a new and safe playground for children. By capitalizing on the talents and resources that are already in a community, KaBOOM! and its funding and community partners sought to build and revitalize a community through the process of building a playground.

For each project, KaBOOM! provided training, materials, and support to corporate and community leaders in their projects.

- The community partner (typically a youth-serving nonprofit organization such as a YMCA or Boys & Girls Club) provided land and worked with KaBOOM! to organize community members to help design, plan, fundraise, and actually build the playground.
- The funding partner (typically a corporation) leveraged a financial investment in the project with its team's expertise and building labor.
- KaBOOM! provided full-service project management for the duration of the project—from the creation and facilitation of planning committees, to playground design and procurement,

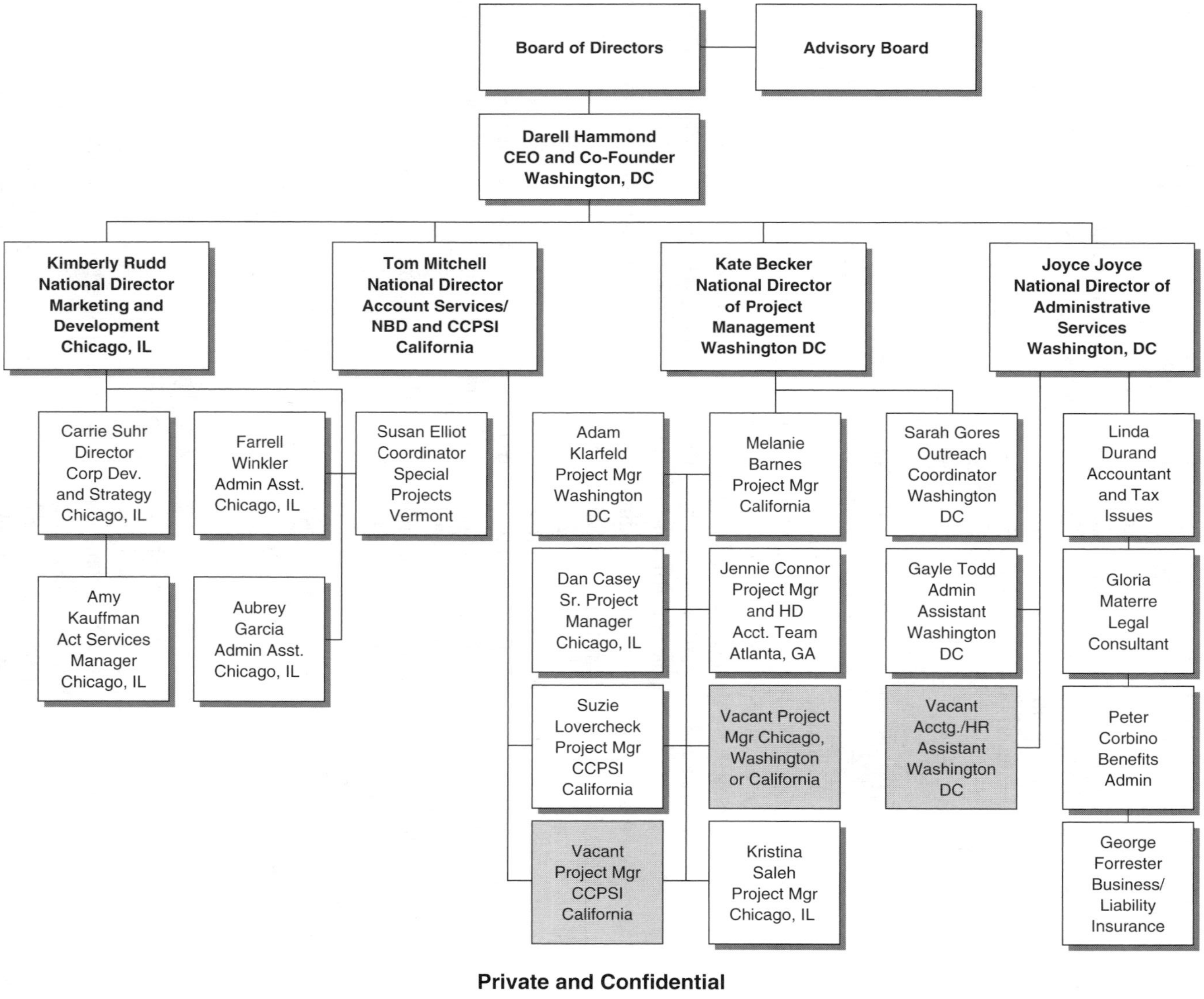

Private and Confidential

Exhibit 5.2.4   Organization Chart and KaBOOM! Team

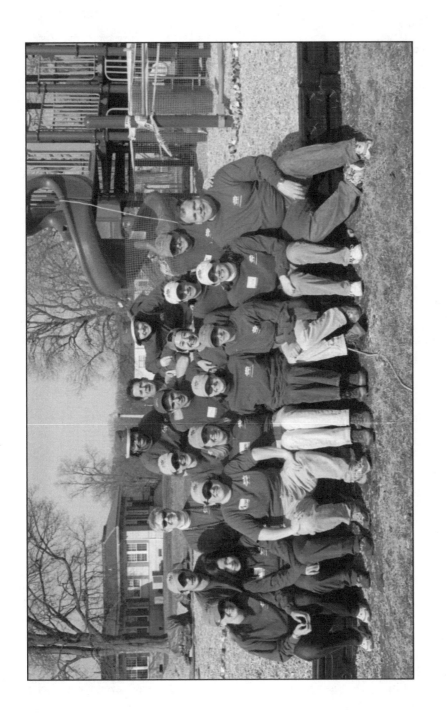

Exhibit 5.2.4

SOURCE: KaBOOM! internal documents.

KaBOOM! Board of Directors	
Suzanne Apple The Home Depot	**Dawn Hutchinson** Cofounder KaBOOM!
Michael Brown City Year	**Erin Patton** Edelman Public Relations Worldwide
Pete D'Amelio The Cheesecake Factory	**Rey Ramsey** One Economy Corporation
Tony Diefell Harvard Business School	**Nancy Rosenzweig** Zip Car
Helen Doria Chicago Park District	**John Sarvey** National Corps/City Year
Peter Farmsworth National Basketball Association	**David Wofford** Wofford Consulting, Inc.
Ken Grouf Yahoo!	**Christopher Zorich** The Christopher Zorich Foundation
Darell Hammond KaBOOM!	

KaBOOM! Advisory Board	
Bob Boulter Jubilee Enterprise of Greater Washington	**Vanessa Kirsh** New Profit Inc.
Fred Druck Playground Environments	**Dale Miller** Playworld Systems
Marian Wright Edelman Children's Defense Fund	**Jean Shappet** Playground Design and Safety Consultant
Bob Goodwin Points of Light Foundation	

Exhibit 5.2.5   KaBOOM! Board of Directors and Advisory Board (April 2002)

SOURCE: KaBOOM! internal documents.

to insurance considerations, to supervision of the construction process, and more.

KaBOOM! also managed SPRUCE©, a national, multimarket playground-improvement program that had helped rehabilitate 1,500 playgrounds. KaBOOM! planned to pilot an Urban Skatepark Program, which would use the community-build process to facilitate skateboard park construction projects, each of which would include design events with teenagers, construction days, and pre- and postbuild

KaBOOM! Playground Dream Builders

Melanie Barnes, Project Manager A native of Omaha, Nebraska, Melanie says that as a child on the playground, she was a game leader—a natural role for the second oldest kid in a family of seven children. All grown up, she's still a leader, an alumnae of the AmeriCorps*NCCC program, and a nationally certified playground inspector. The mantra she keeps at the top of her mind while at work? "It's for the kids," she says often. And that it is, for Melanie's work at KaBOOM! centers on managing community-build playground projects on behalf of and with several funding and community partners. She began volunteering with KaBOOM! in 1997 and became a Boomer in 2000.

Kate Becker, National Director of Project Management Proud of her Ohio roots, Kate has lived in the District of Columbia for eight years. Her first memory on a playground as a child is being pushed higher and higher by her sister who would then run underneath the swing leaving Kate tickled into a fit of giggles. Kate's involvement with KaBOOM! goes back five years, first as a volunteer and then by coordinating the 18- to 24-year-olds she managed to come out and serve on KaBOOM! projects. From the aspect of being the director of the AmeriCorps*NCCC Capital Region Campus, Kate was always impressed with the level of organization and the immediate impacts that KaBOOM! has in a community and is thrilled to be a part of it.

Dan Casey, Senior Project Manager A native of Chicago, Dan says that as a child on the playground, he was a behind-the-scenes kid who enjoyed playing hide-and-seek and other games of mystery (and mischief). A mathematics whiz with a degree from the University of Illinois, his quiet demeanor hides the fact that he lives on the edge and has been known to risk just about anything for a good laugh or sports bet. At KaBOOM!, Dan manages community-build playground projects on behalf of and with several funding and community partners and is a nationally certified playground inspector. He became a Boomer in 1999.

Adam Klarfeld, Project Manager A native of Kansas City—both in Missouri and Kansas!—Adam says that as a child on the playground, he was the kid to beat, the one who wanted to win at racing, climbing, nearly everything! At KaBOOM!, that competitive nature means he aims to create the best playgrounds we build. A graduate of the University of Pennsylvania, Adam says that four years in Philly toughened him up a bit, preparing him for the hard-nosed world of consulting for trucking and telecommunications industry clients at Mercer Management Consulting. After time in suits and meetings, Adam has changed gears and opted for a career in T-shirts and construction meetings with KaBOOM!

Jennie Connor, Home Depot Project Management & Account Services A native of Tennessee, Jennie Connor likes to flip out . . . and over and under. You see, as a child on the playground, Jennie was the girl who could do flips for hours and was most partial to the monkey bars. Today, she manages KaBOOM! community-build playground projects and plays a critical coordinating and account services role for all KaBOOM!–Home Depot partnership programs. A graduate of Furman University in South Carolina, Jennie parlayed her studies in communications into a position at The Home Depot prior to her work with KaBOOM! Having logged more than two years in coordinating community relations for The Home Depot, and two nonstop months on the road traveling and working with all KaBOOM! offices, Jennie is well prepared for her new role. A Boomer since Fall 2001, she works from the Atlanta Store Support Center and is working toward her national certification in playground inspection.

Suzy Lovercheck, Project Manager A native of Palo Alto, California, Suzie says that as a child on the playground, she was a tomboy, always wanting to challenge the boys in soccer, handball, and football, as well as keep up with the girls playing jump rope and tether ball. She is willing to try almost anything once, especially when it comes to food! Suzie graduated from the University of California-Davis

---

Exhibit 5.2.6   KaBOOM!'s Staff (April 2002)   *(Continued)*

(Continued)

in 1999 and went on to complete two years with AmeriCorps*NCCC, where she challenged herself alongside her teammates in both work and play. At KaBOOM!, Suzie is focusing on the Child Care Playground Safety Initiative, a program funded by the David and Lucile Packard Foundation for northern California child-care centers. She became a Boomer in February 2002.

Kristina Saleh, Project Manager Embracing dual homelands of San Lorenzo, California, and Phillipsburg, Montana, Kristina says that as a child on the playground, she was a possum . . . hanging and dangling from every possible item. Kristina cites as her favorite mantra this quote from Robert Frost: "The world is full of willing people, some willing to work, the rest willing to let them." This graduate of Knox College helped lead public relations for Project Vote Smart during the 2000 election. Now she's leading a litany of efforts to boost play opportunities for children by managing community-build playground project on behalf of and with our funding and community partners. She became a Boomer in 2001.

KaBOOM! Administrators of Play

Darell Hammond, Founder & Chief Executive of Play A native of Chicago, Darell says that as a child on the playground, he was a rock thrower and climber, as well as a Boy Scout with a knack for community service, outdoor fun, and old-fashioned leadership. Today, he leads a troupe of Boomers in throwing rocks (at unsafe playgrounds) and climbing (to reach more people about our mission). It's proof that childhood fun can lay the groundwork for great things! Darell is married, a popular speaker at conferences and universities, and a nationally certified playground inspector. At KaBOOM!, he is responsible for all operations for and growth of the nation's leading nonprofit organization of its kind. Darell founded KaBOOM! in 1995 with board officer Dawn Hutchison. Darell is a board member of The Independent Sector, a consortium of the nation's leading nonprofit organizations.

Susan Elliot, Special Assistant to the CEO A native of North Andover, Massachusetts, Susan says that as a child, she was a high-flyer on the playground, fond of the wooden swings that she and her grandmother—who ran the community center—visited regularly. Those wooden swings have been replaced with modern designs, but the desire to fly high, move fast, and catch the wind remains in Susan, who bikes, skis, and snowboards with her sons Nathan and Conner with a passion. A new talent at KaBOOM!, Susan will provide support to the KaBOOM! board of directors and the senior management team. She became a Boomer in 2001.

Joyce E. Joyce, National Director, Administrative Services A native of Elkton, Maryland, Joyce says that as a child on the playground, she was a swinger who aimed high and showed no fear, always asking to be pushed higher and faster. An only child for whom the playground was the perfect social activity, Joyce's favorite saying comes from a childhood icon, Winnie the Pooh: "Things are always so much more grand and wonderful when your friends are there to share them." Last year, life got grander with new husband Butch, new stepson Daniel, and new last name Joyce, making her the only double-named Boomer! At KaBOOM!, Joyce manages administrative and financial operations for the four KaBOOM! offices, making her extremely popular among staff on paydays. She became a Boomer in 1999.

Gayle Todd, Administrative Assistant A native of Amherst, New York, Gayle was the child usually found playing games on the playground—hopscotch and jump rope games were only set aside for a don't-try-this-at-home game called "ghostrider." After earning a degree from the State University of New York at Oswego, she traveled for a few years and ended up in Vermont working for KaBOOM! funding partner Ben & Jerry's Homemade, Inc. Gayle now keeps KaBOOM!'s national headquarters in good running order as the office's administrative assistant. She became a Boomer in 2001.

Exhibit 5.2.6

Farrell Winkler, Administrative Assistant A native of Palos Heights, Illinois, Farrell says that as a child on the playground, she was a tomboy. Today, she believes that life is too short to worry about the wrinkles in your jeans. A recent graduate of DePaul University, Farrell is an aspiring mystery writer who loves children and hanging out with her niece, in particular. At KaBOOM!, Farrell provides marketing support to the KaBOOM! team and handles administrative responsibilities for its Chicago office. She became a Boomer in 2001.

KaBOOM! Pep Squad

Sarah Gores, Community Development Coordinator A native of St. Paul, Minnesota, Sarah says that as a child on the playground, she was a tree climber and a builder of forts in lilac bushes. Today, she puts her knowledge gained on the job and through her playground safety certification to work by building playgrounds and butterfly gardens and more. She is the only Boomer with a cat *and* a motorcycle, and the one entrusted to spread the word about our work to community organizations. At KaBOOM!, Sarah manages outreach and service to community groups that are interested in the KaBOOM! model of community-build playgrounds. She became a Boomer in 2000.

Amy Kaufman, Account Services Manager A native of Chicago, Amy says that as a child, she used the playground to let her imagination soar. This creative spirit carries over into her life, especially into her work at KaBOOM! Amy is an avid traveler who loves visiting the world beyond her own neighborhood. The exploration and discovery of traveling help her to connect with people from all walks of life. At KaBOOM!, Amy puts that energy to work, as she will help to systematize account services and communicate with funding partners to discuss the progress of their programs. She became a Boomer in January 2002.

Tom Mitchell, National Director, Account Services & Project Management A native of Coronado, California, Tom says that as a child on the playground, he was a swinger who loved to climb fast and high, feeling the air rushing into his face on the upsweeps. His childhood memories are vivid with playground time spent with his dad (the man who took him high in swings!) and grandfather (who endured Tom's constant requests to go to the playground). All that time flying high might explain Tom's favorite mantra: "If it doesn't kill you, it only makes you stronger." He flexes his muscles for KaBOOM! by managing our relationships with funding partners and donors and helping to encourage new funding partners to support KaBOOM! playgrounds. He became a Boomer in 1999.

Kimberley Evans Rudd, National Director, Marketing & Development A native of Chicago, Kim says that as a child on the playground, she was a screamer—the kid who screamed loud and proud going down the gigantic slide at Belle Island in Detroit, where she grew up. Now her favorite people to play with are her husband David and their five-year-old twins, who make their own fair share of screams and squeals. Her favorite mantra was something her grandmother said daily to encourage family participation in chores: "Many hands make light work." At KaBOOM!, many hands help with Kim's work in leading KaBOOM! marketing efforts, promoting community playgrounds, child's play, and the other great reasons for supporting KaBOOM! She became a Boomer in 1998.

Carrie Suhr, Director of Corporate Development & Strategy A native of Baltimore, Maryland, Carrie says that as a child on the playground, she was a lightning-fast slide racer and an architect of sandbox cities! Never one to be intimidated by the speed of slides or the challenges of sand, Carrie's favorite motto has become "Ain't nothing to it but to do it." Now, she's doing "it" at KaBOOM!, managing efforts to begin new marketing partnerships with corporations that result in increased funding and support for community playgrounds. Carrie became a Boomer in 2001.

Exhibit 5.2.6

Case Study

Exhibit 5.2.7   KaBOOM! Core Strategies

SOURCE: KaBOOM! internal documents.

events with athletes to promote the maintenance and programming of the skateboard park.

Education

KaBOOM! helped communities independently replicate its community-build playground process through a free Getting Started Kit publication, five Tool Kit manuals, an annual Playground Institute training conference, a playground challenge grant program, its Web site, and demonstration playground builds. (See **Exhibit 5.2.10.**)

The annual Playground Institute provided community and nonprofit leaders with an overview of basic organizing skills such as fund-raising, publicity, and volunteer recruitment, along with an opportunity to learn how to build community

- June 14, 2001
  First meeting of Playground Planning Committee.

- July 2–3, 2001
  Members of Planning Committee worked with K-4th graders in summer school at Francis Scott Key to design their dream playground.

- July 10, 2001
  Design Day and Kick-off Community Meeting at Francis Scott Key.

- August 3, 2001
  Goal: To complete playground design and order equipment.

- August–September 2001
  Recruit volunteers, raise funds, organize and plan Build Day.

- October 2001
  Site preparation and removal of unsafe play structure by SF Unified School District.

- October 2001
  Build Day, installation of new play structure by 200 community volunteers.

- Ongoing
  Maintenance of play structure, continued improvement of play yard, community-strengthening events.

Exhibit 5.2.8   Timeline of Sunset Neighborhood Community Playground Build

SOURCE: KaBOOM! internal documents.

Exhibit 5.2.9   Building the Playground   *(Continued)*

(Continued)

Exhibit 5.2.9

SOURCE: KaBOOM! internal documents.

Welcome! By responding to this Getting Started Kit Questionnaire, you are creating a profile about your project. When you send the profile to KaBOOM!, we will review and track your organization's project in an effort to provide support, information, and other resources (including possible funding) for your project. To complete the questionnaire and get your profile in our "playground pool," please do the following:

Answer the questions below, on your letterhead.

Take photographs of your site (print or digital).

Obtain a letter of support from your executive director, CEO, or board officer.

Sketch an overhead layout of your site, showing the playground area and site measurements in relation to any buildings, streets, trees, parking lots, and other major structures.

Put it all in an envelope and mail to:

KaBOOM! Playground Profile
333 S. Wabash, Suite 16 South
Chicago, IL 60604–4107

Or, submit online to info@kaboom.org.
If you have any questions regarding your Playground Profile, please call 202–659–0215, ext. 225.

Questions

1. Describe your group, its mission, history, and background. If your group is part of a local or national organization, please describe your branch of the organization (such as "one of 12 schools in the District "or "the fourth largest chapter and the only one serving the Fox River Valley").
2. Describe your organization's relationship to the community in which the build is located.
3. Describe your organization's experience with volunteer programs.
4. Describe the children you serve: their ages, ethnic backgrounds, and any special needs or talents they may have.
5. Describe the impact a new playground will have on those children and on your community.
6. Describe how you think the KaBOOM! community-build process compliments the vision and plan for your new playground.
7. If your site is selected for a project, how much and what kinds of involvement and support do you expect to have from people in your organization and/or community?
8. Do you currently have a playground on the site, or is this the first playground that will exist on this site?
   a. If there is a playground, please describe it: the existing equipment and its approximate age, the dimensions of the site, and the surface below the equipment (wood chips, grass, concrete, asphalt, dirt, sand, etc.)
   b. If there is no existing playground, please describe your future playground site and its dimensions. Do you currently own or lease this property? What is on the property now? (grass, dirt, abandoned car, sprinkler system, trees, etc.) What was there before? (abandoned building, vacant lot, gas station, etc.)
9. Tell us about your project's budget? What percentage of your budget do you expect to raise from fund-raising activities, foundation grants, corporate gifts/sponsorships, individual donors, contributions from your lead organization (such as a national office, a school district office, or a city department); your totals should equal 100%. If you already have begun to raise funds, how much have you raised?
10. Please include the names, daytime phone numbers, and e-mail addresses of two people we can contact with questions and for status updates on the progress of your playground project.

Case Study

Exhibit 5.2.10   "Getting Started Kit" Questionnaire

SOURCE: KaBOOM! internal documents.

playgrounds, receive free resource publications, and even qualify for thousands of dollars in grant monies.

More than 1,300 community leaders had participated in the Playground Institutes, and 28 trained communities had received grant support from KaBOOM!, The Home Depot, the American Academy of Dermatology, and Playworld Systems. For Playground Institute graduates, KaBOOM! had provided training and guidance throughout the process of building the playground, ensuring that the design met safety standards, community requirements, and budget guidelines. It also had ensured maximum purchasing power for the playground equipment, materials, and safety surfacing, and sometimes it had even supervised the installation of the new playground by the corporate and community volunteers.

Looking into the future, KaBOOM!'s proposed new strategy would modify the institute's curriculum and launch a national training series that would increase the organization's "surface area" by offering daylong regional trainings that would let local leaders access the expertise of the KaBOOM! staff and learn to replicate its community-build playground model. KaBOOM! would continue to provide challenge grants and would add value in managing grants by working with the recipients in all aspects of the build.

In spring 2002, KaBOOM! also was developing an interactive Web-based project planning tool that it was considering marketing as a free service for public use. The tool, which would also be used in conjunction with all KaBOOM! programs, offered playground planners a robust platform for community organizing, project management, as well as dynamic templates for proposals, recruitment materials, and a free playground project Web site.

Advocacy and Awareness

When KaBOOM! advocated, it spoke out for the value and benefits of play; it promoted awareness of what makes a safe, developmentally appropriate playground with high play value; and it provided commentary on the legislation behind playground safety and playground spending. KaBOOM! had cosponsored media events and published and distributed brochures with the U.S. Consumer Product Safety Commission. It had raised awareness about equity in play on more than 1.2 million pint packages of the new Ben & Jerry's ice cream flavor, and via its funding partners, media relations, and national broadcast and print advertising.

Under the proposed strategy shift, KaBOOM! would promote the creation of a legislative initiative that would call upon states, local governments, and schools to develop and maintain safe playgrounds that were designed to provide greater access to all children, with special focus on underprivileged and underserved children. In spring 2002, it was launching a new service on its Web site, powered by CapWiz, that would allow supporters to write elected officials and media in support of "healthy play opportunities."

To increase awareness about the playground deficit, KaBOOM!, together with The Home Depot and Peter D. Hart Research Associates, was planning to measure the perceived U.S. playground deficit in fall 2002. This study would provide information on the quantity, quality, and safety of the available playgrounds and also explore the perceptions of the health impact of playgrounds. Finally, KaBOOM! and a research team at the University of Southern California's Institute for Prevention Research had proposed a five-year study to the Centers for Disease Control and Prevention that would measure the efficacy of playgrounds as environmental interventions to increase children's physical activity and decrease their body mass; if funded, the study would begin in 2003.

Competitors

One unintended consequence of success for KaBOOM! had been increased competition in playground builds. A group of for-profit companies and nonprofit organizations offered similar products, threatening the KaBOOM! position. This competition increased when KaBOOM! documented its community-build process in Tool Kit publications that were sold to the public through the KaBOOM! Web site: <www.kaboom.org>. These publications included: (a) KaBOOM! Playground Owner's Manual, (b) The Getting Started Kit, (c) Community-Build Playground Manual, (d) Community Fundraising Idea Kit, and (e) A to Z Community Assets & Resources Handbook. Some of its main competitors were the following:

• *Learning Structures* Founded in 1972, Learning Structures had built more than 600 playgrounds and had offered services tailored to support each step of the community-build process: planning, design, construction supervision, and budget management.[12] KaBOOM! had led their first three projects in partnership with Learning

Structures. The company targeted community customers, providing them with similar services to those of KaBOOM!

• *Leathers & Associates* This for-profit company had 30 years of experience designing and building playgrounds with community volunteers. They focused on serving higher-income communities and were "considered the Lincoln Navigators of the swing-set-and-monkey-bar crowd."[13] They had built over 1,600 playgrounds, which were financed mostly by the communities.

• *Jack Morton* This for-profit company, and other event management companies like it, helped firms improve performance, increase sales, and build brands by creating events, environments, and interactive experiences that motivate and transform employees and customers.[14] Although they did not build playgrounds, they had a strong database of current and prospective customers and competed with KaBOOM! by offering companies motivational events similar to the playground builds for their corporate events.

• *Landscape Structures* Founded in 1971, Landscape Structures provided playground equipment for parks, schools, and childcare centers. This company was a leading playground equipment company that employed 425 people, had a national network of independent sales organizations, and was one of the largest makers of playground equipment, with sales of almost $96 million in 2001. KaBOOM! had built its 3rd through 120th playgrounds in partnership with the company. This respected for-profit company now offered to help customers manage volunteer installation processes to boost equipment sales.

• *Boundless Playgrounds* This nonprofit organization was created in 1997 and sought to increase public awareness of the need for playgrounds where children of all abilities could laugh, play, and grow together. In addition, they provided direct services to people, groups, and companies who want to design and develop these playgrounds. The goal was to ultimately have fully integrated, universally accessible playgrounds in reach of every child in the United States. Boundless Playgrounds provided help in the following areas: coaching and support in project management, universal play environment design, community partnerships, volunteer recruitment, community relations, and promotion and fund-raising.[15] Up to year-end 2001, they had completed 30 playgrounds and had 50 more in active development. Furthermore, in August 2001, they completed their first corporate-sponsored playground in Providence, Rhode Island, with the support of Hasbro, a company that designs, manufactures, and markets toys.

Business Model

KaBOOM! had gotten attention in the nonprofit sector as an organization whose business model let it fund programs and operations without relying on traditional sources of charitable contributions. Necessity had been the mother of invention for KaBOOM! in its start-up phase: Philanthropic foundations had hesitated to commit grant support to a young organization, and program officers had shared that they considered play a luxury, not a critical grantmaking issue priority. In response, KaBOOM! studied the nonprofit organizations it most admired—Habitat for Humanity, Children's Miracle Network,

Share Our Strength, and Make-A-Wish Foundation—and began building a transactional business/social sector partnership model that revolved around the sale of a marketable product, rather than the receipt of a charitable gift.

Excited to pursue a more efficient, market-driven approach to the way nonprofits raise funds and run programs, Darell would challenge staff, board, and partners by asking, "If all we were doing was moving money from a fixed universe of charitable funds, and redistributing it to communities, what really—at the end of the day—is our added value?" So, rather than applying for funding from foundation and government grantmakers, the KaBOOM! team generated more than 90% of the organization's operating budget from earned income, project fees, licensing agreements, product sales, and cause-related marketing partnerships structured with corporate partners.

Of the total income that KaBOOM! earned during 2001, 71% came from corporations, 16% from communities, 12% from foundations, and 1% from other sources. The majority of the revenue was raised through a fee-for-service model. That is, KaBOOM! sold playground project packages that included KaBOOM! management fees, expenses, and equipment costs. Sponsorship of a typical playground project ranged in total cost from $40,000 to $55,000 per build.

KaBOOM! also generated revenue by offering companies license to participate in KaBOOM! programs and to use the KaBOOM! trademark, logo, and information in connection with product packaging, advertising, retail program and promotional contests, and other consumer

Exhibit 5.2.11   Ben & Jerry's KaBerry KaBOOM!

SOURCE: KaBOOM! internal documents.

marketing activities in exchange for licensing fees, royalties, and promotional support for the KaBOOM! mission. These cause-related marketing partnerships generated 2% of KaBOOM! total revenues. One example of a deal of this type was the introduction by Ben & Jerry's Homemade of a new ice cream flavor called KaBerry KaBOOM! in April 2001 (see **Exhibit 5.2.11**). In spring 2002, KaBOOM! was negotiating a similar licensing agreement with Snapple Beverages, Inc.

In addition to corporate funding, KaBOOM! asked communities to help pay a fraction of the costs of building the playgrounds. Usually, communities paid between $5,000 and $15,000, depending on their capacity to pay, the size of the project, time available for fund-raising, and the financial gap needed to complete the playground.

The third most important source of revenue for KaBOOM! was foundation grants. However, most of these resources were in turn given by KaBOOM! to communities that participated in the annual Playground Institute organized by KaBOOM! These communities wanted to build playgrounds but were not part of the direct build efforts by KaBOOM! The size of the cash support ranged from $5,000 to $15,000 per community.

Individual donations represented less than 1% of KaBOOM! income, and it received no government funding.

The cost structure of KaBOOM! was about two-thirds variable, varying directly and proportionally with the number of playgrounds built. About 15% of the costs were semivariable, and about 20% were fixed. Some of the costs generated by KaBOOM! operations were actually paid by its corporate partners; for example, KaBOOM! office space in Chicago and Atlanta was provided free of charge by CNA Insurance and The Home Depot, which also provided tools and materials without cost to KaBOOM!

Partnerships

KaBOOM! followed a three-step development cycle that moved individual relationships with potential funding partners from initial contact, to contractual partnerships, to renewal. These steps included: (1) encouraging a prospective partner to see a playground build in action, (2) piloting a partnership with a single playground project, and (3) customizing an approach to future build partnerships that maximized employee and community relations wins for the funding partner.

Hammond explained, "Strategy number one is to bring a potential partner to a build. It is important that they see it, experience it, and understand its power to strengthen employee and community relations."[16] As Hammond explained, "It is a funnel effect. A lot of the partners do not initially invest in the full mission up front. They see KaBOOM! as an avenue to achieve a specific goal," such as gaining goodwill or motivating employees at the end of a corporate retreat. KaBOOM! then worked to expand their investment in the cause. With the exception of a small number of funding partners who made a onetime commitment (such as a family that built a playground in memory of their son), nearly every funding partner in KaBOOM! history had come back to sponsor more than one playground project (see **Exhibit 5.2.12**). Additionally, from one year to the next, an average of 76% of KaBOOM! funding partners renewed their support for KaBOOM! (see **Exhibit 5.2.1**).

Hammond described the role of partnerships to the KaBOOM! model: "When corporations pour more than money into a community, putting their people, values, and creativity there, too, it can be powerful for everyone involved. Communities learn new strategies for their development, and employees feel better about where they work and what the company stands for. It's really a sort of infectious pride that spreads to everyone who touches that playground."

Internally, KaBOOM! had five categories for its resource-generating partners:

• *Team Build Partners* sponsored playground projects exclusively. These partners typically had short planning horizons and the ability to allocate $50,000 at a time from marketing, human resources, or community affairs budgets. While these partners were very important as a source of resources and potential long-term partnerships, the relationship was market based. Darell stated, "Companies outsource these events to KaBOOM! and KaBOOM! receives a fee for its services." This group primarily included companies such as Motorola, which had sponsored six builds, and associations such as the American Academy for Orthopedic Surgeons, which built three accessible playgrounds in conjunction with its annual conference and planned to continue working with KaBOOM! for the remainder of the decade as part of a commemorative period educating the public on bone and joint injuries.

• *Media Partners* helped build awareness of the KaBOOM! cause through media coverage. This group included companies such as Cumulus Media, which had provided $400,000 of radio coverage in 35 markets.

• *Marketing Partners* helped build the KaBOOM! brand through cause-related

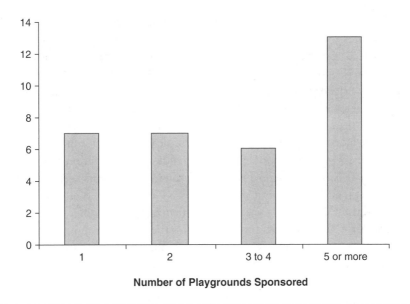

Number of Playgrounds Sponsored

Exhibit 5.2.12   Distribution of Funding Partners by Number of Playgrounds Sponsored

SOURCE: KaBOOM! internal documents.

marketing initiatives. This group included companies such as Odwalla, Walgreen's, Target Corporation, Fairytale Brownies, Radian Guaranty, and others.

• *Donors* provided unrestricted cash contributions. This group included companies like Ryobi, as well as individuals and small foundations.

• *Long-Term Partners in Play* were funding partners who had made substantial long-term commitments to the KaBOOM! cause, sponsoring builds as well as education and advocacy initiatives. In addition to monetary contributions and volunteers, these companies provided in-kind donations of their core products, strategic advice, introduction to new partners, brand-building marketing programs, and operational support. For KaBOOM!, these were

the most vibrant, creative, productive, sustainable partnerships—the model for what the team hoped they could cultivate with other partners. The Home Depot, CNA Insurance, Target Corporation, Ben & Jerry's Homemade, and The David and Lucile Packard Foundation had all invested in KaBOOM! at this level.

THE HOME DEPOT PERSPECTIVE

Bernie Marcus and Arthur Blank, two executives laid off from a regional hardware chain in Atlanta, Georgia, founded The Home Depot in 1978. As of 2002, it was the world's largest home improvement retailer with net sales in 2001 of $53.6 billion and almost 1,400 stores that cater to do-it-yourselfers, as well as home improvement, construction, and building maintenance professionals.

To fulfill its need of being socially responsible, The Home Depot created in 1992 Team Depot, an organized volunteer force comprised of its associates.[17] Through them, the company participated in social service activities that included affordable housing, at-risk youth, the environment, and disaster recovery. Jonathan Roseman, who headed community affairs at The Home Depot, explained that KaBOOM! was a great organization to partner with because its business model was "easy to execute, meets a community need, and employees from The Home Depot love it."

Since the first playground build in 1996, the partnership between The Home Depot and KaBOOM! had grown continuously. By year-end 2002, the partners were on course to complete their 100th playground together. In keeping with the way that The Home Depot supported each of its four national nonprofit partners, the company supported the KaBOOM! playground cause not only with cash but also with high-quality building materials and the sweat, strength, and talents of their associates. They provided high-level counseling and support through the participation of Suzanne Apple, vice president of community affairs of The Home Depot until January 2002, and a member of the KaBOOM! board of directors since 1997; they gave pro bono office space for KaBOOM! in Atlanta; they were working to develop special partnerships for KaBOOM! with its vendors and with entertainment and sports promotional partners, such as NASCAR; they created two television commercials about community-build

playgrounds (which aired in 1999 and 2000); and in the beginning, they had even assisted by filing the incorporation papers for KaBOOM!

The Home Depot measured through random satisfaction surveys that KaBOOM! consistently scored very high on improving employee satisfaction. "Supporting the building or restoration of community playgrounds represents very accurately what The Home Depot is all about," commented Jonathan Roseman. Through these activities the company showed that it was about meeting community needs, bringing people together, empowering them, and helping realize their dreams. KaBOOM! had consistently delivered events that attracted media coverage from *Time, Newsweek,* CNN, NBC's *The Today Show,* the *Washington Post,* the *New York Times,* and many others.

When The Home Depot had a leadership change with Robert Nardelli becoming the CEO, both organizations sought to keep the partnership strong through the transition by looking for ways to improve the partnership and to create custom-made solutions to their respective needs. For example, in July 2001, The Home Depot and KaBOOM! designed a project that would help celebrate the first Home Depot store opening in the District of Columbia, while addressing a serious playground deficit in the Anacostia neighborhood where this store's customers and employees lived and worked. The Home Depot committed activation fees from its NASCAR sponsorship to underwrite a racing-themed playground that was built by hundreds of community and Team Depot volunteers. NASCAR legend Tony

Stewart and team owner Joe Gibbs joined Home Depot CEO Robert Nardelli on the playground site, mixing cement, raising racing flags, and helping to secure media coverage on *CNN Headline News,* in *USA Today,* the *Washington Post,* and more. Members of Congress and local elected officials also took part in a "board-cutting" dedication ceremony. For The Home Depot, the project advanced government relations, delivered substantial media coverage, leveraged their sports sponsorship, and gave them the opportunity to make a high-impact community improvement working side by side with its new neighbors. For KaBOOM!, the high-profile project provided a strong platform for raising awareness of the cause through major media, to roll out customized playgrounds, and, most importantly, to help a community clear out dumpsters, trash, and concrete, and to create a safe, fun place for more than 500 children to play.

In 2001, The Home Depot and KaBOOM!, along with Outback Steakhouse and Cumulus Media, piloted Project Playground, a national playground-improvement program designed to replicate the wins of The Home Depot–KaBOOM! partnership in mid-sized markets. In 2002, The Home Depot was so pleased with the results of the partnership that it decided to extend the reach of the partnership by introducing 75 of its vendors to KaBOOM! through a playground build. Jonathan Roseman explained that The Home Depot welcomed more companies partnering with KaBOOM! because that was the best way to have an impact on the current playground deficit in the United States and improve the safety of children's play.

The CNA Perspective

CNA was a leading global insurance organization founded in 1897 to provide businesses and individuals with a broad range of insurance products and insurance-related services. The company had more than 16,500 employees, and in 2001, it generated $13.2 billion in revenues, making it the fourth largest U.S. commercial lines insurer.

CNA managed its philanthropic activities through the CNA Foundation, which was a nonprofit organization with net assets of more than $25 million and annual giving of around $2 million to support mainly programs that focused on the needs of children. Of these resources, almost one-fifth were channeled to KaBOOM! in 2000.[18]

Then CNA chairman and CEO Dennis Chookaszian said, "The CNA commitment reflects our dedication to giving something back to our communities, giving our children a safe today and a better tomorrow through KaBOOM! community-building playgrounds."[19] Through this partnership, CNA had supported 55 playgrounds builds since 1997.

The way CNA partnered with KaBOOM! was a good example of how most of the long-term partnerships develop. According to Karen Harrigan, CNA Foundation program officer, they contacted KaBOOM! in 1997 because they were looking for a community-based team building project for the celebration they were holding in honor of the company's centennial.

Although the company executives, who represented offices nationwide, were initially not particularly enthusiastic about going anywhere at 6:00 A.M., 700 CNA employees arrived at the selected site: the Bryn Mawr School in Chicago's South Shore neighborhood. With so many volunteers, the employees built two playgrounds, painted fences, painted a map of the United States on the ground, and even ripped up moldy carpeting inside the school.

At the end of the day, the feeling was "so positive and energizing," said Harrigan, "that the officers all wanted a project for their cities." Having tapped into the resources of a nationwide executive workforce, KaBOOM! had created a huge network of CNA resources, volunteers, and organizers who pledged to build 25 playgrounds nationwide and 25 more in Chicago, where CNA was headquartered. According to Harrigan, KaBOOM! provided CNA with "a solid, reliable mechanism for employees who have been asking for ways to volunteer; decentralization of their philanthropic efforts; excellent team-building opportunities; extension of client, business partner, and vendor relationships; and enormous media opportunities."

For KaBOOM!, support from CNA has provided direct benefit to its mission—more playgrounds exist because of CNA's involvement—as well as more capabilities for the organization. CNA provided the office space and furnishings for the KaBOOM! Chicago operation. It also had underwritten the production of its educational brochure for community leaders, the *Getting Started Kit,* and its brochure to encourage corporate "team-building" projects, and had sent dozens of CNA employees to the annual KaBOOM! Playground Institute, a training conference on community-build playgrounds.

Target Corporation

A mass merchandiser with nearly 1,000 stores and 214,000 employees, Target Corporation had grown a four-year partnership with KaBOOM! In 1999, Target invited KaBOOM! to participate in their "A Million Hearts" cause-related marketing campaign. During the week of Valentine's Day, KaBOOM! rallied supporters across the country to cast ballots in support of community playgrounds in Target stores, resulting in a donation to KaBOOM! of nearly $137,000. Target Corporation built their first 17 playgrounds with KaBOOM! later that year, in a one-week, cross-country blitz involving thousands of employee volunteers—from their Minneapolis headquarters to their local sales floors.

In 2000 and 2001, Target and KaBOOM! rolled out the third phase of the partnership: Operation Playground. This nationwide marathon day of service was designed to create safe, clean parks and playgrounds for kids. About 25,000 volunteers from Target stores, Mervyn's, and Marshall Field's stores rebuilt or improved more than 1,400 playgrounds in 80 cities and towns.

Ben & Jerry's Homemade, Inc.

A Unilever subsidiary that manufactures ice cream, Ben & Jerry's gives 7.5% of its pretax earnings to philanthropic causes. Since 1998, Ben & Jerry's had built nine playgrounds with KaBOOM!—both in conjunction with its retail partners (Jewel-Osco, Kroger, QFC, and 7-Eleven) and its franchise operators. Ben & Jerry's also launched an ice cream flavor in 2001 called KaBerry KaBOOM!, which was sold in pints nationally and carried in its Scoop Shops. Proceeds from the KaBerry KaBOOM! ice cream benefited specific playgrounds, as well as general operations.

The David and Lucile Packard Foundation

With assets of approximately $6.2 billion as of December 31, 2001, and total grant awards of $454 million in 2001, the foundation had been a KaBOOM! partner since 2001. The foundation had awarded funding to KaBOOM! for its coordination of a major educational program, the Child Care Playground Safety Initiative, which would work with more than 1,000 child-care centers in northern California toward the construction of 169 new playgrounds by December 2003.

THE FUTURE

Hammond and the KaBOOM! board needed to weigh carefully the proposed strategic shift toward replication via community playground builds and toward an aggressive advocacy role. They recognized that part of marketing its new partnership opportunities would require defining new value propositions for funding partners.

Promoting community builds and advocacy were far different undertakings from the direct playground builds. Even the planned skateboard parks could be seen as different. How could KaBOOM! best package sponsorships of these new initiatives so that they would have comparable appeal and business results for current and future funding partners? How would KaBOOM! measure the impact of its newer initiatives toward ensuring that they support, rather than dilute, its mission? Should the organization seek government funding? If KaBOOM! hoped to reach large numbers of consumers with its advocacy and community-build programs, how could it afford the expense of mass communication? Furthermore, how might the organization's new direction affect its position among for-profit and nonprofit entrants into the community-build playground field? Finally, how would a staff team structured and trained primarily to sell and lead top-notch community playground projects best prepare to fundraise for and implement education and advocacy initiatives?

NOTES

a. Darell's work on behalf of KaBOOM! had been featured in several books, including *Built from Scratch*, by Bernie Marcus and Arthur Blank, and *Common Interest, Common Good*, by Shirley Sagawa and Eli Segal. He was working on his first book about his life's experiences, from traveling with Hillary Rodham Clinton to examine playgrounds in Northern Ireland to making it onto *Crain's* list of 40 top business leaders under age 40.

Case Study

In 2001, KaBOOM! received the Chairman's Commendation from the U.S. Consumer Product Safety Commission, only the sixth such award presented since 1996, for its work in playground safety. In 2000, the Peter F. Drucker Foundation honored the organization's annual training conference, the KaBOOM! Playground Institute, with a special innovation award. In 1999, Darell was one of five national winners of the "Making a Difference" Award by Diet Coke and was profiled in *People* magazine and the *Wall Street Journal*.

1. Hillary Rodham Clinton, Belfast, Northern Ireland, September 3, 1998. (2002, March 6). Viewed at: <http://clinton5.nara.gov/textonly/WH/EOP/First_Lady/html/generalspeeches/1998/19980903.html>.

2. DeBord, K., & Amann, N. (2002, March 18). *Benefits of play in children: Age specific interventions.* Viewed at: <http://www.ces.ncsu.edu/depts/fcs/humandev/disas4.html>.

3. Wang, G., & Dietz, W. (2002). Economic burden of obesity in youths aged 6 to 17 years: 1979–1999. *Pediatrics, 109*(e81). Viewed at: <http://www.pediatrics.org>.

4. Mayors to build west side playground in Chicago for the U.S. conference of mayors. (1998, April 23). *PR Newswire.*

5. *A fifth national survey of playgrounds.* U.S. *Public Interest Research Group.* (2002, March 16). *The Consumer Federation of America.* Viewed at: <http://www.pirg.org/reports/consumer/playground2000/playgroundreport2000.PDF>.

6. US scary playgrounds. (2000, October 18). *Associated Press Newswires.*

7. Waltzman, M. L., et al. (1999). Monkeybar injuries: Complications of play. *Pediatrics, 103*(e58). Viewed at: <http://www.pediatrics.org>.

8. *A fifth national survey of playgrounds.*

9. *Wanna know why playgrounds are so important?* (2002, April 30). KaBOOM! Viewed at: <http://www.kaboom.org/display_item.asp?item_id=32>.

11. KaBOOM! (2002, February 25). Viewed at: <http://www.kaboom.org/ about.asp>.

12. Learning Structures. (2002, April 29). Viewed at: <http://www.learningstructures .com>.

13. Leathers & Associates. (2002, April 29). Viewed at: <http://www.leathersassociates.com/index.html>.

14. Jack Morton. (2002, April 29). Viewed at: <http://www.jackmorton.com>.

15. Boundless Playgrounds. (2002, May 20). Viewed at: <http://www.boundlessplaygrounds.org/home/home.html>.

16. Darell Hammond, as quoted by The Urban Parks Institute. (2002, April 21). Viewed at: <http://pps.org/topics/funding/fundstrat/kaboom>.

17. *Company overview.* The Home Depot. (2002, April 30). Viewed at: <http://www.homedepot.com>.

18. Form 990-PF, 2000, CNA Foundation. (2002, April 30). Viewed at: <http://www.guidestar.com>.

19. Dennis Chookaszian, quoted by KaBOOM! (2002, April 29). Viewed at: <http://www.kaboom.org/display_item.asp?item_id=17>.

CHAPTER 6

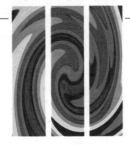

Managing Growth

In this chapter, we will explore some of the primary motivations for pursuing social enterprise growth and some of the unique challenges associated with growing social enterprises. Growth is related to, but distinct from, enhancing organizational impact through the alliance approaches that we examined in the previous chapter. Growth typically entails "creating new service sites in other geographic locations that operate under a common name, use common approaches, and are either branches of the same parent organization, or very closely-tied affiliates of a parent organization."[1] Growth is often a particularly compelling challenge in the social sector because urgent demand for a social enterprise's products or services puts constant pressure on the organization to grow. This pressure may explain in part the common phenomenon that social enterprise growth is often initiated even before a clear strategy for growth has been developed.[2] Consequently, social enterprise growth is sometimes undertaken in an ad hoc manner, thereby compromising the potential social impact that could be achieved. Poorly managed growth can detract from an organization's ability to create greater social impact over the long term or, worse, can even threaten the viability of the social enterprise itself. Furthermore, the initial growth path that an organization pursues has far-reaching consequences for the organization into the future. Thus, it is useful for social entrepreneurs to explore and understand some of the implications of their growth strategy before undertaking growth. In this chapter, we will examine some of the key issues to consider when pursuing organizational growth. We close the chapter with an overview of the chapter's two case studies.

SOCIAL ENTERPRISE GROWTH IN CONTEXT

In the United States, there are more than 1.3 million nonprofits, 80% of which have annual budgets of less than $100,000.[3] By virtue of their small size, many nonprofit organizations remain limited to the communities in which they were first established and rarely, if ever, achieve any appreciable scale. While small organizations may adequately serve the needs in a particular community, some organizations aspire to achieve large-scale impact by reaching far beyond the community in which they were founded. Yet rapid and large-scale growth among new nonprofits is rare. Out of 183,000 nonprofits started in the United States over the past 30 years, less than three fourth of 1%, or 21 organizations,[4] have grown beyond a budget of $20 million in annual expenditures (a size that is still small by corporate standards).[5] The highest-ranked nonprofit in the Nonprofit Times 100, YMCAs in the United States, earned revenues of $4.8 billion in 2005, whereas the lowest-ranked company on the *Fortune* 100 had revenues of $21 billion.[6] In the past two decades, there have been renewed efforts to spur the growth of innovative social enterprises. Many philanthropists and practitioners in the social sector have sought to apply business models, which enabled the phenomenally rapid growth of many new ventures in the private sector, to help social sector organizations achieve similar success in scaling their impact. A variety of new approaches have emerged, many of which we have already examined in previous chapters, ranging from venture philanthropy, to social entrepreneurship, to capacity-building grants for taking small nonprofits to scale.[7] While alliances can be a powerful and cost-effective approach to achieving enhanced impact for organizations, as discussed in the previous chapter, direct growth of the social enterprise itself is sometimes the preferred strategy for achieving greater social impact for a variety of reasons.

WHY GROW?

For many social enterprises, the growth imperative has driven the organization's efforts from its inception. Most often the organization's social mission motivates organizational leaders to expand their organization as much as possible. Oftentimes, initial success in establishing their organization and delivering services leads to demand pull from new communities seeking their services. At the same time, operational issues at the organizational level, such as the need to achieve economies of scale to attract and retain staff, may drive social entrepreneurs to pursue organizational growth. In other cases, funder expectations or personal ambition on the part of the leadership may be key motivating reasons for pursuing organizational growth.[8] Regardless of the reason or combination of reasons driving an organization to grow, it is imperative that before pursuing growth, social entrepreneurs are clear on whether organizational growth is the most efficient, effective, and sustainable approach to achieving increased mission impact.

CHALLENGES TO GROWTH[9]

Management Challenges

To begin, it is useful to have a realistic understanding of some of the key challenges in undertaking organizational growth. Growth requires a tremendous investment of management time and resources in a range of activities— everything from mobilizing resources for growth, to developing a strategy and infrastructure for growth, to implementing the growth plan, not to mention the ongoing challenges of leading a larger enterprise. While these are all activities that are worthy of a social entrepreneur's time, they can also be dramatically different from the day-to-day operations of the social enterprise and potentially distract from the core mission of the organization. Evidence from the commercial sector, for which there is a well-developed institutional structure designed to enable the growth of new commercial ventures, has shown that despite the sector capacity for enabling growth, organizational growth poses significant challenges. Research suggests that geographic expansion is much like establishing a start-up, in that the firm must select a location, recruit and train personnel, establish organizational legitimacy, motivate and supervise employees, and establish a structure to accommodate future growth. Geographic expansion further requires that all of these tasks be accomplished at a distance from the headquarters location. Thus, the organization's leadership is faced with the dual challenge of managing an existing business and a start-up, the latter of which is complicated by the fact that whether the growth is domestic or international, the new geography presents an unfamiliar location and untested market potential, among other challenges.[10] However, despite recent technological advances that facilitate communication, research has shown that there are still very real, and potentially high, costs to managing over a distance, especially as they relate to cultural, political, geographic, and economic differences across organizational locations.[11]

Resource Challenges

Just as senior management must expand its role from overseeing the day-to-day operations of the organization to building and leading a larger enterprise, so too must the role of the board shift from a more direct involvement in programs to fund-raising in order to sustain the growth and governance of a larger enterprise.[12] The challenges for social entrepreneurs can be even more demanding than for their private sector counterparts, as lack of institutional sources of growth capital and managerial talent are among the many obstacles to a social enterprise's growth. As was indicated in Chapter 3, the availability of adequate sources of growth capital for social enterprises is severely limited, with relatively few funders in the sector interested in providing capital for investing in growth.[13] Even among funders who provide the capital to initiate growth, few are willing or able to provide the funding to a larger organization on an ongoing basis. Organizational growth often demands bringing in additional managerial expertise, from a chief operating officer to other staff with specialized skills. Additionally, developing the organization's infrastructure, from formal systems to technology and communication infrastructure, to performance measurement systems, are among the critical tools for managing growth.[14] Growth can be a very costly undertaking in terms of the financial and human capital requirements that are necessary to achieve effective and sustainable mission impact.

FORMULATING A GROWTH PLAN[15]

Once the decision to pursue growth has been made, considerable strategic planning is required to ensure that growth will lead to the desired outcomes. The following section lays out a basic framework for thinking about social enterprise growth along two key dimensions: "What to grow" and "How to grow."

What to Grow

The first dimension requires that social entrepreneurs define specifically what they need to grow in order to increase their organization's mission impact. In some cases, it may be that the entire organizational model must be replicated because the organizational culture, structure, and programs work interdependently to generate social value, whereas in other instances, it may be sufficient to scale a specific program, or even a set of principles or guidelines. The concept of the "minimum critical specification" developed by Jeffrey Bradach,[16] cofounder of the nonprofit management consulting firm Bridgespan, can help social entrepreneurs think through this issue. Social entrepreneurs should seek to identify the fewest key elements that will generate the desired social impact. While it is likely that a vast array of elements contribute to social impact, it is useful and important for the social entrepreneur to define the social innovation at its most basic level in order to clarify what the nondiscretionary and discretionary elements of expansion will be. Identifying what core competencies and value the organization brings and, equally important, as indicated in the previous chapter, what contributions others might bring to delivering on the social mission are cornerstones of an efficient and effective strategy for growth. Given the large scale and complexity of most social issues, social enterprises should consider how to grow the organization's impact by working with and through others.

How to Grow

Once the critical elements of the social innovation are identified, it is then necessary to identify how to spread the social innovation as efficiently, effectively, and sustainably as possible. This strategy can vary along a continuum, from tightly managed and controlled growth to looser forms of knowledge dissemination and technical assistance. Key points along the continuum include (a) dissemination: packaging and disseminating the program or principles, (b) affiliation: building a network of independent entities that are linked through some type of formal relationship, and (c) branching. At the extreme, dissemination is a strategy that exerts the least direction and control over the growth process, whereas branching entails replicating entire organizational units. A social enterprise growth strategy may fall upon more than one point along this continuum, as it is not uncommon for organizations to pursue multiple avenues to growth. To clarify the distinctive aspects of each approach, we will look at examples of each of these categories of growth in the discussion below.

Dissemination

Dissemination involves packaging and distributing knowledge and information with the goal of adoption by others. A dissemination strategy can include training or technical assistance as mechanisms to facilitate increased adoption. Growing the organization's impact through dissemination requires relatively few resources compared to more direct growth such as affiliation or branching. This low-resource approach can enable an organization to spread its impact more quickly and more widely. A key trade-off with this approach is that the disseminating organization has little control over how the program is implemented in a new location and relies on other entities to adopt and develop the program or service independently. KaBOOM!, a case study that we examined in Chapter 5, illustrates how an organization can utilize a dissemination strategy to grow its impact beyond what it could accomplish directly. In 10 years, the organization has built nearly a thousand play spaces. With a build rate of approximately 150 play spaces per year, the organization has acknowledged that it cannot achieve its vision of "a great play space within walking distance for every child in America" simply by scaling up its direct-build activities. The financial and human capital constraints are the key limitation to pursuing organizational growth to reach the vision. Thus, the organization also seeks to expand its social impact beyond what it could achieve through direct playground builds. KaBOOM! has developed a deliberate strategy for seeding other communities to build and rehabilitate play spaces on their own. Thus, it has invested heavily in an online project portal, toolkit manuals, trainings, and technical assistance to provide the knowledge and support that others can use to implement the KaBOOM! approach on their own. This dissemination strategy has enabled KaBOOM! to motivate and support thousands of others to build and rehabilitate play spaces in their communities. According to Darell Hammond, founder and CEO of KaBOOM!, "We give people access to enable them to use the model and independently replicate it. We feel that the best form of flattery is imitation; if people are inspired by our community-build model, then through low-cost distribution, we can provide them with a recipe to use it."[17]

Affiliation

Affiliate structures can range from very loose coalitions of organizations to more centrally managed, franchise-like networks. A substantial amount of social sector activity worldwide occurs through affiliate structures (operations that are coordinated and run at the local level), but it is affiliated nationally or internationally through a shared brand, mission, and set of standards and values. Habitat for Humanity International, the world's leading housing nonprofit, grew by establishing a network of more than 2,000 affiliate organizations in over 100 countries worldwide. The organization's work at the community level is accomplished by local affiliates. Each affiliate is an independent nonprofit organization, operated and governed at the local level. The affiliate coordinates all aspects of Habitat home building in its local area and is responsible for everything from fund-raising, building site selection, partner family selection and support, house construction, and mortgage servicing. Habitat for Humanity International's headquarters, located in Americus, Georgia, provides information, training, and a variety of other support services to Habitat affiliates worldwide. In Habitat's case, all affiliates are asked to "tithe," that is, to give 10% of their contributions to fund house-building work in other nations. Some affiliates in developing countries also receive funding grants from Habitat for Humanity International. The specific arrangements between affiliates and the headquarters office vary from organization to organization and can range from more centrally controlled to very loosely affiliated organizations. A key advantage to growth through affiliates is the fact that the approach mobilizes and leverages resources locally to establish and manage new affiliates. By reducing the resources and management required from headquarters, growth through affiliates has the potential to achieve more rapid and larger-scale growth than through branching.

Branching

The distinction between a tightly managed affiliate network and a loosely managed branch organization is somewhat blurred, as these structures lie along a continuum. Nonetheless, growth through branching entails the highest degree of central control and can be the most resource intensive because a branch structure typically maintains control and responsibility over finances, operations, and strategy at the headquarters level. Thus, growth through branching may require significantly more fund-raising and human resource management costs from the perspective of the growing organization, because it is orchestrating and developing a new organization organically. However, branch organizations do not necessarily have to be tightly managed. The Nature Conservancy, a leading conservation organization, has branch offices in all 50 states, the Virgin Islands, and 22 countries. The organization is governed by a single national governing board, and the branches are all subsumed under a single legal entity. Despite the formal structure, the organization's growth over the past 50 years hinged on a model of decentralization with all the work on the ground being implemented by local branches. Former CEO John Sawhill's "loose-tight" management philosophy translated into granting branches significant autonomy to foster entrepreneurial activity among dedicated staff and volunteers at the local level, yet the organization's overall strategy and values were managed tightly to ensure that the organization as a whole was delivering on its mission. Growth through branching requires the most resources and initiative from organizational headquarters, and yet at the same time, it enables the organization to have the greatest control over the newly formed organization.

Affiliation or Branching? Or Both?

Although dissemination is a growth approach with the potential for the greatest reach, social entrepreneurs often pursue organizational growth through affiliation or branching because of concerns about control and quality. Thus, in the section below, we examine some of the trade-offs between the two approaches. Of course, these approaches are not mutually exclusive and are sometimes pursued in conjunction with each other. We will also examine a dual strategy approach below.

There are numerous trade-offs to consider in thinking about whether to grow the organization organically, such as through branching, or through looser forms of organizational growth, such as affiliation. Franchising has become a common structural form in the commercial sector that overcomes some of the common challenges to growth by branching described above. Franchisees invest their own capital and retain the day-to-day control of their business, while paying a small percentage of revenues in return for use of the brand name, operational support, and product specifications from the franchisor. Among the rationales for growth from franchising are to reduce production and inventory costs, speed product development, and expand new markets.[18] Relative to branching, franchising has been documented by researchers as having provided a source of capital for expansion,[19] enabled more rapid growth relative to branching,[20] entailed lower monitoring costs,[21] and yielded higher profits.[22] Among the challenges faced by a franchisor is balancing the franchisees' desires for autonomy with the franchisor's desire for standardization, consistency, and control in an effort to preserve its goodwill and brand equity.[23] Research in the restaurant and hotel industries, which indicates that franchise chains have lower quality than owned chains, provides evidence of this struggle to balance quality control and franchise autonomy.[24]

This model is relevant to social enterprise in that it is analogous in many ways to the affiliate structure that is commonly pursued as an approach to social enterprise growth. The challenge of balancing local autonomy with central control is among the most salient management issues in multisite nonprofits.[25] Researchers have explored the strategic rationale for franchise and branch structures of large multisite social enterprises. They have argued that franchise affiliates mitigate many of the organizational and economic problems facing multisite nonprofits.[26] Among large nonprofit organizations, affiliate models were both more prevalent than wholly owned branches and, on average, had substantially more sites operating in different geographic locations.[27] Research by Bradach has also pointed out that many private sector businesses have benefited from the plural form of organization, operating both franchises (affiliates) and company-owned branches simultaneously, and that the same dynamic might hold in the nonprofit sector.[28] Branches can serve as models, testing grounds for new ideas, and conduits for keeping the central office in tune with actual delivery of service, while the looser affiliates can enable faster growth and foster innovation. More recently, Bradach developed a framework for thinking strategically about nonprofit replication consisting of three key issues that need to be addressed once a program has demonstrated results and a clearly articulated theory of change: (1) defining the growth strategy, (2) designing the network of organizational units, and (3) the role of the national office.[29] Regardless of what structure a social entrepreneur pursues with growth, the importance of the national office in leading program expansion, facilitating organizational learning and communication, and building organizational infrastructure and systems in a multisite organization cannot be overemphasized.[30] Because the implications of any given structure are far reaching, the national office must be very deliberate and mindful of building and investing in a structure that ensures that the social value being generated by the larger entity is greater than the sum of the individual parts.

Growth must be managed strategically in order to truly enable an organization to achieve its potential for mission impact. It is useful for social enterprise leaders to consider a range of strategic options before undertaking any form of growth. They must be careful when pursuing growth for growth's sake. Organizational growth does not necessarily translate into greater mission impact. Social enterprises have a range of opportunities for growth beyond traditional corporate models for growth. In the corporate context, organizational growth is the key mechanism for enhancing shareholder value. For social enterprises, mission impact can be achieved through a range of growth strategies as described above. There are many ways for a social enterprise to achieve greater mission impact without necessarily scaling the organization itself. The challenges to growth are well documented, and consequently, the pursuit of growth is not something to be taken lightly. Social entrepreneurs must always remember to focus on mission impact first and formulate their strategy for growing their mission impact as efficiently, effectively, and sustainably as possible.

CASE STUDIES

In the following cases, the range of strategic issues that a social entrepreneur must consider when launching a growth strategy are illustrated in detail. Key issues include the role of the center and the relationship between the center and field units and the governance structure necessary to manage a network of geographically dispersed units. The first case, STRIVE, focuses on a network of organizations that provide employment training and placement for hard-to-employ young urban adults. STRIVE has grown to 13 affiliated sites in New York City and four STRIVE-inspired, but independently run, organizations in eastern U.S. cities through an ad hoc approach as opportunities have presented themselves. This poses potential challenges for the organization, as issues of brand management across a network and quality control arise. The organization is faced with the challenge of shoring up its current network of affiliates and partners to maintain the integrity of the STRIVE model and brand and formulate a coherent strategy for engaging in future growth. As you read the case, consider the following questions:

1. What is your assessment of how STRIVE's service model and organizational structure adjusted to each stage of its growth?

2. What was the role of the funding partner mix in the evolution of the strategy?

Sustainable Conservation—Where Next? offers a contrast to the STRIVE case, in that it focuses on a nonprofit that has pioneered an innovative industry and government partnership approach to conservation, and after 10 years of operating successfully out of a single site, it is considering its strategic options for national expansion. The organization is taking a very measured approach to growth by identifying a range of strategic options for whether and how to achieve greater scale and social impact. Reflect on the following questions as you analyze the case:

1. In your view, is SusCon ready for expansion? Why or why not?

2. If SusCon were to expand, which growth option would you recommend and why?

NOTES

1. Taylor, M., Dees, G., & Emerson, J. (2002). The question of scale: Finding an appropriate strategy for building on your success. In G. Dees, J. Emerson, & P. Economy (Eds.), *Strategic tools for social entrepreneurs: Enhancing the performance of your enterprising nonprofit*. New York: Wiley.

2. Bridgespan Group, commissioned by the Edna McConnell Clark Foundation. (2005). *Growth of youth-serving organizations*. Retrieved April 19, 2006, from the Bridgespan Group Web site: http://www.thebridgespangroup.org/PDF/Clarkpdfs/Growth%200f%20Youth-Serving%200rgs%20-%20White%20Paper.pdf.

3. O'Flanagan, M., & Taliento, L. (2004). Nonprofits: Ensuring that bigger is better [Electronic version]. *McKinsey Quarterly*, Number 2.

4. Baumann, H. (2005, March). The growth capital market in the U.S. [Electronic version. *Alliance, 10*(1), 37–39.

5. Kramer, M. (2005, February 3). Scaling social impact [Electronic version]. *The Chronicle of Philanthropy*.

6. *The Nonprofit Times Top 100*. (2005, November 1). Retrieved April 20, 2006, from the Nonprofit Times Web site: http://www.nptimes.com/Nov05/sr_npt100.html.

7. Kramer, M. (2005, February 3). Scaling social impact [Electronic version]. *The Chronicle of Philanthropy.*

8. Taylor, M., Dees, G., & Emerson, J. (2002). The question of scale: Finding an appropriate strategy for building on your success. In G. Dees, J. Emerson, & P. Economy (Eds.), *Strategic tools for social entrepreneurs: Enhancing the performance of your enterprising nonprofit.* New York: Wiley.

9. This section draws on the working paper: Wei-Skillern, J., & Anderson, B. B. *Nonprofit geographic expansion: Branches, affiliates, or both?* Harvard Business School Working Paper #27.

10. Barringer, B. R., & Greening, D. W. (1998). Small business growth through geographic expansion: A comparative case study. *Journal of Business Venturing, 13,* 467–492.

11. Ghemawat, P. (2001, September). Distance still matters: The hard reality of global expansion. *Harvard Business Review, 79*(8), 137–147.

12. Bridgespan Group, commissioned by the Edna McConnell Clark Foundation. (2005). *Growth of youth-serving organizations.* Retrieved April 19, 2006, from the Bridgespan Group Web site: http://www.thebridgespangroup.org/PDF/Clarkpdfs/Growth%200f%20Youth-Serving%200rgs%20-%20White%20Paper.pdf.

13. Baumann, H. (2005, March). The growth capital market in the U.S. [Electronic version]. *Alliance, 10*(1), 37–39.

14. Ibid.

15. This section draws on the article: Dees, G., Anderson, B., & Wei-Skillern, J. (2004, Spring). Scaling social impact: Strategies for spreading social innovations. *Stanford Social Innovation Review, 1*(4), 24–32.

16. Ibid.

17. Author interview with Darell Hammond, December 2003.

18. Baucus, D. A., Baucus, M. B., & Human, S. E. (1996). Consensus in franchise organizations: A cooperative arrangement among entrepreneurs. *Journal of Business Venturing, 11*(5), 359–378.

19. Kaufmann, P. J., & Dant, R. P. (1996). Multi-unit franchising: Growth and management issues. *Journal of Business Venturing, 11,* 343–358.

20. Shane, S. (1998). Explaining the distribution of franchised and company-owned outlets in franchise systems. *Journal of Management, 24*(6), 717–739.

21. Rubin, P. (1978, April). The theory of the firm and the structure of the franchise contract. *Journal of Law and Economics, 21,* 222–233; and Brickley, J. A., & Dark, F. H. (1987). The choice of organizational form: The case of franchising. *Journal of Financial Economics, 18,* 401–420.

22. Michael, S. C. (2000). The effect of organizational form on quality: The case of franchising. *Journal of Economic Behavior & Organization, 43,* 295–318.

23. Dant, R. P., & Gundlach, G. T. (1999, January). The challenge of autonomy and dependence in franchised channels of distribution. *Journal of Business Venturing, 14*(1), 35–68.

24. Michael, S. C. (2000). The effect of organizational form on quality: The case of franchising. *Journal of Economic Behavior & Organization, 43,* 295–318.

25. Grossman, A., & Rangan, K. (2001, Spring). Managing multisite nonprofits. *Nonprofit Management and Leadership, 11*(3).

26. See, for example, Oster, S. M. (1992). Nonprofit organizations as franchise operations. *Nonprofit Management & Leadership, 2*(3), 223–238; Young, D. R., Bania, N., & Bailey, D. (1996). Study of national nonprofit associations. *Nonprofit Management & Leadership, 6*(4), 347–365; and Young, D. R. (1989). Local autonomy in a franchise age: Structural change in national voluntary associations. *Nonprofit & Voluntary Sector Quarterly, 18,* 101–117.

27. Oster, S. M. (1996). Nonprofit organizations and their local affiliates: A study in organizational forms. *Journal of Economic Behavior and Organization, 30,* 83–95.

28. Bradach, J. L. (1999). *Going to scale.* Harvard Business School Working Paper, Social Enterprise Series, #9.

29. Bradach, J. L. (2003). Going to scale: The challenge of replicating social programs. *Stanford Social Innovation Review, 1*(1), 18–25.

30. Letts, C. W., Ryan, W. P., & Grossman, A. (2000). *High performance nonprofit organizations: Managing upstream for greater impact.* New York: John Wiley & Sons.

Case Study 6.1.

STRIVE

The best social program is a job.

—Eugene Debs

On a sunny morning in June 1997, training was in session at STRIVE, a New York City employment program for hard-to-employ inner-city residents. STRIVE was operated by the East Harlem Employment Service (EHES),[1] which was located in the basement of an old brick high-rise apartment building in the James Weldon Johnson Housing Project on East 112th Street. It could be reached by walking past knots of young men talking and mothers sitting on benches watching their children play, around the back of the building, and down a half-dark stairway. Turning right, one arrived at a clean but worn-looking room with institutional yellow concrete walls and linoleum floors, where 30 STRIVE participants, mostly young, mostly black or Hispanic, sat in rows of folding chairs. They listened intently as their instructor challenged one of the participants on why he hadn't bothered to wear a tie that morning.

In his office at the other end of the hall, EHES director Rob Carmona was on the phone with Chairman Sam Hartwell,

SOURCE NOTE: Copyright © Harvard Business School Publishing, case number 9-399-054. Used with permission.

Senior Research Fellow Robert Burakoff prepared this case as the basis for class discussion rather than to illustrate either effective or ineffective handling of an administrative situation.

discussing next week's board meeting. Over the past 13 years, Hartwell, Carmona, and others had built STRIVE from a single-site, shoestring operation in Harlem into a network of 15 sites in New York and other U.S. cities. The network had grown gradually and somewhat informally, its core program evolving and gaining acceptance over time. During the past few months, however, things had changed. The advent of welfare reform provided government, nonprofits, and funders with a heightened sense of urgency about putting disadvantaged people to work quickly. At the same time, STRIVE received a wave of publicity culminating in a highly favorable segment on CBS's *60 Minutes,* one of the most watched and influential programs on American television. As a result, STRIVE had been swamped by interest from across the United States. Hartwell and Carmona felt that the organization was at a crossroads. In addition to deciding how best to take advantage of the spike in interest, STRIVE needed to decide how fast it should grow, and what kind of organization it wanted to be going forward.

THE EAST HARLEM EMPLOYMENT SERVICE

The Creation of EHES

STRIVE was cofounded in 1984 by Sam Hartwell, a successful Wall Street financial executive.[2] Hartwell had volunteered for various charities, especially those serving inner-city minority youth. As his career advanced and his involvement increasingly took the form of board membership, Hartwell had become bored and frustrated with the apparent inability of social service

agencies to improve the lives of inner-city people. Hartwell had been impressed, however, by the efforts of the Henry Street Settlement House on the Lower East Side to train and place at-risk youth. Henry Street coupled job-readiness training with workshops in carpentry, typing, and sewing designed to develop good work habits and attitudes. When Hartwell proposed bringing the Henry Street program to Harlem, its director said that the organization did not want to expand but that it would help Hartwell start his own program.

Hartwell took a year's hiatus from his career and worked with Lyle Gerts, the former head of Henry Street's employment program, to plan the start-up. Together they found donated space in the James Weldon Johnson Housing Project and formed a small start-up board that included executives from Lehman Brothers, the New York Urban League, the housing project's community center, and Henry Street. In addition to presenting detailed financial and operational projections, EHES's business plan asserted that government-funded employment programs, while desperately needed, suffered from shortcomings that left the most at-risk youth underserved. EHES proposed to demonstrate an alternative to these programs. EHES opened its doors by the end of 1984 with Gerts as the only full-time employee and $120,000 raised from Hartwell's friends, corporate associates, and foundations. It adapted the Henry Street training model, using computers and video cameras instead of woodworking tools and typewriters, and shortened the training to three weeks to fit its limited resources.

EHES evolved gradually over the next four years. By 1988, it was making over 200 placements a year (see **Exhibit 6.1.1**). It was governed by a 10-person board chaired by

	1985	1986	1987	1988	1989	1990	1991	1992	1993	1994	1995	1996	Total
East Harlem Employment Service (New York City)[a]	56	86	137	208	202	188	284	409[b]	426	428	425	485	3,334
STRIVE Employment Group Affiliates (New York City)[a]							1,188	1,389	1,874	2,172	1,672	2,091	10,386
Three Rivers Employment Service (Pittsburgh)				124	139	149	NA	NA	NA	NA	NA	NA	2,240
Chicago Employment Service							89	108	155	119	150	275	896
Boston Employment Service											144	195	339
Metropolitan Career Center (Philadelphia)[c]													—
Total													17,195

Exhibit 6.1.1 Job Placements for STRIVE Organizations: 1985–1996

SOURCE: East Harlem Employment Service.

a. SEG placements consist of SEG affiliates' placements plus EHES placements.

b. STRIVE II was launched in 1992.

c. MCC/STRIVE was launched in January 1997.

	1996	1995
ASSETS		
Current assets:		
Cash and cash equivalents	$753,601	$724,828
Grants receivable	1,000,000	0
Other current assets	17,260	21,312
Total current assets	1,770,861	746,140
Fixed assets:		
Computer equipment	100,535	94,094
Video equipment	30,141	15,833
Office furniture and equipment	32,102	34,527
Leasehold improvements	19,119	12,119
	181,897	156,573
Less: Accumulated depreciation and amortization	89,445	116,556
Net fixed assets	92,452	40,017
Other assets:		
Deposits	1,442	1,442
Total Assets	$1,864,755	$787,599
LIABILITIES AND NET ASSETS		
Current liabilities:		
Accounts payable and accrued expenses	$195,590	$43,943
Net assets:		
Unrestricted	848,912	665,198
Temporarily restricted	820,253	78,458
Total net assets	1,669,165	743,656
Total Liabilities and Net Assets	$1,864,755	$787,599

Exhibit 6.1.2a   East Harlem Employment Service, Inc.—Statement of Financial Position, December 31, 1996 and 1995

SOURCE: East Harlem Employment Service.

Hartwell and had a small advisory board of influential corporate CEOs. It raised most of its $278,000 budget from foundations (56%), corporations (30%), and individuals (9%) (see **Exhibit 6.1.2**). Its staff of six included the key people who would shape the organization and play leadership roles up to the present.[3] As the organization embarked on a decade of expansion and replication, the program it delivered to its participants had essentially taken the form it would maintain through June 1997.

Exhibit 6.1.2b   East Harlem Employment Service, Inc.—Statement of Income and Expenses, 1985–1997

	1985	1986	1987	1988	1989	1990	1991	1992	1993	1994	1995	1996	1997 Budget
Public support													
Foundations	84,280	99,800	107,000	156,621	222,667	535,443	689,116	1,288,485	1,127,223	1,238,488	1,442,831	2,828,150[a]	2,081,700
Corporations	38,500	69,500	98,000	83,700	71,500	136,700	143,000	171,050	127,500	154,000	149,000	80,865	—
Churches	1,000	3,500	7,000	6,000	4,000	7,000	1,500	4,000	2,000	4,500	2,000	5,000	—
Individuals	8,338	24,475	32,490	26,230	27,053	32,770	36,020	22,750	14,210	33,601	22,584	44,190	—
Total support	132,118	197,275	244,490	272,551	325,220	711,913	869,636	1,486,285	1,270,933	1,430,589	1,616,415	2,958,205	2,081,700
Revenues													
Investment	865	3,225	2,170	2,059	3,390	4,247	9,923	8,790	11,118	(3,651)	23,802	26,620	29,000
Other	—	—	2,500	3,368	—	21,921	—	—	2,466	7,500	99,539	45,232	31,000
Total revenues	865	3,225	4,670	5,427	3,390	26,168	9,923	8,790	13,584	3,849	123,341	71,852	60,000
Total support and revenues	132,983	200,500	249,160	277,978	328,610	738,081	879,559	1,495,075	1,284,517	1,434,438	1,739,756	3,030,057	2,141,700
Expenses													
Personnel	70,678	125,183	166,474	193,950	249,342	343,042	378,492	442,038	493,192	498,025	581,467	715,224	743,600
Professional Services	8,440	20,693	16,561	17,299	17,897	22,333	27,504	22,199	29,353	36,906	44,230	50,696	45,800
Occupancy charges	—	—	4,840	3,000	3,182	3,000	3,000	18,000	13,000	11,400	12,500	25,180	25,000
Depreciation	3,587	6,363	9,916	13,205	14,643	12,375	13,686	11,872	12,577	15,757	16,908	19,926	19,000
Payments to SEG partners	—	—	—	—	—	126,063	378,867	565,380	694,000	690,310	734,550	636,000	650,000
Payments to ASAP partners	—	—	—	—	—	—	—	—	—	—	—	199,824	315,500
Direct ASAP expenses	—	—	—	—	—	—	—	—	—	—	—	252,563[b]	564,700[b]
Other	36,117	39,411	51,208	49,899	55,823	56,198	114,193	82,857	130,960	100,577	134,162	205,135	615,200[c]
Total expenses	118,822	191,650	248,999	277,353	340,887	563,011	915,742	1,142,346	1,373,082	1,352,975	1,523,817	2,104,548	2,978,800
Excess of Income over Expenses	14,161	8,850	161	625	(12,277)	175,070	(36,183)	352,729	(88,565)	81,463	215,939	925,509	(837,100)

SOURCE: East Harlem Employment Service.

a. Accounting rules require the entire $1,000,000 Ford Foundation ASAP implementation grant to be included as income in 1996, the year it was committed, although $774,367 of the related expenses would not be reported until subsequent periods. This results in an excess of income over expense in 1996 and a deficiency in the 1997 budget.

b. Includes all of EHES's direct expenses for ASAP for the year, regardless of type (e.g., includes personnel).

c. Includes $400,000 for launching and operating a new site in Central Harlem.

The STRIVE Program in 1997

Three tenets underlay the STRIVE program and were reinforced at every opportunity. The first was that employment offered the best and quickest leverage on the problems of the urban poor and that "the best training for work was work itself." STRIVE targeted people who wanted to get a job quickly, with the idea that more-advanced vocational skills could be acquired at work and education could be tackled at night or on weekends. STRIVE also believed that the biggest barriers to employment for this group were attitude and job readiness, collectively known as "soft skills," rather than job-specific "hard" skills. As Carmona said to a recent class, "As your boss, I'm going to be spending more time with you than I am with my wife. What do I care most about? Your computer skills? No way! I'm asking myself, 'Do I *like* you? Can I *work* with you?'" Finally, the STRIVE model confronted people with the "baggage" of their negative experiences and attitudes in a way that encouraged self-examination, "ownership," and change.

STRIVE served predominantly African American and Latino men and women ages 17–40. Approximately 60% of its participants were female. Many were single parents, welfare recipients, and/or high school dropouts. Many had been victims of family abuse, alcohol or drug dependency, or crime, and a significant number had been incarcerated. Few had any continuous history of employment.[4] One of the few limitations imposed by STRIVE was that it did not accept applicants who could likely get good jobs without the program's assistance. The program consisted of recruitment, training, job development, initial placement, and long-term follow-up.

Recruitment

In 1997, EHES operated two STRIVE sites in Harlem (the 112th Street headquarters and STRIVE II in West Harlem) but recruited participants citywide. It got most of its applications through a small help-wanted ad appearing in the New York Daily News. The organization also used public service announcements, publicity at church and community groups, referrals from nonprofit and government agencies, and word of mouth. Typically the first contact with STRIVE was over the telephone, with as many as 400 calls per training cycle. Less than half of the callers took the next step of visiting STRIVE to fill out an application and interview with staff. Unsuitable candidates were rejected or referred to other resources at this stage, including people who appeared to be overqualified, disruptive, under the influence of drugs or alcohol, or whose current circumstances made full participation impossible.

The final step in the recruitment process was the orientation, a three-hour session held the Friday before the program start date. The orientation, which was attended by as many as 100 applicants, was conducted in the same interactive, confrontational style of the STRIVE training described below. It allowed applicants to decide if they wanted to commit to the program and if trainers were to assess the attitude and abilities of the applicants. Applicants who wished to continue (approximately 70%–75%) reported to one of the two EHES sites the following Monday morning.

Training

In addition to developing appropriate attitude and basic job-search and retention skills, STRIVE sought to introduce participants to the demands of the workplace. Training met from 9:00 A.M. to 5:00 P.M., five days a week for three weeks. Participants received a transportation subsidy but no other stipend or expenses. They were required to wear "interview attire" every day (dress shirt, tie, and dark pants for men; conservative dress or blouse and skirt for women). One trainer had primary responsibility for the class but could draw on other staff for their expertise or to vary the classroom dynamics. Most trainers came from backgrounds similar to the participants'; many were STRIVE graduates themselves. Trainers followed a basic curriculum but could adapt it to their own teaching styles or the needs of the class.

During the orientation and the first week, the training focused on attitude, discipline, self-presentation, self-awareness, and teamwork. All sessions were highly interactive. Rules were read and discussed. Clothing, behavior, posture, and speech were critiqued. Participants were expected to sit up straight, speak in a clear voice without slang, look the trainer in the eye, and accept criticism. Sessions addressed the factors that prevented young people from getting and holding jobs, the socioeconomic condition of the group, and the connections that tied participants to one another. A partner system was introduced, which held each participant responsible for the actions of a colleague. Perhaps the most memorable session for participants was "Stand and Deliver," which required them to talk about themselves to the whole group for five minutes as frankly and personally as possible. These presentations often dealt with extremely painful experiences in the participants' lives and were highly emotional; they served to vent negative feelings and help the class bond together based on their common experiences.

The trainer addressed any infraction of the rules or display of negative attitude as soon as it occurred by swiftly and forcefully confronting the offender and dismissing any excuses. Other participants were asked to comment on the offending behavior and describe proper behavior.[5]

For example, several people invariably arrived late during the first few days of training. The trainer told the late people to stand in the back until a break in the class discussion, then addressed each in turn:

Trainer: Ten minutes late your first
                 day on the job? I can't
                 believe this. If you're late the
                 first day, you're fired, man!

Participant: The train was late.

Trainers told participants that their graduation depended totally on their actions. The clear message was "stick to the rules or leave." Some infractions were punished by small fines, but those who presented continuing problems were terminated ("fired," in the parlance of STRIVE) to maintain this sense of responsibility. Except in severe cases, other STRIVE staff "played catch" with terminated participants, sitting down with them to discuss the reasons for the action and inviting them to return to class or reapply when they felt that they were ready to meet STRIVE's requirements.

Toward the end of the first week, most "attitudinal stragglers" had been separated from the program.[6] In the second week, the trainer increasingly took the role of counselor rather than disciplinarian, explaining why certain issues were important and rebuilding participants' self-confidence. Participants learned how to write a résumé and cover letter (including how to deal with nonexistent work histories or periods of incarceration), and after basic word-processing instruction, they created their own on the PCs in STRIVE's computer room. There were also role plays in which participants "sold" the qualifications of fellow participants to colleagues playing "board members," and small groups invented an entry-level job at a dummy company, interviewed several classmates for it, and explained the reasons why they chose the successful candidate. Participants brought in job ads, discussed them with the class, underwent mock interviews for one of the positions, and got feedback from colleagues and staff. In the final week, the class also participated in two video projects intended to build teamwork and self-confidence: a 20-minute video planned, shot, and edited by the class with no intervention from the trainer and "Man on the Street," in which participants interviewed people on a busy downtown street corner about their job-search experiences.

The training ended with graduation, which included family and friends, certificates, and a potluck meal.[7] For many STRIVE participants, graduation was clearly an emotional event, marking the end of an intense, "transformational" experience. Some reported that it was the first time they had graduated from an educational program of any kind. Some younger participants said that STRIVE was one of the few times in their lives that they had experienced a supportive relationship with an adult.

Placement and Follow-Up

STRIVE's job developers were responsible for developing employer relationships, identifying job opportunities, and matching participants with openings. They targeted entry-level or semiskilled positions with opportunities for advancement, preferably full-time with benefits (see **Exhibit 6.1.3**). "Dead-end" positions, such as security guard or fast-food jobs, were avoided except as a last resort. Although job developers sometimes got in the front door through a high-level board contact, ultimately STRIVE's customer was the human resources officer. STRIVE's pitch emphasized its performance numbers, its graduates' motivation and job readiness, the absence of any fees, and the lack of risk: STRIVE would "take back" any hire that didn't work out. As each training session advanced, the job developers got to know the participants and began to match them up with opportunities in the pipeline. Participants were also encouraged to develop and pursue their own leads. In a typical class, up to 70% would be hired within a month after graduation, with an additional 10% finding work in the following month.

STRIVE's Graduate Services followed up on graduates for two years, calling them regularly to check if any problems had developed and to update employment and wage status on the database. Work-related problems were addressed by job developers and graduate services staff. Graduates who quit or were fired could return to STRIVE for counseling and replacement; in fact, replacement was viewed as an integral part of the program, and staff would say that for some graduates, the training really didn't start until the person was fired from their first job. Personal or family problems were referred to an on-staff social worker who provided counseling and referrals. During the first few weeks, follow-up calls were made as often as necessary to keep tabs on the graduate; thereafter, calls were made

Employer	Graduate Position
Asphalt Green	Registration Clerk
Bed, Bath & Beyond	Sales, Customer Service
New York City Board of Education	Software Tech, Office Administration
British Airways	Customer Service, Telephone Sales
Bronx Health Plan	Mailroom Clerk
CableVision	Customer Service, Data Entry
Chase Mellon	Customer Service, Data Entry
Choice Courier	Mailroom Clerk, Time Service
Cita Corp.	Data Entry, Bank Teller, Customer Service
Effective Management	Telephone Operator, Security Officer
Ellis Island	Food Service/Cashier
Federal Express	Courier, Driver, Customer Service
Hunt Point Cooperative Market	Receptionist, Data Entry, Accounts Payable
Ikon Night Rider	Document Specialist
Interfaith Neighbor	Receptionist, Maintenance, Office Aid
J.P. Morgan	Line Server/Food Services
Manhattan Ear, Nose & Throat Hospital	Nurse's Attendant, Mailroom Clerk, Clerk/Typist
Merrill Lynch	Receptionist, Clerk/Typist
Michael Lee & Company	Clerk/Typist, Secretary
Mt. Sinai Hospital	Clerk/Typist, Secretary, Maintenance
Paradon	Stockroom, Sales
Prudential	Clerk/Typist, Secretary
Smith Barney	Figure Clerk
United Parcel Service	Driver
World Travel Club	Receptionist, Messenger

Exhibit 6.1.3   Illustrative List of Recent Employers of EHES Graduates

SOURCE: East Harlem Employment Service.

quarterly. After two years, STRIVE no longer initiated contact or tracked graduates; however, graduates could continue to use STRIVE services for as long as they liked, and many dropped in to use the computers or to chat with staff.

EHES's 1996 annual report quoted an initial placement rate of 80% at an average wage of $7.80/hour, with retention after two years consistently averaging 75%–80% over the organization's history. Placements for 1996 totaled 485. EHES stated its cost per placement as $1,500.

The Organization

EHES prided itself on having a flat, unbureaucratic, low-overhead organization that could place people for a fraction of the cost of other alternatives. EHES employed 26 people: 13 at STRIVE I/EHES headquarters; 5 at STRIVE II; and 8 at ASAP, a two-year initiative funded by the Ford Foundation to help STRIVE graduates enter career-track jobs. Twelve staff members were STRIVE graduates; the great majority came from backgrounds similar to those of STRIVE's clientele. EHES did not have a formal organizational chart, and in fact, many staff members had multiple roles—for example, all senior staff members spent a substantial amount of time on replication and technical assistance to other STRIVE sites.

The four senior staff members had all been with the organization since 1988 or before. Hired as executive director in 1986, Rob Carmona had overcome a past history of substance abuse to earn a master's in social work at Columbia University and to build a career in youth counseling. In addition to overall leadership of the organization, Carmona was STRIVE's chief spokesperson, promoter, and deal maker. The staff credited Carmona's unrelenting "tough but fair" approach as a major influence on both the STRIVE training and organizational culture. Deputy Director Lorenzo Harrison, who combined an inner-city background with an MPA from New York University, was responsible for administration and played a lead role in recent replication efforts. Frank Horton, a graduate of the first STRIVE class, was the director of training and leading exponent of the STRIVE classroom technique.[8] Lawrence Jackson, who had grown up in the James Weldon Johnson housing project, was site director for 112th Street and EHES's de facto director of day-to-day operations. EHES had no on-staff CFO but retained a local accounting firm whose principal performed many of a CFO's functions. Nor was there a dedicated development staff; fund-raising was conducted by senior staff and board leaders, with Sam Hartwell and Rob Carmona taking the lead.

EHES's expenditures had grown to over $2.1 million in 1996. Expense breakouts stated that over $1.5 million was attributable to direct program services, and approximately $180,000 to technical assistance, $300,000 to administration, and $90,000 to fund-raising. The budget for 1997 was just under $3 million, with most of the increase due to ASAP and a proposed new EHES STRIVE site in Central Harlem.

Funding came from a mix of foundations, corporations, and individuals (see **Exhibit 6.1.4**), with foundations (including the United Way) providing 93% of 1996 income and accounting for almost all of the budget growth since 1987. Although a relatively small part of STRIVE's support, corporate and individual gifts tended to be steady and were thought to strengthen STRIVE's credibility and relationships. Foundation grants could be large but were often short term, and EHES's leaders sometimes felt the need to pitch "something new" to keep program officers interested. Hartwell said he had learned early that national funders would support a locally based organization only if it was likely to have a wider impact by serving as a model for others. EHES received no direct government support. This was unusual: Most nonprofits providing training and placement to the disadvantaged received a substantial amount of government money via the federal Job Training Partnership Act (JTPA), state welfare programs, or other sources.[9]

STRIVE felt that its ability to produce performance numbers and communicate candidly were key to its credibility and helped attract money and other forms of support. It sent quarterly and annual reports to its supporters on the progress of the organization. In all of its external communications, STRIVE's message reinforced a few basic facts with the insistence of a drumbeat:

Clark Foundation (SEG and EHES)		$1,000,000
United Way (SEG and EHES)		178,000
Ford Foundation (ASAP planning grant)		275,000
Ford Foundation (ASAP implementation)		1,000,000
Other Foundations		
Tiger Foundation	75,000	
J.M. Kaplan Fund	50,000	
Underhill Foundation	45,000	
Hearst Foundation	35,000	
Anonymous	35,000	
New York Community Trust	30,000	
9 other grants	58,500	
Total		328,500
Corporations		
J.P. Morgan	25,000	
Merrill Lynch	25,000	
Philip Morris	25,000	
American Express	20,000	
Chase Manhattan	15,000	
6 other grants	9,250	
Total		119,250
Individuals		
1 gift > $10,000	30,000	
5 gifts at $1,000–$10,000	7,000	
46 gifts < $1,000	9,665	
Total		46,665
Churches		5,000
TOTAL		$2,952,415

Exhibit 6.1.4   EHES: Sources of Support, 1996[a]

SOURCE: East Harlem Employment Service.

a. Funding tallies are based on money committed rather than cash received and do not match exactly the support figures reported on EHES's income statements.

- Hardest-to-employ clients
- Three-week attitudinal training
- Two-year follow-up

- 80% placement
- 80% retention
- $1,500 per person
- No government funding

REPLICATION

Between 1987 and 1997, STRIVE pursued two avenues of expansion: the creation of the STRIVE Employment Group in New York City and the creation of independent STRIVEs in four major U.S. cities. "From the beginning," said Hartwell, "we thought of doing something so well that others would come to see it and want to do it themselves. At the time it seemed crazy, considering how small we were."

New York City Expansion

In 1990, STRIVE proposed and received a major grant from the Clark Foundation[10] to establish a network of STRIVEs that would put 10,000 people to work in New York City over four years. Based on a cost of $1,200 per person, the plan called for $4 million from Clark spread out over four years, matching on a one-to-two ratio money to be raised by the STRIVE sites. The grant was four times larger than any of Clark's previous grants. "But it was a good fit," said Executive Director Joe Cruickshank. "We like providing operating support, and we fund organizations over long periods of time, sticking with them through short-term challenges. We don't tell people what to do. The bottom line for our board is that every grant should help people. STRIVE's numbers showed that they were doing that. Plus, we trusted the people; they had been very open with us."

At first, EHES planned to create new sites to meet their placement goal, but the logistics of launching and operating so many sites were daunting. Instead, EHES began recruiting partners for a network of existing organizations (to be known as the STRIVE Employment Group [SEG]) that would deliver the STRIVE program at their own sites. Organizations they approached were interested in the Clark money and intrigued by STRIVE, but they had concerns about how the program would fit with their existing services and funding, as well as unspoken questions about the smaller, younger EHES as network leader. In order to get relationships started, EHES compromised on program specifics but held firm on two requirements: long-term postplacement help and at least some element of attitudinal training. The Clark Foundation agreed to extend the grant to six years to give EHES more time to put the network together. EHES and Clark also allowed affiliates to count preexisting funding and government grants toward the challenge, recognizing that most relied extensively on government funding and were not confident they could match the Clark grants with new, private money. Despite a slow start, SEG records showed that it had made 10,455 placements by the end of the first Clark challenge grant in 1995. Clark approved a second major grant for $1 million a year for five years starting in 1996, with the goal of putting an additional 18,000 people to work with 80% retention. The grant stated the expectation that STRIVE's dependence on Clark would decline by the end of that period.

By June 1997, SEG consisted of eleven sites,[11] including the two EHES sites. EHES provided SEG affiliates with start-up and ongoing technical assistance in training, placement, follow-up, and graduate information systems, which in turn helped EHES track SEG's performance. Each affiliate had a letter of agreement with STRIVE, was committed to an annual placement target and budget, and was assigned a specific level of Clark support by EHES, which retained some of the Clark money to fund its own centers and SEG management costs.[12] Affiliates submitted reports on actual placements, retention, and expenditures, and EHES staff conducted site visits to observe training and review sample files. In addition to a yearly retreat for SEG organizations, there were also informal interactions, especially among the more highly committed organizations.[13] Some affiliates had also hired STRIVE graduates or former EHES staff to help deliver their STRIVE programs. There were pluses and minuses to running a STRIVE program within a larger multiservice agency. On the plus side, there were opportunities to share overhead with the agency's other programs, greater flexibility in staffing, and the ability to draw on the agency's existing expertise and networks. However, STRIVE program heads at SEG affiliates reported feeling tugged by the dual accountability to STRIVE and their own organizations.

There was considerable variation in the STRIVE programs at the nine sites run by affiliated agencies. Even affiliates who followed the model closely adapted STRIVE to their particular circumstances. For example, the Stanley Isaacs Neighborhood Center softened the classroom interaction to accommodate its settlement house culture and the younger age of its participants. The Center on Children and Families replaced the video projects with additional job-search activities and added posttraining workshops and field trips. Other SEG sites departed more significantly from the STRIVE model because of their different client populations and

funding constraints. For example, the site operated by the National Association for Drug Abuse Problems accepted clients from 12-step treatment facilities throughout the city and offered a three-day STRIVE-like seminar, followed by placement and follow-up. The South Bronx Overall Economic Development Corporation offered expensive hard-skills training for the cable industry and used attitudinal training as a way of screening participants for these longer programs. Midtown Community Court used STRIVE as a component in its alternative disposition program for less serious offenders; they offered long-term training in reprographics into which they incorporated attitudinal components.

Stanley Isaacs' director of youth employment, Howard Knoll, saw the biggest issue facing SEG as quality control: "EHES knows the placement and retention numbers, but it's possible to produce those numbers without adding value in the classroom. In the end, the training is Frank Horton. He's brilliant, but he can't be replaced and you're limited to the number of staff who've been in close contact with him." For its part, EHES considered variations among SEG affiliates as a necessary part of working with existing organizations and serving new populations and thought that most SEG members were gradually moving closer to the STRIVE model. EHES felt that it needed to be flexible in SEG oversight: They gave affiliates significant leeway in their allocation of STRIVE and non-STRIVE costs and were patient with short-term problems with placement or retention numbers. But they also said that they policed the relationships to maintain SEG's integrity, citing several cases where affiliates were monitored for questionable practices or suspended until their STRIVE programs were reorganized.

Replication in Other Cities

"As soon as we had one STRIVE up and running," said Sam Hartwell, "I started thinking about launching another. In each case I had a fingernail grip on how to get started in the new city." The first city where STRIVE supported a replication was Pittsburgh (1988), where Hartwell grew up and had many contacts among the town's major foundations and wealthy families. Second was Chicago (1991): He had lived there earlier in his career, and his daughter had a friend who was interested in relocating to start a STRIVE there. Another daughter was working at a law firm in Boston and gathered a group of partners to explore launching a local STRIVE (1994). In Philadelphia, an acquaintance put him in touch with a civic leader, who in turn recommended an agency that might want to launch a STRIVE program (1997).

Before Philadelphia, each of these STRIVEs was an independent nonprofit created expressly to deliver the STRIVE program. In each case, Hartwell made the initial contacts, and Carmona, Hartwell, and others traveled to the city frequently during the year prior to the launch. They talked to interested parties about STRIVE, helped gather a core group that would become the organization's board, and approached key funders and civic leaders. Boston lawyer Kitt Sawitsky remembers the factors that drew him to STRIVE and helped him, as chair of the Boston STRIVE, attract other people:

It seemed like a way of using the power and connections I had been accumulating in my professional life to get at the root economic causes of the problem without having to become a social worker. I liked their style: There weren't a lot of meetings or structure to work through. The fact that it was privately funded and there was no national board or central control was another plus: People felt they could put their reputations on the line because there weren't any strings attached to the New York program, and the local foundations preferred funding a Boston-based effort. Sam was a big factor, too. It's hard to put your finger on how he does it. It's not charisma and he doesn't talk a lot, but he has a way of creating trust and opening doors.

EHES staff provided technical assistance to the new STRIVEs on start-up and ongoing operations; except in special circumstances, there was no charge for EHES staff time or expenses. Pro-formas for a new launch called for a $175,000 budget, three staff members, and 2,500 square feet of space, which would grow to six people and a budget of $260,000 in three years. This low initial investment was a major selling point for early supporters of a new STRIVE. Although EHES had taken the first steps toward drafting an affiliation contract, it was never completed, and no formal agreement existed between EHES and the new STRIVEs. However, Hartwell or Carmona would sit on the new site's governing or advisory board and there was some communication between staffs. Except in Pittsburgh, the new programs identified themselves prominently as STRIVE programs. In Chicago and Boston, the organizations often referred to themselves merely as "STRIVE" rather than using their full legal names.

In all four cities, the programs had modified the model to fit their circumstances. All had dropped EHES's video projects in favor of activities more directly related to job search, such as informational interviews with local employers or downtown field trips for job interviews. Pittsburgh, Chicago, and Philadelphia had lengthened the program by a week or more to allow more time for attitudinal change and skills remediation. Perhaps most important, all four organizations modified EHES's "in your face" style to fit their different populations and organizational cultures. In most cases, this meant that staff continued to call participants on inappropriate behavior but used a less aggressive manner and paid more attention to the instructor's position as role model.[14] Each of these organizations illustrated different approaches and issues in bringing STRIVE to new cities.

Pittsburgh

Three Rivers Employment Service, with a budget of approximately $800,000 and a staff of 11, was headed by Executive Director Wilma "Bunny" Carter, an outgoing and entrepreneurial woman who had led the organization since 1988. During its first few years, it followed the STRIVE model closely, but the two programs had long since diverged, and by 1997, STRIVE was rarely mentioned in Three Rivers' materials.

Three Rivers' core offerings consisted of a six-week job-readiness program and half-year hard-skills courses in office technology, computer networking, and computer maintenance. Participants represented a broad range of skill levels. Though there were some attitudinal components to the training that were similar in spirit to STRIVE's, they were integrated into other program content as "employer expectations." Three Rivers had also offered a wide variety of more focused programs—such as a diversity program for state employees and a yearlong school-to-work program for troubled high school students—and had its own replication program that helped other organizations set up employment services in Pennsylvania and neighboring states. About 80% of the Three Rivers' participants were referred to it by state, county, or city government agencies. Government support provided an estimated 60% of the budget, with the balance coming mainly from foundations.

Leaders from Three Rivers and EHES publicly praised each other's good works, but little connection remained between them. Said Hartwell:

They're doing great things and people in Pittsburgh love them, but it's not really STRIVE. Even though I'm on the board, I haven't received an annual report or any information on job placements or funding for the past five years. My impression is that they weren't able to continue raising private money, and they started a lot of new programs to take advantage of government dollars. From their perspective, they would probably say that I was helpful in the beginning but then kind of disappeared when we started Chicago.

According to the organization's founding board chair, Bob Pease, "Three Rivers has grown because Bunny has not been satisfied with the status quo. She wants to have an effect on people's lives and isn't afraid to innovate."

Chicago

The Chicago Employment Service (CES) ran two sites with a staff of 18 people headed by Executive Director Steve Redfield and just over $550,000 in annual expenses. Chicago followed the STRIVE model in its broad outlines despite some differences, such as dropping the intense Friday morning orientation. ("We start right out on Monday morning creating a supportive environment where you can tell people the truth and they can hear it," said Redfield. "We were seeing 50% attrition, so we changed how fast and hard we hit them.")

CES had created or participated in a number of special initiatives in which it partnered with local foundations or community-based organizations to deliver services. According to Redfield, these initiatives were most often driven by funding:

We don't have a corporate champion like Sam or a Clark Foundation, so we have to be more opportunistic. Sometimes we've tinkered to add a new element to attract funding, but ideally, we deliver our basic product to a specified group within our same basic population. We don't want to have a lot of different products or treat people differently depending on what program they're in. Still, it can get messy in practice.

The biggest experiment was with government funding, in which Redfield said they first got involved in order to "get to know the devil, even if we decided against it eventually." Starting with a performance-based contract with the Illinois Department of Public Aid to train and place 40 people in 1993, CES undertook state contracts in each succeeding year. Initially the state made phased payments upon participants' enrollment, graduation, and placement. However, it soon began paying one lump sum for successful placements only, which meant that CES was not getting paid for some of its most challenging clients. CES's state contracts peaked in 1996 at 200 placements and 31% of its revenues, but it had found it progressively harder to fulfill the contracts and began to scale back. Though CES found welfare funding more flexible and outcomes oriented than JTPA money, it still required specialized case management, which led to higher costs and other problems. CES had concluded that in the long run, it preferred to reduce its reliance on government contracts.

In 1994, CES's board had decided to do a slow intake and to focus on the needs of its current graduate pool rather than extend services to entirely new populations. Accordingly, the staff created the Career Path project to see if STRIVE's typical clients could improve their wages through a combination of employment, training, and education. The program identified work and training tracks to advance participants to career-level positions in promising business sectors[15] and recruited STRIVE graduates who felt they needed more skills. CES counselors worked one-on-one with Career

Path participants to develop individual career plans and provide ongoing support and mentorship. Although there was no cut-off in service, the program was designed to be useful for a period of three to five years. The target wage was $18,000 a year ($9 an hour). At the end of 1996, Career Path had an ongoing caseload of 125 and expenses of just under $90,000 a year. Initial results were encouraging but not conclusive. Participants experienced higher placement and retention rates than regular STRIVE graduates, but they were earning lower wages, mainly because they were subordinating short-term wage growth to longer-term career development in the early stages of the program. Only 10% had reached the $18,000 benchmark. Moreover, as welfare time limits were implemented in Illinois in 1996, program participants' engagement in education began to fall off.

CES placed a high value on operations data and had recently embarked on a $100,000 investment in MIS, including a networked PC on every staff desktop. For management purposes, they were able to cut data several different ways to track office and individual performance and understand the real costs of various activities. In addition to following the current employment and wage status of each graduate, CES tracked whether each job was a first, second, or third position, how long it took to get, and how long it lasted. Externally, CES sought to present simple and compelling numbers that would not overstate performance or lead to negative surprises. To that end, CES had modified several of the usual STRIVE methods for stating placement and retention figures.[16]

Boston

Of all the city start-ups, Boston Employment Service (BES) bore the most resemblance to the original EHES program. In less than three years it had grown to a staff of six and a $270,000 budget, funded entirely by private money. Its 1996 placement numbers were strong at 195, or 30% over goal. However, the board and staff had become concerned. First, replacements accounted for almost half of the placement numbers. Second, class sizes typically ranged from 10 to 15 participants, most of whom came from nearby neighborhoods. These facts suggested that BES's main challenge was a shortage of applicants rather than funding or jobs.

In part, this was attributed to record lows in unemployment and strong competition for even low-skilled employees. The board worried that in the current economy, many people were getting quick, no-future jobs but would not have STRIVE skills and resources to fall back on if they were fired or laid off. Another factor was the program's location in Dorchester, a predominantly low-income residential section of Boston consisting of more than a half dozen insular neighborhoods that were hard to reach by public transportation. The board also thought that it needed to do a better job forging relationships with community-based organizations and agencies that could refer participants to STRIVE. The board felt that CES needed to meet these challenges through growth and planned to move forward with its long-term goal of launching several new sites to bring STRIVE's total Boston placements up to a thousand a year. It was looking into several opportunities, including opening a BES-run site in a highly accessible section of Roxbury and helping the largest local homeless program launch a STRIVE site to serve its clients.

Philadelphia

The Philadelphia STRIVE was unique among the four cities in that it was launched by an existing nonprofit organization.[17] The Metropolitan Career Center (MCC) served a total of over 500 people a year with a staff of 35 and a $2.2 million budget. Its executive director, John Rice, was a Presbyterian minister with an MBA who had cofounded the organization in 1974. After a pilot program during the first half of 1997, MCC had decided to add STRIVE as an ongoing program, hiring two new people and appointing a longtime MCC employee as STRIVE program director.

MCC's other employment programs ranged from 12 weeks to a full year and included offerings in job readiness, retail, office technology, and computers, some of which included a GED component. The clientele was overwhelmingly African American single mothers on public assistance. MCC tracked placement, average wages, and other outcomes for these programs, which were highly regarded in Philadelphia. Over 75% of MCC's funding was from government sources. With recent activity in the employment field focused on the "Work First" strategy of getting people into jobs quickly, MCC needed a short, intensive program that would complement its traditional strength in longer hard-skills training. MCC saw STRIVE as a way to experiment with Work First and "get it

right," free from the strictures of a government contract. In addition to the usual program adjustments, however, MCC had the challenge of adapting STRIVE to an existing organization with its own culture and values. According to Rice:

> Our organizational style and culture were different: For example, EHES was led predominantly by men, whereas most of our managers and staff are African American women. We had reservations about Work First and needed to address them in program design. But STRIVE understood this and expected us to use our judgment to adapt the program. The result was that the staff migrated toward STRIVE because they were drawn to it, not because it was imposed from above. From their point of view, getting involved with STRIVE has made us aware again of the importance of the attitudinal issues.

Nonetheless, Rice had continuing concerns about how MCC and others would reconcile long-term skills development with the Work First strategy:

> Eventually, you have to find a way to work in more training and education. Otherwise, you end up with a two-class system: One group goes to college and spends four years full-time developing their skills. The other gets a series of quick, low-paying jobs. Though theoretically they can continue their education on weekends and at night, how is a low-income single mother going to have time to do that?

THE CHALLENGE OF THE DEAD-ENDED CLIENT

As the STRIVE network expanded in the early 1990s, a troubling phenomenon surfaced at EHES. The STRIVE model had always assumed that attitudinal training and two years of work experience would result in self-sufficiency for participants. As a growing number of graduates reached the end of the two-year follow-up period, EHES found that some had reached a dead end. EHES's Lorenzo Harrison observed:

Here's a guy who's done everything STRIVE has told him to. He has good work habits, maybe a GED, and he's working as a stocker in a drugstore for a buck or two over minimum wage. He's living alone in poverty or with relatives, and has no chance of moving up in his job. We asked ourselves if we were really succeeding in our mission of improving people's lives.

Several STRIVEs had made efforts to address this challenge, including Pittsburgh's entry into hard skills and Chicago's Career Path.

ASAP and the Ford Foundation

In 1994, Rob Carmona approached Ron Mincy, a senior program officer at the Ford Foundation,[18] seeking support for STRIVE's core program and the challenge of increasing wages for its graduates. Mincy had also recently been approached by Jobs for Youth, a Boston agency that had been successful placing young people in Boston's booming healthcare industry. According to Mincy:

I had a limited amount of money to deploy in the employment and training area, and I could either "go deep" with one or two big grants or spread the money around. I knew that Ford couldn't fund the core program at STRIVE. Separately, STRIVE and JFY were not attractive grants. But together, they were very attractive.

Mincy had a deep interest in "sectoral development," which stressed working with employers in high-job-growth industries to identify employment needs and develop hard-skills training and recruiting relationships that responded to them. Mincy was concerned, however, that sectoral development programs did not reach people at the low end of the skills distribution. He saw a STRIVE/Jobs for Youth partnership as a way to push sectoral development down to lower-skilled people, by combining JFY's expertise in sectoral hard-skills training with STRIVE's expertise in attracting and providing attitudinal training to a broad range of low-skilled people. This combination also broadened support within the foundation. Moreover, Mincy knew that, unlike many welfare-related job-training programs, STRIVE served a significant number of men. Bringing men into the welfare and employment equation was a major goal for Mincy, and he thought that STRIVE might play a role in future Ford efforts in that area.

Supported by two Ford planning grants totaling $450,000, a working group drawn from the agencies and Ford designed the ASAP program (for "Access, Support, and

Advancement Partnership") to train and place people in career-track jobs paying $22,000 plus benefits.[19] In addition to delivering services, ASAP would encourage a knowledge transfer between the partner agencies. Although some friction developed between STRIVE and Jobs for Youth during the planning stage, Ford approved a $1 million grant to fund the first year of the two-year demonstration project, with the understanding that the partners would raise another $1 million for the second year. ASAP began operation in November 1996 at a New York site operated by STRIVE and a Boston site operated by JYF, with first-year placement goals of 90 and 40, respectively.

Participants were required to have a GED as well as a year's work experience after graduating from STRIVE's or JFY's basic job-readiness program. Both sites delivered four weeks of "Advanced Attitudinal Training," based on STRIVE, but modified to focus on corporate career advancement. Participants then received 6–20 weeks of industry-focused hard-skills training in one of three training niches: Financial Services, Envirotech, and Telecommunications. In some cases, the training was contracted out to a community college or trade school; in others, curricula were designed by the agency and delivered by a mix of in-house and contracted instructors. Sectoral Employment Developers at each site were to link ASAP with employers in the target industries, help participants develop career plans and find employment, and identify new target industries. Graduate Services staff were to provide support and guidance during the program and follow-up after placement.

Although outcomes and an evaluation of ASAP's first year were not due until the fall,

some initial feedback was available by June 1997. The program was operational at both sites and had been able to place many of its graduates. Although the average participant did not hit the $22,000 target, many were hired at salaries above $20,000. But the ASAP partners faced a number of challenges. Both sites had difficulty attracting eligible participants and relaxed their entrance requirements. Communications between the two sites had dropped off, and most decisions were made on a site-specific basis. Among other staffing problems, the original ASAP director in New York was replaced in April and a Boston site director had still not been hired. Neither partner was able to raise significant funding for the following year. There was also considerable variation in the types and quality of services offered at the two sites. For example:

- Boston ASAP staff had significant difficulties delivering attitudinal training.
- New York had been less successful in sectoral development, including the creation of relationships with industry employers.
- In Boston, some participants had quit their jobs to attend training, which was scheduled during the day.
- New York Envirotech participants were disappointed because the training, which was contracted to an automotive industry–sponsored program, prepared them for mechanic jobs falling far below the target wage.
- Telecommunications, which was contracted to a New York community college, experienced high attrition due to the advanced math required.

Although total placement numbers were on track, they included a large number of people in New York who made use of the ASAP placement services but had been through little or no ASAP training. Excluding these placements, the number of placed ASAP graduates fell far short of the goal at both sites.

STRIVE's new ASAP director, Eric Arroyo, observed that there were plenty of jobs paying $22,000 but that STRIVE didn't necessarily have the people with the right skills for them. He saw a much bigger opportunity to advance people from $13,000 to $18,000 in such industries as hotel, travel, and tourism. While EHES continued to pass Ford ASAP funding through to Boston, the two sites for the most part would operate independently for the remaining year of the project.

ESCALATING RECOGNITION AND DEMAND

Rob Carmona said, "I remember during the first year or two saying to people: 'I don't know when or how, but someday this thing is going to blow out crazy on us.'"

The year leading up to June 1997 was eventful for STRIVE. A wave of state-based welfare reform initiatives culminated in federal legislation that was signed into law in August 1996. The Personal Responsibility and Work Opportunity Reconciliation Act imposed a five-year lifetime limit on benefits and stiff work requirements on adult recipients, while it authorized states to spend a certain percentage of federal welfare funding to support job training and placement. These provisions gave all levels of government and nonprofit service providers powerful incentives to put welfare recipients to work quickly. STRIVE was increasingly invoked as a model for the emerging Work First philosophy. It was singled out by the Department of Labor and the Government Accounting Office as a particularly effective agency, caught the eye of Secretary of Labor Robert Reich, and its leaders were invited to the White House to talk with senior presidential aides.

STRIVE's rising visibility culminated on May 4 with the highly favorable coverage on *60 Minutes*. The program, with its dramatic footage following a class from orientation through graduation and employment, provoked more viewer response to CBS than anyone could remember in the network's history. Representatives from major movie production companies came to Harlem with proposals to turn the STRIVE story into a feature film. In little more than a month, EHES received over 2,000 telephone calls from across the country, many of them from civic leaders, local governments, and community organizations wanting to bring STRIVE to their communities. According to EHES's Lorenzo Harrison, they represented a new challenge for STRIVE:

> We don't know these people. We have a brand name and they want it. Some of them think "tough love" training is a panacea but don't seem to understand the importance of follow-up. We're asking ourselves: Who are they and why do they want this? Is it just to raise money or help them with a short-term problem—or do they really believe in it?

To help EHES cope with this challenge, the Ford Foundation made a $200,000 "capacity grant" to help it plan the next phase of its growth and build organizational capacity, while maintaining its focus on the ASAP initiative.

One positive byproduct of the publicity was increased receptivity at foundations and corporations. According to Sam Hartwell, national funders that were unconvinced a few years ago were now paying attention as he invoked STRIVE as a national model and proposed six-figure grants. More and more, however, Rob Carmona felt that government would have to play a role in funding the ongoing operations of local, independent STRIVEs:

When you're small, you can hustle enough private money to keep going, but it gets much harder when you're bigger and have been around for a while. Long term, the mix for local STRIVEs should probably be about 35% government and 65% private. Ultimately government has a big responsibility for this kind of program.

The Board Meeting

The June 18 board meeting was scheduled as an all-day retreat at IBM's Palisades facility. In addition to the usual attendees, Steve Redfield was flying in from Chicago and Kitt Sawitsky was coming down from Boston. Several board members had urged STRIVE to "get serious" and develop formal criteria and procedures for affiliation, a national advisory board, and possibly a new national organization to manage replication and serve as the umbrella for local STRIVEs. Though

doubtful about the last suggestion, both Carmona and Hartwell felt that STRIVE faced big decisions:

- How should EHES respond to the current wave of interest? Should it charge for technical assistance? How should the assistance be delivered? Should they focus on groups that wanted to launch full-fledged STRIVEs, or should they also serve groups who simply wanted to learn from the model?
- How fast should STRIVE grow? Could it go from starting a new STRIVE every three years to starting several a year? Should it change the way new STRIVEs were created or their relationship to EHES?
- Were any structural changes required to support STRIVE's future growth?
- What should STRIVE do to address the needs of its "dead-ended" clients, both next year and after ASAP?
- How should the organization be funded—both short term and long term? What role should government funding or large foundation grants play?

Although the board would not make final decisions on all of these issues, it was clear that next week's discussion would be a defining one in STRIVE's evolution.

NOTES

1. People usually referred to the organization simply as "STRIVE." This case sometimes

refers to East Harlem Employment Service (EHES) to distinguish it from the STRIVE program model or the network of other STRIVE organizations.

2. Hartwell had graduated from Harvard Business School in 1956, worked at several Wall Street firms (including as a managing director at Merrill Lynch), and in 1979 launched his own firm providing consulting on major investment banking projects.

3. In addition to Hartwell and the staff, Michael Frey, former director of Henry Street, played an important role in STRIVE's early years both as its board president and as a part-time consultant. He left the organization in 1991 and was succeeded by current board president Jack Flanagan.

4. Although nationwide unemployment in the middle of 1997 was a low 4.7%, STRIVE operated in a more difficult environment: The unemployment rate for New York City was 8.8% and rising, and the city's job growth over the past year was about half the national average. In addition, nationwide black and Hispanic unemployment was about twice that for whites, while the unemployment rate for black teens was 28.4%.

5. For example, several people invariably arrived late during the first few days of training. The trainer told the late people to stand in the back until a break in the class discussion, then addressed each in turn:

Trainer: Where do you live?

Participant: Fulton Street.

Trainer: Watch your tone and don't roll those eyes. This is not a training session, this is a job. What train do you take?

Participant: The 4 to the 6.

Trainer: That's only 30 minutes! I live on Staten Island; I have to take a boat, a train, and a bus!

Other participant: I came from Queens and I made it on time. You should have left more time. The first impression is the most important.

6. In fact, it was not uncommon for 10%–15% of the participants to drop out during the program, most of them during the first week. STRIVE saw this attrition not as a failure but as evidence that the program was "working at the cutting edge of its target population."

7. An optional three-day add-on workshop, "For Women Only," offered by a female on-staff clinical social worker, addressed the unique challenges facing working women and introduced them to additional resources.

8. According to Horton, "It takes the right kind of person to do this training. There are different ways, it's not a formula—but you know it when you see it in a person. Then you can mold it and shape it. The STRIVE method has been spread like an African folktale—a combination of watching others, hearing about it, and doing it yourself. You're not really a STRIVE trainer until you've been doing it for 18 months."

9. JTPA funding was administered through a complex revenue-sharing system involving federal, state, and local components. Extensive regulations governed client eligibility, permissible services, and reporting requirements. In 1996, the average adult JTPA program participant received 435 hours of training (often part-time and spread over six months or more). Retention was measured as of 13 weeks

after termination. Funding for JTPA programs for the disadvantaged had declined over the past few years, in part because a number of studies had cast doubt on the impact of these programs.

10. Clark was a New York City family foundation that prided itself on its small staff (two professionals making $4.4 million in grants annually) and low profile (the foundation had no printed literature or annual report). It had been funding STRIVE at the $10,000–$15,000-a-year level since EHES's incorporation.

11. SEG membership had changed gradually over time, with several new affiliates joining and three dropping out since 1990.

12. Clark funding for SEG and EHES was supplemented by funding provided by United Way of New York City.

13. According to Charles Modiano, the STRIVE director at the Center for Family and Children: "The key to making STRIVE work is people who understand it and are completely committed. With Rob, Lorenzo, and Frank, you see it immediately: They're very real, very dedicated, and there's real humility there. It's contagious. I try to pass it on to the staff myself and get them into contact with STRIVE people every chance we get."

14. Comments from executive directors included: "We like to say that if New York is the Marines, we're the Coast Guard: It's the same basic truth whether you shout or whisper." "There can be some stress, but it can be done without Frank Horton's drama." "We don't use confrontation as a training tool; that's counterproductive."

15. In healthcare, for example, a patient transporter could train to become a certified nursing assistant, earn her GED, become a licensed practical nurse with a one-year course of study, and eventually earn an associate's degree and become a registered nurse.

16. First, when quoting placement numbers to external audiences, CES included only first-time placements and excluded replacements of graduates who previously had quit or been fired. Most STRIVEs included replacements in their overall placement numbers. Second, to calculate retention, CES broke graduates down into quarterly cohorts and reported how many people were still working two years after the quarter they were initially placed. Most STRIVEs divided their graduates into two-year cohorts and expressed their retention rate as the percentage of that cohort still employed at the end of the period. (Neither method required the graduate to be employed in the same job over the two-year period.) CES's materials stated 73% placement and 70% retention rates.

17. When Sam Hartwell approached Jim Bodine, a prominent business and civic leader, about setting up a new STRIVE, Bodine replied that there were too many organizations already and recommended working with the Metropolitan Career Center, which he felt was the best employment training and placement agency in the city. Bodine did agree to head up a STRIVE advisory committee for MCC and play a leadership role in raising private money for the STRIVE program.

18. Ford was the largest U.S.-based foundation with over $6.6 billion in assets. Ford had over 500 staff members making $280 million in grants worldwide in such areas as urban poverty, social justice, public policy, education, and international affairs.

19. A third partner in New York provided a youth development perspective in the planning phase but played a smaller role in implementation.

Case Study 6.2.

Sustainable Conservation—Where Next?

Sustainable Conservation advances the stewardship of natural resources using innovative, pragmatic strategies that actively engage businesses and private landowners.

—Mission Statement

It was a little after 10 P.M. on September 27, 2002, when Ashley Boren, executive director of Sustainable Conservation (SusCon), a San Francisco–based environmental nonprofit organization, sat down to review the latest draft of the five-year strategic plan (**Exhibit 6.2.1**) she was presenting to the board of directors (**Exhibit 6.2.2**) the next morning. The plan outlined five primary goals for the organization and detailed the next steps toward achieving them. Ashley Boren's long-term vision was for SusCon's pragmatic approach to reducing the environmental impact of the industries with which it worked to become nationally recognized. Rather than fight corporations and private landowners with legal challenges and

1. **Focus on a Few Industry Sectors and Address Multiple Environmental Issues Within Those Sectors.** Identify industries that are having a significant environmental impact, in which traditional tools are not sufficient, and where change promoted through collaboration and incentives has the potential to yield significant gains. Pilot successful solutions, and, as appropriate, move from pilot projects to broad adoption/implementation. Build on successes and relationships to address multiple environmental issues within each industry sector. Focus on both land-based industry sectors, including agriculture, and industry sectors that affect urban environmental quality, including transportation.

2. **Leverage Learnings and Success by Moving Beyond California.** Identify and pursue best ways to adapt and replicate successful solutions outside of California. Pursue opportunities strategically using expertise and partnerships.

3. **Raise Visibility of the Organization; Become Widely Recognized Among Environmental Funders and Partners for Our Unique Approach and Results.** Create a compelling brand identity and exploit partnerships, marketing, and media coverage to significantly enhance visibility for SusCon's work.

4. **Advance Past Start-Up Phase; Become a Well-Funded Organization With a Strong Infrastructure to Manage Growth.** Succeed in a concerted effort to increase the quantity and diversity of funds raised with the aim of building capacity, developing more depth in staff, and increasing flexibility in expenditures.

5. **Foster and Advance a Culture of Collaboration, Creativity, and Innovation to Achieve Results.** As we do externally with our partners, we will strive to promote these cultural attributes within our organization. It is particularly important that we promote this type of culture as we grow to ensure that we do not lose or dilute those factors that have been critical to our success. Internally and externally we strive to truly understand each other's viewpoints. We value a vigorous and open debate about ideas because it enables us to develop better, lasting solutions. To foster creativity and innovation, we trust each individual's desire and ability to succeed, and we support varying work styles and approaches.

Exhibit 6.2.1   Proposed Five-Year Goals for Sustainable Conservation

SOURCE: Sustainable Conservation 2002–2007 Strategic Plan.

demonstrations, SusCon worked collaboratively with these constituents and with federal, state, and local governments to devise economically feasible solutions to environmental problems that protected the environment. One of SusCon's business partners observed: "Their approach to solving environmental problems— working with industry to determine incentives to get industry more in compliance or more conscious of impacts on the environment—is a real strength in terms of SusCon's likelihood for long-term success.

They have got very sharp staff and are clearly dedicated."

Based on preliminary conversations with board members, Boren was confident that the board would accept four of the five strategic goals without much resistance or debate. Those included narrowing the organization's industry focus, raising visibility, strengthening sources of funding, and continuing to foster a strong culture. The issue that she anticipated would generate the most discussion was scaling the organization geographically. Boren needed to discuss with

Mr. Charles Ahlem	Founder and Partner, Hilmar Cheese Company
Mr. Frank Boren	Past President, The Nature Conservancy
Ms. Laura Hattendorf	Former Executive Director, Sustainable Conservation
Ms. Jennifer Hernandez	Partner, Beveridge & Diamond
Dr. Michael Hertel	Manager of Environmental Affairs, Southern California Edison Co.
Ms. Cynthia Hunter Lang	Ranch Owner
Ms. Felicia Marcus	Executive Vice President & Chief Operating Officer, Trust for Public Lands
Mr. Charles McGlashan	Consultant in Sustainability
Ms. Sunne Wright McPeak	President and CEO, Bay Area Council
Dr. Gerald Meral	Executive Director, Planning and Conservation League
Mr. Rich Morrison	Senior Vice President (Retired), Bank of America
Ms. Tina Quinn	Cofounder, SusCon
Mr. Russell Siegelman	Partner, Kleiner Perkins Caufield & Byers
Mr. Stanley Van Vleck	Partner, Kahn, Soares & Conway, LLP

Exhibit 6.2.2   Board of Directors

SOURCE: Sustainable Conservation.

her board the desirability and feasibility of expanding beyond California in the difficult funding environment of 2003.

SUSCON'S POSITIONING AMONG ENVIRONMENTAL NONPROFITS

SusCon was a small but innovative player in the large, vibrant sector of nonprofit organizations that focused on improving the natural environment. Among the most common and successful strategies these organizations employed to address environmental threats caused by economic activity were lobbying state and federal legislatures to reduce harmful environmental impacts from business by imposing stricter rules, regulations, and penalties; directly challenging businesses through court litigation; educating and training consumers to choose sustainable products; purchasing, preserving, and restoring endangered lands; mounting direct-action appeals, such as protests to publicize environmental issues; and

partnering with businesses to reduce their negative impact on the environment.

Advocacy

In the United States, the federal and state governments had primary responsibility for enacting environmental laws to preserve forests, rivers, and wildlife habitat. Federal and state legislatures were also empowered to mandate stricter emissions rules for businesses. Nonprofit conservation organizations such as the Wilderness Society, Sierra Club, and National Wildlife Federation lobbied state and federal representatives to vote for greater environmental protection in relevant pieces of legislation.

Litigation

Organizations such as Earth Justice Legal Defense Fund and the Natural

Resources Defense Council (NRDC) emphasized resolving environmental problems in
court. These organizations filed lawsuits
against businesses they believed to be responsible for environmental damage, seeking
financial compensation or court mandates
ordering that the damage be reversed and prevented from occurring again. Lawsuits not
only hurt companies financially but were also
a source of negative publicity and strained
relationships with regulators and shareholders. These organizations also litigated
against government agencies to uphold current laws and further limit emissions, chemical discharges, and other practices believed to
have adverse environmental impacts.

Land Acquisition

Habitat and open space were often protected by buying land outright or paying
landowners not to develop their properties.
This strategy was employed by organizations
such as The Nature Conservancy and Trust
for Public Land. The Nature Conservancy
conducted extensive research to identify
areas with the greatest numbers of valuable
flora and fauna threatened by development
and agriculture. Once identified, these areas
were purchased and managed by the organization or by a government agency to which
the nonprofit transferred its rights.

Education and Training

Environmental education was emphasized
by many organizations in the belief that individuals educated about the importance of
protecting natural resources would adapt

their lifestyles to be more sustainable. Venues
for environmental education included
schools (kindergarten through 12th grade),
nature museums, aquariums and wildlife
parks, published reports on environmental
topics, and media coverage of such reports.
Rarely the sole strategy of large conservation
organizations, education tended to be viewed
as complementary to other programs.

Direct Action

Organizations such as Greenpeace mobilized people to actively engage in protests,
demonstrations, and even blockades to draw
attention to environmental issues. This
approach aimed to heighten publicity around
a problem or issue and thereby motivate individuals and governments to act. Greenpeace,
for example, had long focused on banning
whaling worldwide, its volunteers following
whaling ships and working to release whales
that had been caught. Incidents of volunteers
being shot or injured brought international
attention to the problem and resulted in
international treaties banning whaling.

Business Partnerships

Some environmental organizations came
to believe that environmental gains could
be made by collaborating more with businesses. Though litigation often achieved
the environmentalists' goals, it had increased
tension between business and environmental
organizations and led many corporate leaders to resist calls to improve their environmental performance. To counter the belief
that protecting the environment was not

good business practice, environmental organizations often partnered with companies willing to explore the viability of sustainable business practices.

A Multifaceted Approach

For the past decade, the largest conservation organizations had been pursuing their environmental ends through multiple strategies, given the growing complexity of the environmental problems emerging. (See **Exhibit 6.2.3.**) These organizations developed portfolios of programs and initiatives that encompassed a host of approaches, ranging from litigation to business partnerships. An example was Conservation International; its 10 program areas ranged from a Center for Environmental Leadership in Business to programs that focused on education, ecotourism, research, and conservation investment.

SusCon's Approach

SusCon was one of the few environmental organizations that collaborated with business at the industry level to find solutions to environmental problems and demonstrate that these solutions could work by delivering tangible, on-the-ground results. Although highly focused on pragmatic, economically viable solutions for business, SusCon realized that environmental issues often involved multiple stakeholders and that results were best achieved when all parties collaborated to devise the solutions. SusCon's approach was to be a catalyst for such partnerships. For a range of environmental issues—from waste

runoff from dairy farms, to mercury in vehicles, to stream restoration—the organization identified industry players, regulators, and other nonprofits and worked with them to devise solutions that satisfied the interests of all constituents.

Instead of competing with other environmental nonprofits, SusCon proactively partnered with them on issues to which it could bring its unique capabilities. In early 2003, the organization began to work with Californians Against Waste (CAW) on legislation intended to level the economic playing field for auto dismantlers. Licensed businesses faced unfair competition from unlicensed operators, who were not required to comply with environmental regulation of potentially hazardous runoff from dismantled vehicles. (See **Exhibit 6.2.4** for a description of the Auto Recycling Project.) An environmental advocacy group focused on waste reduction, recycling, and resource conservation issues, CAW had more than 20,000 members in California, and its core competency was lobbying for legislation and policy on these issues. SusCon offered in-depth knowledge of the auto recycling industry and its accompanying environmental impacts as well as established partnerships with the major industry associations. By combining their strengths, SusCon and CAW sought to increase the likelihood of passing the legislation and getting the industry to support the effort.

SUSCON'S FOUNDING AND EARLY DEVELOPMENT

After presiding over the world's largest conservation organization, The Nature

Exhibit 6.2.3 Focus of Environmental Nongovernmental Organizations

	2001 Net Income ($ M)	2001 Assets	Litigation	Education/ Training	Science	Business Partnerships	Land Purchase	Advocacy/ Lobbying	Citizen Mobilization
1 The Nature Conservancy	$547	$2,935				○	■		
2 Trust for Public Land	161	280					■		
3 Greenpeace	158	120		○	○			■	■
4 The National Audubon Society	129	212		○	○	○		■	
5 World Wildlife Fund	118	254			○	○		■	○
6 National Wildlife Federation	105	99		○	○	○			
7 Conservation International	69	132			○	○	■		
8 The Conservation Fund	65	189		■	○	○	■		
9 Sierra Club	64	85						■	■
10 Environmental Defense Fund	41	51	○		○	○		■	○
11 NRDC	39	77	■					■	
12 Earth Justice Fund	22	32	■						
13 Wilderness Society	17	23		○				■	
14 Sustainable Conservation	1.2	0.3				■			

Key:

Existing programs		Primary organizational focus

SOURCE: Casewriter.

Auto Recycling The objective of the Auto Recycling Project, launched in January 2001, was to promote lasting, cost-effective solutions that reduced the amount of polluted runoff leaking from end-of-life vehicles. Auto recycling yards provided a valuable service by keeping end-of-life vehicles out of landfills, but many were not using best-management practices to prevent the toxic liquids in the cars from polluting waterways. The runoff resulted in significant water contamination affecting aquatic life, polluting water sources, and threatening public health.

Before SusCon's involvement, the dismantling industry, regulators, and environmentalists met almost exclusively in courtrooms. Under the leadership of Project Manager Nathan Arbitman, SusCon developed a productive partnership with the State of California Auto Dismantlers Association, which represented nearly one-third of licensed auto dismantlers in California. Under the partnership, government, industry, and environmental stakeholders agreed on what constituted the best structural, best-management practices. SusCon created technical-assistance materials for these best-management practices and worked to develop incentives to motivate their adoption.

Brake Pad Partnership (BPP) This partnership was a multistakeholder effort to understand the impact on the environment of brake-pad wear debris generated by passenger vehicles. SusCon worked with manufacturers, regulators, stormwater management agencies, and environmentalists to develop an approach for evaluating potential impacts on water quality using copper in South San Francisco Bay as an example. Brake pad manufacturers committed to adding this evaluation approach to their existing practices for designing products that both were safe for the environment and met performance requirements.

Partners in Restoration (PIR) SusCon developed the Partners in Restoration Program in collaboration with the Natural Resources Conservation Service. Many privately owned lands in California needed conservation work to help protect and restore water quality, creekside vegetation, and the natural functioning of essential habitat for wildlife. But the complexities of obtaining permits for these practices often discouraged landowners from doing anything at all. PIR, which SusCon developed in collaboration with the Natural Resources Conservation Service, simplified the permit process and made it easier for private landowners to protect valuable ecosystems by carrying out environmental enhancement projects on their property. By coordinating regulatory review of permits for conservation projects, PIR removed a major barrier to voluntary conservation and served as a catalyst for high-quality erosion control and habitat restoration work on private lands.

Developed initially in Elkhorn Slough, a biologically important watershed that suffered from some of the worst erosion in the western United States, in four years the program resulted in 28 conservation projects that prevented more than 40,000 tons of soil from burying sensitive creekside and wetland habitat and enhanced more than 1.5 miles of stream bank. The program was piloted in additional watersheds to refine and learn how best to replicate the model. A survey completed by SusCon in January 2001 identified nearly 30 more watersheds in California in which PIR might yield significant environmental benefits, and a strategy was developed for best tackling the expansion. Over the course of four years, the program evolved from inception and testing into its final phase: statewide replication. The ultimate goal was to make PIR available anywhere it was needed to further conservation.

Exhibit 6.2.4   Current Sustainable Conservation Projects

SOURCE: Sustainable Conservation.

Conservancy, from 1986 to 1990, Frank Boren founded SusCon in 1992 to advance the stewardship of natural resources using innovative strategies to actively engage businesses and private landowners in conservation. Before assuming the presidency of The Nature Conservancy, he had spent most of his professional career as a real estate developer and corporate attorney, a background that gave him a passion for using the power and capabilities of the private sector to preserve the nation's natural resources. Frank Boren believed that conventional tools for solving environmental problems—litigation, legislation, and land acquisition—did not adequately address the private sector's impact on the environment. SusCon sought to fill this void by working with the private sector on the environment's behalf.

SusCon initiated its first projects in January 1992 with three staff members and a $25,000 budget. In 1993, Frank Boren met Laura Hattendorf at Stanford University, where she was completing her MBA, and recruited her for the position of executive director. That same year, the organization became a project of the Tides Center, a nonprofit that provided fiscal and administrative support to new organizations that had not yet incorporated as nonprofits. SusCon quickly developed a distinctive approach that emphasized creating collaborative partnerships for applying business strategies to environmental priorities. Between 1993 and 1998, SusCon worked with private landowners and companies such as Wells Fargo Bank and Lloyd Properties on land conservation and assessment issues. In 1998, it obtained independent nonprofit status 501(c)(3).

Ashley Boren (Stanford MBA, 1989), daughter of Frank Boren, joined SusCon in 1997 as deputy director. Previously she had spent more than seven years with Smith & Hawken, a mail-order and retail gardening company, working in the areas of new-business development, inventory planning, and retail merchandising. Over the next three years, she comanaged SusCon with Hattendorf. In the fall of 2000, Hattendorf retired as executive director and joined SusCon's board.

OPERATIONS

Building an Interdisciplinary Team

Almost all of SusCon's project staff had private sector experience (**Exhibit 6.2.5**). Ashley Boren believed that an individual who had worked for a business would be better able to understand the constraints under which businesses operated, identify opportunities for change within businesses, and build the partnerships needed to realize change. She also sought people with experience or knowledge of how government and regulations worked, since the public sector had a profound impact on how businesses operated. "We recruit staff who reflect the constituencies with which we collaborate so that we can better understand the various economic models and cultures with which we are working and can develop solutions that will work for business and be supported by other stakeholders," Boren explained.

We promote innovation by giving project managers significant autonomy and encouraging them to take risks. Finding

ASHLEY BOREN, Executive Director

Ashley came to Sustainable Conservation from Smith & Hawken, where she spent eight years in the areas of new-business development, inventory planning, and retail merchandising. After earning a BA in human biology from Stanford University, she began her career with the Nature Conservancy's International Program in 1983 working in program development and fund-raising. Ashley left the Nature Conservancy in 1987 to attend Stanford Business School, from which she received an MBA and Certificate in Public Management as well as an MA in applied economics.

NATHAN ARBITMAN, Project Manager, Auto Recycling

Nathan came to Sustainable Conservation with a wide range of experience in the environmental field, having worked in environmental capacities for the National Wildlife Federation, the Rhode Island Attorney General, the Dial Corp., and Tetra Tech EM, Inc. Nathan received a BA in political science from Brown University.

SARAH CONNICK, Senior Project Manager, Brake Pad Partnership

Sarah's background in environmental science and policy included six years as a study director with the National Academy of Sciences' Water Science and Technology Board. Her doctoral research focused on the use of collaborative processes for making water policy in California. She holds an AB in chemistry from Bryn Mawr College, an MS in environmental engineering from Stanford University, and a PhD in environmental science, policy, and management at the University of California, Berkeley.

ALLEN DUSAULT, Senior Project Manager, Dairies

Allen began his career as a soil scientist and moved on to senior positions with the Massachusetts Department of Environmental Protection, Laidlaw, and the New Hampshire Project Authority. Prior to joining Sustainable Conservation, he was a consultant to corporations and government agencies in California, including IT Corp., Santa Barbara Public Works, and Browning-Ferris Industries. Allen has an MBA from the University of Redlands, an MS in resource management from the University of Guelph, and a BS in soil science from the University of Wisconsin at Madison.

KEN KRICH, Program Associate, Dairies

Ken started his business career in the natural foods industry. He spent 15 years in financial and operational positions in the computer industry, most recently as CEO of ComputerWare, a chain of retail computer stores. Before arriving at Sustainable Conservation, Ken was a visiting specialist at the University of California Energy Institute, researching California's restructured electricity market. Ken has an MBA in finance from the University of California, Berkeley, and a BA in sociology from the University of Chicago.

BOB NEALE, Director, Partners in Restoration

Prior to coming to Sustainable Conservation in 1998, Bob was land manager for Peninsula Open Space Trust, a land conservancy in San Mateo County. Before he changed careers into the conservation sector, Bob was a founder and partner of Thunderbolt Transport, a local trucking company. He graduated from San Francisco State University with a BA in English.

CAROLYN CALLAHAN REMICK, Senior Project Manager, Partners in Restoration

Carolyn has managed restoration and planning efforts at two Bay Area consulting firms, Zentner and Zentner, and CONCUR, and specializes in multiparty dialogues on permitting issues. She holds a BS in conservation and resource studies from the University of California, Berkeley.

Case Study

Exhibit 6.2.5   Staff Biographies   *(Continued)*

(Continued)

SARAH BETH LARDIE, Development and Communications Director

For more than a decade, Sarah Beth has been successfully raising money and increasing visibility for a wide variety of political candidates on the local, state, and national levels as well as for traditional nonprofits operating in the United States and around the world including the Coalition for Homeless Children and Families, Youth for Understanding, and the Jane Goodall Institute. Sarah Beth holds a BA in social work and a BA in labor studies from Rutgers University and an MPA from the University of Pittsburgh.

JANET FOSTER, Development and Communications Manager

Janet Foster works closely with the development and communications director to raise funds for the organization and support its marketing efforts. Janet has a background in fund-raising and writing, having worked for such organizations as the Women's Building, Forests Forever, the Committee in Solidarity With the People of El Salvador, Working Assets, and Swords to Plowshares. Janet earned a BA in French literature and English at Scripps College in Claremont and spent a year abroad at La Sorbonne, L'Universite de Paris.

MOJGAN VIJEH, Financial Consultant

Mojgan manages financial accounting and reporting for Sustainable Conservation. Prior to joining SusCon in March 2001, she was chief financial officer for the Family Violence Prevention Fund for five years. Mojgan has more than ten years of nonprofit accounting experience and is working in a consulting capacity for other nonprofit organizations and in the corporate sector.

KARENA GRUBER, Operations and HR Manager

Karena oversees all daily operations of the office to ensure a smooth working environment. Previously she was the customer service manager at Rent Tech, an on-line apartment-finding service in San Francisco. Karena received a BA in cinema from San Francisco State University.

KIM COLLINS, Office Manager

Kim works closely with the operations and human resources manager to keep the office running smoothly and provide tech support and database management. Kim holds a BA in anthropology from Trent University and a Certificate in Museum Management and Curatorship from Sir Sandford Flemming College.

Exhibit 6.2.5

SOURCE: Sustainable Conservation.

the right person with private sector know-how and environmental interests can be challenging. So far, however, we have been able to do it. And, from the number of calls I get from people looking for this type of work, I am hoping we can continue to be successful. To date, we have always been able to fill a position with a solid hire, and the searches have not been long.

Our salaries are competitive with those offered at other nonprofit environmental organizations but not with the business world, especially with consulting, investment banking, and positions that have an equity upside. We are steadily increasing salaries to be as competitive as possible, but our current funding sources would probably not support "business world" salaries. As we increase our individual gifts and develop other unrestricted sources, we should be able to do more here.

SusCon had attracted strong talent due to its pragmatic, results-oriented approach as well as its location. Three of seven program staff had earned MBAs, one had a PhD, and two others held master's degrees. They had come to the organization because they wanted to make a difference through their work. Reflected Kenneth Kirch, former CEO of ComputerWare, who had become a SusCon associate:

I have always been interested in resource and energy issues. At SusCon, I can work on projects involving these issues and also apply the skills I acquired from the business world. The work is difficult, and you have to push hard to make things happen, but it became very rewarding once I started getting calls from around the country from people who consider me the expert on energy production from animal waste.

SusCon was also able to attract summer associates from leading MBA programs. Over the past four years, it had hired nine summer associates: three from Stanford GSB, two from the Haas School at Berkeley, two from Kellogg, one from Michigan, and one from Harvard Business School. "It was a priority of mine to work for an organization that shared my personal values of commitment to the environment," remarked a second-year MBA student from Haas who worked at SusCon in the summer of 2002.

In the short 10 weeks of my internship, I wanted to contribute to the greater goal of disproving, by example, the myth that environmental and economic objectives are always at odds. My internship at SusCon was meant to be. What better place to work than an organization dedicated to identifying and developing voluntary conservation programs with the potential to generate economic benefits, allowing economic incentives and market forces to drive higher environmental performance. In addition to the rewarding work, SusCon's location in the heart of San Francisco offered an unparalleled combination of opportunities: a beautiful place to live and work with access to a thriving metropolitan center and the great outdoors.

Realizing that some of the talent SusCon had attracted had been drawn to the organization in part because of its location, Boren was unsure how expanding into new locations would affect the hiring process. The abundance of high-quality academic institutions in the Bay Area had made it easy for SusCon to hire qualified graduates from Berkeley and Stanford, but the cost of living had become prohibitive in the last few years, and many people had left the area to look for jobs in more affordable locations. Opening an office in a location with a lower cost of living could attract employees whom SusCon had previously not been able to recruit.

Raising Funds

Although funding for SusCon had more than doubled since 1998, with revenues

Bank of America Foundation	Monterey Bay National Marine Sanctuary Water
Bay Area Stormwater Management Agencies	Quality Protection Program
Elizabeth & Stephen Bechtel, Jr., Foundation	Morro Bay National Estuary Program
Blue Oak Foundation	National Fish & Wildlife Foundation
California Coastal Conservancy	Andrew Norman Foundation
Community Foundation Silicon Valley	The David and Lucile Packard Foundation
Compton Foundation	Peninsula Community Foundation
Mary A. Crocker Trust	PG&E Corporation
Dominican University of California	Roxbury Charitable Foundation
Joseph Drown Foundation	Sacramento Stormwater Management Program
The Bradford M. Endicott Charitable Lead Trust	San Francisco Estuary Project
Environment Now	The San Francisco Foundation
Ford Motor Company Fund	Sand County Foundation Bradley Fund for the Environment
The Fred Gellert Family Foundation	
The Wallace Alexander Gerbode Foundation	Santa Clara Valley Urban Runoff Pollution Prevention Program
Richard & Rhoda Goldman Fund	
Walter & Elise Haas Fund	State of California Auto Dismantlers Association
Haynes Foundation	The Summit Foundation
The William and Flora Hewlett Foundation	Robert and Patricia Switzer Foundation
The Home Depot	U.S. Environmental Protection Agency
The James Irvine Foundation	Vallejo Sanitation and Flood Control District

Exhibit 6.2.6   Major Institutional Donors 2001: Foundations, Corporations, and Governments

SOURCE: Sustainable Conservation.

reaching $1.2 million in 2002, the organization still relied heavily on a small group of donors (see **Exhibit 6.2.6**) mostly based in California.

Most of SusCon's funding came from foundations, which preferred to fund specific projects for a limited number of years. SusCon's finances, like those of many nonprofits, were affected in 2002 by the downturn in the stock market, which had reduced the availability of foundation grants and the amount of individual giving (see **Exhibits 6.2.7** and **6.2.8**). Thus, SusCon failed to achieve the growth it had anticipated, with revenues in 2002 flat compared with those in 2001. Even so, the organization had performed better than larger environmental organizations, such as NRDC and the Wilderness Society, which had both seen a decline in funding in 2002.

Boren had set as a goal to develop a diversified funding base and increase

	1998	1999	2000	2001	2002
Support and Revenue					
Corporate	$ 69	$ 91	$ 69	$ 170	$ 149
Foundation	284	346	537	690	683
Government	78	85	34	90	201
Individual	66	92	199	189	166
Fee for service	12	44	23	5	2
Investment income	3	5	9	12	4
Total Support and Revenue	**$512**	**$663**	**$871**	**$1,156**	**$1,205**
Expenses					
Program expenses	$317	$445	$550	$ 856	$ 885
General and administrative	125	160	176	158	172
Fund-raising and development	47	57	94	79	90
Total Expenses	**$489**	**$662**	**$820**	**$1,094**	**$1,147**
Net Income	**$ 23**	**$1**	**$ 51**	**$ 62**	**$ 58**
Beginning fund balance	52	75	76	127	189
Current year income	23	1	51	62	58
Ending Fund Balance	**$ 75**	**$ 76**	**$127**	**$ 189**	**$ 247**

Exhibit 6.2.7   Sustainable Conservation Historical Statements of Activities (in thousands)

SOURCE: Sustainable Conservation.

funding from the government sector and individuals. As SusCon's projects were demonstrating tangible success, the government was increasingly awarding it grants to replicate that success. To exploit the major opportunity individuals still presented, Boren knew the organization would need to create a "full-service" fund-raising operation that included expanded opportunities for donor recognition and involvement, major-donor research, and cultivation and planned giving. To help her execute this

goal, she had hired an experienced development and communications director, Sarah Beth Lardie, who had more than 10 years of fund-raising experience at national and international organizations (see **Exhibit 6.2.5** for Lardie's biography). "Eighty-five percent of all money raised in the United States every year comes from direct individual donations," observed Lardie.

That 85% consists of large donations and small. It's true that a single large

	1998	1999	2000	2001	2002
Assets					
Cash and cash equivalents	$ 86	$172	$ 263	$ 230	$237
Grants and contracts receivable	302	130	548	652	265
Pledges receivable	—	—	143	106	47
Other receivables	4	11	13	1	2
Prepaid expenses	6	11	14	20	17
Fixed assets (net of depreciation)	8	14	34	20	4
Total Assets	**$406**	**$338**	**$1,015**	**$1,029**	**$572**
Liabilities and Fund Balance					
Accounts payable	102	61	49	35	25
Accrued wages and PR liabilities	–	–	9	15	26
Deferred grant revenue	229	201	687	790	274
Total Liabilities	**$331**	**$262**	**$745**	**$ 840**	**$325**
Beginning fund balance	52	75	76	127	189
Net income/loss current year	23	1	51	62	58
Ending fund balance	$ 75	$ 76	$127	$ 189	$247
Total Liabilities and Fund Balance	**$406**	**$338**	**$872**	**$1,029**	**$572**

Exhibit 6.2.8   Sustainable Conservation Historical Balance Sheets (in thousands)

SOURCE: Sustainable Conservation.

Case Study

donation can make a huge impact on a small organization, but it's the steady stream of small donations that keeps most nonprofits afloat—while larger gifts are used as springboards for growth. Currently, SusCon does not have a large enough pool of individual donors to nourish the organization and provide for future growth. We need to balance individual donors, foundations, corporate and government funding, and expand our unrestricted assets to pay for the expansion of our operations outside California.

Achieving Visibility

SusCon was not well known in the environmental arena or to the public at large. The organization was relatively unknown even in California, where most of its projects were located, and had virtually no name recognition in other parts of the country.

Historically, SusCon had devoted few resources to building its brand and marketing itself, instead focusing its limited resources on testing its approach and achieving results. Moreover, it had chosen projects based entirely on the seriousness of the environmental problem and the match with SusCon's problem-solving approach. Finally, because it worked predominantly through partnerships, often behind the scenes, SusCon had shied away from seeking credit for its work, choosing instead to direct attention to its partners. Remarked a government partner, "They lack recognition, lack a widely known reputation for what they can do. If they were better known, they might be in a better position to promote their goals."

Believing that to achieve greater impact, SusCon needed to become well known to the environmental funding community, the industries it wanted to influence, and the general public, Boren had, since 2001, been devoting time and resources to increase visibility. When not leading fund-raising efforts, Lardie turned her attention to improving SusCon's visibility. She pursued relationships with the media, placing several stories about SusCon's work in local media and specialized magazines in her first six months with the organization. Previously, SusCon managers had granted interviews and contributed to articles on an ad hoc basis. Lardie became the point person for media communication and sought to ensure that media mentions conveyed a consistent message about SusCon's work.

Lardie also launched a branding campaign, hiring a marketing agency to develop a SusCon logo and tagline that would be readily recognizable to potential donors. She explained:

The word "sustainable" has become overused since SusCon was founded and so is no longer a distinctive name. The organization also lacks a logo, tagline, and consistent image and tone in public materials. By developing the brand, we can increase visibility both among our partners and among potential donors. A well-defined brand is indispensable if we are to expand.

Industry Sector Focus

In its early years, SusCon had tackled a variety of environmental issues in a number of industries. The work had included projects as diverse as conservation-based real estate development, an energy retrofit of a multitenant office building, and wetlands restoration on private lands. In 1998, the organization narrowed its focus to water quality and habitat, with a particular emphasis on reducing nonpoint source water pollution. Nonpoint source pollution was an area in which traditional environmental tools such as regulation and litigation had exhibited limited effectiveness. Although this focus served SusCon well for a time, enabling it to develop a solid track record and establish a good reputation both with the industries with which it worked and with other organizations concerned with water quality, by 2001 management had begun to perceive it to be limiting. A focus on industry sectors instead of environmental problems was determined to be a better strategy, and SusCon's 2002 strategic plan outlined this new philosophy to the board. "We want to retain a focus but expand beyond water quality and habitat," Boren explained.

We believe we can offer the most value to the environmental arena by focusing on a few industry sectors and building on the relationships and successes we develop in those sectors to tackle the variety of environmental issues associated with each. By staying within a particular industry sector to address the breadth of environmental issues it faces, we can further develop and utilize our industry knowledge and the valuable partnerships we develop.

Project Selection and Implementation

Prior to 1998, SusCon had selected projects based more on the expertise and interest of its staff than through a systematic, research-based process. In 1999, under Boren's leadership, the organization developed a detailed methodology for deciding which projects to undertake (see **Exhibit 6.2.9**). Following a period of brainstorming during which staff identified serious, unaddressed environmental problems linked to specific industries, project ideas were prioritized using 11 criteria. The projects with the highest priority were researched and analyzed more closely, often by summer associates from leading MBA programs. The interns investigated an industry and relevant environmental issues thoroughly enough to gain an understanding of the barriers that prevented businesses from engaging in more environmentally sustainable practices and to identify opportunities to create incentives to change business practices. Projects with favorable assessments were presented to the organization's board for approval. Once funding was secured for a new project, Boren searched for an individual to lead it. That individual could either come from within the organization or be recruited through an external search.

New managers devised an initial strategy for addressing the environmental problem using the recommendations from MBA summer associates who had explored the issues in detail, suggestions from SusCon's other managers, and information gleaned from specialized literature as well as their own background and experience. Management identified the constituents to be involved in resolving the problem. These could include the targeted industry, individual firms, state or federal agencies, and other nonprofits. As partners joined the project, they helped SusCon refine its strategy by sharing their perspectives on the environmental problem. Through this process, the final solution gained the support of most or all partners and minimized obstacles to eventual implementation.

Since the problems SusCon tackled were highly complex, projects could last from two to eight years. Thus, managers tended to stay on the same project for many years and lacked a clear path for transitioning to new work once a project was completed. Project managers operated with considerable autonomy and rarely documented their precise strategies or the reasons for those strategies.

In 2002, Boren introduced performance metrics that required all projects and the organization to set targets and track progress, activities, and resources used. This system was a step toward more actively monitoring SusCon's impact on the industries and constituents with which it worked and facilitated communication of results to

Step 1:   Brainstorm project ideas. All ideas go on a master list.

Step 2:   Prioritize which ideas we will dedicate resources to evaluating based on the following criteria:

1. Does the project address a serious and important environmental issue?
2. Is the problem a good match for SusCon's approach?
3. Is the problem unaddressed or unsuccessfully addressed?
4. Is there potential for national impact?
5. Is there potential for replication?
6. Is the project a good match for SusCon's mission, purpose, and goal?
7. Is there staff interest and passion for the idea?
8. Is the proposed project innovative and exciting?
9. Do we believe there are decent prospects for funding the project?
10. Does the project fit with SusCon's organizational strategy?
11. Does the project build on SusCon's expertise or add to our expertise?

Step 3:   Conduct initial assessment for top priorities. The initial assessment will evaluate the project's feasibility and potential for improving the environment. The analysis focuses on understanding the nature and extent of the environmental problem, the basic structure and economics of the industry involved, and the range of conservation tools that might be employed to solve the problem.

Step 4:   Conduct detailed feasibility. For ideas that continue to meet criteria, conduct a detailed feasibility study that includes thoroughly researching the environmental problem, evaluating the management practices within the industry, and analyzing the external and internal forces that drive decisions in that industry. The goal is to identify barriers to change, incentives to motivate new actions, strategic partnerships, and points of leverage where intervention would be most effective. We also begin to look for potential funding sources for the project.

With this information in hand, we, with the board's approval, make a decision about whether to pursue the project. This decision depends largely on the degree of impact we think SusCon can have on solving the problem. Can we provide the tools/incentives that will change the way a business or industry makes decisions that affect environmental quality?

Step 5:   Program design. We define our role and the strategies we will pursue, set up partnerships, and begin raising project-specific funding.

Step 6:   Program implementation. With funding in hand, we implement the project. Depending on the project, implementation can take from six months to three years.

Case Study

Exhibit 6.2.9   Sustainable Conservation Project Selection Process

SOURCE: Sustainable Conservation.

Dairies Project Metrics

Impact
Environmental Improvements
Tons of manure processed
Amount of nitrogen converted from manure
Amount of methane captured
Amount of electrical generating capacity offset (kWh)

Business Practices Changed
Number of methane digesters installed
Number of companies/farms that have changed business practices
Number of initiatives completed
Number of organizations replicating SusCon methods/projects/solutions

Economic Efficiency
Expected net present value of project
Costs incurred by affected firms/farms to implement change
Financial benefits/averted costs from implementing change
Amount of funding made available to industry/company/farm through partnership

---

Activities
Percent of desired stakeholders involved
    Regulatory agencies
    Nonprofits (in this case, state universities)
Other industries (in this case, utilities)
Number of legislative/policy change successes
Number of outreach activities (information sessions, training)

Capacity
Financial Health
    Total operating budget
    Percent of future years' budget committed

Visibility
    Number of press mentions
    Number of articles published by staff

Expertise
    Number of training days
    Project spin-offs

Exhibit 6.2.10   Dairies Project Sample Metrics Template

SOURCE: Sustainable Conservation.

current and potential funders. Managers had to quantify the impact of a project by calculating metrics such as miles of stream restored or tons of runoff prevented from entering waterways. Boren believed that this analysis would help SusCon be more rigorous in evaluating its work and selecting future engagements. (**Exhibit 6.2.10** presents a sample metrics template.)

Current Projects

At the beginning of 2002, SusCon had four active projects in its portfolio: (1) a partnership with California's auto recycling industry that aimed to reduce polluted runoff from end-of-life vehicles; (2) a partnership with national brake pad manufacturers, government agencies, and environmental organizations that aimed to create an agreed-upon protocol for evaluating potentially harmful effects of elements used in automobile brake pads; (3) a program to streamline the permitting process for California landowners willing to voluntarily implement conservation practices on their lands; and (4) an initiative that aimed to reduce pollution from California dairies. (Details of the first three projects are provided in **Exhibit 6.2.4**.)

The Dairies Project, one of SusCon's more recent and most successful projects, exemplified what the organization stood for: working collaboratively with industries; bridging the gap between government, industry, and the environmental community; and developing economically viable solutions that delivered environmental benefits. Moreover, the prospect of the project's being expanded outside of California was favorable. Dairy industry associations in Arizona and New

Mexico had expressed interest in working with SusCon to improve the environmental practices of farmers in those states. Working with these types of organizations could provide the basis for expansion.

DAIRIES PROJECT

Issue

Most dairy farms in California were located in the Central Valley, an area that grew more than half of the nation's fruit, nuts, and vegetables and raised 15% of the nation's dairy cows. California dairies generated in excess of $4.5 billion in revenues in 2001, and the state boasted more cows than any other state. These 1.6 million cows, each of which produced 120 pounds of solid and liquid waste per day, were responsible for as much waste per year as 35 million people. Cow waste, unlike human waste, was not treated. Dairy farmers generally stored it in large lagoons and spread it as fertilizer on their fields. When the tons of manure produced by California's dairy cows was not dealt with correctly, rainwater washed pollutants from the waste—primarily nitrates and salts, but also E. coli, salmonella, phosphorous, potassium, ammonia, hormones, and antibiotics—into nearby streams. Pollutant-laden runoff flowed to creeks and streams and into groundwater supplies and threatened both aquatic species and human health.

Dairies also added tons of particulates, ammonia, reactive organic gases (ROGs), and other pollutants to the air. These pollutants contributed to the formation of smog and were linked to high rates of asthma and other respiratory diseases. According to the California Air Resources Board, dairies appeared to be one of the leading sources of ROGs and ammonia in the Central Valley.

Devising a Solution

After an MBA summer associate analyzed the dairy industry and SusCon recognized that there was an opportunity to improve water quality in California by collaborating with the industry, Boren hired Allen Dusault in July 2000 to lead the effort. Dusault had spent many years working on environmental issues in California and on the East Coast. He held a degree in soil science and an MBA and had worked as director of composting for the Massachusetts Department of Environmental Protection, in which capacity he had developed the state's green and agricultural waste composting program. This background helped him to narrow down the viable strategies for addressing the dairy waste problem in California.

To understand their concerns and solicit ideas, Dusault engaged dairy farmers and dairy associations around the state in lengthy conversations. These conversations enabled him to share and refine his strategies for addressing the agricultural waste problem and add new ideas to his arsenal. Dusault also read industry publications and consulted experts nationwide about the issue. Once he had finalized the set of initiatives he wanted to implement, he initiated formal partnerships with the farmers and organizations he had contacted earlier to implement the solutions he had devised. These initiatives attracted the attention of state and national agencies, which subsequently joined the partnerships.

Initiatives

Dusault took an innovative approach to resolving the waste problems of the California dairy industry. He and his team promoted revenue-generating and cost-saving technologies and management practices to motivate dairy farmers to adopt more environmentally sound and economically sustainable methods of waste management. The two most successful initiatives were methane from manure and composting.

Methane from manure. SusCon developed a program to promote the construction and use of methane digesters that captured the methane released as animal waste decomposed. The methane was then combusted to produce energy. In the course of a year, a 1,000-cow dairy could produce enough energy to power 100 average households while reducing the emission of methane, a greenhouse gas. The digester could power all of a dairy producer's on-farm needs, offsetting energy consumption and reducing energy costs by as much as $50,000 for an average farm. In states in which utilities would buy back power from distributed sources, dairy farmers could sell their excess energy and generate revenue. Methane digesters also reduced air pollution, greenhouse gas emissions, and water pollution.

Composting. SusCon also promoted composting to dairies as a cost-effective and environmentally sound way to manage manure and convinced two municipalities to combine dairy waste with city green waste to produce a high-quality compost product. Through microbial action, composting broke down yard waste, manure, and other organic products into a rich soil amendment that provided nutrients, decreased soil erosion, promoted disease resistance in plants, and increased the water retention of soil.

Partnerships

To implement these initiatives, Dusault developed partnerships with the dairy industry and the key stakeholders responsible for monitoring, educating, and regulating dairy farmers. SusCon pursued a formal relationship with the California Dairy Quality Assurance Program (CDQAP), a voluntary partnership that comprised dairy industry representatives, federal and state government agencies, and two universities (**Exhibit 6.2.11** lists all participants). Formed to improve the dairy industry's environmental stewardship and care of animal health and welfare and to help safeguard public health, CDQAP had proven to be an excellent forum for introducing and gaining support for SusCon's Dairies Project. The partnership had focused primarily on education, offering courses to hundreds of dairymen across the state. More than 1,000 dairies had participated in the training. CDQAP had also established a program for certifying dairies with sound environmental and waste management practices. As of February 2003, 121 of the state's dairies had been certified. SusCon was the only environmental organization invited to join the partnership.

SusCon also developed partnerships with the leading dairy producer organizations in California. Collectively, members of Western United Dairymen, the Milk Producers Council, and the California Dairy Campaign accounted for more than 90% of the state's dairy industry. Together with Western United Dairyman and the Milk Producers Council, SusCon had successfully pushed for legislation to encourage farmers to adopt methane digesters. The combination of industry and an environmental group advocating for the same thing was unusual and powerful.

SusCon also collaborated with the University of California at Davis, the California Department of Food and Agriculture, Synagro (a commercial organics management firm and operator of state-of-the-art composting and methane digesters), and the U.S. Department of Agriculture's Natural Resources Conservation Service, among others, to identify, research, and promote methods and technologies that would improve manure management practices.

Results

Less than two years after launching its Dairies Project, SusCon had achieved considerable success. Forming partnerships with parties that typically considered environmental organizations the enemy was a big accomplishment, but the organization had achieved much more. With the support of the dairy associations and the CDQAP, SusCon had convinced California governor Gray Davis to approve through legislative measure SBX-5, which created $15 million in state funding to provide cost-share assistance for the

Industry Organizations	Academic Organizations
Alliance of Western Milk Producers	California Polytechnic State University
California Dairy Campaign	University of California at Davis
California Dairies, Inc.	
California Dairy Research Foundation	
California Farm Bureau Federation	
California Manufacturing Milk Advisory Board	
Clover Stornetta Farms	Regulatory/Government Organizations
Dairy Council of California	California Department of Food and Agriculture
Dairy Institute of California	California Environmental Protection Agency
Hilmar Cheese Company	California Department of Fish and Game
Land O'Lakes, Western Division	U.S. Department of Agriculture
Milk Producers Council	USDA Natural Resources Conservation Service
Northern California Holsteins	U.S. Environmental Protection Agency
Western United Dairymen	
Allied Industry Organizations	Public Interest Organizations
California Cattlemen's Association	Sustainable Conservation
California Veterinary Medical Association	
National Meat Association	

Exhibit 6.2.11   CDQAP Members

SOURCE: Adapted from California Dairy Quality Assurance Program (CDQAP) Web site, http://www .cdga.org/committee/.

construction of methane digesters. Dusault served on the technical advisory committee that approved the digesters. Since the legislation was signed, in the Chino Basin of southern California two municipally operated methane digesters with the capacity to produce more than four megawatts of power had begun to collect waste from the high concentration of dairies. Four additional methane digesters were under construction in the Central Valley, and five more were approved for funding. When all were completed, they would be able to collectively process 400,000 tons of animal waste from 36,000 cows annually, producing the energy requirements of 2,000 households and offsetting more than $1.6 million annually in energy costs to dairy farmers.

So that farmers could get credit for the energy they sent back to utilities, SusCon worked with government agencies, the major California utilities, and the industry to extend net metering regulations, which, at the time, applied only to wind and solar power and not to methane digesters. Net metering effectively ran farmers' electric meters backwards when the digesters were producing energy and putting it into the electric grid. After arguing the case for digester net metering in front of the state legislature, Dusault, with the help of influential members in the partnership, succeeded in pushing through the state legislature measure AB2228, which established a pilot program that permitted owners of methane digesters to participate in utility net energy metering programs.

Another indicator of the success of the methane digester initiative was emerging interest in the program from dairy organizations in other states. One industry group in New Mexico had contacted Dusault seeking assistance with and advice on their farmers' waste management problems. "State agencies in New Mexico have tried promoting methane digesters, but the programs and incentives provided by the state are often unknown to our farmers," explained the organization's executive director.

For a couple of years we have been trying to help our members take advantage of environmental technologies. We even hired an independent consultant who analyzed the profit potential for our members if digesters were built. However, we have been losing the battle with the local utilities and have no way of providing subsidies for the capital investment in digesters. SusCon's program in California sounds like the solution we need in New Mexico. We need to form partnerships to get financing and to convince the utilities to participate.

To promote composting, SusCon partnered to develop the concept with several commercial composters including Nilsen Farms in Sacramento Valley and Grover Landscaping in Modesto. Dusault also secured market development funding from the U.S. Environmental Protection Agency (EPA) for a facility that would combine loads of green waste with dairy and turkey manure. EPA officials in Washington, D.C., were so impressed with this work that they flew out to tour the farm and talk with SusCon about its approach. Dusault recently had received approval from the County of Merced's Board of Supervisors to have the Merced landfill's composting operation accept dairy waste to mix with the city's green waste. SusCon planned to document the economic and environmental benefits of this program to help promote it to all relevant cities in the Central Valley.

Dusault hoped that the critical mass of methane digesters, satellite composting sites, and new legislation would provide enough working examples and incentives to motivate many in the industry to follow suit. He believed, like Boren, that by passing favorable regulations and educating partners in environmentally sustainable practices and technologies, SusCon could create the momentum that would eventually enable the Dairies Project to grow on its own, freeing up more staff to plant the seeds of the program in new states or industries.

OPTIONS FOR EXPANSION

Boren contemplated the strategic options she would present to the board to complement the discussion of the potential national expansion of one or more of SusCon's initiatives. A brainstorming session with her staff had produced a lengthy list of expansion strategies and narrowed the list to two options that merited immediate analysis. In addition to these options, Boren had to consider the possibility of not scaling up in the short term but focusing instead on further developing SusCon's capabilities in California. Some of her management staff were skeptical about going national, arguing that a continued focus on California could strengthen the organization's position in the state and enable it to improve and develop existing programs and prepare them for long-term national expansion.

Option 1: Scale Up Through Partnerships With Nonprofits in Other States

SusCon could expand its reach by partnering in other states with like-minded nonprofits that could adopt and implement its programs and initiatives in their communities. Boren believed that partnering with such organizations could be a cost-effective way to test the feasibility of replicating a SusCon initiative outside of California. She knew that there were many environmental organizations working creatively around the country and hypothesized that there might not be a need for SusCon to open an independent office in locations where such organizations already existed.

Option 2: Expand by Opening Wholly Owned Branches

Another possibility was to open wholly owned branches in other states. Dairy trade associations in New Mexico, Arizona, and Idaho with which SusCon had been in contact had expressed interest in working with Dusault and his team. They wanted to focus on improving the environmental

compliance of local producers to mitigate the risk of regulatory action and on helping build methane digesters to offset energy costs. Opening an office in one of the western states might be an attractive option that merited further research.

Option 3: Do Not Scale Up in the Short Term

SusCon could focus its short-term efforts on refining its approach in California and accumulating more knowledge and experience to position it for expansion in the longer term. In 2001, the state's economy ranked among the 10 largest in the world, contributing 12% of U.S. gross domestic product. The state had the largest agricultural industry in the country, and its air and water were among the most polluted. Moreover, SusCon's work in the industries on which it wanted to focus was far from complete. Project managers had identified promising opportunities for working with the automobile and transportation sectors. Existing projects could also be expanded to cover more communities and landscapes in the state. In this difficult economic environment, SusCon could focus on documenting its processes and principles and work on disseminating them to other environmental nonprofits, rather than pursue geographic expansion.

NOTE

Nonpoint source (NPS) pollution, unlike pollution from industrial and sewage treatment plants, has many diffuse sources. NPS pollution is caused by rainfall or snowmelt moving over and through the ground. As the runoff moves, it picks up and carries away natural and human-made pollutants, finally depositing them into lakes, rivers, wetlands, coastal waters, and underground sources of drinking water.

CHAPTER 7

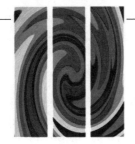

Measuring Performance

Social entrepreneurs and socially entrepreneurial organizations are characteristically filled with new ideas—indeed, the incubation of new ideas is generally their fundamental purpose, and new ideas are therefore their lifeblood. But bringing ideas to some reasonable fruition requires some ability to focus, to define which ideas are the ones the organization is currently pursuing and, correspondingly, which are not. The new ideas of today constantly compete with the new ideas of yesterday for the time and attention and developmental resources and talent of the organization. Early in the entrepreneurial cycle is a time for the creation of new ideas, but at some point, the time comes to take the best ideas and make them happen. When we turn to developing the ideas and getting them ready for "prime time," for rollout into the world at large, we need to focus on whether they are working and how they can be improved, and to do that, we need to specify what they are supposed to be accomplishing. Without a definition of our purpose—of what we mean by a "good result" or by "good performance"—we cannot create management processes that will systematically generate and improve results over time. If we cannot say, reasonably clearly, what we are trying to do, then we probably cannot build systems and mechanisms to help move us forward. If, by contrast, we can specify reasonably succinctly what we have set out to do, then we will be able to build managerial systems that help us discover whether we are accomplishing what we intended, identify those aspects of what we are doing that are contributing to our success (and those that are not), and help us focus on what we can do to improve our performance. In the end, every social entrepreneur needs to know how he or she is doing in order to do better. In this final chapter, we describe methods that entrepreneurial organizations can use to get the benefit of this kind of managerial focus.

The German philosopher Friedrich Nietzsche (1844–1900) put this point very directly:

> The most common form of human stupidity is forgetting what we were trying to accomplish.[1]

This statement is a very useful reminder to leaders. If we look at the statement from the other direction, it suggests that perhaps the most important thing that leaders can do is to help themselves and others stay focused on their goals and objectives—that is, on their intended results. We can formulate this as defining "Question Zero"—so numbered because it comes before all other questions that the organization needs to ask and answer:

> **Question Zero:** What, *exactly,* are we trying to accomplish?

One of the important roles of leaders—and leadership or management or performance systems—in an organization is to consistently remind people of what the key objectives are, to help them stay focused—lest they fall prey to the forgetfulness that Nietzsche pointed to and (implicitly or explicitly) begin to serve other objectives instead.

If an organization can provide a reasonably succinct and coherent—and shared and believed!—answer to Question Zero, then it can begin to build a system of measuring and managing its performance. The answer to Question Zero *defines* performance: it tells us what counts as performance. The task that remains is to measure it, track it, and figure out how to improve it. In a for-profit organization, defining performance is relatively straightforward. In a social enterprise, by contrast, one of the signature and enduring challenges is to give a sufficiently crisp description of the desired performance—one that would allow us to specify measures showing when the desired results are being produced.

In this chapter, we will outline a general framework for building systems in social enterprises that measure performance and relate those measures to the underlying activities of the organization, thereby providing a focused approach for managing the organization for excellent performance.

ACCOUNTABILITY AND PERFORMANCE

Once the intended results—the desired "performances"—have been defined, the organization (and the people in it) can begin to be held accountable (both by themselves and by others) for the level of performance and for raising that level over time. Since performance is the goal, we need to be careful to build systems that provide accountability for performance—that is, for *results*. That may sound obvious, but too often, where it is difficult to provide clarity about what results we want to achieve (that is, where we have difficulty giving a good and clear answer to Question Zero), we fall back instead on defining accountability for *processes*: Did we complete the actions that we had planned? This question is important; as we shall see, we do need to track and examine the actions we are taking and activities we are involved in, but it is not enough, because it is focused on actions rather than on results. Holding people accountable in these terms will produce *procedural* rather than *results* accountability. Effective management will require *both* procedural *and* results accountability, and too often we see systems that have far too much emphasis on completion of processes and too little attention focused on whether those processes actually produced results.

We also need to be careful about how we craft the accountability systems so that we do not create the wrong incentives. Often, we see people introducing what they refer to as "accountability" or "performance" systems that, when examined closely, have a largely punitive orientation. These systems are essentially saying, "This organization has not been performing because it has not been held accountable, and our new system is going to hold people accountable and boost their performance." Too often, the underlying supposition in this approach is that the organization and its employees have not been trying hard enough, that they need performance goals and incentives to encourage greater effort, and that it would be easy to improve performance if people were just willing to make more effort to do so. This diagnosis could indeed be correct, but it may also not be. Table 7.1 outlines a range of reasons why performance may not be as good as we might like, dividing the challenges along two dimensions: the level of motivation, on the one hand, and the difficulty of knowing how to improve performance, on the other. Organizations could have either high or low motivation to produce high performance, and the difficulty of knowing how to improve performance could be either great or small, and this divides our circumstances into four different situations.[2]

The first case shown in Table 7.1 is easy: If motivation is high and it is easy to know how to improve performance, presumably performance will be good, so Case 1 gives us little to be concerned about.

The idea that underlies many "accountability" reforms—the idea that performance can be improved simply by increasing pressure, by setting objective goals and holding people accountable for meeting them, with rewards if they do and sanctions if they do not—effectively assumes that all that is missing to provide higher performance is motivation, that effort alone will boost performance. The underlying assumption is that we are in Case 2, where motivation alone, which can be supplied by objective measures combined with carrots and sticks (that is, by incentive schemes), will create performance improvements.

Table 7.1   Need for Different Forms of Performance Systems

	Degree of motivation to produce high performance:	
Degree of difficulty in knowing how to improve performance:	High	Low
Easy	Case 1: no problem	Case 2: need for incentives
Difficult	Case 3: need for learning mechanisms	Case 4: need for both incentives and learning mechanisms

What if, instead, people are highly motivated (as they often are in entrepreneurial social enterprises) but it is not easy to know how to improve performance (that is, we are in Case 3, in the terminology of Table 1)? What will happen in such an organization if we set objective measures and put pressure on people to meet them? Such a regime would be enormously frustrating to our well-intentioned workers. Trying hard is not enough; they are highly motivated, and they are already doing that. They need tools to help them detect what activities actually would or could improve (or are improving) performance. Pressuring them to create a performance that they already want to generate but do not know how to produce will quickly feel unfair and abusive.[3]

Often, of course, we will face both problems: We will need to maintain motivation (because not all workers are self-motivated, though in the social sector they are often very highly motivated indeed) *and* we will need to create mechanisms to make performance and improvements in performance more visible, to help people determine what seems to be "moving the needle," what activities seem to be enhancing performance. Thus, we need to build performance measurement and management systems that provide for motivation but that also allow for—indeed, encourage and facilitate—systematic learning. Rewards and sanctions alone—the narrow form of accountability—will generally be out of place; at best, they will be a necessary component but rarely sufficient by themselves.

BUILDING SYSTEMS FOR MEASURING AND MANAGING PERFORMANCE

A system for assessing and enhancing performance begins with a good understanding of the distinctive value or goal that the organization intends to produce—the "value proposition" for the organization, or the "impacts" that the organization hopes to create. What is unique or unusual about what the organization does (in particular, about what it produces) that makes it especially valuable? With this fixed goal in mind, the organization must next try to understand how this result—this distinctive value—is produced. What activities are responsible for generating the intended results—and through what process(es), what set of cause-and-effect links? As the organization develops its understanding of how its activities are linked to the outcomes it hopes to be generating, it is developing its "logic model"—its theory of how the activities it engages in will result in producing the value that it has defined as its distinctive contribution.[4] There are many different ways to divide the flow of cause-and-effect relationships and many ways to label them. In the end, the specific scheme for labeling may not be particularly important. What *is* important is the careful development of the organization's assumptions about how its work translates into effects. Figure 7.1 shows one commonly used framework and choice of labels for depicting the logic of causal flows, starting with the factor inputs (labor, capital, etc.) and how they are combined in "activities" to produce "outputs." Outputs are the most direct consequence of the activities: They flow directly from the completion of the activities. If a literacy program holds evening classes, then the activity is running the class—and the output is the person-hours of instruction absorbed by participants. Outputs, in turn, it is hoped (and assumed), produce *outcomes*—in the case of adult literacy programs, the intended outcomes are presumably people who are able to read or whose reading has been significantly improved. This outcome is not the final goal or purpose of the program, however; most literacy programs are motivated by a desire to help the participants find jobs and, more generally, improve their quality of life. These more distant goals might be referred to as "impacts."

As we move from inputs through the stage of the inputs being organized into activities, the activities generating outputs, the outputs generating outcomes, and the outcomes generating impacts, we tend to go

1. Farther out in time (it takes longer for the effect to take place or to be noticed)

2. Away from the center of the organization, and toward the rest of the world

3. Down in the degree of our control (for example, we control inputs, but not impacts)

4. Down in measurability (it is generally harder to observe and objectively measure results that are farther down the value chain and that may be more tenuously associated with the action)

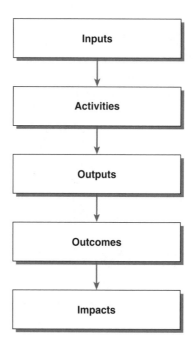

Figure 7.1   The General Logic Model Framework or "Value Chain"

5. Up in abstraction (the concepts themselves tend to become less immediate and practical—"quality of life" is a more abstract concept than "reading scores")

6. Down in the degree to which we can confidently attribute causation (there are many different causes influencing the long-term quality of life of participants in our literacy campaign, and the farther we go down the value chain, the harder it is to be sure that the changes we are seeing were generated by our actions)

As Figure 7.1 indicates, we can trace the flow of cause-and-effect relationships straight through the logic model. Different suggested performance management frameworks may differ in terminology and in the specific steps that they recommend for building a system to enhance performance, but all performance measurement and management systems (a) provide some framework for a set of cause-and-effect relationships; (b) explore how those relationships can be studied; and (c) through a better understanding of how the organization's distinctive value is produced, suggest how its performance can be systematically improved—both through the development of new approaches and through refining existing techniques.

An important insight of performance management is that we *can* use the framework in Figure 7.1 in *either* direction—and that we *should* use it in *both* directions. First, we can examine it in the order in which it is given above—that is, we can watch the execution of activities and see how efficient the process is and see whether it is producing the anticipated results—outputs, outcomes, and impacts. We will refer to this as the "execution" direction. Importantly, however, we can also use the framework in the other direction. Starting with the goal or desired impact, we can work *backwards* up the value chain to try to figure out what outcomes would be likely to generate that impact, what outputs would be likely to generate those outcomes, and so on. We will refer to this as the "planning" direction—the search for new activities that would more reliably, more efficiently, or more consistently generate the desired impacts. To emphasize that it works backwards from the desired ends, this process is sometimes referred to as "reverse planning"—that is, planning the organization's activities by starting with the desired results and working successively backwards to identify the activities that will produce those results. We use the execution direction to study and assess the impacts we are creating; we use the planning approach to seek new and better activities, processes, and methods that might produce more of the desired impacts. Strong organizations use both approaches—either alternating between them or running them simultaneously. In what follows, we will first examine the challenge of building a performance system focused on the execution direction, and we will then return to a brief discussion of its use in planning.

The logic model identifies logical cause-and-effect connections along the value chain. Once a reasonable logic model has been constructed, we can begin to test its assumptions and premises, and thus seek the best approaches within it, by developing measures at each end of the cause-and-effect links. The logic model embodies a series of assumptions—if we do X, then the results will be Y. But are they, in practice? Empirically, when we do X, does Y result? Performance *measurement* is directed at producing an empirical basis for assessing how well our current activities are working, and performance *management* is directed at using measurement in the context of a logic model to produce the very best possible process for generating our desired results—improving existing processes and inventing and testing new ones. This treats the intended results as the central goals; the processes are seen as means toward the intended ends, not as ends in themselves.

The testing of the assumptions of the logic model begins with the process of specifying measures on both ends of each cause-and-effect relationship. For example, to see if activities are conducted efficiently, we examine the relationship between the inputs consumed and the activities produced; to do so, we need ways of counting the inputs and ways of counting the activities. No system can keep detailed records about every conceivable input to its processes or count every aspect of every activity (logging every phone call, for example, or every meeting or discussion)—even though these "activities" are part and parcel of what the organization is doing to advance its objectives. Thus, we have to determine which inputs we particularly want to monitor and which activities it makes sense to track, and then develop appropriate measures for each of them.

Of course, we cannot always directly measure the inputs, the activities, or the outcomes. Sometimes, we have to count *indicators* rather than direct measures. For example, we may not be able directly to assess whether people in our personal financial management program are able to plan their finances better. We may have to settle for collecting data about their capacity to carry out a classroom exercise on balancing a checkbook. But if we choose (or design) indicators that are reasonably closely associated with the underlying phenomenon we are trying to influence, we can be correspondingly confident that the indicator is pointing us in the right direction. The key features of the measures we choose thus include that they are

1. Reasonably objective

2. Related to the most important aspects of the work and its results

3. Reasonably closely linked to the underlying phenomenon we are trying to examine—that is, in the case where we can't directly observe the phenomenon of interest, the indicators we choose for it are reasonably reliably linked to it

4. Not unduly expensive (in time, effort, and direct expenditures) to track, capture, record, keep, and analyze

5. Observable within a reasonable time horizon

6. Not too numerous

Since our performance management framework consists of a series of (hypothesized) cause-and-effect links, the key step in driving our learning from the data about how things are actually happening is to find measures meeting these criteria at each end of each of our cause-and-effect links and see if indeed they are related as we suppose. If we hypothesize that "doing A causes B," we can

of our activities), focuses on *results*—the external outputs and the more or less directly discernible external outcomes of our actions. This zone embodies the information and analysis necessary to support our management of the results we are producing, and thus guides managerial decision making and supports learning about how well our actions are being translated into accomplishments.

Program Evaluation

The third zone, which lies beyond the usual limit of our ability to collect results data, is focused on *program evaluation*. Generally, this will require special efforts to collect and analyze data, often involving a formal (and possibly expensive) statistical study. This zone allows us to test what would otherwise be only assumptions and theories, allows at least episodically an assessment of our broadest and most far-reaching accomplishments, and, correspondingly, supports possible reevaluation of our general strategy.

Performance management, in general, should focus on making sure that adequate data and analysis and attention are focused in the first ("administrative") and second ("results management") zones. While the administrative focus is important and constitutes a part of what we need to do to carry out effective performance management, the administrative focus by itself would leave us as an introspective organization. Truly focusing on performance requires attention to the consequences occurring outside the organization, not just to its internal processes. This, in turn, requires developing, collecting, and analyzing data about external outputs and outcomes ("results")—close enough to the organization that we can measure them and be confident that our actions are in fact driving them, but not so close in that they confirm only that we completed our internal processes (without assessing results).

HOW FAR OUT SHOULD WE PUSH
THE NORMAL DATA HORIZON?

The "normal" data horizon is as far as we can "see"—or, at least, measure and collect data—on a reasonably real-time basis. With greater effort and resources, we can generally push the horizon farther out, collecting data on somewhat more remote consequences. How much effort should we expend on expanding the "visible" results zone by collecting more data on a regular and frequent basis? Obviously, our decision about this will be influenced by many factors—for example, on how easy it is to specify the more remote consequences, develop measures for them, and collect the data. Importantly, however, it should also depend on the degree of confidence we have in the act of faith we are making in the domain of our cherished theories. To the extent that we are highly confident that if we achieve outcome X, it will cause impact Y, then measuring the production of outcome X will be a good proxy and may be all we need to do; measuring impact Y would then be largely superfluous and a waste of resources. Of course, we should never be completely confident of something that is only a theory or act of faith—it may be wrong, or it may *become* wrong as a result of changes in the world, so we need to reevaluate our confidence in it at least episodically. But if we have good reason to believe in the further implications of the outcomes we are producing, then for most managerial purposes, it may be best to focus on the easier, less expensive, more directly measurable external outputs and outcomes, rather than making every possible effort to push the data horizon farther out.

"CLIENT SATISFACTION" AS A MEASURE OF ORGANIZATIONAL EFFECTIVENESS OR SUCCESS

Many socially oriented organizations collect data on "client satisfaction" with the services the organization is delivering. Where do such measures fit into our logic model frame? Some socially oriented organizations appear to treat client satisfaction measures as a goal in themselves, or as a more or less complete indicator of organizational success. If that were appropriate, then client satisfaction should be regarded as an impact, located at the end of the organization's value chain—as an end in and of itself. In general, however, the goal of social organizations is not to satisfy their clients per se, but to achieve some larger social purpose, often by providing services to an identified client. Thus, while the client's welfare is presumably an important consideration and her perception about it an important indicator, her satisfaction is not necessarily very strongly linked to or an accurate reflection of the larger intended impact of the program. When the program's intent is indeed to produce benefits for a specific client group *and* that group is in a good position to judge the quality and value of the benefits they have received, their satisfaction may be seen as an impact, and measures of it may be accurate and important impact measures. When the client is *not* in a good position to judge the value of the program—as might be the case, for example, when the program is designed to *prevent* a bad outcome (rather than to create a good one), so that its success for a particular client may not be very visible to the recipient—then serving the client's interests is still the intended impact, but client satisfaction may not be a very reliable guide. And in many cases, serving the self-perceived interests of the individual client may be an instrument toward a larger end, rather than an end in itself, in which case, the purpose should not be to maximize client satisfaction but to maintain it at an appropriate level.

An emergency housing program illustrates this distinction. The clients being served may indicate incomplete satisfaction and say that they would be more satisfied by more spacious and comfortable arrangements. But maximizing the client satisfaction of the people currently being served would consume resources that could be used instead to serve additional clients. Thus, the client satisfaction of the current client group is not a central and independent goal for this program: Providing adequate and safe housing for the largest possible number of displaced people is the true intent. In this situation, measures of client satisfaction could not and should not be taken as measures of ultimate success. At most, attaining a requisite level of satisfaction would be necessary condition for success, contributing to the further impacts of the program that are its true intent.

THINKING THROUGH AN EXAMPLE OF PERFORMANCE MEASUREMENT AND MANAGEMENT

Consider a program designed to increase the rate of college attendance by disadvantaged young people. Such a program might be motivated by the belief that college attendance will improve the future quality of life of the students and will strengthen the communities they will subsequently live in by producing adults who can help those communities function more effectively. What would a performance management scheme look like for such a program, and how would we go about constructing it?

Assuming that the program has been designed (or is already operating), our first step is to lay out our "logic model"—our story of how we believe the program will create (or is creating) value. We need to look broadly at the inputs that might be used (counselors, volunteer mentors, instructors to teach remedial or college-enrichment classes, classrooms, and so on) and at the activities into which those inputs are or will be organized (counseling sessions, test-preparation sessions, courses or counseling on how to fill out college applications, sessions on seeking financial aid and figuring out how to assemble the financial resources necessary to attend college, etc.). Next, we would outline our theory about how those activities will translate into outputs—for example, that math review and test-preparation classes will raise standardized test scores, and sessions on how to complete applications will improve the quality of applications or raise the average number of applications filed per student in the program (or both). These intended outputs, in turn, are anticipated to produce the relevant outcomes—acceptances to colleges and subsequent enrollment. Presumably, the intent of the program extends further to its impacts—to the participants graduating from college, leading more prosperous and productive lives by virtue of their greater training, and acting as community resources.

Having developed the overall outline of the logic model, our next challenge is to identify in more detail the relevant inputs that we want to measure and track. The financial system will have identified and collected data on some of these, but it may not, for example, track volunteer hours, which might be an important input for a program of this kind. Once the relevant set of inputs has been defined, a reasonably objective, useful, and hopefully inexpensive measure of each input needs to be specified, and data must be collected to track and support analysis of the inputs focused on. In the case of a college attendance program, the relevant resource might consist of staff and volunteer time (with some key skill sets, like counselors, separately tracked), classroom space, computers and other educational equipment, and so on. Relevant units of input use must be developed for each input that will be tracked.

The next challenge will be to identify the separate activities the program involves and to devise ways of counting the relevant activity levels. How many students are involved, and in which activities, and for how many hours per week and for how many weeks? Are total classroom hours an adequate measure, or do we need to track classroom activities of different kinds separately? The answer will depend on what our logic model assumes about the effects of different activities, and those assumptions will drive the level of differentiation and detail we need to keep in defining activity measures.

Once activities have been specified, we can articulate and define more carefully the outputs that the activities are intended (and presumed) to generate. Internal outputs might include the number of student-hours of mathematics instruction, attendance at counseling sessions, and test-preparation activities completed. External outputs might include standardized test scores and college applications completed.

Finally, we can specify the outcomes that we are hoping the program will generate—college acceptances (perhaps weighted by the ranking of the colleges), college matriculation, and college graduation. These measures, some of which will be available within a year of the start of the program, and all of which should be available within a few years at most, can provide useful feedback to the program design and operation. Which kinds of colleges are most open to these applicants? Can we work with those colleges who don't seem to understand the virtues of our applicants, so that more of them can be admitted? Are there some additional forms of preparation that might improve the chances of our participants attending better colleges? Data about our results that inform these kinds of questions will help us to develop a better-designed and better-operated program, whose redesign and increasing success is driven by careful examination of how things are working—rather than having to be guided by theory (and guesswork) alone.

In the longer term, we may also wish to track what we hope will be the ongoing success of the program's alumni. Obviously, this will take longer to discern and will be more difficult to collect, as it is likely to become more difficult to maintain contact with alumni as they get further out in time from the program—and we had better not wait for feedback of this form before we try to figure out how to engineer operational improvements in the ongoing program. But we might want to inquire, at least episodically, about some of the longer-term impacts. Are there some college degrees that seem to be more valuable in generating success for program alumni? Is there a set of colleges, or a type of college, or a particular size of college at which program alumni seem to be most successful? We will not have new data every week, or even every year, about these questions, but inquiring about them periodically may allow us to refocus the program by taking advantage of what we can learn about its largest and most enduring successes.

PERFORMANCE, EXECUTION, AND PLANNING

A key advantage of having an effective performance management system is that by being explicit and systematic about our theories of how our programs are creating value, we can check on whether they are working as we thought they would, and we can therefore improve them as we go along. We have described this as the "execution" direction—watching the combining of our inputs into activities, watching the activities in operation, and observing the outputs and outcomes. Careful ongoing performance management as the organization executes its existing programs provides opportunities for identifying what is working well and what is working less well. It guides our experimentation with other approaches, our improvement of elements that are not functioning as well as we had hoped, and/or our rebalancing of efforts toward those things that are working well and away from those that are working less well.

A major insight of performance management (described briefly earlier) is that we can also use the logic model framework of Figure 7.1 in the opposite direction—as a guide to planning. At the beginning of our work—when designing a new program or initiative—and at least periodically thereafter, it is important to consider or revisit the overall program design to make sure it is sound or to see if any more significant changes in it might be justified. A performance management approach can be useful as a guide for this form of analysis—using the logic model and performance management scheme in what we described earlier as the "planning" direction. Stephen Covey, the best-selling author of books about self- and organizational-improvement, famously advises that we "start with the end in mind" and construct plans to achieve the chosen goals. Mountain climbers and military planners describe this as "reverse planning"—start with what engineers call the "endstate vision," and work backwards, figuring out what must come before in order to attain the vision. If, on Day 30, we wish to be at the top of the mountain with enough food and equipment to climb back down, where does that imply that we need to be on Day 29? We should be in Camp V, with two people, a tent, enough oxygen to reach the top the next day, enough food for tomorrow and the climb back down. Where does that imply we need to be on Day 28? And so it goes—working backward from the goal to the steps necessary to reach it.[6]

Thus, organizations need to track their performance on an ongoing basis in the *execution* direction—watching as activities generate outputs, and outputs generate outcomes, seeing which activities are being executed best and are producing the best results, making adjustments as indicated and trying new activities to see if they produce better results. In addition, they need to operate in the *planning* direction, at least episodically, to reconfirm their goals and to rethink whether, given their goals and aspirations, their current activities are the best program to be implementing. The adjustments arising from examining the activities in execution are likely to be incremental, while discoveries or inventions arising from *re*examining the activities in the planning direction are more likely to result in more revolutionary changes—especially if goals are reexamined and changed in the process. Some organizations find it best to carry out both forms of analysis simultaneously and continuously (but often in different offices, with the execution analysis carried out by operating managers and the planning analysis carried out by a separate group). Other organizations find it most valuable to carry out the performance-oriented execution analysis on an ongoing basis, and to go into "planning mode" more episodically.

A SIMPLE "BALANCED SCORECARD" FRAMEWORK FOR SOCIAL ENTERPRISES

There are many ways in which the general approach to performance management described here can be implemented in social enterprises. Many organizations choose their own terminology and structure, customizing it to match their specific circumstances and situation. A number of social enterprises, however, have adopted an approach related to the "Balanced Scorecard," a framework developed by Robert Kaplan and David Norton that has subsequently been adapted to nonprofit and social enterprises as well (with various modifications).[7] The idea of the balanced-scorecard approach is that it proceeds by reverse planning from the organization's ultimate objectives. In the private sector, these objectives are generally financial, so that the financial results for the firm form the top of the balanced scorecard hierarchy. In the social sector, by contrast, financial results are not generally an independent *goal*; they act instead as a *constraint* that must be attended to in order to produce the organization's intended goal of achieving its mission. The balanced scorecard consists of a series of what Kaplan and Norton describe as "perspectives," with each linked to an underlying set of actions and activities that cause or enable it. Thus, in constructing a balanced-scorecard-oriented performance management system for social enterprises, we should begin by reverse planning from the creation of mission value, and we might term the measures we construct of these outcomes and impacts the "mission perspective." Underlying the mission value created would be the activities or operational processes of the organization, and our measures related to these activities would constitute our "operations perspective." To support these operations, and improve them over time, Kaplan and Norton suggest a "learning and growth" perspective focused on the recruitment and development of new skills and capabilities. Finally, undergirding the whole enterprise, the financial perspective focuses on the resource flows necessary to sustain the activities and support the mission. Figure 7.3 shows a general framework for developing a balanced-scorecard-oriented performance management system for a social enterprise. The performance "loop" is closed by the flow from the creation of mission value to the financial perspective; that is, the organization must find some way in which to translate the performance of its mission into a flow of financial resources necessary to sustain its activities (and survival).

To apply such a framework, the organization needs to define measures within each perspective and indicate its assumptions about how the measures within each perspective are linked to the perspectives above it. How will the organization track the achievement of its mission? Which operational processes are linked to each aspect of mission performance? What new skills (learning and growth objectives) must either be recruited into or developed within the organization to improve or enable the operations it wants to undertake? And what are the connections between the delivery of mission value and the creation of financial flows that will sustain the organization?

Using this general framework—as customized to its own circumstances—the organization can both build and track the progress of its strategy. By defining its activities as projects and initiatives, and connecting them to mission objectives, it can track the success of its actions, identify actions that are not being successful (and modify or eliminate them), and identify mission objectives that do not seem to be adequately supported by existing activities. Each project should be associated with the following elements:

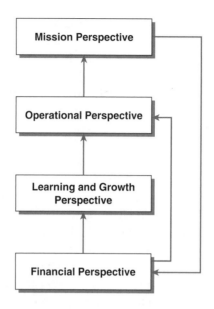

Figure 7.3   A Balanced Scorecard-Oriented Performance Management Framework
for Social Enterprises

- The activity measures that capture and describe its operations
- The output, outcome, and impact measures that indicate its contribution to advancing mission objectives
- The learning and growth initiatives and measures that will indicate the organization's investment in evaluating and improving it

USING THE PERFORMANCE MANAGEMENT FRAMEWORK TO CREATE ALIGNMENT AND BUILD STRATEGY

A major difficulty for many social enterprises is maintaining *alignment* among the resources, activities, and goals of the organization. Social enterprises inhabit a world with multiple stakeholders, supporters, and clients with differing perceptions about priorities, purposes, and methods, and their managers often find themselves pulled in many different directions, urged to use their resources to pursue disparate goals. Maintaining a reasonable degree of focus in such an environment is an enduring challenge, and a well-crafted balanced scorecard (or other performance management system customized to the organization's circumstances) can be a very useful device to help managers, board members, supporters, and other stakeholders understand, assess, and improve the organization's theory of action. A reasonably fully articulated performance framework can help people who care about the organization and its purposes answer three central questions:

1. *What activities are not related to our goals?* A well-designed performance system shows which activities *are* related to the organization's goals—and thus correspondingly helps identify and eliminate those activities that do *not* seem to be very closely related to the organization's main purposes.

2. *What goals are not adequately supported by our activities?* A good performance system shows which of the organization's purposes do not seem to have enough activities associated with them, and can thus encourage the invention and development of new ways of trying to achieve the stated purposes.

3. *What processes need additional improvement?* An effective performance system focuses attention on further streamlining and improving the processes that *do* seem to be working and *do* seem to be related to the organization's major goals.

A strong performance management framework articulates and reveals (and, thus, opens to scrutiny, testing, and examination) the organization's ideas about how its resources and activities are being translated into accomplishments, and thus encourages a dialogue inside the organization and between the organization and its supporters about its efficiency, effectiveness, focus, and goals. Consistent encouragement by senior management to speak to and develop the performance framework focuses internal and external discussions on the organization's efforts and accomplishments, emphasizing the need for alignment.

As an organization works its way through defining its activities and their intended results (and develops the associated measures necessary to track them), it is engaged in an exploration of its whole "business"—it is building a set of understandings and hypotheses about the most important strategic issues it faces: How does our collection of actions line up with, and to what extent is it accomplishing, our mission objectives? Building such a framework can thus be enormously useful in helping an organization to develop a more coherent, consistent, and shared understanding of what it is doing and why it is doing it. To put it in Nietzsche's terms, the organization is building a way to remember what it set out to accomplish—a way to remember its *intentions* in a way that helps guide both its *operational actions* and its *developmental efforts and investments*. Such a framework can help create and maintain the alignment of resources and actions to outputs, outcomes, and impacts—that is, to the central goals and purposes of the organization—thus helping to address one of the greatest challenges in creating organizational excellence for social enterprises.

CASE STUDIES

The case studies that follow provide the reader with an opportunity to think about the construction of performance management systems and the development of the associated performance measures for two quite different organizations. The National Campaign to Prevent Teen Pregnancy is an organization that was started by a group of people who wanted to reframe the political debate about how the social challenges of teenage pregnancy should be addressed—and who wanted to construct a program based on data and evidence about what approaches actually work (rather than on rhetoric and untested beliefs and preferences). They organized a very impressive board of directors who could help them to develop sources of funding and to reach into the world of politics and into the sphere of media ranging from newspapers to Hollywood movies, and they set about trying to develop an effective collection of evidence-based activities that would significantly reduce the incidence of teenage pregnancy. As you read through the case, think about the following questions:

1. What is the logic model of the campaign? How carefully have they articulated it?

2. Have they developed a good set of mission objectives and measures of their progress toward those objectives?

3. How would you go about building a performance measurement and management system for this organization?

At the end of Chapter 5, on building alliances, we presented a case on KaBOOM!, an organization that creates playgrounds, at an early stage of its development. We now return to KaBOOM!, which has made progress in expanding its activities and now faces a new set of questions about how to organize its measurement systems to help it focus its attention on its most important management challenges. As you read through the case, think about the following questions:

1. What are the most relevant activity and performance measures for KaBOOM! to focus on?

2. Should KaBOOM! try to track such impacts as childhood activity and obesity, or should it concentrate on closer-in measures of outputs and outcomes?

3. To the extent that KaBOOM! should, in your view, pursue a networking or alliance strategy to expand its mission impact, how should that be reflected in its performance measurement and management system?

4. Sketch the outline of the performance measurement and management system you would propose for KaBOOM! What outputs or outcomes or impacts would you specify, and how would you propose to measure them? What activities would you monitor, and what measures would you use to track them?

NOTES

1. This quotation was located by my colleague John Donahue, who reports that it appears in section 206 of Nietzsche's *The Wanderer and His Shadow*, the second sequel to *Human, All Too Human*, published in 1880. The original German refers to "Vergessen" (forgetting), "Dummheit" (stupidity), and "Absichten" (intentions)—so a more direct translation would be that "the forgetting of intentions is the most frequent form of stupidity." The treatment in this section closely follows a discussion in Herman B. Leonard, *Question Zero*, mimeo, February 2003.

2. For a related discussion, see Herman B. Leonard, *Four Divergent Challenges of Performance Management*, Kennedy School Executive Session on Performance Management, June 2000; and Herman B. Leonard, *Motivation, Learning, and Performance Management*, Kennedy School Executive Session on Performance Management, June 2000.

3. It may be particularly difficult to shift to a performance orientation in organizations where jobs are described by the functions to be performed (rather than by the results that are supposed to be generated)—so that the work people have agreed to do is defined in terms of activities rather than intended results.

4. For an excellent description of the construction and use of logic models, see WK Kellogg Foundation, *The Logic Model development guide*. Retrieved July 9, 2006, from www.wkkf.org/Pubs/Tools/Evaluation/Pub3669.pdf.

5. This kind of systematic exploration of the efficacy of a program we are running often creates an ethical dilemma. To the extent to which we are confident that our program is working, reducing the amount available to (or denying it altogether to) some recipients is likely to reduce the benefits they receive. Is the learning about the program (or proof of its efficacy) that we gain worth this loss in benefits produced? The more

certain we are that the program is working, the sharper is the ethical dilemma posed by experimenting to explore or prove its effectiveness. On the other hand, if we are uncertain about the impacts, it may be crucial to develop better data about the program's efficacy. The ethical challenges are particularly difficult in the face of issues like experiments concerning new and potentially life-saving treatments (for example, for cancer or for HIV/AIDS).

6. This process is consistent with a crucial theorem from optimal control theory in operations research—that an optimal path is optimal from each point in the path to the end point. This implies that the optimal path can generally most easily be constructed by starting at the end point and figuring out what the last optimal step to arrive at it would be. This provides a new end point (one step farther back), and the process can then be repeated until the starting point is reached.

7. There is a wide literature describing the private sector version of this approach. See, for example, Kaplan, R. S., & Norton, D. P. (1992, January–February). The balanced scorecard: Measures that drive performance. *Harvard Business Review*; and Kaplan, R. S., & Norton, D. P. (1996). *The balanced scorecard: Translating strategy into action*. Boston: Harvard Business School Press.

Case Study 7.1.

The National Campaign to Prevent Teen Pregnancy

INTRODUCTION

It was November 18, 1999. Sarah Brown, director of the National Campaign to Prevent Teen Pregnancy, and Isabel Sawhill, the campaign's founder and now part-time president, had just adjourned another successful board meeting. Board members had engaged in a lively discussion of the campaign's successes to date and its future strategy, but still, Brown and Sawhill felt that members had not said enough about setting priorities for the campaign's moving forward. The central

questions were, "Should they maintain all their current programs or begin focusing on only one or two?" and "How should they go about assessing their impact?"

Brown and Sawhill were very pleased with the campaign's progress over the past three years. The campaign was increasingly recognized as a successful initiative helping to catalyze a variety of efforts aimed at preventing teen pregnancy in the United States. Moreover, teen pregnancy rates were coming down. (See **Exhibit 7.1.1** for rates since 1972.)

However, two questions still plagued them—as always, they were asking themselves

AUTHORS' NOTE: Copyright © Harvard Business School Publishing, case number 9-300-105. Used with permission.

Research Associate Susan Harmeling (MBA 1991) prepared this case under the supervision of Professor John Sawhill as the basis for class discussion rather than to illustrate either effective or ineffective handling of an administrative situation.

what role the campaign had played (if any) in this good news and which of its many activities were having the greatest impact. And, no matter what the campaign's direct impact had been, U.S. rates were still much higher than those of any other industrialized country (see **Exhibit 7.1.2**)—much work remained to be done.

Despite the difficulty of measuring the campaign's impact, Brown and Sawhill were forging ahead with a bold program that combined strong research on the causes of teen pregnancy with a multifaceted approach to attack the problem on various fronts.

At the board of directors' meeting that had just adjourned, Brown, Sawhill, and members of their board had discussed the organization's mission statement. They had also revisited the campaign's basic strategy and program. Finally, the staff had developed a preliminary set of performance indicators that were shared with the board.

Although the leadership hoped that the campaign had had a significant impact on the teen pregnancy problem nationwide, the organization's $2.8 million budget was relatively small, and its 19 employees were being stretched thin, unable to respond to the many requests for speeches, technical assistance, and visits to specific communities. As Tamara Kreinin, the campaign's director of state and local affairs, said, "With the staff we now have, which is basically two of us for state and local affairs, we are only able to be *reactive* to requests for support rather than *proactive* in our approach to building community programs from the ground up."

Some board members had argued that it was only through very strategic, *wholesale* investments in research, education, and broad-based media campaigns rather than through the kind of *retail* efforts that the campaign was being drawn into that a

- The Campaign's Mission: To prevent teen pregnancy in the United States.
- The Campaign's Specific Goal: To reduce the teen pregnancy rate by one-third by 2005 from its level in 1996.

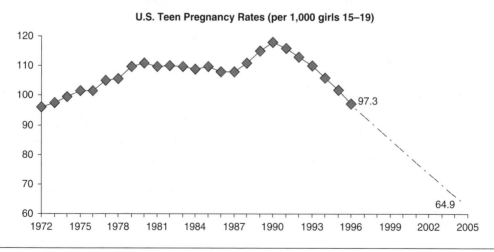

U.S. Teen Pregnancy Rates (per 1,000 girls 15–19)

Exhibit 7.1.1   Mission and Goals

SOURCE: Henshaw, S. K. (1999). *Special report: U.S. teenage pregnancy statistics with comparative statistics for women aged 20–24.* New York: The Alan Guttmacher Institute.

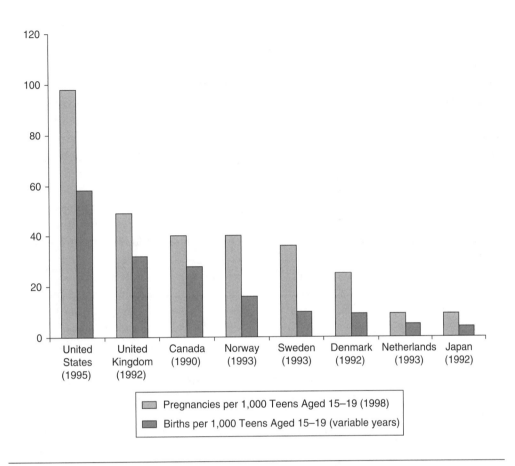

Exhibit 7.1.2   Declining Teen Pregnancy Rates in Industrialized Countries

SOURCE: The National Campaign to Prevent Teen Pregnancy. (1997). *Whatever happened to childhood: The problem of teen pregnancy in the United States.* Washington, DC: Author.

small organization could make a difference in a country as large and diverse as the United States. Others felt that it was important for the campaign to invest even more in its "on-the-ground" retail activities in specific communities. Many felt that both were needed, but with limited resources, picking the right balance between whole-sale and retail activities was critical.

So the question for the campaign's leaders remained: Should they continue to work on everything from public policy to media

partnerships to grassroots support, or should they focus their limited resources on one or two areas? And how would they ever know what impact their work was having?

BACKGROUND

Isabel Sawhill, a senior fellow and economist with the Brookings Institution, had worked for many years on public policy and public policy research. Her research on inequality and poverty had convinced her that reducing teen pregnancy was one of the most highly leveraged ways to reduce child poverty and other related social problems.

Following a long career in academia, Sawhill went to work as an associate director at the U.S. Office of Management and Budget (OMB) in 1993. During her time at the OMB, Sawhill interacted frequently with William Galston, a domestic counselor to the president, and Jody Greenstone, another White House colleague. She recalled:

> Bill helped to get the president interested in the issue of teen pregnancy and convinced him to mention it in his 1995 State of the Union address. The president made a very strong statement about the problem and when pollsters measured real-time public reaction to the president's statement that "teen pregnancy is the most important social problem we face as a nation and it can't be solved by government alone," there was huge public resonance.

Sawhill, Galston, and Greenstone all left government in 1995, and they decided, "with encouragement from the White House," to "start something" to address the teen pregnancy issue. Greenstone began the process with encouragement from Galston, and Sawhill later became involved after Greenstone took a new job as COO of Americast, a media start-up in Los Angeles.

Following a meeting with the president in the fall of 1995, at which there was a lively discussion of the issue among several dozen leaders from business, the foundation world, and other sectors, Sawhill took responsibility for organizing a new initiative and recruited Sarah Brown to help. Brown, a Stanford MPH, then at the Institute of Medicine, had just finished a comprehensive report called "Best Intentions" on the subject of unintended pregnancy and its effects on child and family well-being.

Between October 1995 and February 1996, Sawhill and Brown worked on a prospectus for the national campaign with a "little bit of planning money" they had gotten from several foundations and a private donor. The Urban Institute, where Sawhill held an endowed chair at the time, gave her a leave of absence to pursue the project. "I was very happy about this turn of events," she said, "because I didn't want to just keep writing—I wanted to *do* something."

Sawhill and Brown completed the prospectus (see **Exhibit 7.1.3** for excerpts) and shared it with a planning group (many of whom had attended the original White House meeting in 1995) at a meeting in January 1996 hosted by Dr. David Hamburg, then president of the Carnegie Corporation of New York.

Sawhill explained:

> Everybody loved the basic idea we had in the prospectus about the organization whose sole purpose would be to reduce the teen pregnancy rate in the United States. The only problem at this juncture was that we didn't have a penny. We needed resources to get this thing going. So we began fundraising, and within six months, we had raised funds from three or four foundations and felt secure enough financially to move forward.

This proposal lays out the rationale and need for a national campaign and describes its mission and guiding principles, its proposed activities, and its leadership, organization, and funding.

A. Why the National Campaign to Prevent Teen Pregnancy?

There are at least eight reasons to mount a national campaign:

1. **The magnitude of the teenage pregnancy problem is great.**

    *   More than 40% of young women in the United States become pregnant before they reach age 20, producing the highest teenage pregnancy rate of any industrialized nation. In 1988, the teenage pregnancy rate in the United States was more than twice that of England and Wales, twice that of Canada, and almost 10 times that of Japan.
    *   The teenage pregnancy rate has increased over the past two decades, and by 1991, it reached about 115 pregnancies per 1,000 young women ages 15 to 19; in 1976, the comparable rate was about 101 per 1,000.
    *   Half of the almost one million pregnancies among teenage women each year end in birth and a third end in abortion; the rest end in miscarriage.
    *   The *birth rate* among teenagers is also very high compared to other industrialized nations, and as of 1993, it stands at about 60 births per 1,000 teenage girls ages 15 to 19.

2. **The consequences of teenage pregnancy and childbearing are serious and contribute to many of the nation's enduring social problems.**

    Teenage pregnancy and childbearing go hand in hand with high levels of risk for all those involved, particularly the teenage mother and her baby. The mothers are more likely to live in poverty and to depend on public assistance. They are much less likely to finish high school or to attend college and have lower earnings once they finish school. Younger mothers are also quite likely to have a second birth relatively soon, which can further impede their ability to finish school or embark on a steady work life. These burdens on the mothers obviously affect their children, who inherit a legacy of poverty and social disadvantage. The children of teenage mothers, for example, are at greater risk of various health and developmental problems, including low birth weight and infant mortality.

3. **The public is deeply concerned about the current state of the family in America and sees teenage pregnancy as an important part of a larger crisis in values and community well-being. These somewhat diffuse but powerful concerns have not been channeled into useful action.**

    Although the data and perspectives summarized above should be enough to focus the nation's energies on reducing teenage pregnancy, there is another dynamic that motivates action as well. High levels of teenage pregnancy seem to symbolize our gnawing sense that somehow our families and communities are coming apart—(a) that we are failing to transmit a sense of values to the next generation, (b) that parents have less influence over their children than they wish, (c) that teenagers are not being made to understand that pregnancy and childbearing are among the most important tasks of adult life requiring years of devotion, and (d) that our culture is not speaking clearly about all of these issues either to teenagers or to adults. Think of how often teenage pregnancy appears in the conventional list of social challenges: crime, drug use, school failure, and—always—teenage pregnancy. It has almost become a code word for unresolved social problems, especially those that are closely linked to poverty.

Exhibit 7.1.3   A Prospectus for the National Campaign to Prevent   *(Continued)*
            Teen Pregnancy—February 1996

(Continued)

4. **There are too few leaders at the national level willing to state forcefully and repeatedly that teenage pregnancy is wrong and that the nation must take action to address this serious social problem.**

   Teenage pregnancy will not drop dramatically unless there is persistent, visible leadership to focus the nation's attention on this problem. Unfortunately, there is not enough such leadership at present. Few high-profile national figures speak forcefully and repeatedly about the critical need to reduce teenage pregnancy. Although many local and state groups are active in this area, and numerous expert groups continue to focus on the problem at the national level, their activities are rarely supported by powerful voices cheering them on, giving them visibility, and echoing their messages nationwide.

5. **Reducing teenage pregnancy requires the help and power of the media, but forging partnerships with the media is a national task that individual communities cannot be expected to shoulder on their own.**

   Television, movies, music videos, radio, magazines, and other media have assumed overwhelming importance in the lives of Americans as the media have become ever more pervasive and persuasive. Indeed, interaction with some form of mass media has become the predominant leisure-time activity for all Americans. Teenagers spend more time in front of the television than interacting with their parents; many spend up to two hours a day watching music videos; and few parents discuss with their children the messages that the media convey or set rules about media viewing. Moreover, several recent surveys of the sexual content of the media confirm what we all sense—that there is a great deal of sexual material in the media; that sex between unmarried people without consequences or contraception is the norm in the entertainment media; and that sexual activity is rarely depicted in the context of loving, committed relationships.

6. **Although there are some state and community coalitions focused on reducing teenage pregnancy, more are needed, and all require a higher level of support, power, and visibility.**

   Some states and communities have broad coalitions that address teenage pregnancy prevention. Some of these coalitions are sponsored by the state itself and include heavy representation of state agencies (such as the coalitions in California, Virginia, Alabama, and Florida); others are entirely in the private, voluntary sector (although public officials are often involved), such as the coalitions in North Carolina and Minnesota. These coalitions undertake a wide variety of tasks—training and technical assistance, information sharing, advocacy, and networking among individual community-level programs.

7. **Even though major disagreements about values and behavior impede the ability of communities to take actions to reduce teenage pregnancy, there is at present no national dialogue on these issues and no systematic efforts to build common ground and to search for ways to move forward.**

   Many of the struggles over ways to reduce teenage pregnancy have centered more on differences in values, cultural traditions, and religious beliefs than on such practicalities as cost or data about "what works." Indeed, it is in this domain that the nation seems most stuck—unable to find common ground, to listen respectfully to differing points of view, or to tolerate diverse opinions about how best to reduce teenage pregnancy. A number of thoughtful people have suggested that these intangibles are as much a part of the problem and solution as is, for example, developing better information on effective programming at the local level.

Exhibit 7.1.3

> **8. The knowledge base of how to reduce teenage pregnancy though community-based programs needs to be strengthened, which requires new investments in program evaluation and more efforts to put current knowledge in the hands of states and communities.**
>
> There is a solid consensus that more investments need to be made in program evaluation generally, and that knowledge derived from already completed evaluations needs to be synthesized on an ongoing basis and made more accessible. Two groups especially need such information: (1) those who wish to put programs in place at the state or local level and are looking for model programs or "best bets" and (2) public and private funding entities who must make decisions about future investments in both programs and program evaluation.
>
> In sum, we believe that the National Campaign to Prevent Teen Pregnancy is well justified and addresses a serious national problem. Such a campaign can (a) fill an important leadership void, (b) connect powerfully with existing public concerns about the future of American families, (c) support and stimulate action at the state and local levels to reduce teenage pregnancy, (d) harness the power of the media to help, (e) strengthen the knowledge base for community intervention, and (f) open a dialogue on issues of religion, culture, and public values as they relate to teenage pregnancy.

Exhibit 7.1.3

The group was plagued from the beginning with assumptions that it was part of the Clinton White House, perhaps a new presidential commission. But the newly formed organization was in fact entirely private and realized that its success and durability would depend on its remaining apolitical.

Sawhill and Brown saw as one of their first priorities the creation of a distinguished board of directors. Wanting the campaign to be a distinctly nonpartisan group, they recruited a number of prominent members of each political party, and with the help of Dr. David Hamburg, Sawhill convinced Tom Kean, the former Republican governor of New Jersey, to serve as their chairperson. (See **Exhibit 7.1.4** for current board members.) The first board meeting was held in February 1996 and then the real work began—raising money, recruiting staff, finding office space, getting 501(c)(3) status, and setting up administrative systems.

Up and Running

In the prospectus, Sawhill and Brown first sought to answer three main questions: (1) What should the specific mission of the new organization be? (2) What were the reasons for the alarmingly high teen pregnancy rate in the United States? and (3) What did such information imply about the most effective ways to attack the problem?

Sarah Brown explained:

At the beginning, we knew we had to get clear about our mission. We decided it would be *to prevent teen pregnancy in the United States*. This was as opposed to "preventing teen

(Text continues on page 357)

Case Study

Linda Chavez

Linda Chavez is president of the Center for Equal Opportunity and is a syndicated columnist for *USA Today*. She writes often for many other publications, including the *Wall Street Journal*, the *Washington Post*, the *New Republic*, *Commentary*, and *Reader's Digest*. She also makes regular appearances on *The McLaughlin Group, CNN & Co., Equal Time*, and *The News Hour with Jim Lehrer*.

Annette Cumming

Annette Poulson Cumming is an alumna of the University of Utah, where she received both a BS degree in nursing and an MBA. She was an intensive-care nurse and nursing administrator for 11 years before changing to a career in business and real estate. She is a prominent business leader who also volunteers for philanthropic organizations and is a generous contributor to numerous community causes. She now serves as vice president and executive director of the Cumming Foundation in Jackson, Wyoming.

Nationally, Annette Cumming has chaired the newly created Planned Parenthood Foundation, serves on the boards of the Planned Parenthood Federation Action Fund, the U.S. Ski and Snowboarding Team Foundation, and ACCION International U.S. Venture Leadership Council (a microlending organization). She has served on the boards of Planned Parenthood Federation of America and the Alan Guttmacher Institute.

William Galston

William Galston is a professor in the School of Public Affairs at the University of Maryland at College Park and currently serves as director of the Institute for Philosophy and Public Policy. He previously served as the deputy to the president for domestic policy (1993–1995) and director of economic and social programs at the Roosevelt Center for American Policy Studies (1985–1988), and he taught at the University of Texas at Austin in the Department of Government (1973–1982).

David Gergen

David Gergen currently serves as editor-at-large at *U.S. News & World Report* and as a regular conversationalist on the PBS series *The News Hour with Jim Lehrer*. In addition, he recently joined the faculty at Harvard University, as a professor of public service, teaching at the John F. Kennedy School of Government.

In the past, he has served in the White House as an adviser to four presidents: Nixon, Ford, Reagan, and Clinton. Most recently, he served for 18 months in the Clinton administration, first as counselor to the president and then as special adviser to the president and the secretary of state. He returned to private life in January 1995.

From 1984 to 1993, Gergen worked mostly as a journalist. For some two and a half years, he was editor of *U.S. News*. During that period, he also teamed up with Mark Shields for political commentary every Friday night for five years on the *MacNeil/Lehrer News Hour*.

Whoopi Goldberg

Whoopi Goldberg began performing at age eight in New York with the Children's Program at the Hudson Guild and the Helena Rubinstein's Children's Theatre. She continued to work in theatre including a Broadway show that featured original material written and created by Ms. Goldberg. *The Color Purple* launched Ms. Goldberg's film career, resulting in an Oscar nomination and the 1985

Exhibit 7.1.4   The National Campaign to Prevent Teen Pregnancy—Brief Board Biographies, November 1999

Golden Globe Award for Best Actress in a Dramatic Motion Picture. Since then, she has starred in and received various awards, including an Academy Award, a Grammy Award, a number of Golden Globe Awards, and several NAACP Image Awards, for pictures such as *Jumpin' Jack Flash, Fatal Beauty, Ghost, The Long Walk Home, Sister Act,* and *Sarafina!* She has also worked in the genre of television receiving nominations for various awards with her work on *Star Trek: The Next Generation,* an episode of *Moonlighting,* and an episode of *A Different World.* In 1987, Ms. Goldberg, Billy Crystal, and Robin Williams cohosted HBO's now historic "Comic Relief" benefit for the nation's homeless. This benefit, along with Comic Relief II, III, IV, V, VI, and VII, has raised more than $25 million.

Katharine Graham

Katharine Graham has been chairman of the executive committee of the Washington Post Company since September 1993. The Washington Post Company is a diversified media organization whose principal operations include newspaper and magazine publishing, broadcasting, and cable television systems. The company owns the *Washington Post;* the *Gazette Newspapers;* the *Herald; Newsweek; Newsweek International;* television stations in Detroit, Houston, Miami, Hartford, San Antonio, and Jacksonville; and cable systems serving subscribers in midwestern, western, and southern states. Previously, Mrs. Graham was chairman of the board (1973–1993), chief executive officer (1973–1991), and president (1963–1973) of the Washington Post Company. She was publisher of the *Washington Post* newspaper from 1969 to 1979. After attending Vassar for two years, Mrs. Graham graduated from the University of Chicago. She worked as a reporter for the *San Francisco News* and later joined the staff of the *Washington Post,* working in the editorial and circulation departments.

David A. Hamburg

David Hamburg served as president of Carnegie Corporation of New York from 1983 to 1997. He received his AB and his MD degrees from Indiana University. Prior to Carnegie, he was professor and chairman of the Department of Psychiatry and Behavioral Sciences at Stanford University (1961–1972); Reed-Hodgson Professor of Human Biology (1972–1976); president of the Institute of Medicine, National Academy of Sciences (1975–1980); director of the Division of Health Policy Research and Education; and J.D. MacArthur Professor of Health Policy at Harvard University (1980–1982). He served as president, then chairman of the board of the American Association for the Advancement of Science (1985–1986). Dr. Hamburg has been a trustee and vice chairman of the board at Stanford University.

Alexine Clement Jackson

Alexine Clement Jackson is the national president of the YWCA of the USA and has been an active volunteer in the Washington, D.C., community for more than 20 years. Her recent volunteer service includes the following: chairman of the 1994 Wolf Trap Ball; cochair, 135th Anniversary Celebration of the YWCA of the USA; chair, 125th Anniversary Gala Dinner for Howard University College of Medicine; and cochair, Salute to American Fashion. Current board memberships include Wolf Trap Foundation for the Performing Arts, Washington Ballet, Washington Concert Opera, United Arts Organization, American Cancer Society/D.C. Division, Washington Charitable Fund, Black Women's Agenda, and United Negro College Fund (D.C. Advisory Board).

Sheila Johnson

Sheila Johnson is the executive vice president of corporate affairs for Black Entertainment Television, Inc. (BET), an advertiser-supported, basic cable television network launched in January 1980 that

---

Exhibit 7.1.4   *(Continued)*

(Continued)

serves as both a cultural and an information source for black consumers. *Teen Summit* is BET's award-winning, talk/performance show that focuses on African American teens. Aired each week, the hosts are joined by celebrity guests and a teen panel to engage in frank discussions about critical issues affecting young people.

Judith E. Jones

Judith E. Jones is a clinical professor at Columbia School of Public Health and is the director of the National Program Office of the Robert Wood Johnson Foundation's National Head Start Initiative to Prevent Substance Abuse. She also serves as senior advisor to the Carnegie Corporation for the Starting Points State and Community Partnerships for Young Children grants program.

Leslie Kantor

Leslie Kantor, Planned Parenthood of New York City's (PPNYC) vice president of education, provides overall vision and direction to a department that provides workshops to over 8,000 New Yorkers annually, trains professionals and parents to be effective sexuality educators for youth, and explores ways to make reproductive health services accessible for adolescents. She also oversees the agency's projects related to educating the public and healthcare providers throughout New York City about emergency contraception and new initiatives to reach out more effectively to men. Ms. Kantor is often invited to provide keynote speeches and trainings for professionals across the country. She has provided training and technical assistance to over 300 communities in 47 states.

Nancy Kassebaum-Baker

Nancy Kassebaum-Baker, a former U.S. senator (R-Kansas), was introduced to the world of politics at an early age. The daughter of Theo Cobb and Alfred Landon, former Kansas governor and 1936 Republican presidential nominee, Senator Kassebaum grew up listening to political discussions between her father and the many politicians and journalists who came to visit. Her environment created the intense interest in politics that led her to a bachelor's degree from the University of Kansas in political science and a master's degree in political history from the University of Michigan.

Thomas H. Kean

Former New Jersey governor Tom Kean is currently president of Drew University, a post he has held since 1990. Kean's leadership is shaping Drew into one of the nation's leading small universities. *U.S. News & World Report* listed Drew among the "up and coming" universities nationwide. *Newsweek* rated Governor Kean among America's five most effective governors. Governor Kean is on the board of a number of organizations including the Robert Wood Johnson Foundation, the World Wildlife Fund, United Health Care Corporation, and the National Endowment for Democracy.

Douglas Kirby

Douglas Kirby, PhD, is a senior research scientist at ETR Associates in California. He has directed nationwide studies of adolescent sexual behavior, sexuality education programs, school-based clinics, school condom-availability programs, and direct mailings of STD/AIDS pamphlets to adolescent males. He has been the principal investigator or co–principal investigator of large evaluations of *Postponing Sexual Involvement*, a curriculum designed to delay the onset of sexual intercourse; of *Safer Choices*, a comprehensive school-based program designed to reduce unprotected intercourse; of a middle school curriculum for high-risk youth; and of school condom-availability programs.

John D. Macomber

John Macomber is currently the principal of JDM Investment Group, where he has served since 1992. He served as chairman and president of the Export-Import Bank of the United States (1989–1992)

Exhibit 7.1.4

and chairman and CEO of Celanese Corporation (1973–1986) and is a former senior partner of McKinsey & Co. (1954–1973). Mr. Macomber is chairman of the Council for Excellence in Government and is a director of Bristol-Myers Squibb Company, the Brown Group, Inc., Lehman Brothers Holding Inc., Pilkington Ltd., Textron Inc., and Xerox Corporation.

Sister Mary Rose McGeady

Sister Mary Rose McGeady, a member of the Daughters of Charity of St. Vincent de Paul, became president and chief executive officer of Covenant House on September 1, 1990. Sister Mary Rose earned her BA in sociology from Emmanuel College in Boston and her MA in clinical psychology at Fordham University in New York. Subsequently, she pursued doctoral studies in the same field at Fordham and the University of Massachusetts. She holds over 17 honorary doctorates from outstanding universities, including St. John's, Niagara, and DePaul.

Jody Greenstone Miller

Jody Miller is the former acting president and chief operating officer of Americast, the start-up video and interactive services programming venture of Ameritech, BellSouth, GTE, SNET, and the Walt Disney Company. In that capacity, Ms. Miller was responsible for overseeing the venture's technology, programming, marketing, and operational deliverables; managing the technology group; and strategic planning and business development. Prior to Americast, she served in the White House as special assistant to the president and deputy to the counselor, David Gergen. As. Mr. Gergen's top aide, she advised him on all major policy and political matters, including healthcare, the budget, and NAFTA.

John Pepper

John E. Pepper currently serves as chairman of the executive committee of the board at Procter & Gamble. Pepper became chairman of the board of Procter & Gamble in September 1999, after serving as chairman and CEO since July 1995. Prior to becoming CEO, he served nine years as president and the last five years as head of P&G International. During his leadership of the company's international business, P&G doubled its sales and profits outside the United States. This growth included continued gains in established markets, particularly Europe, as well as developing new markets in eastern Europe, Russia, China, India, and Latin America.

Mr. Pepper is a member of the board of directors of the Xerox Corporation and Motorola Inc. He is deeply committed to community service, particularly education, and served as cochair of the Governor's Education Council of the State of Ohio. He is a trustee of the Yale Corporation, cochairman of the Cincinnati Youth Collaborative, a trustee of the Christ Church Endowment Fund, and a member of the Business Roundtable.

Stephen W. Sanger

Stephen W. Sanger became chairman and chief executive officer of General Mills on May 28, 1995. Sanger joined General Mills in 1974 and progressed through a variety of positions in marketing management across the company's consumer food businesses, including president of the Big G Cereal Division and president of Yoplait USA. He was elected to the board of directors in 1992 and was named president of General Mills in October 1993.

Victoria P. Sant

Victoria P. Sant is the president of the Summit Foundation and the Summit Fund of Washington. Mrs. Sant serves as national cochair of the Board of Population Action International, where she is a

Exhibit 7.1.4

(Continued)

(Continued)

member of the Executive, Development, Governance, and Budget & Finance Committees. In addition to her role as a board member of the National Campaign to Prevent Teen Pregnancy, she serves as a trustee of Stanford University and is on the boards of the Foundation for the National Capital Region, the Phillips Collection, and WETA.

Isabel V. Sawhill

Isabel V. Sawhill is currently a senior fellow in economic studies at the Brookings Institution. She is also president of the National Campaign to Prevent Teen Pregnancy. Previously, Dr. Sawhill was a senior fellow occupying the Arjay Miller Chair in Public Policy at the Urban Institute. Before returning to the Urban Institute in 1995, she was an associate director at the Office of Management and Budget for two years, where her responsibilities included all of the human resource programs of the federal government, accounting for one-third of the federal budget. Before joining the Clinton administration, Dr. Sawhill directed several large research projects at the Urban Institute. She is the author or editor of numerous books and articles including *Welfare Reform: An Analysis of the Issues*, *Challenge to Leadership: Economic and Social Issues for the Next Decade*, and "The Economist vs. Madmen in Authority."

Isabel C. Stewart

Isabel Carter Stewart is national executive director of Girls Incorporated. As someone who attended a girls' high school, attended a women's college, taught at a girls' high school, and spent 10 years on the campus of Spelman College, Ms. Stewart has firsthand knowledge of girl-focused environments and their impact on girls' lives. As national executive director of Girls Incorporated, Ms. Stewart advocates on behalf of girls and works to introduce and expand program outreach to meet the many challenges facing girls and young women today.

Judy Woodruff

Judy Woodruff, a veteran of more than 20 years in broadcast journalism, is CNN's prime anchor and senior correspondent. She coanchors *Inside Politics*, the nation's only daily program devoted exclusively to politics, airing from 5:00 to 5:30 PM (EST) with Bernard Shaw, and *World View*, an hourlong international newscast that examines the major stories and issues around the world, from 6:00 to 7:00 PM (EST) with Shaw.

Andrew Young

Andrew Young has spent more than 35 years in public service. Following his graduation from Howard University and Hartford Theological Seminary, he pastored small Congregational churches in Marion, Alabama, and in Thomasville and Beachton, Georgia. Later he moved to New York City to become associate director of the Department of Youth Work for the National Council of Churches. In 1961, Young returned to Atlanta to work as a top aide to Dr. Martin Luther King, Jr., during the civil rights movement. He served as executive vice president of the Southern Christian Leadership Conference.

Exhibit 7.1.4

births," because that would have put us squarely in the middle of the abortion debate and we emphatically did *not* want to be there. We did not want our organization to become mired in the polarization that this issue so often produces; we wanted to bring people with very different views to the same table.

In addition, we did not want to duplicate the efforts of organizations in the business of providing family planning or reproductive health services, as important as these activities are. The goal we decided upon was to *reduce the teen pregnancy rate by one-third by the year 2005.* This gave us a way to measure collectively how we are doing against the goal. We felt this was an achievable goal because the United States has a teen pregnancy rate so much higher than that of any other industrialized country.

As Brown explained, "the initial strategy grew naturally out of the prospectus and the reasons it outlined for the high teen pregnancy rate in the United States." These included the following:

- A culture that tends to **glamorize sex but avoids discussing its consequences:** The campaign would work with the entertainment and media industries to change the messages being delivered to teens.
- **Too little knowledge about what works** to reduce teen pregnancy: The campaign would encourage more research and would synthesize

what had been learned for use by communities.

- A country that is very much divided in its beliefs on what should be done—abstinence versus contraception, Christian right versus secular left, and so on. These value disagreements are heightened by the fact that the United States is a deeply religious country, and religious issues and values color public life and discourse in many complicated ways. The campaign would air these disagreements openly but in a respectful rather than a confrontational way.
- Not enough understanding of and support for what is going on at the grassroots level: Though national leadership and aid are helpful, **all programs and efforts are ultimately local.** The campaign would combine a top-down strategy focused on popular culture with a bottom-up one centered on state and local action.

THE TASK FORCES

Once they believed they had identified the causes of the high teen pregnancy rate, Brown and Sawhill created four task forces to address each of the four problem areas listed above. As Brown explained, the task forces were a "distinctive part of the campaign's structure and key to leveraging a small staff and getting buy-in from various sectors." Some 65 volunteers agreed to serve on the task forces.

Each of the four task forces was comprised of some of the most prominent leaders in the field/industry. For example, the State and Local Action Task Force included local government leaders, leaders of national organizations with a network of local affiliates, and local grassroots leaders. On the Religion and Public Values Task Force were prominent religious leaders, philosophers, and others with diverse perspectives on the issue. On the Media Task Force were media moguls and leaders in the entertainment industry, and on the Effective Programs and Research Task Force were leading scholars and intellectuals in the field.

In addition, as Sarah Brown explained, the goal was to include on the task forces "at least some people beyond the 'usual suspects' in this field." By this, she meant that instead of recruiting only traditional providers of family planning services or sex education, the campaign wished to bring to the table a variety of people representing all sides of the debate as well as those from outside the field. As Sawhill explained:

> We call this our "big tent" philosophy and it has been absolutely critical to any success we have had. We have helped people to understand that the battles between those who believe in abstinence and those who believe in contraception are not only unnecessary but also terribly counterproductive. The reality is that more of both are needed.

Furthermore, both Sawhill and Brown felt from the beginning that only a politically and professionally powerful group of people could help them make headway both in influencing policy and in fund-raising.

DESCRIPTION OF THE TASK FORCES

1. The Religion and Public Values Task Force

The purpose of this task force was to spark a discussion on the role of religion and values in teen pregnancy prevention. Relying on the credibility of the task force's leadership and its diverse membership (members included Joan Brown Campbell of the National Council of the Churches of Christ; Amitai Etzioni, founder of the Communitarian Network; Sister Mary Rose McGeady, president and CEO of Covenant House; and Wade Horn, president of the National Fatherhood Initiative), the campaign had begun to shift the "polarized and static debate" to a more productive discussion on how—across ideological, religious, and moral differences—to help teens avoid pregnancy.

Chaired by William Galston, the task force spent its first 18 months working through a white paper on the different belief systems in the United States. The final product, a document that was eventually called "While the Adults Are Arguing the Teens Are Getting Pregnant," included, as Isabel Sawhill explained, "views from the right, the left, and everything in between." As the foreword to the report stated, the purpose of the paper was "not to propose a single definition or course of action, but . . . rather to provide a short, usable description of competing moral and religious understandings, and the interaction between these understandings and empirical evidence, in the debate over what to do about teen pregnancy. And it is to suggest a range of strategies for making progress in the context of ongoing moral disagreements."

Regarding the priorities of the Religion and Public Values Task Force moving forward, Chairperson William Galston explained:

> We are now in the middle of a discussion about the relationship between our activities and the broader aims of the organization. In the first two years, when very diverse groups were arguing over the best way to attack this problem, we spent a lot of time crafting a general statement ("While the Adults Are Arguing") that would take a broad, nonpartisan approach, that all of our members would accept. We needed a genuine meeting of the minds and this was an essential building block for our work moving forward. This was Stage One—it was more of a "wholesale" strategy.
>
> We made a decision about a year ago that Stage Two would involve active engagement with faith leaders and faith communities across the country—more of a "retail" strategy. We initially decided that this would entail convening a national summit of faith leaders, but later revised those plans to include six regional meetings that would eventually lead to the national summit. These regional meetings, a few of which are already completed, are a way to broaden our contacts, to discover what are the real issues that faith leaders face in this area and to see what we need to do in order to convene an effective national meeting at a later date. . . . We

also run what we call "structured community dialogues" to help settle conflicts over value differences.

In fact, the staff of this task force had been extremely busy over the past year organizing these regional meetings. The first of these meetings brought together faith leaders from throughout Louisiana for a daylong meeting in New Orleans. The second regional meeting was held in Indianapolis and was cosponsored by Mayor Goldsmith's Front Porch Alliance. The third and fourth meetings took place in Tucson, Arizona, and in Santa Fe, New Mexico. In addition, the campaign had been invited to help communities who were having difficulty agreeing on what to do about teen pregnancy—for example, what kind of sex education there should be in the schools. So they had hosted a number of conflict reduction workshops, including one in California and one in Arizona.

These "on-the-ground" retail activities were complemented by the task force's discussion of the need to get clearer about how religion affects teen pregnancy and what faith-based organizations can contribute to the solution. For this reason, discussions were under way about some new publications that would review the research on these issues and document in the form of case studies some especially interesting or effective faith-based efforts at the community level.

2. The Media Task Force

The goal of the Media Task Force was to bring "new media partners" to the campaign and to help get campaign messages into the media that were most popular with the organization's "core audiences," parents and teens. In addition to delivering the traditional messages of teen pregnancy prevention, the campaign worked to educate and mobilize the creators of entertainment media about the causes and the consequences of teen pregnancy.

For example, with the help of Jody Greenstone Miller and other key members (including Patricia Fili-Krushel, president of the ABC Television Network, and Susanne Daniels, president of Entertainment for the WB network), the task force had created opportunities for the staff to brief many writers and producers of television shows. These briefings led to partnerships with those networks and efforts to integrate campaign messages into such popular shows as *Dawson's Creek, Felicity,* and other prime-time programs that appealed to teens in particular.

The media work enabled the campaign to reach tens of millions of people and thus was a highly leveraged way of changing the conversation about teen pregnancy. However, one question from the beginning was, "What should the message be?" Marisa Nightingale, the campaign's director of media programs, explained:

When we started the campaign three years ago, everyone wanted to know what our message was. We found out very early that there are in reality a variety of messages that are constructive. There is no single message that works across the board. So, we offer a variety of ideas on prevention. There are certain messages aimed at parents, others for boys, still others for girls,

for sexually active vs. non-sexually active teens, etc.

We decided to start by trying to reach parents as our research showed that parents and families have a great impact on teens' risk for pregnancy. So we created a publication called "Tips for Parents" to help parents talk to their teens about the issue. We then began to tailor our messages to teens after doing research on their attitudes, motivations, what resonates with them, what doesn't, etc.

We are delivering our messages mainly through the entertainment industry as it is a very cost-effective way to get the word out there. The majority of the cost of our entertainment media work is my salary and travel expenses! I meet with the industry executives face to face and urge them to work with us on creating story lines with positive messages about preventing teen pregnancy. Thus, the main job of the Media Task Force is to introduce me to the decision-makers in the industry and help forge partnerships with media leaders.

Jody Greenstone Miller, cochair of the Media Task Force, agreed:

The Media Task Force has been incredibly successful thus far and the challenge moving forward is to figure out how to continue that momentum. This work is highly based on "whom you know" and it is thus incredibly opportunistic. The campaign has been quite good at capitalizing on the opportunities that come up, but I often wonder how long we can keep up this success.

Certainly, there had been many successes to date. Examples included articles in such popular magazines as *Teen People* (8.4 million readers per month) and *Parenting Magazine* (1.46 million readers per month). They also included influencing the content, messages, or story lines in various prime-time television shows, soap operas, and documentaries (*7th Heaven, Dawson's Creek, Felicity, One Life to Live,* and the documentary *Teen Files: The Truth About Sex*). The campaign was also experimenting with public service announcements (PSAs), which were being developed on a pro bono basis by Ogilvy & Mather. One PSA featured pro basketball star Grant Hill and was launched in *Teen People,* distributed nationally through Tower Record Stores, and was slated to be published in other magazines such as *Spin, Vibe, Blaze,* and *Sports Illustrated.* The goal of PSAs was to reinforce messages coming through the entertainment media.

3. The State and Local Action Task Force

The purpose of this task force was to "support and celebrate existing efforts in states to prevent teen pregnancy" and to "stimulate more initiatives to reduce teenage pregnancy at the state and local level." Members included a wide variety of community leaders and a few representatives of national organizations with extensive field networks. For example, Alexine Jackson, president of the YWCA of the USA; Elayne Bennett, president and founder of Best Friends Foundation; and Leslie Kantor, vice president of education at Planned Parenthood of New York City, all serve on the task force.

The national campaign wanted to use this task force as a means to create a true national movement by fostering a sense of connection to national activities as well as to a larger network of efforts across the country. They did so by "providing state and local programs, coalitions and leaders with a wide variety of materials and ideas, as well as hands-on assistance and motivation." Perhaps the most important of these materials was a guide for local community leaders called *Get Organized: A Guide to Preventing Teen Pregnancy.* This 17-chapter "tool kit" features up-to-date information and specific strategies for action on a broad range of teen pregnancy prevention topics from how to develop a sustainable coalition at the local level to what is known about the effectiveness of various education, family planning, or youth mentoring programs. The task force realized that the campaign couldn't be a presence in every community and felt that materials such as *Get Organized* were a highly leveraged way to achieve its objectives. These "wholesale" strategies were an important complement to the site visits and hands-on assistance that the campaign was providing in many states.

Since its inception, the campaign had visited 43 states (some more than once), given speeches, provided technical assistance, conducted workshops, revitalized some state-level coalitions, and responded to numerous requests for information. It had also developed a list of 450 key contacts at the state level and shared materials with them through the campaign's website and in bimonthly mailings of campaign materials.

The State and Local Action Task Force had struggled with where to focus its efforts. The task force had decided that the greatest attention should be given to "target states," those states with the highest teen pregnancy rates or those whose rates were declining most slowly. However, this targeting strategy was often easier in theory than in practice. As Leslie Kantor, cochair of the State and Local Action Task Force, explained:

We want to focus on the states that need the most help in terms of the highest rates, etc. but the reality is that we are not necessarily going to those states. What happens is that the "squeaking wheel" often gets the grease. For example, we have focused heavily on South Carolina in the last year or so, largely because we have relationships with local politicians there, and the community has been very active in developing a coalition to deal with this problem. But South Carolina is definitely not one of the worst states in the country in terms of teen pregnancy rates. Texas, for example, is a big state with a huge teen pregnancy problem, but there, we do not have as much of a "way in."

Kantor continued:

The key question for our task force, and for the campaign as a whole, is, "Should we be a think tank or should we actually try to help people in their communities?" Until now, we have tried very hard to do both. We are

in the process of evaluating the campaign's state and local work to determine how effective it has been. We are asking, for example, Should we produce more publications like our *"Get Organized"* kit for local community leaders, or should we continue to try to meet with people face to face? We are also looking at better ways to use our Web site to bolster the work of the task force and to serve as a resource for people when we are unable to meet with them face to face. There are many more decisions to be made.

The campaign's deputy director, Sally Sachar, was charged with facilitating this decision making by preparing a report that would lay out the options for future work and the pros and cons of adopting a different mix of retail versus wholesale activities. She commented,

We are now asking the question, "Which is the most efficient? A wholesale strategy? A retail strategy? Or some blend of the two?" Many organizations like ours are struggling with this question, and we are facing the fact that both approaches have real appeal. But at the end of the day, an organization probably can't invest equally in both.

4. The Effective Programs and Research Task Force

Believing that research should be the very foundation of the campaign's strategy, this task force was devoted to providing a "solid foundation of evidence, derived from rigorous research, that could support and inform the campaign's policies and activities." The initial goal of this task force was to produce a summary of all the research on which types of community-level programs had worked and which hadn't to prevent teen pregnancy. This summary, called *No Easy Answers*, is a best-seller (80,000 copies to date) and quickly became a valuable resource for everyone involved in teen pregnancy prevention across the country.

Equally important was the task force's commissioned research on the relationship between the campaign's program activities (such as work with the media or with faith-based groups or with parents) and the reduction of the teen pregnancy rate. For example, the campaign's report, titled "Families Matter," reviewed a body of literature suggesting that parents have far more influence over adolescent values and behavior than they have generally assumed. It was this and other research that gave the campaign some confidence that their strategies were well chosen.

Douglas Kirby, chair of the Effective Programs and Research Task Force, explained the research focus of the campaign and outlined the task force's goals over the next three to five years:

> I got involved in the campaign because I very much support its goals. The first thing that attracted me to the idea is the "big tent" philosophy that tries very hard to bring people with widely differing views together. The second thing I like is the strong research focus—research leads to policy—we do what the research tells us to do. Finally, I am impressed by the leadership, particularly Sarah and Belle.

We have two major aims for the Research Task Force over the next few years. The first is to continue to conduct new analyses of existing data sets. The second is to review existing research in the field—that is, to review multiple studies on a given topic in a search for the collective "truth" about that topic. For example, in the past, we have done work on the influence of the family, peers, and the media on teens and their attitudes toward pregnancy. This involved both data analysis and research reviews. In the future, we may look at work on schools, youth development programs and the influence of religion. We are also going to create a sequel to "*No Easy Answers*" this spring.

Our work on the Research Task Force is vital to the campaign as a whole because it forms the basis for all the other task forces and their work. In other words, they largely decide how to develop their programs and activities after reviewing the research work we do. I think that is the campaign's single biggest strength and what gives it its focus.

The chairs of the task forces were automatically given a seat on the board of directors (as well as the executive committee of the board). Task forces met from one to three times per year to review recent work completed and develop plans for future activity. Each task force had a campaign staff member to support it and carry out agreed-upon projects. The campaign staff members also used the task forces to help advance the campaign's agenda. For example, members of the Media Task Force introduced Marisa Nightingale, the campaign's director of Media Programs, to other industry leaders in order to work toward spreading the campaign's message to as many media outlets as possible. Sister Mary Rose McGeady, the Religion and Public Values Task Force member, convinced the Catholic bishops to send the campaign's materials to every Catholic diocese in the country.

OTHER PROGRAMS

In addition to the activities of the four task forces, the campaign had established three other programs: communications, public policy, and youth leadership. Thus, there were a total of seven program areas in all, although the last three were not as resource intensive as the first four.

1. Communications

The communications department is responsible for publications, marketing, press outreach, and a rapidly growing Web communications effort (see www.teenpregnancy.org). The campaign has been featured in articles, editorials, and opinion pieces in most of the major newspapers and in hundreds of local papers. The Web in particular seemed a logical place for expansion, as Bill Albert, the campaign's communications director, explained:

For the past two years, our Website has seen exponential growth. We have gone from 300,000 to over 500,000 hits per month and were up to 1.2 million

last month. At first, we just wanted to communicate who we are and what we are trying to do. We are now using the Web to distribute materials like Tips for Parents, and have a section devoted only to teenagers, a weekly teen survey, and a section called "Now Showing" which lists the television programs soon to be aired with a story line on teen pregnancy.

This has been wonderful for us in large part because it decreases the demands on our time. Although I still talk to journalists quite often, I can also urge them to get information on our Website which saves me a lot of time.

The Website also contains fact sheets on specific topics (such as teen pregnancy and childbearing among Latinos). It provides state-by-state information on teen pregnancy, childbearing, and contraception, including maps of county rates where possible and contact information for those needing still more information at the local level. Furthermore, it provides an easy way to order the campaign's publications and to donate money. It provides an interactive weekly survey and discussion forum for teens, and it is continuously being improved through the addition of new features such as E-postcards and advertising banners that can be placed on the Web sites of other organizations or search engines. The Web site was also the primary fulfillment vehicle for PSAs and entertainment media outreach.

2. Public Policy

Another area where the campaign felt that it could make a difference with its limited resources was in influencing the national debate on programs and policies that affect teen pregnancy. For example, the 1996 welfare reform law contained a number of important provisions affecting state efforts in this area. And more recently, Congress had appropriated more funding for after-school programs that the campaign's research had shown to be one way of reducing teen pregnancy. To take advantage of these kinds of opportunities, the campaign had established two bipartisan congressional advisory panels, one in the House (chaired by Representatives Nita Lowey [D-NY] and Mike Castle [R-DE]) and one in the Senate (chaired by Senators Joe Lieberman [D-CT] and Olympia Snowe [R-ME]). Both panels were 50% Republican and 50% Democrat. The campaign had done a number of events with both groups, briefed both members and staff, and worked with them on legislative ideas.

3. Youth Leadership

In addition, the campaign had created a Youth Leadership Team (YLT) to serve as advisors on many aspects of its work. The YLT was made up of teens from varied backgrounds and was meant to "foster greater involvement of youth in teen pregnancy prevention both on a national level and within their own communities" and to "ensure teen participation when campaign policies and programs are designed, implemented, and evaluated." A new group of teen leaders was recruited each year and was brought to Washington to advise the campaign and learn more about the issue, including how to be effective advocates within their own communities or youth-serving organizations. Teens were nominated by any of the more than 50 youth-serving organizations with which the campaign was in touch. The YLT members were then sent back into their local communities to advocate for this issue. For example, one of the teen leaders was responsible for getting Ann Landers to run the entire content of the campaign's pamphlet containing advice from teens to teens in her regular column. Since the column was read by 90 million individuals, this was another example of a highly leveraged way of educating teens and their parents.

ASSESSING THE CAMPAIGN

By late 1999, the campaign had been in operation for more than three years. It had achieved a certain amount of financial stability, visibility, and respect for its work. It had a strong board and staff, had a long list of publications, was regularly cited in the press, and had developed a real following among practitioners at the grassroots level. But Sawhill and Brown were not entirely satisfied. With encouragement from several board members, they decided to use the fall 1999 board meeting to revisit their strategy, program activities, organizational capacity, and impact.

Strategy

The campaign's strategy as outlined by Isabel Sawhill at the board meeting was still very much based on the diagnosis of the problem outlined in the original prospectus that had led to the establishment of its four

Case Study

task forces. But, she argued, the campaign needed a still more explicit "theory of social change" that related its programmatic activities to its ultimate goal of reducing teen pregnancy. She walked the board through a flow chart (**Exhibit 7.1.5**) that showed the logic behind the campaign's strategy. She went on to explain how its efforts had been modified to reflect, first, the results of research commissioned since the prospectus was written and, second, the campaign's assessment of its strengths vis-à-vis other organizations in the field.

The campaign's leaders had come to the conclusion that the primary, although not exclusive, focus of their work should be to try to increase the motivation of teens to avoid pregnancy. They had chosen this focus for three reasons. First, several campaign publications, including *No Easy Answers* and *Whatever Happened to Childhood*, had suggested that lack of access to contraception and ignorance about sex and pregnancy were no longer the major factors causing teens to become pregnant. For example, condoms, the preferred contraceptive method among teens, especially in the era of AIDS and other sexually transmitted diseases, were widely available in stores. And analysis of past data suggested that teens were better informed than ever *and* had better access than ever to birth control. However, because of a shift in social norms, they were more sexually active and less motivated to avoid pregnancy than in the past (the proportion of girls ages 15–19 who were sexually experienced increased from 32% in 1972 to 54% in 1990, and there had been a similarly large increase in the social acceptance of early pregnancy and out-of-wedlock childbearing). Second, they felt that other

organizations such as Planned Parenthood and the Sexuality Information and Education Council of the United States were doing a good job of advocating for more family planning services and sex education in the schools. Finally, they determined that the cost of running programs to reach each individual at-risk teen would simply be prohibitive, and this necessitated that the campaign find more global strategies for influencing attitudes and behavior. (See **Exhibit 7.1.6**.)

The campaign had concluded that this lack of motivation to avoid pregnancy related, in turn, to various factors ranging from pop culture to peer influence to lack of supervision. Each of these factors suggested a set of implied solutions, such as influencing the popular media, changing peer culture, and devoting more resources to effective after-school or other youth programs (see **Exhibit 7.1.7**). Here again, research had affected the campaign's choice of intermediate objectives and the program activities needed to achieve them. For example, a report commissioned from the Harvard School of Public Health on the efficacy of social marketing or media campaigns had given the campaign some added confidence that its strategy of working with the media was a reasonably sound one, although questions remained about just how influential such efforts were. And new research showing the importance of peers in influencing who becomes sexually active or gets pregnant suggested the need to give more emphasis to working with teen leaders and influencing peer group norms and attitudes.

Throughout the board of directors meeting on November 18, 1999, various board members spoke on what they saw as the

Using research to link action to results while not duplicating the efforts of other organizations

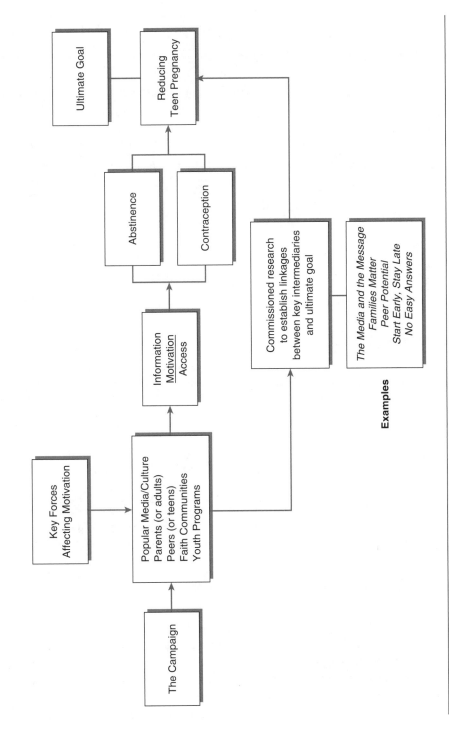

Exhibit 7.1.5   Dimension One: The Campaign's Strategy

But we do not run programs. Reaching every teen who gets pregnant would be too expensive:

Number of girls who turn age 15 each year	Number expected to become pregnant (40%) by age 20
1.9 million	760,000
Annual cost of Big Brothers/Big Sisters $1,000 per person	Annual cost of Quantum Opportunities $10,000 per person

Cost of serving 40% expected to become pregnant for five years:

Big Brothers/Big Sisters $3.8 billion	Quantum Opportunities $38 billion	Mixed Approach[a] $21 billion

Exhibit 7.1.6

a. Highest-risk kids in expensive programs; others in less expensive programs.

Possible Reasons	Implied Solutions

• Ignorance
• Insufficient access to contraceptives
• Lack of motivation related to:
 	
  o A popular culture that glamorizes sex while ignoring consequences
  o Parents who are uninvolved or who feel powerless
  o Peer influence
  o Teens who are unclear about their own values
  o Lack of supervision and few alternatives to sex and pregnancy
	• Sex education/information
	• Family planning clinics; condom distribution
	• Strengthen the motivation to avoid pregnancy by:
	  o Influencing the media to change the way sex and pregnancy are portrayed
	  o Encouraging parents to talk about sex, love, and relationships
	  o Training teens to speak out
	  o Engaging faith communities, parents, and others
	  o Mentoring, community service, after school, and other youth programs

Exhibit 7.1.7   Diagnosis: Why Are U.S. Rates So High?

campaign's main strengths. Several of them noted some of the campaign's distinctive attributes: its nonideological approach, its emphasis on research, its catalytic nature, and its focus on building highly leveraged partnerships. John Pepper, chairman of the executive committee of the board and recently retired CEO of Procter & Gamble, noted, "I have never seen a nonprofit organization that gets as much bang for its buck as the campaign does. You all are really able to leverage the limited resources you have and do amazing things." And Vicki Sant, president of the Summit Foundation, a Stanford trustee, and National cochair of the Board of Population Action International, commented, "I am impressed by the campaign's truly substantive approach and in particular by the fact they are focusing so early on evaluating what works and what doesn't." Dr. David Hamburg, president emeritus of the Carnegie Corporation, added, "I have never seen an organization that has accomplished so much so quickly." But virtually everyone agreed that the campaign was right to be asking the hard questions about its effectiveness and its program priorities.

The Campaign's Program

The campaign's activity program included the seven elements already described, four of which were based on the task forces and the other three being Communications, Public Policy, and Youth Leadership. At the board of directors meeting, a number of issues and challenges came up in each program area. The discussions dealt, in part, with the tension between "wholesale" and "retail" strategies. For example, in the state and local programs, should staff continue to travel around the United States facilitating meetings for community leaders? Or should they use limited resources to produce resource materials for wide distribution to local program leaders and/or improve their Web site and publicize it more effectively? Or should they launch "saturation" programs in a few key communities that could serve as models for others?

Several board members, including the three members of the State and Local Action Task Force (Alexine Jackson, Leslie Kantor, and Annette Cumming), felt that the state and local work needed more staff and resources. But they realized that a "Swat Team" could never reach every community in a country as large as the United States. Other higher-yielding strategies would be required.

Others wondered if the campaign didn't need to devote even more effort—through either traditional academic or market research—toward understanding what made a difference and why the rates had been coming down recently. David Gergen, Judy Woodruff, Katharine Graham, and Linda Chavez, in particular, pressed on these more basic research questions. Many found the campaign's highly leveraged media partnerships, which were showcased for the board in a short video presentation, to be the most exciting and promising aspect of the campaign. But they were acutely aware that it would take much more than a few episodes on *Dawson's Creek* to turn around the culture. Pepper, in particular, was impressed with the media work and the performance measures that had been put in place but suggested that the campaign get more involved with a new effort on the part of a group of corporations trying to use their advertising dollars to promote more family-friendly programming on television.

With regard to public policy work, Judy Jones thought that as important as it was, it was just as well that the campaign did not have an ambitious effort under way in this arena, given everything else it was doing. However, Sarah Brown and Isabel Sawhill as well as the new deputy director, Sally Sachar, brought strength to this area both in terms of their personal contacts in the political arena and their skill and experience in policy work. As Sarah Brown explained, they were indeed "very interested in public policy":

It's in our genes! So you'd think perhaps that we'd do more of it than we do. But in fact, we didn't burst onto the scene with a strong emphasis on public policy. Why? I think we were busy at first just getting the facts straight and reshaping the public debate. Our first priority was to revitalize a field that was troubled and sluggish, at least on a national level, and get the public interested in it again. And the way to do this was *not* to get caught up in the abortion wars or to write dry policy briefs on the issue. In addition, a lot of people in DC were already doing high-quality policy work so we felt that at least it was getting some attention. We didn't agree with what everyone was saying or doing but at least there was a lot going on here. So we decided to tackle Hollywood before Washington.

Having said that, we are beginning to work more on public policy now, though we must always balance it with all the other work we are doing.

As one example, in January 2000, the campaign would run a one-day conference for states on how to use surplus welfare monies to fund community programs that prevent teen pregnancy. As Brown explained, "A lot of states tell us they need

money more than anything, and while we can't directly give them money, we can help them learn how to secure funds themselves." In addition, the campaign was working with members of Congress on a bill that would provide more federal money to evaluate and eventually fund promising programs.

Organizational Capacity

The campaign's 19 employees were very busy trying to keep up with its many activities. There seemed to be some disagreement as to whether they were indeed stretched too thin or not. Sarah Brown felt that she had an "effective staff working on a variety of issues," but she didn't feel that they were "burning the weekend oil or anything." However, Tamara Kreinin, director of state and local affairs, commented that for staff members like her who were required to travel extensively for the job, the feeling was very much one of being overstretched. "To have more staff doing what I am doing would clearly be helpful and would take some of the pressure off."

With a FY 2000 budget of $2.8 million (see **Exhibit 7.1.8**), the campaign would not be able to hire additional staff. The campaign had done much to leverage their own staff, from the support of the volunteer task forces to pro bono work by the Ogilvy & Mather advertising agency to cost cutting on travel and administrative expenses. But still under debate was whether or not they should attempt in the next few years to significantly ramp up the size of their staff. This was somewhat of a catch-22. In order to be in a position to hire more staff, they would need to raise more

Expenditure		Totals
Personnel Budget		
Salaries	$1,048,319	
Fringe benefits[a]	256,455	
Total personnel budget		$1,304,774
Nonpersonnel Budget: Direct Costs		
Staff travel	62,605	
Leadership conferences	132,750	
Printing and publications	238,098	
Office space	193,049	
Professional services	272,000	
Total direct costs		898,502
Nonpersonnel Budget: Operating Costs		
Total operating costs[b]		309,003
Task Force Budget		
Task force operating expenses[c]	8,000	
Task force travel	135,340	
Total task force budget		143,340
Total personnel, nonpersonnel, and task force budgets		$2,655,618
Capital renovation budget		134,770
Total FY2000 budget		$2,790,388

Exhibit 7.1.8   National Campaign to Prevent Teen Pregnancy—Proposed FY2000 Budget—
Summary

a. 2000 fringe benefits rate is 25%.

b. Operating costs include postage, computers, supplies, photocopying, etc.

c. Task force operating expenses include task force meeting and operating expenses.

money, an activity that in itself would require additional staff. Moreover, it might require changes in the board and/or necessitate that Sawhill and Brown devote a lot more time to fund-raising (not a prospect they relished or felt was realistic given their other responsibilities).

Finally, even were they to achieve success (and there was no guarantee of this), it was never clear where to draw the line. A few more individuals staffing the state and local work wouldn't solve the problem of reaching every community, or even most communities, in America. There would never be enough people to do the job. But questions about the scale of the effort remained. Could an organization this small have a real impact, and if not, where could they find the resources to expand the effort? The campaign's development officer, Jamie Brown, was already working full-time writing proposals and researching new funding opportunities and felt that most of the obvious targets had already been

Case Study

explored. Moreover, the campaign's leadership believed that one reason they had been successful was that the size of the organization had forced them to be entrepreneurial and strategic and had made the campaign a fun place to work. They risked losing these three ingredients in a larger organization. Still, it was likely that some additional resources could be found and the question was, "How could they best be used?"

The Campaign's Impact

This was perhaps the toughest dimension along which to measure the campaign—what real impact had it had? As Isabel Sawhill had illustrated in her presentation to the board, contraceptive use was up, sexual activity was down, and rates of teen pregnancy were falling. But it would never be clear whether any improvement in these rates was directly attributable to the campaign's efforts. The best that could be done was to first measure the effects of the campaign's programs on a set of intermediate objectives, such as media content influenced, and then to use research to link those intermediate objectives (e.g.,

what teens see on television) to teen attitudes and rates of sexual activity, contraceptive use, and pregnancy. Subsequent discussions with board member Steve Sanger, CEO of General Mills, suggested that the campaign might be able to work with General Mills' market research department on this particular set of questions.

Finally, the campaign staff had developed a set of performance indicators in each program area (see **Exhibits 7.1.9** and **7.1.10**) that they were using to track how well they were doing against the intermediate objectives established for each program. And, as several board members had emphasized, one of the campaign's most distinctive strengths was its use of research to link these intermediate objectives to its ultimate goal of reducing teen pregnancy. But Sawhill knew that it would be very difficult to answer the question of where the campaign was truly having the greatest impact, and thus where they should focus their efforts moving forward. She and Sarah Brown still had a lot to talk about as they reflected on a board meeting that had provided plenty of food for thought.

Communications

- Goals: Raise public awareness
- Sample Activities: *New York Times* editorial, Ann Landers columns
- Performance Indicators: Press outreach, website activity, size of mailing list, number and diversity of clips

Media Program

- Goals: Change the culture, create new social norms
- Sample Activities: Storyline on *One Life to Live;* Grant Hill PSAs for boys
- Performance Indicators: Media partnerships, content influenced

Religion and Public Values

- Goals: Reach parents, other adults, and faith communities and encourage them to articulate their own values
- Sample Activities: Ten Tips for Parents, Nine Tips for Faith Communities
- Performance Indicators: Production and distribution of pamphlets; structured community dialogues (conflict reduction workshops)

Research

- Goals: Get the facts straight and use research to inform strategy and practice
- Sample Activities: No Easy Answers, research-based technical assistance to states and communities
- Performance Indicators: Research publications produced and sold, new or more effective approaches adopted in states and communities

State and Local Action

- Goals: Stimulate more, and more effective local action; build a national movement
- Sample Activities: Snapshots from the Frontline, Get Organized
- Performance Indicators: Site visits, production and distribution of materials to key contacts, community feedback, new or more effective local coalitions or campaigns

Youth Leadership

- Goals: Develop teen leaders, influence youth culture
- Sample Activities: Thinking About the Right Now, Teen In-Site, Youth Leadership Team
- Performance Indicators: YLT members and meetings, contests for teens, teen use of website

Public Policy

- Goals: Shape public policy or public funding priorities
- Sample Activities: Lowey/Castle bill, welfare amendments, Ways & Means testimony, member briefings
- Performance Indicators: Briefings, testimony, legislation, events

Exhibit 7.1.9   Goals, Activities, and Performance Indicators

Case Study

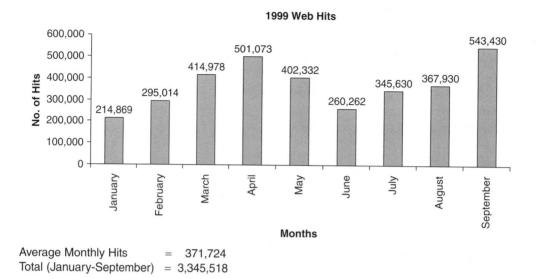

1999 Web Hits

Average Monthly Hits   =   371,724
Total (January–September)   =   3,345,518

Exhibit 7.1.10a

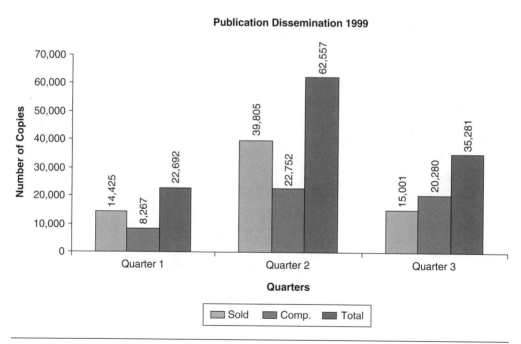

Publication Dissemination 1999

Exhibit 7.1.10b

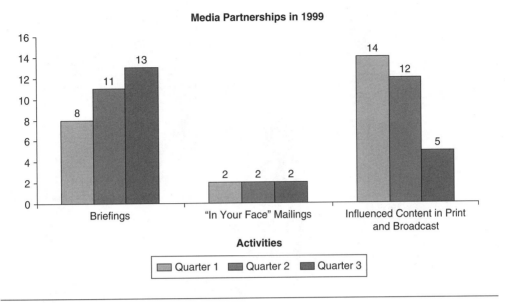

Exhibit 7.1.10c

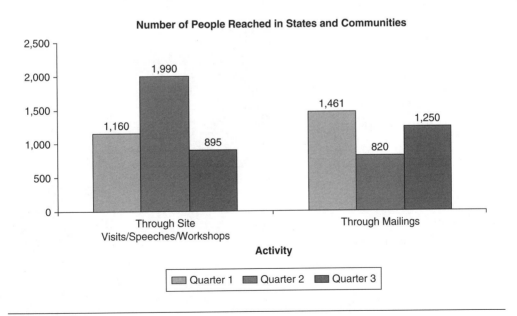

Exhibit 7.1.10d

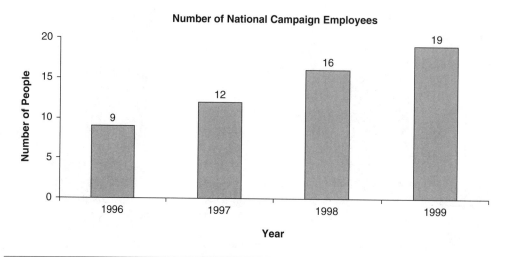

Exhibit 7.1.10e

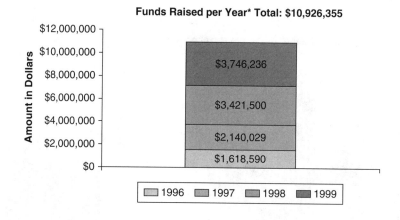

Exhibit 7.1.10f   Selected Performance Indicators

*Some grants are multiyear grants.

Data for 1999 are preliminary.

Case Study 7.2.

Playgrounds and Performance

Results Management at KaBOOM!

We do this work becau nce in the world; how can we go further faster?

—Darell Hammond, CEO and cofounder, KaBOOM!

Darell Hammond stepped onto the elementary school playground and took a long, slow look around. It was 8 A.M. on an unusually warm fall day in 2002 and the playground was deserted, but Hammond knew that the children would start arriving soon to admire their new playground. Dotted with purple, blue, and orange swings, slides, and seesaws, the playground had been built just the day before by an army of volunteers dispatched by The Home Depot, the national hardware

AUTHORS' NOTE: Copyright © Harvard Business School Publishing, case number 9-306-031. Used with permission.

Professors Herman B. Leonard, Harvard Business School, and Marc Epstein, Rice University, and Research Associate Laura Winig, Global Research Group, prepared this case. HBS cases are developed solely as the basis for class discussion. Data in this case have been disguised. Cases are not intended to serve as endorsements, sources of primary data, or illustrations of effective or ineffective management.

retailer, together with parents and community volunteers. Hammond thought it would be the best place for him to collect his thoughts for his early morning board of directors meeting.

This wasn't the way a CEO typically prepared for a board meeting, but KaBOOM!, the not-for-profit Hammond founded in 1995 with partner Dawn Hutchison, wasn't a typical company. KaBOOM! was a splashy, high-profile social enterprise, often featured in local and national news stories for its work—namely, building playgrounds in "kid-rich, playground-poor" neighborhoods around the country. The organization had overseen the construction of 441 playgrounds (see **Exhibit 7.2.1** for construction by year) and was working hard to keep up with demand. The board was pleased with the organization's growth and accomplishments but lately was showing signs of being overloaded by the deluge of information it was receiving from management—everything from playground build reports to piles of press clippings. The board wanted to assess the organization's performance without being overwhelmed with data. Hammond knew they needed to develop a performance measurement system, but how would they get there? Hammond glanced at his watch and realized that the meeting was about to start. He closed the playground gate behind him and headed for the boardroom.

Building KaBOOM!

KaBOOM! was born of a tragedy. After reading a newspaper article about two children who suffocated in a hot car after climbing in to play, Hammond and Hutchison began their quest to fight for each child's right to have a safe and fun place to play. They envisioned that if KaBOOM! was successful, all children in America would have fun and healthy play opportunities through the support of their communities.

Although there were approximately 250,000 playgrounds in the United States—located on public and private school grounds, in child daycare facilities, in municipal and state parks, and in other private and public recreation spaces—only 65,000 were deemed fit for use; 75% of playgrounds had fallen into disrepair, leaving too few playgrounds to serve the 52 million U.S. children between the ages of 2 and 12.[1] "If children are our future, why are we allowing them to play in garbage-strewn lots, abandoned cars, bushes riddled with crack vials and needles, and boarded-up buildings? It is unacceptable for children to grow up without a safe place to play," said Hammond.[2]

With $25,000 in start-up money, Hammond and Hutchison launched KaBOOM! and fashioned a new model for building playgrounds, creating partnerships with a host of *Fortune* 500 corporations,

	Inception to 1998	1999	2000	2001	2002
Playgrounds	115	64	63	90	109

Exhibit 7.2.1   KaBOOM! Playground Builds by Year
SOURCE: Company documents.

which funded playground and skatepark construction—called "builds"—on a fee-for-service basis. KaBOOM! matched its funding partners with community partners (the recipients of the playgrounds) who recruited children from their community to design their dream playground. (See **Exhibit 7.2.2** for images of children playing on a KaBOOM! playground.) After eight weeks of collaborative planning, 175 volunteers (half from each partner) would transform an empty lot into a playground in 6 hours.

Hammond noted that one important aspect of the organization's theory of change—that individuals and groups can and want to make a difference—relied on tapping leadership from within the local community. "By focusing on building a discrete project on a discrete timeline, we activate hundreds of volunteers to get involved in their communities—many for the first time," said Hammond. KaBOOM! hoped that by stimulating civic involvement, more play spaces would be built at a faster rate.

Community partners paid for 15% of the cost of their playground, while funding partners, who viewed their relationship with KaBOOM! as an opportunity to contribute to their communities while building their brands, developing their human resources, and enhancing their public relations efforts, paid 85%. (See **Exhibit 7.2.3** for KaBOOM! income statements.)

The organization's 2002 operating revenue of $5.8 million was comprised almost entirely of earned income and project fees collected from its largest funders—The Home Depot, Nike, Target, Computer Associates, and Sprint—and a network of other corporate, foundation, and association

funding partners. By 2003, KaBOOM! would become the largest producer of community-build playgrounds in the United States, leading 25,000 volunteers annually in the construction of playgrounds and skateparks mostly in low-income and urban areas. The organization, headquartered in Washington, D.C., with satellite offices in Atlanta, Chicago, and San Francisco, employed 21 full-time staff members.

KaBOOM! was pursuing a three-pronged strategy it referred to as "Lead, Seed, and Rally." The Lead prong of the strategy called for KaBOOM! to lead by example—building playgrounds by providing planning expertise, matching funding partners to communities, and managing the playground builds directly. While this model gave KaBOOM! control over build schedules, quality, and event publicity, it was a time-intensive process, as each project manager could complete an average of just 18 playground builds annually at a cost of about $60,000 each. Early on, Hammond's team realized that it could not reach its vision by building playgrounds on its own; the human resource and equipment costs as well as the finite financial resources of its funding partners would limit its growth. "We deliberately chose NOT to open additional offices," explained Hammond. "Instead, we took our cue from the 14,000 requests we received for technical assistance on building playgrounds and developed our Seed strategy."

The Seed prong of the KaBOOM! strategy called for the organization to provide support, planning tools, and encouragement to community groups, but it removed KaBOOM! from the role of project planner

Exhibit 7.2.2   Children at a KaBOOM! Playground

SOURCE: Company documents.

	1999	2000	2001	2002
Operating Revenue				
Funding partner earned income	1,731	2,268	5,063	3,488
Community partner earned income	258	318	627	880
Other earned income	364	23	66	699
Grants: corporate, foundation, and other revenue	109	117	255	233
In-kind contributions	269	190	358	526
Total Operating Revenue	2,732	2,915	6,368	5,825
Operating Costs				
Construction total	1,900	1,855	2,681	3,867
Grant expense	70	49	140	21
Other program-specific costs	325	483	691	1,492
Management & general costs	610	664	716	562
Development costs	457	347	465	550
Total Operating Costs	3,364	3,398	4,693	6,492

Exhibit 7.2.3   KaBOOM! Four-Year Income Statement, 1999–2002 ('000s)

SOURCE: Company documents.

and builder. "The Seed strategy placed a higher level of responsibility on the community group to do it themselves," said Hammond. KaBOOM! provided just enough support to ensure that the community could successfully complete a build. The organization published free information on all aspects of its community-build model and encouraged communities to adapt the model to meet their individual needs. KaBOOM! provided do-it-yourself handbooks, training programs, technical assistance, challenge grants, and online tools, including a Project Planner. KaBOOM! also planned to track builds that resulted from its Seed strategy but knew that these were going to be more difficult to measure since, for example, not everyone who attended a training session

would successfully complete a build. Further, since the Seed activities built a pipeline of potential community partners for Lead builds, there was overlap between the Lead and Seed prongs of the strategy.

The third prong of the KaBOOM! strategy was an advocacy program that would later become known as "Rally." Planned for implementation by 2006, Rally called for KaBOOM! to partner with individuals it called "Playmakers," who would go beyond onetime volunteering to serve as community or national advocates for increasing the number of play spaces. These Playmakers would form local mayoral-recognized "Play Boards" that would take responsibility for increasing play in their cities and towns. Each city or town would then apply to KaBOOM! for recognition as one of

America's "Most Playful Cities." The Rally strategy was a sophisticated public relations program that KaBOOM! hoped would help "ripple out" its message from local neighborhoods to the city and national levels—ultimately generating more play spaces.

Although the advocacy strategy had not yet been launched, KaBOOM! wasn't lacking for attention. In 2001, it received the Chairman's Commendation from the U.S. Consumer Product Safety Commission for its achievements in playground safety, and in 2002, KaBOOM! was named one of America's 100 best charities by *Worth* magazine. The company even persuaded Ben & Jerry's Homemade, Inc., a Vermont-based ice-cream maker, to name an ice-cream flavor (strawberry and blueberry ice cream with white fudge–covered crackling candy and a blueberry swirl) after it: KaBerry KaBOOM!

The Board's Challenge

KaBOOM! had been growing quickly and professionalizing its operations, staff, and board of directors in the process. By 2002, its board of directors was a diverse group, with members ranging from a supermarket executive to an entrepreneur to the CEO of an organization trying to bring Internet access to affordable housing units (see **Exhibit 7.2.4** for a list of board members and their affiliations). The board met quarterly to discuss the organization's performance and future, and at each meeting it was presented with a torrent of reports, analyses, and other performance information (see **Exhibits 7.2.5** and **7.2.6** for fiscal years 1999 and 2000 performance measures). Hutchison,

who by then had joined the board, recalled, "As a board, we were getting too much information and didn't know what to pay attention to." Fellow board member Nancy Rosenzweig agreed: "We wanted to be able to determine in what ways KaBOOM! was most successful and healthy. We wanted to know how we could tell if problems existed. The board has ultimate accountability, but we're part-time volunteers. We needed timely, accurate, and useful information to perform our function. As this got frustrating, we decided to get more involved, and a few board members began collaborating with management to figure out what would give us the best pulse of the organization."

In fall 2002, Hammond and the board decided to develop a performance measurement system to report consistent data points, measured over time, that would enable the board to evaluate the organization's health and effectiveness. Ideally, the report—which came to be referred to as the "KaBOOM! Formula"—would present and prioritize key performance drivers, establish year-to-year benchmarks, monitor organizational performance, and help set strategic goals.

Tony Deifell, one of the founding members of the board, offered to collaborate with Hammond to build the performance measurement system. Deifell, a recent graduate of Harvard Business School's MBA program, was eager to work on the project because it would give him an opportunity to see if his combination of for-profit and social enterprise training could be used to develop an innovative measurement system for KaBOOM! Hammond emphasized the importance of the task:

Director	Title	Organization	Year Joined Board
Suzanne Apple	Vice President of Community Affairs	The Home Depot	1997
Bruce Bowman[a]	Vice President of Operations	Wild Oats Community Markets	2002
Michael Brown	President	City Year	2002
Peter D'Amelio	President and COO	The Cheesecake Factory	2000
Tony Deifell	Vice President of Business Development	Ballistic Entertainment	1996
Kim Dixon[a]	Vice President	Sprint, Great Lakes Area	2002
Helen Doria	Special Assistant to the General Superintendent	Chicago Park District	1996
Peter Farnsworth	Vice President, Business Development	National Basketball Association	2001
Ken Grouf	Co–Executive Director	City Year New York	1997
Darell Hammond	Cofounder and CEO	KaBOOM!	1996
Dawn Hutchison	Cofounder, KaBOOM!, Consultant		1996
Erin Patton	President and CEO	The Mastermind Group LLC	2001
Rey Ramsey	CEO	One Economy Corporation	2001
Jonathan Roseman[a]	Director of Communications and External Affairs	The Home Depot	2002
Nancy Rosenzweig	Vice President of Marketing	Zipcar	2000
David Wofford	President	Wofford Consulting, Inc.	2001
Christopher Zorich	Chairman	The Christopher Zorich Foundation	2000

Exhibit 7.2.4   KaBOOM! Board of Directors, 2002

SOURCE: Company documents.

a. Joined board on November 15, 2002.

"We feel pressure to perform at a very high level [because of our mission], so whatever tracking system we develop had better be meaningful and significant in driving performance—not just a kind of easy take on measuring our jobs."

As CEO, Hammond was charged with managing up through the board and down through the organization. "I'm the swing," he explained. "I'm back and forth. The board needs to use a performance measurement system as a way to manage the strategic direction of the organization. Yet managers need to use it to manage the business on a day-to-day basis. Our challenge was to create a system that would provide management with very detailed measures that could, in turn, be aggregated and presented as an

Administration and Operations	Project Management
Balance of cash flow	Level of vendor involvement
Growth in reserve funds	Diversity in vendors
Employee ratio to projects; capacity for new projects	Lead time required for planning a build
	Lead time required for ordering equipment for a build
Margin per project	Retention of funding partners
Margin per employee	Renewal rate
Project Management	Increase in support
Number of projects completed by year	Diversity of support (in-kind versus cash)
Projects completed versus planned	Number of referrals
Level, amount of community fund-raising	Staff development and retention
Outcome of playground projects	Retention rate
Community impact and satisfaction	Promotions rate
Number of referrals from community partners	Completion of performance evaluations
Number of new partnerships formed	Assessment of performance evaluation ratings
Growth of Club KaBOOM! database	Employee morale

Exhibit 7.2.5   "Vital Sign" Data Presented to the Board, Managers, and External Constituents, 1999

SOURCE: Company documents.

analysis to the board. The analysis should tell the board where KaBOOM! is at the moment and where it needs to go next."

Before the board recessed for the winter holidays, board chair Peter D'Amelio, CEO of The Cheesecake Factory, offered a word of caution: "People will do what you measure; be careful what you measure because it's going to drive people's behavior." Deifell added, "The performance measurement system shouldn't be a list of isolated measures; it should be a dynamic feedback loop that helps the organization pay attention to what is most important for running a successful social enterprise."

Setting Goals

The board started the process by revisiting the goals of the organization. "We knew we needed to start by answering the deeper question of what success means to the business. This is much clearer in for-profits than nonprofits," said Deifell, and then asked: "What did we want KaBOOM! to be as an organization? Were we more about playgrounds, community leadership, civic engagement, children, or all of the above? If we don't know where we're going, any path will get us there." Hammond added his perspective:

Operational Data	Measure
Playground builds	63
Volunteers	12,600
Value of volunteers' service	$1,261,260
Children impacted	63,000
Calls to the KaBOOM! Outreach Hotline	279
Getting Started Kits shared with community groups	3,282
Getting Started Kit responses received by KaBOOM!	5%
New business proposals sent	109
Builds resulting from new business proposals	53
New sponsors	26
Value of donations from individual donors	$54,560
Special event funds raised	$22,330
Project sponsors	16
Sponsor retention rate	100%
Publicity impressions	26,473,580
Increase in publicity over FY1999	66%
Print, broadcast, and Internet stories about KaBOOM!	224
New marketing materials developed	9
Staff count	14
Playground challenge grants	7
Number of people attending training events	151
Number of e-mails requesting support	1,202

Exhibit 7.2.6   Examples of Operational Data Collected by KaBOOM! Staff, 2000

SOURCE: Company documents.

We were trying to be more strategic as an organization, and we were about to kick off our planning to hone our three-pronged Lead, Seed, and Rally strategy. We knew we were making a difference, but how would we know if we were doing it most effectively or even improving? If we put strategy and measurement behind our work, could we go further faster as an organization?

The board members realized that the strategy was a moving target and struggled with the question of whether a measurement system should reflect or drive the strategy and underlying vision and mission (see **Exhibit 7.2.7** for the organization's guiding principles). "It's a constant evolution," remarked Deifell, noting that the exercise of developing a measurement system was causing the board to simultaneously reevaluate its strategy and hone its vision and mission. Hammond pointed out that the KaBOOM! measurement system would also need to be aligned with its growth strategy, so it would need to be

Mission:

Every child through the participation of their communities should have healthy play opportunities.

Vision:

Our vision is to help develop a country in which all children have, within their communities, access to equitable, fun, and healthy play opportunities, with the participation and support of their families and peers.

Core Values:

Play—fundamental to children's healthy development.

Access to play opportunities—equity is vital for all children.

Community action and participation—the process is as important as the product.

Family involvement in playground—training, education, and advocacy are key.

Exhibit 7.2.7   KaBOOM! Guiding Principles
SOURCE: Company documents.

flexible and forward thinking, as well as help shape the advocacy program that formed the final piece of its three-pronged strategy. "We need to design a measurement system that will help us realize the KaBOOM! we want to build, not just measure the organization we already have," he said. Hammond's goal was to create a substantial, professional measurement tool that could be used to improve organizational performance rather than simply to "prove" success to external audiences. Rosenzweig explained:

KaBOOM! wants to be best-in-class—on the cutting edge of the nonprofit sector. The organization has a for-profit bias, probably because of its social enterprise focus. Many of our managers and board members are MBAs. We're headed by a CEO, not an executive director, because Darell wants to model KaBOOM! after the for-profits. It's taking us out of the old paradigm of charity and moving us into social enterprise. We do business WITH businesses. Yes, we look for grants to fund education and advocacy, but in the social enterprise model, our partnerships are with industry. Darell meets with top CEOs and wants to be able to speak their language.

Hammond elaborated: "I want our measures to be internally driven, not funder driven. I want a measurement system that is supported by the organizational culture so that the board, myself, and our staff 'own' the data from the outset." The board also emphasized that it would require the financial indicators to be presented in the context of a financial analysis or, better yet, a formal framework. "We knew we would need to provide more than a series of gauges to look at; we would need to give some guidance as to the implications of the measures," said Deifell, who noted that he had been considering adapting the DuPont Formula, a system of analysis used widely among for-profit corporations. The formula looked at the interrelationship between operating management, asset management, and capital structure management, the underlying meaning of which Deifell believed was relevant to a social enterprise.[3]

Rosenzweig noted that the board wanted the data and analysis to be presented on an annual or semiannual basis and hoped that the system could serve as a signaling system for the board. "Its power will be in its ability to keep the organization focused on its mission and strategy and hold managers accountable to measures being on or off target," she said.

Deifell and Hutchison formed a new board task force to work with Hammond on a solution. They met to discuss next steps and decided they needed to brainstorm a list of performance measures as well as a schema for interpreting them—essentially creating a draft performance measurement system. "Without some sort of framework to provide a rationale for organizing metrics, every measure can seem important viewed out of context," Deifell pointed out. They set to work, determined to be ready to present their work at the February board meeting.

NOTES

1. "Playing It Safe: The Sixth Nationwide Safety Survey of Public Playgrounds," The Consumer Federation of America and U.S. Public Interest Research Group Education Fund, June 2002, available from the U.S. Public Interest Research Group Web site, http://uspirg .org/uspirg.asp?id2=7219&id3=USPIRG&/, accessed August 4, 2005.

2. "Mayors to build west side playground in Chicago for the U.S. conference of mayors, city leaders to build a KaBOOM! playground in Chicago," PR Newswire, April 23, 1998, available through Factiva, http://www.factiva.com, accessed August 8, 2005.

3. In the analysis, three financial ratios—profit margin, total asset turnover, and equity multiplier—are multiplied to equal return on equity. Chris Peterson, "DuPont Analysis and its Interpretation," Michigan State University, available at http://www.msu.edu, accessed October 24, 2005.

Index

About the Authors

Jane C. Wei-Skillern is Assistant Professor of Business Administration in the General Management Unit and Social Enterprise Group at the Harvard Business School. She teaches her MBA elective, Entrepreneurship in the Social Sector, at Harvard Business School and the Kennedy School of Government. She also teaches in the HBS Social Enterprise executive education program, Strategic Perspectives in Nonprofit Management (SPNM). Wei-Skillern earned her BS in Business from the Haas School of Business at the University of California at Berkeley, an MA in Business Research and a PhD in Organizational Behavior, both from the Graduate School of Business at Stanford University. Prior to joining the faculty at Harvard, she was an Assistant Professor of Organizational Behavior at London Business School.

Wei-Skillern's research is focused in the field of Social Enterprise. Her research has examined the topics of nonprofit growth and management of multisite nonprofits and most recently has been focused on nonprofit networks. She is currently studying how building a range of strategic networks can be a powerful lever for nonprofits to achieve greater social impact. A strategic network is distinguished from traditional partnership approaches in that it entails a shift in mind-set from the organization as the hub for social value creation to the organization as a node within a larger network of critical and complementary entities that must work collaboratively to achieve mission impact. Her research explores how trust-based strategic networks that leverage resources in innovative ways to achieve mission impact can be created and managed.

James E. Austin is the Eliot I. Snider and Family Professor of Business Administration Emeritus at the Harvard Business School. Previously he held the John G. McLean Professorship and the Richard Chapman Professorship. He has been a member of the Harvard University faculty since 1972. He was the Cofounder and Chair of the HBS Social Enterprise Initiative. Prof. Austin has been the author, coauthor, or editor of 16 books, and he has written dozens of articles and book chapters and over a hundred case studies on business and nonprofit organizations. He has taught courses on Entrepreneurship in the Social Sector, Governance of Nonprofit Organizations, Management in Developing Countries, Agribusiness, Business Ethics, International Business,

Business-Government Relations, Marketing, Nutrition Policy, and Case Method Teaching. In addition to Harvard, Dr. Austin has taught and advised managers, government officials, and multilateral agencies throughout the world. He is one of the founders of the Social Enterprise Knowledge Network (www.sekn.org).

He earned his Doctor of Business Administration and Master of Business Administration from Harvard University with Distinction; his Bachelor of Business Administration from the University of Michigan with High Distinction; and he was elected to Beta Gamma Sigma. Austin has been the author or editor of 16 books, dozens of articles, and over a hundred case studies on business and nonprofit organizations. His prior research focused primarily on management problems in developing countries, agribusiness, and nutrition policy. His current research deals with social enterprises with emphasis on the creation, management, and governance of nonprofit organizations and on the role of business leaders and corporations in the social sector.

Herman B. ("Dutch") Leonard is the Eliot I. Snider and Family Professor of Business Administration at the Harvard Business School and the George F. Baker, Jr., Professor of Public Sector Management at Harvard University's John F. Kennedy School of Government. In addition, he serves as faculty cochair of the HBS Social Enterprise Initiative. He teaches extensively in executive programs at the Business School and the Kennedy School and around the world in the areas of general organizational strategy, governance, performance management, crisis management and leadership, and corporate social responsibility. His work on leadership focuses on innovation, creativity, effective decision making, and advocacy and persuasion. His current work in leadership and management is focused on the relationships among governance, accountability, and performance and emphasizes the use of performance management as a tool for enhancing accountability. He has also worked and taught extensively in the area of crisis management and on issues related to corporate social responsibility. Professor Leonard is a member of the Board of Directors of Harvard Pilgrim Health Care, a 900,000-member Massachusetts HMO; of the Hitachi Foundation; and of the ACLU of Massachusetts. He was for a decade a member of the board of directors of the Massachusetts Health and Educational Facilities Authority and of Civic Investments and was a member of the Massachusetts Commission on Performance Enhancement.

Howard H. Stevenson is the Sarofim-Rock Professor of Business Administration at Harvard Business School, Senior Associate Dean, Director of Publication Activities, and the Vice Provost for Harvard University Planning and Resources. A member and former chair of the Entrepreneurial Management Unit, he has served as the school's Senior Associate Dean and Director of

External Relations, chair of the Latin American Faculty Advisory Group, Senior Associate Dean and Director of Financial and Information Systems, and faculty chair of Executive Education's Owner/President Manager (OPM) Program. Professor Stevenson's research focuses on the life patterns that create enduring success, entrepreneurship, and predictability. He has authored or coauthored more than 150 case studies, numerous articles, and nine books— including *Just Enough: Tools for Creating Success in Your Work and Life* (with L. Nash) and *Make Your Own Luck: 12 Practical Steps to Taking Smarter Risks in Business* (with E. Shapiro). He has created several successful companies. Currently he is a director of Camp Dresser & McKee and Landmark Communications. He is a director of National Public Radio, a trustee of the Massachusetts chapter of the Nature Conservancy, Mt. Auburn Hospital, and Trustee Emeritus of the Boston Ballet. He served as director and president of the Sudbury Valley Trustees.